Jason Elliot

Mirrors of the Unseen

Journeys in Iran

PICADOR

ed 2006 by Picador
Pan Macmillan Ltd
Pan Macmillan, 20 New Wharf Road, London NI 9RR
Basingstoke and Oxford
Associated companies throughout the world
www.panmacmillan.com

ISBN-13: 978-0-330-48656-9
ISBN-10: 0-330-48656-X

Copyright © Jason Elliot 2006

The right of Jason Elliot to be identified as the
author of this work has been asserted by him in accordance
with the Copyright, Designs and Patents Act 1988.

Endpapers: an eighteenth-century view of the Chahar Bagh in Isfahan
(Claude Sauvageot, after Pascal Xavier Coste), copyright © Bridgeman Art Library.

1 3 5 7 9 8 6 4 2

A CIP catalogue record for this book is available from
the British Library.

Typeset by SetSystems Ltd, Saffron Walden, Essex
Printed and bound in Great Britain by
Mackays of Chatham plc, Chatham, Kent

For R.

AUTHOR'S NOTE

There is nothing like writing a book about another country to extend the frontiers of one's ignorance, and this is all the more true when the chosen country is as rich in history, culture and territorial variety as is Iran. Early and innocent plans for both travel and research there suggested almost infinite horizons; and though circumstance soon reduced the scale of the endeavour, the glimpse of them remains as a humbling reminder of their extent.

I had imagined, when I began the journeys described here, that to travel in Iran would be both problematic and hazardous: it is neither. So well trodden and authoritatively described by others are the routes I followed that my re-tracing of them can only be described as pedestrian. This revelation, however, granted me the opportunity to explore a narrower range of subjects in areas which, in the course of things, I came to feel had been neglected elsewhere.

There are, as a result, many conspicuous omissions, as well as discoveries reluctantly compressed into footnotes or infiltrated into moments of historical fantasy. Happily, the former are generously addressed elsewhere by a growing number of more specialized works; the latter are intended to be taken in a spirit of informed diversion.

To acquire a sense of a culture's enduring characteristics requires time; and the journeys I have described took place over several years and at different seasons. These were mercifully unimpeded by the present and temporary confusion, and aided along the way by the hospitality and kindness of Iranians all over the country.

To my host and his family in Tehran, I owe a special debt of gratitude. Thanks are also due to Cecil Hourani for first introducing me to Louise Firouz; to Simon Shercliff at the British Embassy in Tehran, who was generous to me in an hour of need; and to my agent, Gillon Aitken, who was generous to me in several more; to the editorial staff at Picador, especially Charlotte Greig and Nicholas Blake; to Professor Leonard Lewisohn for helping me hear the voice of Hafez; and to Stephen Goodchild for providing, on more than one occasion, a safe haven in which to compose the lines which at long last I must now offer up.

J. G. W. E.

Contents

Map xii

One

Tehran

Not Kansas Any More · Common Knowledge

What the Persians have Ever Done for Us · The Weight of Assumption

Street Names, Old and New · Capital Growth · The Sweep of History

Trouble Ahead · Sorush, my Mentor · Heaven's Scent · Which Iran?

The Double Life

I

Two

Tehran · Isfahan

The Faces of the Doomed · Geography · First Glimpses of Isfahan

History of the Chahar Bagh · Half the World · The Naqsh-e Jahan

The Royal Mosque · The Mosque of Sheikh Lutfullah · Gardens of the Unseen

The Vision of Shah Abbas · Grim History

39

Three

Tehran · Gombad-e Qabus · Gorgan
Eastern Alburz · Golestan

Fatter is Better · Louise Firouz · Conspiracy Theory · Steppe Country
Ranch Life · The Rescue of the Caspian Horse · Opium Dog-Hell
A Day at the Races · Romans and Parthians · Mithra Myths
Parabolas and Colonnades · A Forgotten Corner of Iran · Golestan
The Sound of Eons

93

Four

Soltaniyeh · Tabriz · Sanandaj
Takht-e Suleyman

The Traveller's Ritual · Mongol Hoards · Dark Days for Islam
Pax Mongolica · Fantasy: the Persianization of the Mongols
Uljeitu and the Italian Connection · Sunni or Shiʾa? · Ali, Prince of Martyrs
A House of Strength · An Irreverent Host · Muqarnas · Border Manoeuvres
Wine and Women · Daydream at Vanished Shiz

153

Five

Kirmanshah · Hamadan
Tehran · Shiraz

Trouble with Herodotus · 'Weststruck': Shades of Heidegger · The Sons of Adam
The Importance of Being Azerbaijani · The Virgin Castle
A Subterranean Discovery: What Byron Missed · The First Dome
Sasanian Rhapsody · Hafez and the Language of the Unseen · Blame the Greeks
Little Britain · Déjà Vu · Begging For It

209

Six

Aups · Isfahan · Shiraz · Firuzabad

An Unbeautiful Instrument · Phi, Fie ... · Lines Visible and Invisible
The Riddle of the Maidan · Clues and Discoveries · Zizou's Honour
More non-Euclidean Speleology · Caveat Lector: Nasruddin's Pigeon
Aspects of Islamic Art · Epistemological Conundrums · The Problem of Meaning
All Roads Lead to Metaphysics · Dissolving Snowflakes

275

Seven

Persepolis · Yazd · Kerman · Natanz
Kashan · Mashhad

Money Talks · Persepolis · The Shah's Last Hurrah
Operation Ajax: The Un-Democratization of Iran · A Civilized Way to Differ
Dualities · Holy Smoke · Taxis of Evil · Rendezvous in Paradise
Rosewater · The Crazed Ones · Plus ça Change · Lessons in Profanity
To the Shrine · Full Circle

337

Appendage 405

Index 409

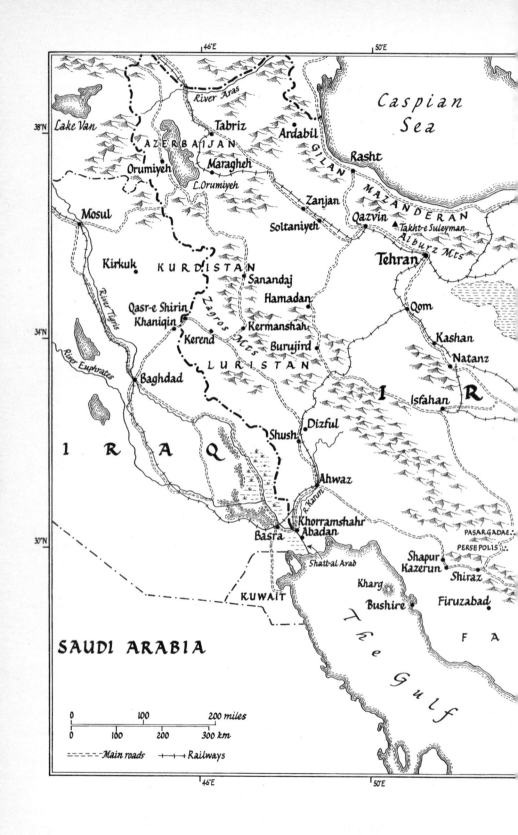

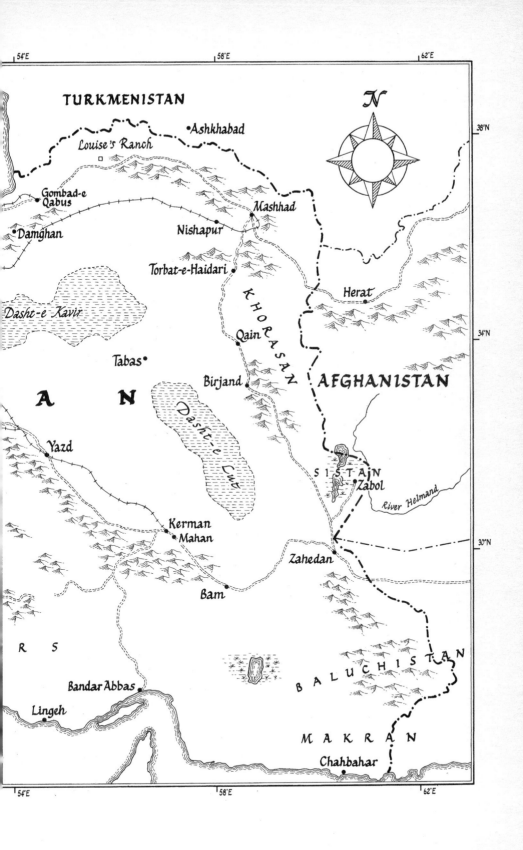

حاصل کارگ کون و مکان این بمه نیست   با ده پیش آر که اسباب جهان این بمه نیست

The harvest from the fields of space and time is not that much
Bring on the wine: the world's affairs do not amount to much

One

Tehran

Not Kansas Any More · *Common Knowledge*
What the Persians have Ever Done for Us · *The Weight of Assumption*
Street Names, Old and New · *Capital Growth* · *The Sweep of History*
Trouble Ahead · *Sorush, my Mentor* · *Heaven's Scent*
Which Iran? · *The Double Life*

جمال یار نذارد نقاب و پرده ولی   غبار ره بنشان تا نظر توانی کرد

The face of the Beloved wears neither a veil nor covering
To glimpse it for yourself, just let the dust of the road settle

AT FIRST, I did not understand the question.

'Been away long?' asked the taxi driver again, more clearly this time. He was studying me now in his mirror with new curiosity. As I settled into the back seat I could make out his inquisitive gaze, his tanned and furrowed brow and the silvery shadow of stubble across his cheeks, lit by the streaking beams of oncoming cars.

'It's my first time,' I said. 'I've never been to Iran before.'

He apologized for the mistake. 'I thought you were Iranian,' he said, 'coming back from America or somewhere. You've got –' his hand made a veil-like gesture in front of his face – 'you've got an Aryan look about you.'

This was a surprise. It was also reminder that I had entered the orbit of a different and more ancient mythology. The very name Iran, I now remembered, was a modern version of the word 'Aryana', Land of the Aryans. But this was all a surprise. Most surprising had been the ease of my own arrival. My flight had been on time, my baggage had arrived swiftly and intact, and I had been waved through immigration with no more than a weary grin from an official.

The shortfall of difficulty had left me with a feeling of suspicion. I had vaguely expected the airport to be draped with revolutionary banners, and to be interrogated under the gaze of booted and unshaven soldiers. I had imagined my possessions spread over long tables and scrutinized by humourless veiled women of the kind who, twenty years earlier, had zealously pieced together the shredded documents from the abandoned American

3

Embassy. But as I walked unhindered out of the customs hall, I met nothing more ominous than a sea of kindly faces, filled with benevolent anxiety and craning from the confining barrier in the hope of a first glimpse of loved ones. Above them, like clusters of fallen blossom on a pond, bobbed dozens of bouquets of fragrant and brightly coloured lilies.

Φ

The warm night air, scented with eucalyptus and diesel, flowed over us as we gathered speed towards the city. The streets were broad, quiet, and lit with yellowish pools of light. Full of the thrill of arrival, I wondered what landmark might first imprint itself at my approach, and searched from the window for some feature of a destination which for years I had been able only to imagine. It was too dark to see much. Beyond the street signs, which were all in English, I could make out the slopes of grassy embankments and sheaves of dusty cypress trees, rising from traffic islands with kerbs painted in black and white. For several miles we weaved through a graceless landscape of shabby rectangularity. Soon rows of concrete buildings began to thicken around us, their rooftops tethered by chaotic webs of wires and telephone cables. Occasionally I glimpsed a string of multicoloured lights, draped from a balcony like a forgotten Christmas decoration. But no domes or slender minarets pierced the eastern sky; only the silhouettes of giant gantries bearing advertisements for washing machines and mobile telephones.

'So, how is Tehran?' I asked.

The driver let out a snort of disgust.

'I expect it's changed over the past few years.'

He sighed cynically.

'It used to be a nice place – in the Shah's time. Now it's all thieves, queers, and swindlers.' About fifteen million of them, according to the most recent census. 'Not like the old days,' he began to ramble, 'when you knew who your neighbours were, and they knew you too. If you had a problem, you could turn to your

4

neighbour. Even for money, if you needed it.' He lifted his hand from the wheel and raked it briefly over a stubbled jawline. 'Now I don't even know who lives next door to me. Peasants from God knows where, who'd sell their own mothers for drugs.'

I laughed in sympathy; but this too was a surprise. Then I remembered I had bought cigarettes at the airport, and passed one forward. It was a ritual which had always helped to break the ice with armed mujaheddin commanders in Afghanistan.

'From England,' I said.

The driver lit one, steering for a few moments with his knees, then examined it with a scowl. 'Those are women's cigarettes,' he muttered. He snapped off the filter, flicked it from his thumb out of the window, and began to puff ruminatively.

'I had a friend who went to England,' he said.

'How did he get along?'

'He got so depressed he committed suicide. It was the way of life. He used to call us up and tell us everyone was on drugs over there.' Then he asked: 'What will you do for alcohol while you're here?'

I said I hadn't thought about it: I had come to Iran to write. No, I wasn't a journalist, nor did I work for the British Embassy. I wanted to write a book about Iran.

'What is there to write about?' he scoffed.

'There's so much . . .' I began. But now, at the threshold of its own fulfilment, the ambition rang oddly in my ears, like a promise made late at night, meeting the glare of day. The breadth of Persian influence — on the art, architecture, literature, poetry, and music of the great cultures of the East — is well known. The vast Ottoman and Moghul empires were modelled on the Persian template, and from Agra to Istanbul and from Samarqand to the Bay of Bengal, a vast bloc of civilization had been impregnated with the legacy of Persian culture.

But what had the Persians ever given to the West? Until not so long ago, generous concessions in tobacco and tea; plenty of cheap oil; a compliant Shah; and, more recently, in the glowering visage of Khomeini, an enduring icon of Islamophobia. It was all a pale similitude of the days when Persia was the intellectual treasury of the world, and its culture a model of sophistication.

It helps to go back a bit: a thousand years, more or less, when the scientists and philosophers of Persia were the outstanding minds of the age. Their learning was distilled from the scholarly heritages of Egypt, Greece, Babylon, India, and China. These ancient polymaths were uniquely placed to serve as a bridge between the cultures of East and West, and did so with far-reaching consequence. Fused in the revelationary crucible of Islam, much of Arab knowledge, so called, was the labour of Persian minds, among them the world's most comprehensive scholars. Transmitted into Europe largely by way of Moorish Spain and rendered into Latin at such bookish metropolises as Cordoba, Zaragoza, and Toledo, their works not only enriched but in some cases formed the very foundations of Western disciplines, and penetrated into every branch of European learning.

It was their universality that impressed; Ibn Sina, better known as Avicenna (whose *Canon* became the world's most widely read text on medicine, and whose *Kitab ash-shifa'* was the largest encyclopaedia of knowledge composed by one person in the medieval period), composed more than two hundred other important works, ranging over language, grammar, phonetics, mysticism, theology, poetry, logic, mathematics, metaphysics, and cosmology. Nasruddin Tusi, one of the most influential medieval astronomers, wrote – in Persian, Arabic, and Turkish – on ethics, psychology, and psychosomatic medicine. Biruni, one of Islam's outstanding philosophers, was also a geographer, historian, natur-alist, physicist, and translator of works on Indian mysticism. Even the most famous Persian theologians, such as al-Ghazali, Europe's Algazel, or Fakhruddin Razi, were known also for their works on law, logic, medicine, agriculture, and anatomy. Omar Khayyām, most commonly thought of in the West as a poet, was one of the great mathematicians of all time.

Φ

Countless other Persians left their mark on the fledgling disciplines of Europe around the end of the first Christian millennium: al-Farabi (Alfarabius) on logic and musical theory; Karaji on hydrology; al-Dinawari on botany, al-Jahiz on zoology and Ibn Haytham (Alhazen) on ophthalmology; al-Kindi on mineralogy, Mansur Shirazi on gemology. A vast corpus of philosophical and metaphysical works also percolated westwards from the pens of al-Kindi, Shirazi, ʿayn al-Qudat Hamadani, and Sohrawardi, whose Illuminationist doctrines were preached to the Oxford school by Roger Bacon; as well as the arcane erudition of Jabir ibn al-Hayyam – the West's Geber – on whose Pythagorean and Hermetic lore the European schools of alchemy were founded, and with whom the enigmatic intellects of Albertus Magnus, Aquinas, Raymond Lull, and Paracelsus are inextricably linked.

But that was more or less common knowledge. Long before the Islamic comet burned through the skies of Western learning, and long after its empowering light had been reduced to a flicker, the westward-bound influence of things Persian can be charted – at least as far back as the time of the Achaemenids, two and a half thousand years ago; perhaps further.

It is an impressive and eclectic legacy: the earliest models of international administration; the banker's cheque; the world's first postal service (from which the United States Postal Service today takes its unofficial motto);* the first international charter of human rights; the first modern astronomical observatory; the first calculating machine; the decimal fraction; the algorithm; the foundations of algebra and trigonometry; the almanac; the astrolabe, forerunner of the mechanical clock; the theodolite; the earliest electric batteries; the windmill and the waterwheel; chain

---

* 'Neither snow nor rain nor heat nor gloom of night stays these couriers from the swift completion of their appointed rounds.' This fifth-century BC quotation from Herodotus' description of Persia's Achaemenid mail couriers is carved onto the entablature of New York's Central Post Office on 8th Avenue and 32nd Street, and is often taken for the official motto of the US Postal Service – which does not, in fact, have an official motto.

mail – unknown even to the Romans until their fateful encounter with the Parthian *cataphracti* – the Parthian shot; the bullfight; the etymological origins of 'paradise', 'magic', and 'scarlet'; the dome built over the squinch, and all the glories of architecture enabled thereby; the flying buttress and, if Merovingian tradition is to be believed, the inspiration for the creed of the Templars, Free-masonry, and the arcane rites of the *fedeli d'amore*; most of the world's finest carpets and miniature paintings, the earliest ceramic glazes, and the origins of delftware and majolica; the 'Arabic' numerals; the 'Arab' horse; the Oxus hoard; the Tusi couple; the Demotte *Shahnameh* and the Freer *Jami*; the Shiraz grape; the carrot; the domesticated rose and, via the empire of the Ottomans, the tulip; the conversion of the godless Mongols to Islam; the Gypsies, according to a tradition of Bahram Gur, the Sasanian king who introduced them to Europe from India; the Baha'i faith; the Koh-i noor diamond of the English crown jewels; the paisley motif; the purple gown of high ecclesiastical office and the tradition of the royal crown; the gardens of the Alhambra and Cordoba; the Taj Mahal; the earliest stained glass; the founding motto of the United Nations; the cult of the Assassins and their Indian derivation, the Thuggees; the octagonal castles of Sicily; Persian cats; Persian blinds; the subterranean Mithreaeums of the Roman Empire and, raised over their ruins, many of the holiest sites in Europe; Mani the Heretic (or prophet, depending on your take), and the fateful persecutions of his Cathar followers in Europe during the Albigensian heresies and the Bogomil anathe-mas; the Phrygian cap, as worn by the stone alchemist of Notre Dame's north tower, the sans-culottes and Delacroix's *Liberté*; Zoroaster; the three Magi (said to have set out from the Iranian city of Qom, and whose bones today rest in Cologne Cathedral); the Virgin birth, the date for Christmas, Christmas lights and the tradition of Christmas trees and, come to think of it, the very foundations of Christian eschatology – heaven and hell, the idea of messianic redemption, angelology, and the sacramental use of wine; the oceanic mystical literature and poetry of Sana'i, Attar, Rumi, Nizami, Shabestari, Sa'adi, Jami, Hafez, Ferdowsi, and of course Omar Khayyām, and from it, the symbolic themes and motifs of Persian Sufism — responsible not only for the pseudo-Persian poetry of Arnold, Shelley, and Tennyson and Fitzgerald's exuberant renderings of the *Rubayyat*, but also, some say, for the curiously antinomian streak to be found in the works of Dante, Chaucer, Shakespeare, Marlowe, Cervantes, Aesop, Ibsen, Blake, Milton, Shelley, Goethe, Nietzsche, Novalis, Vigny, Hugo, Lamartine, Schlegel, Thomas Moore, Emerson, Whitman, Dag Hammarskjöld, C. S. Lewis, Graves, Ted Hughes, Doris Lessing, and Robert Bly, to name a few; the *Thousand and One Nights* (one of the first books to have been translated from Persian into Arabic) and their beguiling narrator, Shahrazād; chess; tennis it seems likely, and certainly polo; and even Kipling's Parsee Pestonji, whose cake crumbs so irritated the Red Sea rhinoceros … all, if one were in the mood for it, could be traced back to Persia.

But I had not yet put these scattered thoughts in order, so I said: 'Art, history, culture — that sort of thing.'

A puzzled look passed over the driver's face; it might have been disappointment.

'I've got friends who are interested in all that,' he said.

He fumbled about the dashboard, and snapped a dusty tape into the cassette player. The car filled with the haunting strains of a slow, stringed melody, to which a man was singing in a high and mournful key, breaking from time to time into a passionate ululating refrain. I had never heard anything quite like it. It was hypnotic and very moving, and beyond the windows the city seemed to be losing its grasp on us, and shrinking from the very frontier of materiality.

'Listen to that,' said the driver dreamily. 'It's not just music, it's *divine*. Have you heard of the poet, Mowlavi?'

'He's called Rumi where I come from,' I said. 'And he's very popular in America nowadays.'

'Then you know there's nothing like it,' he said, cocking his head slightly towards the sound of the verses composed eight hundred years earlier. 'I listen to it when I'm stuck in traffic. It's the only thing to do.' He turned up the volume a little and sighed deeply. 'God,' he said, 'it brings tears to my eyes. Makes me feel like I've died and gone to heaven.'

Soon we reached the hotel. The driver helped me with my bags to the door, and wished me well for my trip. I paid him and offered him the packet of cigarettes. He refused several times; but I already knew of this routine: it was part of the ritual courtesy that Iranians called *ta'arof*. With a final show of reluctance, he accepted, slipped it into his pocket, turned, and, without a backward glance, sped into the darkness.

Inside, what appeared to be a busload of European tourists had overtaken the lobby. I was surprised to find myself among so many foreigners. They were huddling in anxious groups, and a porter was running up and downstairs with their bags. From somewhere a rendition of 'As Time Goes By' was playing over a loudspeaker. A Frenchman and his wife were checking in ahead of me; the receptionist asked for their nationality.

'*Nous sommes citoyens du monde!*' came the reply, but the joke fell flat, evoking only a tolerant smile. The Frenchman wore a photographer's vest with bulging pockets; his wife, in a blatant transgression of public codes that drew all local eyes in her direction, wore a loose scarf, thigh-hugging trousers, and a shirt that reached barely lower than her waist. My own glance was met by the doorman, who was sitting disconsolately at a small table by the entrance. He rolled his eyes heavenward and sunk his head, slowly shaking, into his hands.

My reservation, which I had made from England, was in order. The room was clean and warm, and a small television was showing, on three different channels, a ranting mulla, a football match, and a documentary about gorillas. I opened a window and looked down into the street below. There was a trickle of cars, some men were walking past the shuttered shopfronts, and a few neon signs blinked dumbly above the pavements.

Something held me there for a long time: I am not sure what I was looking for. A hint, perhaps, of something different; an intimation that I had entered a different world from my own.

My last encounter with Asia had been wartime Afghanistan, Iran's eastern neighbour. It was only a few hundred miles away, but now it felt as distant as it did from London. There was no curfew here; no armed men patrolling below my window, no ruined tanks or bullet holes, no front lines around which to plot my trajectory; not even a turban. I heard a thump; it was a slamming door, not the muffled detonation of artillery.

I had arrived in a modern city, where strangers do not invite you into their homes, or ask the range of English guns. No crossfire of enquiry had signalled my arrival. Nor had I yet caught sight of the image of a single glowering ayatollah. Only the practised ritual of women slipping their chadors over their T-shirts as our flight prepared to land had signalled the approach of a different frontier.

The weight of assumptions, when lifted, is apt to leave a hollow feeling. Perhaps the traveller, seeking to affirm his other-ness, requests a toll of unfamiliarity from his surroundings. As I watched the life on the street below thin into stillness, it seemed a fraudulent compulsion. Perhaps I was surprised to find that I was looking at an ordinary street.

It was the last thing I had expected.

Φ

For two days I searched for the refuge of my imagination — a small, family run pension in a leafy cul-de-sac — but found nothing between the extremes of towering luxury hotels and run-down motels whose windows trembled to the cacophony of traffic. Mornings brought a bleaching glare, cruel to eyes and skin accustomed to the gentle vapour of English skies. By day it seemed all the cars of the world had swarmed into the streets, swarming as desperately as salmon on their way to death.

Tehran, I soon discovered, is not a city to explore on foot. Any pleasure of discovery is utterly usurped by the enormous distances between neighbourhoods and the appalling volume of traffic. Out of stubbornness I walked for most of those first days, hoping hour after hour to encounter some tranquil and shady enclave, but finding myself repeatedly at one end, then another, of some vast and charmless street.

I deciphered shop signs as I went. Every other building seemed to be a bank; these are invariably the largest, and evoke a sense of wonder at what such towering, upended concrete shoeboxes can possibly contain. Between them flourish eclectic enterprises, whose signs, in swirling Persian script, make no sense transposed into English, and puzzle for a few moments before the mind switches track: T-O-R-I-N-O P-I-Z-A; B-U-R-G-E-R H-O-W-S; D-A-M-A-V-A-N-D A-N-T-I-Q; T-E-H-R-A-N S-A-N-D-V—I-C-H.

I was looking all the while for the centre, but it is hard to say whether, today, Tehran has one. It has centres, like the heads of a hydra, which are linked by great looping tentacles of motorway in a perpetual state of construction. On early twentieth-century maps, the city's heart coheres around a cluster of stately ministries and foreign embassies, notably those of Britain and Russia, whose walled compounds, even now, stretch over acres. Originally, they were separated by broad tree-lined avenues. But little survives in the congestion and dilapidation of the original centre to connote a heart. From it has haemorrhaged an ocean of concrete, and its pulse has been overwhelmed by the thunder of traffic.

Few monuments of historical appeal have survived this ineluctable wave of progress. Tehran is, after all, only the most recent of Iran's capital cities. Two and a half millennia ago, the founders of the earliest Persian Empire made their capitals far to the south; Cyrus at Pasargadae, and Darius at Susa and Persepolis. Both survive, in ruin, in the heartland of the province of Fars, from which the empire first took its name.

In the early centuries of the Christian era, the Parthians, a nomadic tribe who rose from the empire shattered by Alexander's famous incursion, ruled from Ctesiphon, in today's Iraq; the Sasanians occupied in turn the royal centre until they were scattered by the Arabs in AD 638. For a further four centuries, Persia's Arab overlords ruled from the purpose-built headquarters of Baghdad, though the land was torn by rival local rulers in the east and north. The Seljuks, a nomadic people of Turkic origin, chose Isfahan for their capital in the eleventh century, roughly in the centre of the original empire. The Mongol Ilkhanids, who stormed into Persia in the thirteenth century, favoured Soltaniyeh, then Tabriz, in the north-west. Timur (the West's Tamburlaine) chose Qazvin. The Safavids in the sixteenth, fearful of Ottoman encroachments, moved the capital south again to Isfahan. In the eighteenth century, it was transferred to Shiraz in the south-west. Only at the end of the century was Tehran, under the first of the Qajar kings, declared the capital. It was then a small town of ten thousand souls, sheltered in the leafy folds of the western Alburz hills. And there it has remained.

A century later, in 1890, when Thomas Cook offered its first guided tours of the country, roughly a hundred and fifty thousand people lived in Tehran. It was a twelve-gated city encircled by a moat, ten miles in circuit. By the 1930s, when Persia was officially named Iran, Tehran was a rapidly growing city of nearly half a million. Since then its numbers have vaulted in astonishing leaps. In the late 1970s, its population had grown to five million. A decade later, it had doubled.

Nearing the end of a long and foolhardy circuit, weary feet and a burning neck drove me into the shade of a stall selling fresh fruit juices. The friendly owner plied me with liquidized iced melon. He showed no surprise at meeting a lone foreigner, but at the mention of England, a knowing smile spread across his face, as if to say: I thought as much.

'I had a friend who went to England,' he said. But he didn't know the details. He asked me what I thought of Tehran. It was bigger than I had expected, I said.

'It was good,' he winked, 'under the Shah.'

His grandson, who had been born at least a decade after the Shah's death, hovered by me and took my glass to refill it. 'Yes, it was good before,' he echoed confidently. 'Those mullas have ruined it.'

I was quite lost, and ducked into a taxi. My map, against which I had been checking my creeping progress, was a useless relic. It was twenty-five years old and I could make no sense of it. As we neared the hotel, I recognized the street, marked Kouroche-ye kabir, Cyrus the Great. But it didn't correspond to the signs on the street.

'That was the name before the revolution,' explained the driver. 'Now it's called Doctor Ali Shari'ati Street.'

'Who was he?' I asked, having read nothing yet about the revolutionary intellectual who had risen to fame in the 1970s.

'He was ... a doctor,' came the reply, with a note of dismissiveness.

'Why did they name a street after him?'

'He was an important man – a big man. A thinker. He travelled – abroad. Then...' his hand lifted from the wheel and waved in a motion that suggested infinite worldly complexities, 'then he came back.'

It seemed half the street names of Tehran had been changed since the revolution. I bought a more recent map and that evening unfolded my own next to it, and studied the work of the revolution's cultural copy-editors.

Even a slender knowledge of Iran's history rendered the comparison between old and new names instructive. All references to the nation's imperial rulers, I quickly noticed, had been diligently excised. The city's famous north–south road, formerly called Pahlavi Avenue after the country's extinguished royal family, had become Vali Asr. This giant thoroughfare, which runs from the prosperous northern suburb of Tajrish to the main railway terminal of Tehran's impoverished southern quarter, takes its name from the Mahdi, the messiah figure of the twelfth and final Shi'ite Imam. I followed it with a fingertip on both maps, comparing names. About half a mile to the west, it crossed Shah Reza Avenue, now Islamic Revolution Avenue. Soraya Avenue, after the Shah's wife and Empress, had become Somayye. Shah Avenue, to my south, had been rechristened Islamic Republic. Tehran's most famous monument, named Shahyad in commemoration of the 2,500th anniversary of the Persian Empire, had become the Freedom monument. Amir Abad – Place of the King

— was now Kargar, Worker's Street. Sepah (Cavalry) Avenue had become Imam Khomeini.

This purging of royalty went back further than I had expected. The street named after Nader Shah, whose rule ended the Safavid dynasty in 1736, was now Mirza Shirazi Street, after a nineteenth-century grand ayatollah who defied the British. The name of Shah Abbas, sixteenth-century Safavid ruler and probably the most famous of Persian kings, is similarly extirpated in favour of that of Qa'em Maqam Farahani, a former prime minister, assassinated by royal order. The Street of the Throne becomes the Shrine of the Imam; Takht-e Jamshid, the traditional name of the capital of the Persian Empire, makes way for Taleghani, another revolutionary Ayatollah. Even the name of Ardashir Babakan, founder of the Sasanian dynasty in the second century, is replaced with that of Mir Damad, a seventeenth-century theologian.

But the purge does not end there. The purge, in fact, continues all the way back to Cyrus himself, founding King of Persia, conqueror of Babylon and Assyria, Macedonia and western China, whose rule had ended twenty-five centuries earlier, and who had been officially censored in favour of the enigmatic travelling doctor of my taxi driver.

Foreign imperialist devils have been similarly expunged. France, Churchill, and Stalin Avenues have disappeared; Boulevard Elizabeth II is now Keshavarz — Farmer's Street. Kennedy has become 'Unity' and Eisenhower 'Freedom'; Roosevelt Avenue is now the Madrasseh Motorway: Los Angeles Avenue is now — cheekily, one cannot help thinking — Hejab, 'Street of the Veil'. Bordering the west of the British Embassy is the famous Babisandz Street, after Bobby Sands, whose prison hunger-strikes defied the British government. Anatole France Street is now Qods, 'the Holy'; Goethe has become Shaheed Ahmadi; but the street and square named after Pasteur survive with incongruous tenacity, between Palestine Avenue (formerly Kakh, meaning palace) and Worker's Avenue. Italy Street also survives, as does Argentina Square.

Ghandi Street has usurped the former Park Avenue, but turns incongruously, a little further south, into Khaled Islamboli, the assassin of the Egyptian leader Sadat. It ends as it joins Shaheed Beheshti, formerly 25 Shahrivar — the date on which the Shah inaugurated a radical and ill-fated new calendar, based on the accession of Cyrus the Great in 559 BC.

Yet a paradox soon emerges. The names of all the great Persian-speaking poets have escaped the wrath of the cultural censors. Rudaki, Khayyām, Sa'di, Jami, Hafez, Nasir-i Khusraw, 'Attar, Sana'i, Mowlavi and, of course, Ferdowsi, Iran's most famous poet and literary deity, have all survived. Their preservation suggests, at first glance, a curious intellectual dissonance. Other than kings — who frequently despatched troublesome lerics by imperial decree — few have had a more stormy relationship with the religious orthodoxy than the nation's poets. Their sensual imagery has ever raised the hackles of the righteous, and many of the mystical doctrines expressed covertly thereby have proven inimical to conventional theology. Almost every great lyric poet followed Sufism, the egalitarian principles of which stressed personal intimacy with the Divine, and their works contain much satire at the expense of more worldly and intolerant men of God.

Iran's poets were almost universally — and on occasion, fatally — outspoken against the pedantry and dogmatic bluster of the mulla and the cleric. Their works were by no means irreligious, but have always chafed against the collar of orthodoxy.

For their impudence, one would imagine them to have been the first to be silenced under theocratic rule. Khayyām's bacchanalian evocations border on the orgiastic, and are enough to turn a mulla's beard grey; and Ferdowsi's glorification of the kings of old — of Persia prior to the arrival of Islam — even made his epic *Shahnameh* a favourite symbol of royalist pride under the Shah. His work was in fact shunned, and much scorned, by revolutionary enthusiasts; but it was never officially banned. That Iran's poets were not extinguished — at least cartographically — is evidence of the deep cultural reverence in which they continue to be held.

Φ

Of her visit to Tehran roughly a century ago, the dour and indomitable Isabella Bishop wrote: 'On the whole it impressed me as a bustling place, but the bustle is not picturesque.' There is something to this. On the streets you encounter a feverish energy; no trace of oriental languor hangs about the city's population, which seems consumed by universal haste. Though the faces might be Mediterranean — I thought of Athens at first — the culture of the streets is not. The haste communicates anxiety, not diversion, as if the entire city is racing to discharge the day's obligations as quickly as possible. Harried crowds, not cafe tables, fill the pavements, and only the foreigner has the leisure to stare and wonder.

In the north of the city this dogged clamour lessens; but in the south, where the poverty begins to thicken like a mist and the narrowing thoroughfares grow ever more crowded, one's progress is reduced to a shoulder-bruising shuffle. Heat, dirt, distance, and the ubiquitous curse of pollution conspire against the resolve of the pampered visitor; a taxi offers irresistible refuge. But even this ordinarily straightforward act is a challenge, whose novelty quickly fades.

Taxis do not stop; they sidle. The would-be passenger shouts his destination through the opened window, and the driver decides, according to his needs, whether to stop or move on. Most taxis are shared by six passengers, and ply between the city's main squares and junctions: it helps to know their names, but the visitor does not. Women do not sit between men, so most journeys are preceded by a hurried exchange of places, like the pieces of a Chinese puzzle. There are no meters; the fare is negotiated in advance. Price and counter-price are exchanged above the roar of traffic as both vehicle and passenger creep forward. Frequently a driver whose first offer has been refused will drive on in mock disgust, then stop his car a few feet beyond the passenger, using his stubborn presence as form of leverage. You may relent, or begin the process again. Most of the cars that will stop for you are not, in any case, taxis, but privately owned by men who need the extra cash: it is safe to halve the first price offered.

Conversation is always instructive. My first attempt – I wanted to get to the National Museum – had yielded a cheerful young driver consumed by a knuckle-whitening sense of urgency and a passion for football. He spurred the car into the flow of traffic.

'From England? Seriously? Did you see the match last night?'

I hadn't seen a football match for years, and said I'd missed it. The driver filled me in, with a passionate account of the battle between two European teams, and as he drove he seemed to be reliving the game. Headers sent us diving sideways into different lanes and the thrill of each penalty kicked provoked a lurch of acceleration. What was my favourite team? I didn't really have one, I confessed. He seemed very disappointed, then began to rake my memory for names of English footballers I might know. He knew every goal scored by every player, the names of their wives, lovers and children, and their favourite holiday destinations, and took my ignorance cheerfully.

'What about Maradona? You must have heard of him!' I had, at last. 'That handball didn't make the English very happy! Not with that Falkland Islands business. Some people think he was paid to do it: he can't have done badly. But look at him now! Must be the drugs...'

Didn't I have a favourite player? Never had my knowledge of football, at best impaired, seemed more inadequate. For a few moments my mind was blank.

'Pelé,' I ventured, wondering if he would remember him.

'Brazil–Sweden, 1958,' came the unfaltering reply. 'Stockholm – that was the goal of the century! Right over the defender's head. The second was a header. Seventeen years old and the youngest player ever to win a world cup...'

I was not sure which was more instructive: his knowledge of football or his driving. Years of practice had given him an astonishing confidence in both, and today my understanding of football is linked to ineradicable memories of near death in Tehran.

Seatbelts are hardly ever worn, or grudgingly looped over a shoulder at the sight of a police car up ahead. Traffic lights are only rarely observed. Meeting another car coming the wrong way down a one-way street evokes no surprise, merely annoyance. Junctions are a prolonged exchange of scowls, as eight lanes of traffic head for the centre of the intersection: all looks hopeless at first glance. The drivers, almost all men, have a universally grizzled and exhausted look; lacking the energy to start a fight, their frustration is expressed in glances of exaggerated contempt. Women drivers, in oversized jeeps, negotiate the whole thing with one hand; the other is clamped to a mobile phone, and their conversations are uninterrupted. Everyone, at some point, is on the wrong side of the road. But ten minutes of aggravated jostling, as well as a certain shared faith in the outcome, resolves the initial anarchy. No policeman is summoned: none is expected.

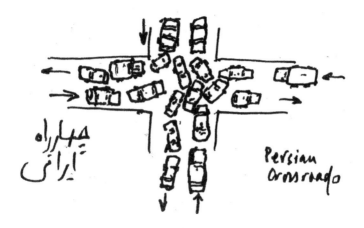

Persian
Crossroads

The sheer volume of cars in the centre of Tehran dampens the threat of high-speed collisions, but along the trembling parabolas of asphalt that link the city's neighbourhoods the traffic echoes the frenzied and violent world of a video game. Cars slew at reckless velocity between the lanes, and swerve to avoid disaster with the suddenness of dragonflies in mid-flight. The drivers descend on each other like fighter pilots, nudging one another's bumpers at sixty miles an hour, and forcing opponents of lesser nerve into the slower lanes with a burst of horn and headlight. Then battle quickly resumes with the car ahead, and the passenger's terror too begins anew.

At dusk, a kind of psychosis descends over the city, like a breeze before a storm, as a million vehicles are impelled collectively homeward. They flee with an urgency that suggests some creeping apocalypse, and the streets swell with weaving headlights dimmed by a veil of fumes.

There is something desperate about all this: it communicates pent-up fury on a huge scale. I often wondered whether it had always been so extreme. I did not yet know it, but was not surprised to find out later that Iran has the highest road-accident rate in the world. A quarter of a million accidents are reported annually, reaping a grim toll of twenty thousand deaths. Day and night municipal tow-trucks patrol the nation's highways like dutiful vultures, awaiting their inevitable carrion of smashed-up metal. Around every Iranian city runs a dilapidated belt of car-repair shops, where the dented and crippled bodies are hammered back into shape and sent back to the front, as it were, a sort of cannon fodder for the gods of the road.

Equally extraordinary is the dispassion with which pedestrians navigate these torrents of flowing metal, daily escaping extinction by a hair's breadth. To observe this spectacle is already painful; to participate is excruciating. At every moment, bodies launch themselves calmly into the lethal fray with scarcely a sideways glance, much less a gesture to convey either warning or – unthinkably – thanks.

It is not bravado or recklessness that prompts them: there is simply no other way. Pedestrian crossings are unheard of. There are occasional subways in the centre of the city, and metal walkways above the larger roads. But they are as rare as oases in a desert. And since what passes elsewhere for the width of a single lane becomes three in Iran, all main streets are transformed into six, sometimes ten interweaving lanes of cars. The flow is ceaseless, and to wait for a break in the traffic across all the lanes is to condemn oneself to a pavement for hours. Each lane must be individually negotiated, like a stepping-stone, while rivers of vehicles flow alongside; the far side is approached in agonizing stages. Frequently, an outer lane, miraculously free of traffic, appears to promise a few moments of relief. This is a bus lane, the flow of which runs contrary to the preceding lanes. A few thundering near-misses quickly refine one's judgement.

Millions are obliged daily to run this heart-constricting gauntlet. Whole families, children, the heavily laden, and old men hobbling at an agonizing pace must all submit to its ritual. And ritual there is, despite its unfamiliar reasoning. 'The whole trick,' someone explained to me much later, 'is to not let the driver think you've seen him, or he'll never slow down. If he thinks you haven't seen him, he has to slow down to let you cross. That's the secret. He doesn't want to hit you.'

Nobody, I agreed, wanted a needless death on their conscience.

'It's not killing you that worries him. It's the paperwork.'

We were creeping now along a busy stretch.

'Look at him,' said the driver scornfully, as a car ahead of us made a dangerous U-turn. 'No signal, and his brake lights aren't even working. That car should be in a garage, not on the road. That would never happen in Europe. There's rules there about that sort of thing.'

There was a sudden screech of tyres, a lurch, and a crunch of impact: we had run into the car in front of us. The driver jumped out, exchanged a few words with the other driver – almost matter-of-factly, it seemed – then stooped down to pocket the fragments of his headlamp. Scarcely a minute had passed before he had settled into his seat and swept us back into the flow. 'What was I saying? That Kevin Keegan – he was never the right man for captain . . .'

At last we came to a swerving halt. As I got out, he was listing the best players of all time. 'Pelé, Cruyff, Charlton, Robson . . . I'll be seeing you,' he said cheerfully, and I thought how absurd the words would sound on the lips of a taxi driver in London. But he was quite right: he picked me up again a few days later, and I was treated to an equally terrifying journey.

Φ

The National Museum was built in 1937 to a Sasanian model, designed by the head of the French archaeological delegation to Iran, André Godard. This was in the heady days when European archaeologists designed Iran's national monuments, and built private castles on the sites they excavated. It is difficult to imagine them submitting to the indignities imposed on the modern tourist. Inside the museum, a sign displayed two entry prices: one for Iranian nationals, and another, ten times more expensive, for foreigners. I never quite got used to this arrangement, and resisted it from the start.

'Are you German?' asked the man who sold the tickets. 'You have a German-looking face.'

'If it helps with the price, I shall be German.'

'The price is sixty thousand *rials*.' That was about ten dollars. 'You are a foreigner: it is nothing for you.'

'And if I were Iranian?'

'Five thousand,' said his assistant, with a malicious grin.

'This museum,' added the other with practised seriousness, 'is the most important museum after the British Museum.'

I pointed out that at the British Museum we charge nothing, and made a long speech about the exigencies of the traveller, his longing to fathom the greatness of Iran's past, and his shortness of cash. They were most sympathetic. They grinned, laughed, agreed enthusiastically with my every point, shook hands with me, and expressed wholesome delight at my visit. Then they exchanged a solemn look, and spoke in unison: 'Sixty thousand.'

It is unwise to compress the history of Iran: it is too vast, and stretches over half the world. Time must be cruelly compressed and the mind's eye anaesthetized to detail before glancing at the nation's past. Popular Iranian history reaches back beyond the grasp of European equivalents to Gayomart, the very progenitor of the Aryan people. He is well known to Iranians through the *Shahnameh* of Ferdowsi, whose epic tale links mythology to recorded history at the time of the Sasanian kings Qay Qubad and Qay Khosrou.

By more concrete measures, the history of the first Iranians can be traced, albeit shakily, three thousand years, to the migrations of the Indo-European tribes of southern Eurasia. This was not the first time, and by no means the last, that the restlessness of these semi-nomadic confederations, as competent in conflict as they were mobile, would impinge on the settled populations of the world. A thousand years earlier, tribes from the same region had rounded the Black Sea, spread through the Balkans and penetrated Asia Minor across the Bosphorus. An eastern branch – the Indo-Iranians, so called – moved round the Caspian and into the Caucasus.

This later wave of Aryans found the territories south of the Hindu Kush already claimed by descendants of earlier migrations, and were forced westward into the heart of what is today Iran. They came with their families, flocks, and cavalries, through natural breaches in the north-east of the country, settling variously, but by no means always peaceably, among the peoples of the Iranian plateau.

Moving west, their progress was checked by well-established states – Assyrian, Urartuan, and Elamite – on whose borders they began to settle. In the area we today call Iran, three ruling clans appear to have emerged: the powerful Medes in the north-west, the Parthians in the east, and in the south, the Persians. Assyrian records list tributes received from the rulers of these peoples in the eighth century BC. The Persians oversaw a small but growing kingdom in the foothills of the Bakhtiari Mountains, where advances in architecture and golden tablets bearing their own alphabet attest to their ingenuity.

From the ruling family of Achaemenes came Cyrus, to whom Median suzerainty rankled. His motives are nowhere recorded, but his ambition was to change the world. In 550 BC Cyrus first defeated, then subsumed the Median army, inheriting the rule of their territories. Three years later his armies marched on the famous Lydian King Croesus, and the Greek cities of the Mediterranean fell reluctantly to Persian arms. The fabulous wealth of Croesus was appropriated to finance the growing empire, and a two-thousand-mile-long royal highway soon linked the Aegean to the king's homeland of Fars. The empire grew under his astute leadership, and within ten years had absorbed Babylon in the west and reached as far into central Asia as the oasis of Khiva, and to the Indus in the east. Conquered rulers, it is recorded, were treated with clemency, and by the Jewish captives of Babylon Cyrus was regarded as a saviour. On the unruly eastern front, thirty years after his accession, he was cut down by the army of the fiery Queen of the nomadic Massagetai.

His son, Cambyses, marched on Egypt, whose armies were defeated at Memphis, and the limits of all the known world seemed within reach. Rebellions flared up at home, but unity was restored by Darius, grandson of the King of Kings. His victories were carved into cliff faces across the empire; his army plundered India, and his navy rounded the Arabian peninsula and reached Suez, where a canal was constructed to link the Red Sea to the Nile. In the empire's heartland he raised a capital built of gleaming basalt, into which the wealth of all the known world flowed in rivers of gold and silver, and whose treasuries were crammed with the annual tributes from thirty countries. This was Persepolis.

The might of this extraordinary empire seemed unstoppable. In 512 BC Darius invaded Europe, but was beaten back by Scythian cavalry on the lower Danube. In 490 the legendary defeat of the vast Persian army by the Greeks at Marathon drove the Great King homeward once more. A decade later, his successor Xerxes raided Athens and burned the Parthenon. But only a few days later, from a silver throne above the straits of Salamis, he watched the Persian fleet decimated by Greek ingenuity. The western frontier remained persistently problematic; but Greece was never attacked again on such a scale.

For a century and a half, Iran remained an unequalled bridge of learning, and cultural exchange between East and West was fertile and widespread. The empire's administration, military organization, coinage, transport, and postal systems were the envy of the world. Persian architecture was adopted in the Far East; Greek men of learning travelled and studied in Persia. Egypt and

Babylon became the cultural and intellectual centres of the world. But dynastic intrigue, corruption, rebellion, and an ever sterner rule had steadily weakened the empire.

Into this fracturing world burst the young Alexander with fateful vigour, spurning the diplomatic offers of the final Achaemenid King, Darius III Codommanus, on whose final humiliation the Macedonian was fixed.

In 331 the king's army was decisively routed at Gaugamela, near the banks of the Tigris, and all of Persia's glories fell into Alexander's hands. His crusade climaxed ingloriously at Persepolis, where the greatest treasuries of the world were sacked and loaded onto the backs of fifteen thousand animals, and the hateful capital abandoned, mired in blood and ash.

The Greek Seleucid overlords inherited Persian territories, but not its heart: the task was too vast, and by a series of drawn-out and bloody campaigns Hellenistic rule withdrew steadily westward. An ambitious nomadic tribe, later called the Parthians, overtook most of the former empire within a century, appropriating the royal Achaemenid lineage en route. Under Mithradates, Persia became a world power, a broker of international commerce, and the old Achaemenid title of King of Kings reappeared on Parthian coinage.

In 53 BC, the same year that Caesar invaded Britain, an arrogant Rome sent its armies to the Euphrates, dismissive of Parthian calibre and seduced by the promise of easy booty. But its legions were checked by the lances of the mailed and mounted Parthian cavalry, then drowned in cataracts of deadly arrows. Twenty thousand Romans died and ten thousand were taken captive in the worst defeat in Roman history. The Parthian military was notorious, but the dynasty's rule was never complete: for five hundred years they fought the Romans in the west and successive nomadic invasions in the east. And in subsuming their Greek overlords and checking Roman might, they had unwittingly incubated a purer Persian revival, nurtured in the very same region of southern Iran where, a thousand years earlier, the Aryan predecessors of the Achaemenid kings had first settled.

The last of the Parthian monarchs died in hand-to-hand combat in AD 224. His victor was Ardashir, the first of the Sasanian kings. A worldly and sophisticated dynasty now arose, and ruled Persia for four hundred years. Religion and state were, for the first time, ingeniously fused, and the ruling kings invested with cosmic authority. Society became rigorously hierarchic, and a centralized bureaucracy and powerful administration oversaw a hugely successful civilization. The powerful Zoroastrian priesthood dispensed royal justice. In the west, the Romans were dealt lasting defeats; in the east, the Kushan kingdom was reduced to a Persian province, and Sasanian art spread as far as the borders of China. The later Sasanian armies besieged Constantinople and conquered Jerusalem; and marched up the Nile to Ethiopia, restoring the borders of Persian rule to Achaemenid vastness.

The most famous kings and generals of this cosmopolitan empire – Firouz, Bahram, Nurshirvan, Rustam – were immortalized in later Persian literature not only for their rectitude and wisdom but also for their prowess as hunters, poets, and musicians. It is a distinctly Persian combination. Their dress and jewellery were exquisite; their imperial headgear fabulously ornate. The life of the Sasanian nobility was cultured and luxurious: from them chess, tennis, and polo were bequeathed to the West.

It was also doomed. The high life of the privileged was financed by a rapacious exchequer, the national armies were exhausted by senseless conflicts, and the misery of an exploited peasantry sent tremors of revolt through an increasingly decadent aristocracy.

Then, at its height, the magnificent edifice begins to sway. It glitters a little longer in a flurry of kings – a dozen in as many years – then collapses with astonishing swiftness. But the coup de grâce was not delivered by any of the civilization's traditional enemies. In 637, when the vaulted and bejewelled palace at Ctesiphon was overrun, it was by a hitherto virtually unknown people. Even today among Persians the memory of their incursion evokes a look of scorn. Their language, religion, and manner was entirely unfamiliar, but their zeal made them unstoppable. At

Nihavand, five years later, the armies of the final Sasanian king were defeated by them, and the body of the greatest empire in the world lay prostrate at its victor's feet. The Arabs had arrived.

If the sweep of this history is extravagant, the portrayal of it at the museum is miserly, and disappoints the eye unaccustomed to finding rapture in pottery shards and Neolithic bronze trinkets. There are some exceptional exhibits: a colossal headless statue of the Achaemenid King Darius, made in Egypt and bearing a cuneiform dedication; a portion of monumental stairway from the palace of Xerxes at Persepolis; a bronze statue of a Parthian noble; a stone capitol from Susa in the form of an addorsed bull; an enigmatic palace mastiff in gleaming black marble; and the undated remains of a prehistoric wanderer, accidentally mummified in a salt mine. But what I had at first taken for a single room turned out to be the entire collection, into which five thousand years of human endeavour had been ignominiously compressed.

Φ

As I left, I heard a voice.

'Was it good?' asked the man who had sold me the ticket. 'Was it as good as the British Museum?'

It was not; and the visitor's book was full of complaints at the price. A pity, you at first think, that in the capital of what was once the world's greatest empire such a paucity of artefacts remain, and that they cannot afford to display them any more creatively. Then, walking next door to the museum of Islamic arts, you realize that the antiquities budget has been allocated elsewhere.

History has been treated more generously here, where the full spectrum of artistic marvels from later centuries — those of the Islamic period — are represented on three marble-paved floors, each crammed with artefacts behind alarmed glass cases, sensitively lit, and all overlooked by watchful guards.

Around a central display of illuminated Qur'āns and manuscripts radiate roomfuls of exquisite ceramics, carpets, brocades, glassware, metalwork, coins, astrolabes, huge stucco friezes, and

panels of lustre-painted tilework immersed in sublime calligraphies. All testify to the passion and ingenuity of the Persian
artist, whose contribution to the art of Islam was in almost every
era superlative. Time and again, Persia falls under the sway of
different rulers; history records twenty different dynastic families
from the outset of Arab rule in Mesopotamia to the present. But
more often than not, the art of the region transcends at every
major historical juncture the creative bounds of its predecessors,
and testifies to a peculiarly Persian talent for seducing and
assimilating its invaders.

The best known of these cultural infusions – those of the
Ghaznavids, Seljuks, Ilkhanids and Timurids – rise not in the
Arab world, but in central Asia. It is an eastern magnet which
draws the artistic centre of gravity of Persia persistently further
from its Arab genesis, as any glance at the physiognomies of faces
in early Persian miniatures will affirm. And in its highest
expressions, all Persian art displays an unmatched delicacy and
refinement. In decoration – perhaps the Persian artist's most
outstanding contribution to art – a highly evolved sensitivity to
both colour and light, a passion for dazzling geometric symmetries, and scripts pushed to the frontiers of legibility bring Persian
art closer to the world of mandalas and hexagrams than to the
Byzantine and Hellenistic traditions in which its roots were first
nourished.

A subtle danger lurks here for Western eyes. The very
opulence of Persian decoration, and that of all the best Islamic
art, has a tendency to bedazzle and overwhelm, to excite a
fascination for the alien and exotic. More rigorous interpretation of any deeper meanings, beyond the undeniable aesthetic
appeal of its shapes and recondite harmonies, has thus tended to
be obscured. Perhaps by its very visual opulence it throws up an
inadvertent barrier to understanding, like the erotic sculpture, so
called, of Lakshamid India, in which early Western observers
found only lewdness.

Whether Islamic art possesses a symbolic language as yet

uncharted — whether it means anything, in other words — beckons the curious mind onto that very territory about which those best equipped to explore — academics and scholars of Islamic art — have been astonishingly reticent. But it is difficult to suppose that an art as prolific and expert as that of the Islamic world was driven by no more than a desire to impress the eye alone.

Great art aims higher. Though the resonance between its hugely varied forms of expression is widely acknowledged, there is no generally accepted theory about any informing principles behind Islamic art, largely because nothing has yet been discovered in Islamic literary sources to explicitly confirm such a principle. The result — officially, as it were — is that the fundamentally abstract nature of Islamic art makes it beautiful, but symbolic-ally mute. Elaborate layers of meaning — entire cosmologies, even — have been uncovered in every form of art from Navajo sand-paintings to Japanese gardens. But I had read nothing to suggest that there was anything to Islamic art other than its beauty, and it seemed a puzzling verdict.

It was early days for this kind of thinking. But it vexed me from the start, and I sensed trouble ahead.

Φ

A strange rushing sound, like the roar of an enormous waterfall, interrupted these thoughts. The guards had gathered wearily around the front entrance, one of two of them with cigarettes cradled in their palms, and all were waiting patiently for me to leave. I went outside, and discovered the roar came from the traffic. It was nearly dusk, and the streets were swollen with jostling cars, like rats fleeing some urban disaster.

I waved down a taxi, agreed a price, and we plunged into the flow. I had been given an address, and an offer of refuge, through friends of friends. It was in the north of the city, but I soon realized the driver had no idea of the route. At each new crossroads, he would mutter the name of the neighbourhood to himself, as if trying to dislodge it from memory.

'Are you quite sure,' I asked him, 'that you know where to go?'

'Of course I know where to go,' he snapped loudly. Then, in rueful tone, said: 'I just ... don't know ... the exact way.'

We stopped to call the address from a public telephone to confirm directions, but the line was inaudible in the noise of the traffic. We tried again, this time at a bookshop, where half a dozen men entered into lengthy speculation over my destination. More than an hour had passed before we reached the north of the city where, as the streets grew narrower, the driver looked more and more anxious.

'Where have you taken me?' he muttered, in the first of a series of skilful attempts to raise the fare. 'This is no longer Tehran.'

'It looks like Tehran to me. Just drive.'

'It might be a dangerous neighbourhood.'

'I will protect you.'

'We have come much further than I expected, and the price of petrol has never been higher.'

'The price was agreed in advance.'

'But it is dark now. The price we agreed was for daytime.'

I had no answer for this.

At last we reached the house. I pressed a buzzer aside an iron gate. There was a clatter of locks, and a man in his sixties with big twinkling eyes and a silvery moustache shuffled across the courtyard. I took him for a watchman, and as I was about to ask him to summon the owner a knowing grin spread over his face, and I hesitated. I was glad I did. It was Sorush: my mentor and host, if I now add it up, for about six months.

I was welcomed into a large and exquisitely appointed home, and left my bags beneath a Qajar painting of a bare-chested, dancing Jewess. We sat on the balcony above a small garden and I shared my first impressions and the grievances I had heard from taxi drivers. Sorush's English was rusty but delightfully learned.

'All Persian love to complain,' he chuckled, 'for them is sport.' He poured generous measures of whisky into a pair of cut-glass tumblers, and we looked out across the northern sweep of the city, which lapped against the darkening slope of the hills.

'For ordinary man, life is work, work, work, unless' – a circling finger evoked a turban above his head – 'he is son of mulla. All business is monopoly of government.' He waved a hand towards the muddy haze that hung over the lowest portion of the city. 'We need a big wind to clean it.'

I had not known the Iran of Sorush's youth: it was an extinguished world. He belonged to a family of influence, and seemed destined to a life of hereditary privilege. He had travelled widely, and watched from abroad as his country collapsed into the revolutionary maelstrom of the late 1970s.

Appalled at the excesses of the time, he had been courted by opposition groups abroad. But politics was not his interest, and exile had made him miserable. Ten years ago, he had chosen to return. Along with countless others of his generation, his familial association with the deposed regime rendered him an outcast under the nation's new leaders. Those like him who had not fled now moved like ghosts within their own society.

'For me was dangerous to return. How many they killed! But too much I loved my country.'

To serve a corrupt government, or relinquish privilege to follow one's conscience? There was a proverb, he told me, familiar to all Iranians: a man either sleeps well, or eats well. But he was not bitter. He had chosen the spiritual consolation of return at the expense of worldly goals, but an air of physical depletion suggested the toll it had taken.

He ushered me outside to a table in his small garden, then disappeared inside. There was another sonorous rattle of ice cubes and he returned with a tray bearing bowls of mulberries and walnuts, and planted the bottle of whisky between us. We watched the silhouette of the hills dissolve into the darkening sky, and soon a web of lights, trembling in the escaping warmth like reflections along a quayside, began to stretch across the lower slopes. Gradually the sound of traffic subsided, humbled now by the evening birdsong. I had expected a chorus of calls to prayer, but there was only a solitary muezzin, whose cry reached us from afar as a thin metallic wavering. Then even this was soon overcome by a sound closer by: the voice of a nightingale in a cypress tree.

Φ

I walked stubbornly for much of the next day. In the late afternoon, somewhere on the vast thoroughfare of Vali Asr, I began to flag. I had not yet calculated that, stretched over London, it would link Parliament Hill to Crystal Palace. A car pulled over.

'Take me somewhere nice,' I said to the driver, and he did. Soon we were in a park on the gently rising slopes of the north, looking down on the shimmering lagoon of the city. Beyond us, a dusty miasma of pollution crouched like a muddy tide against the base of the hills.

We sat and drank tea by the edge of an artificial lake, where couples circled in pedal-boats, or courted furtively on secluded benches. Reza was keen to talk, and I to practise my rusty Persian, which he mocked gently for its Afghan accent. He was a boyish thirty, a little overweight by his own admission, had trained as a dentist, but lacked the money to finish his studies. He bore two scars from his military service, and had narrowly escaped poisoning by gas on the Iraqi front. He wanted nothing more, he said, than to go to England.

Charmed by his gentle manner, I accepted an offer of ice cream at a nearby cafe. We walked to the car, and on the pavement ahead we saw a woman reading what looked like a letter. She was very beautiful, but her face, bewitched by whatever she was reading, was held in an expression of immense sadness.

Beside her sat an old man on an upended crate, tending a pair of budgerigars in a battered cage; a third was perched on his finger. The woman turned, pocketed the piece of paper in her hand, and turned away as we drew nearer.

'Shall we?' asked Reza. It seemed absurd: what would I do

with a pet bird? But he nodded to the old man, who lifted the bird on his finger atop a little box of folded paper slips. He was a *fal-gir*, explained Reza — a fortune-teller. 'You must ask a question,' he said, 'about the future. The answer will be your *fal*.'

As I did so, the bird plucked at the paper slips, lifted one out, and the old man coaxed it deftly from its beak and handed to me. Printed in tiny characters was a couplet from Hafez, I now realized, with a brief commentary.

> O man of fortune, know and be aware that in the near future your troubles will come to an end, and you will reach the goal of your wishes, providing you are righteous in your future efforts. Your star is rising to the ascendant and has left hardship behind.
>
> > If from your neighbourhood the wind would bring a scent
> > I'd give up my life and soul to the winds for the news
> > You're neither before my eye, nor hidden from view
> > You don't remember me, but you won't leave my memory
>
> Your *fal* is very good but an inner longing has made you unhappy. Trust in God that your wish will be granted. You have suffered greatly, but the eventual outcome of your efforts will be successful. Do not forget God.

'That's a good one,' said Reza. 'Everything will work out for you.' He seemed genuinely pleased. My fortune was being told by a tenth-century poet in a twenty-first-century city, and I was struck by the facility with which, among its people, the intervening millennium could be compressed into irrelevance.

We went for ice cream at a local cafe, and then at dusk Reza pointed to a winding road which snaked up the northern hills to a barren ridge. We drove up, reaching the top as darkness fell, and at a roadside stall ate kebabs and smoked a water pipe of sweet tobacco soaked in rosewater. We talked — he, in thoughtfully uncomplicated Persian — of our hopes and things we loved, until we had solved many of the world's ills; and this too was unexpected, as I realized that under the influence of my gently proprietorial host I had not talked so readily about such things with anyone for years. I was very touched when he refused steadfastly to allow me to pay.

We drove back as the air began to chill, and half an hour later we were at the house. A streak of light from the bulb above the door fell obliquely over the car. I thanked Reza for his company and time, but he made no effort to ask for money, so I turned to him across the shadow and said: 'You must tell me how much I owe you.'

'*Qabel-e nadarad*, don't mention it,' he replied, with a deprecatory tilt of his head and a blink of refusal. But I insisted; I had to give him something, if only for the petrol, I thought. He made the same troubled gesture of reluctance, as if by the mention of money I had embarrassed him. For a few moments we were silent.

'Tell me,' I said again.

'Well,' he said at last, coyly, 'if you could just give me the fare from Vali Asr to the park,' and mentioned a figure. I was happy to oblige, and counted the notes into his hand, adding a few more as a measure of my gratitude, and reached for the door.

'And then – *bebakhsheed*, forgive me – there was also the hour's waiting time.' Muttering numbers and times like an incantation, he raised his fingers above the steering wheel in a flurry of calculation. 'At the park – you remember? I make it thirty thousand riyals.'

I counted a few more notes.

'And after that . . . the fare from the park to the cafe.' Soon I was fishing for more cash out of my bag. '. . . and after that was overtime, so . . .' I felt the goodwill draining like water from me as I handed over the final notes, noticing that the troubled look of moments before had entirely vanished from his face. He tucked the money into a shirt pocket, and beamed.

'I'll see you again soon!' he called cheerfully from the window, as I reached the door of the house. But already I hoped I would never see him again. Cursing my naivety, I retreated inside in a fit of inarticulate, English resentment.

Φ

Sorush was downstairs in his shorts, smoking and watching an episode of *The X-Files* in Italian on a huge television. I joined him for a while, then we shared a pot of tea and he asked me about my plans.

Did I want to go to a party, he asked. He had been invited by some friends; we could leave in half an hour if I wanted. I agreed out of curiosity. But I had heard about Iranian parties. Their preferred venue was a basement, lest the music be heard by scandalized neighbours. Lookouts were posted in the street to scan for gangs of roving police, famous for their ferocity on discovering nests of moral corruption. Illicit music and alcohol were smuggled in with great cunning, and consumed at the risk of flogging. At a sudden signal, the entire assembly, in a well-rehearsed drill, would conceal all trace of contraband in specially designed hiding-places; the women would slip beneath their chadors, and everyone would pretend to have been reading poetry. I saw myself clambering down a drainpipe pursued by a bearded and fanatical gendarme, and wondered how Sorush would fare at the moment of crisis.

We left at midnight, and drove for half an hour to a small unlit street, somewhere in the north of the city. There must be few countries in the world where the prospect of attending a party can evoke such feelings of guilty anticipation in the newcomer. But my fears were misplaced, again.

We entered a new apartment block; Sorush adjusted his jacket and cravat, and we began to climb several flights of white marble stairs. Even from the ground floor of the building we could hear the music. It tumbled down to meet us, first as a deepening throb, then resolving as we neared into what sounded like an extravaganza of flamenco. Outside the door, which had been left open, a hat-stand was draped like a Christmas tree with the gold chains of ladies' handbags. Within, I could make out an energetic swarm of bodies, into which Sorush disappeared with a wink. It was impossible to hesitate; an arm ushered me inside, and a glass of red wine was pushed gently into my hand.

The throbbing came from two men seated on cushions on the

marble floor with different drums, one called a *zarb* and the other a *dombaq*, like a giant tambourine; three other musicians played a lute-like *setar*, a *santur*, the prototype of the dulcimer, and a *kamanche*, played with a bow like a violin. To their rousing oriental mode, a tall and beautiful woman was dancing in the middle of the floor, urged on by a riotous clapping of fifty pairs of hands. Others perched on faux Louis XIV furniture. The dancer's bare arms were twirling wildly and her long black dress, shot with silver thread, shimmered electrically. The whole room seemed to be trembling.

A procession of urbane and well-dressed couples continued to arrive, neatly confronted by a tray of drinks circulating aloft on the hand of a waistcoated servant. Every other man carried a black and oddly shaped instrument case, like members of an oriental Lavender Hill Mob, and the fingers and wrists of the women sparkled in golden flashes.

I felt very bumpkinish and sheltered near the door. The entrance ceiling was made of smoked mirrors which receded upwards in octagonal tiers. My glass was refilled as if by magic, and soon from the kitchen emerged an urgent relay of dishes trailing steamy, perfumed wakes. The crowd gathered around a glass-topped table, laden now with mounds of rice like smoulder-ing volcanoes, bejewelled with crimson barberries and saffron threads, or piled in multicoloured layers with pomegranate seeds and slivered orange peel. Ranged around them were platters of salads and meats cooked with fruits and spices. Later, in their place, came pastries, profiteroles, ice creams, and liqueurs.

I wondered if I had ever been to such a civilized gathering, where pleasure was so delicately matched with poise; everything about it suggested a way of life I had naively imagined to be extinct. I had read many of the early twentieth-century accounts of the genteel peregrinations of English travellers – the scholarly Edward Browne, addicted charmingly to opium; or Byron and Sykes, traipsing confidently through the ruins of Persepolis, endlessly quaffing local claret on consulate verandas or turning down offers of tiger-shoots – all evoke a world of irretrievable romance. To outsiders at least, the Iran of the time was associated with nothing but civility and refinement. Privileged travellers of the era picnicked habitually with ambassadors or drank tea with nomad chieftains among the ruins of Firuzabad, admired the sophisticated bloom of Persian art, and strolled the leafy boulevards of Isfahan. All is leisure and untrammelled delight. Even until virtually yesterday, the memoirs of travellers to Iran suggest a quality of the unworldly; scholarly deputations sent from Oxford to measure the dimensions of Assassins' castles, or to investigate the habits of subterranean sightless fish. But nothing I had read or heard of Iran's recent history had prepared me for any trace of romance; darker ideas adhered to the name Iran today. In 1979, Atlantis-like, the charm of the land sank from the world's view beneath the waves of revolution, the murderous excesses of a thuggish secret service, the exile of a generation, and a ten-year war with Iraq medieval in the scale of its carnage. Little in the intervening years had softened the imagery of the implacable gaze of turbaned mullas, of throngs of unshaven fanatics, their fists poised defiantly aloft, their booted feet trampling the embers of their enemy's flags.

Except, perhaps, in Iran itself. A new round of musicians had taken up their instruments, and the beat was quickening, growing louder and wilder by the minute. Men and women had gathered to dance again and were stamping like matadors, or circling one another with gazes interlocked. I moved closer, to a marble-topped bar, where the exhausted musicians had swapped their instruments for tumblers of vodka. The door and windows, through which I expected the Revolutionary Police to come swinging inside, truncheons flailing, had been thrown open, and the music was trailing into the darkness. There was no hint of restraint, much less of the furtiveness which, until that evening, had seemed likely to mark my every encounter. My Iran, and everything I had assumed about it, was dissolving before my eyes.

Suddenly I was aware that a woman had settled onto a stool beside me. She wore a white blouse and leather skirt, and her unlit cigarette wavered towards me at the end of a long black holder. At its far end was a gently smiling face of weary but striking beauty. As I fumbled for matches, she introduced herself in English.

'I feel sorry for the neighbours,' I joked, nodding towards the dancing.

'We *are* the neighbours,' she said, blowing a languorous puff of smoke, Dietrich-style, into the air above us. Her name was Farideh. She was an artist, she said, and divided her time between Tehran and a home on the Caspian. Mirage-like, she seemed to grow lovelier at every moment.

'And you are English, you are a writer, and you want to travel around Iran,' she smiled. It was a gentle smile, but charged with a kindly cynicism. 'Be careful,' she said, 'we have a history with the English.'

I looked across to the dancing with mixture of delight and disbelief. It was not, I told her, quite what I had imagined.

'You are surprised?'

I was, I said. The last thing I had expected to see was people enjoying themselves with such abandon.

'You see,' she blew another puff of smoke upwards, and waved her hand in a languid arc towards the dancing throng, 'here in Iran we lead a double life.' She smiled again. 'Understand that, and you will understand everything.'

Two

Tehran · Isfahan

*The Faces of the Doomed · Geography · First Glimpses of Isfahan
History of the Chahar Bagh · Half the World · The Naqsh-e Jahan
The Royal Mosque · The Mosque of Sheikh Lutfullah
Gardens of the Unseen · The Vision of Shah Abbas · Grim History*

مرا و دل ز تماشای باغ عالم چیست   بدست مردم چشم از رخ تو گل چیدن

What is the Heart's purpose in gazing on the garden of the world?
To gather the flower of your face in the grasp of the eye's pupil!

ALL OVER Tehran, from billboards, vast hoardings, and windowless facades, the eyes of the nation's war dead look onto the world of the living. At first I had thought these giant paintings, some of them thirty feet high, to be of present-day military leaders. But by degrees they became more articulate and I began to realize they were nothing of the sort. They were impossible to miss, though no one had pointed them out to me; to the local inhabitants they had perhaps acquired, like the clamour of the streets they overlooked, the invisibility of the familiar.

The portraits depict faces from among the hundreds of thousands of Iranian soldiers who died in the decade-long war with Iraq. They are heroic, as they are intended to be: giant in scale, ubiquitous, and powerful, as statements with a political dimension are apt to be. But no medals glint on their chests; there are no jaws clenched in martial fervour. Aggression is the last emotion to cross their brows and the youngest are, on the contrary, almost meek, their features suggesting an untempered idealism more fitting to a gallery of poets than of soldiers.

They are family members, whose ordinariness evokes their untimely departure from home. In the faces of the older men, there is an avuncular quality, and their gentle smiles suggest the inner resolve born of great suffering. Such faces do not speak in the conventional language of heroism; the very concept of their portrayal reaches for a different place in the scale of the pathetic. The note is struck by their eyes, which look onto a distant world with a gaze that expresses the singular knowledge of men who have already glimpsed their fate: they are doomed, and know they are doomed.

Sometimes these portraits lie against a sun-coloured, eight-pointed star, bearing in an upper corner the insignia of a military unit. More often it is the imagery in the surrounding field which tells the victim's story. There is little technical merit to these background elements; but their coarseness, executed at times with almost childlike strokes, renders them more articulate. Above the faces of a four-man aircrew, the bulky silhouette of a bomber, its wings streaked by moonlight, tells of an ill-fated night-time mission. In another, behind a pair of youthful faces, stretches a field of blood-red tulips, and from the nearest, a shimmering drop hangs from a rim of petals: dew or a tear? Another man's reckoning is told, beneath the martyr's otherworldly gaze, by a pair of dog tags draped over a landmine. Elsewhere, an amphibious assault unfolds amid plumes of watery detonations, or a ragged line of men return at dusk from an operation along a muddy embankment lined with palm trees. Behind them, rid now of the enemy, lies a ruined village, from whose charred and fractured walls a plume of black smoke ascends into the sky.

Often the symbolism borders on the evangelical: a troop of infantrymen cross an open field on patrol, and through gaps in the clouds above them, the sun's rays stream over them in broadening shafts of golden benediction. Everywhere the message is driven home with calligraphic sayings of the Imam: 'The greatest sin is to forget the heroism of the martyrs'; 'The smiles of the martyrs shine like stars from Paradise'; 'The martyred are like the *suras* of the Holy Qur'ān'. This alliance of religion and slaughter strikes a sinister note, until one remembers that the walls of every other English church are draped with regimental flags, and chiselled with countless elegies to our own glorious dead. But stripped of their political connotation, the iconography of these visual memorials, against which our own seem mute, betrays a predisposition to both nuance and suggestion; an acute sensitivity to suffering, a susceptibility to tragedy. They allude, also, to a different geography of time. The dead are not merely dead: they have been resurrected into the present, where they subvert the usual continuum by carrying with them the knowledge of their impending extinction. Their gaze is purgatorial: it is a strange and haunting manipulation.

I had stopped beneath one such giant portrait and was copying the script into my notebook ('martyrdom is the courageous art of the men of God') when a teenage girl stopped on the pavement next to me, waiting to cross. She wore sunglasses, violet lipstick, and a light-coloured scarf. A phone was clutched to her ear; her nail varnish was a lurid pink, and her chador was no more than a baggy shirt. On the far side of the road a brand-new Peugeot had pulled up, and a pair of young men, phones clipped like pistols to their belts, stepped out to wait. She waved to them, mid-conversation, then skipped across.

This sudden glimpse of youthful purpose, decked with the brash trappings of modernity, had woken me as if out of a daydream. Suddenly I regretted I had not stopped her to ask what she thought of the looming face above. She would have been an infant when the war had ended, nearly fifteen years earlier, and tasted nothing of the immediate horrors of revolution and conflict; she would have little time for the doleful sayings of the kind I had just been writing down. For a moment I wondered what her answer might have been, but it wasn't difficult to guess.

Φ

The duality of old and new is always sharpest in cities, where prosperity goads forward the encounter between fashion and tradition. In Tehran I had the impression of moving at a moment's notice between different worlds. One summer's morning, a friendly neighbour invited me to an open day at one of the city's international colleges. The interior of the compound had diplomatic status, and the usual codes of dress and segregation ceased at the door, through which, as we arrived, a little crowd was funnelling. Within, two hundred students had seized hungrily on the opportunity to mingle, and to the trilling of mobile phones all around were busily reclaiming liberties

unthinkable in public. The young men were all lean and dash-
ingly groomed, and the girls had dressed to kill. Or rather,
undressed. At the door, scarves were being energetically torn off
like the masks of divers coming up for air, sending jet-black
curls tumbling over tattooed shoulder blades. Drab coats were
dispensed in heaps, exposing sequinned singlets, jeans hung lower
than a gunslinger's belt, more tattoos – further down now, I
couldn't help noticing, and as elaborate as Lindisfarne Gospel
illuminations – and a good number of bejewelled navels, flashing
from slender midriffs.

But the pleasure in this to the unaccustomed eye was offset by
the disturbing sight of half a dozen girls with surgical tape across
the bridges of their noses. The marks of that ugly vice, jealousy,
were never so cruelly expressed as on such fine-boned features. At
least that's what I thought, until I counted an equal number of
male victims, and wondered who had been breaking their noses,
too.

'They all have it done nowadays,' explained my host for the
occasion. 'Being able to afford a plastic surgeon is a status
symbol.' Much later, I even saw a mannequin in a shop window
with the telltale splints and tape across its nose.

When it was time to leave, the girls took up their scarves and
coats, disappearing beneath them like flowers whose petals close
as evening falls. It was strange and a little sad to see them go.

Today, the rules – on dress codes, parties, and public displays
of affection – have lost much of their revolutionary potency.
Their interpretation makes for some odd social barometers, like
the amount of hair showing in public from beneath women's
headscarves, which diminishes perceptibly when the government
is going through one of its periodic spasms of intolerance.
For obvious reasons these rules on public conduct affect life
deeply – though perhaps not as deeply as the outsider usually
imagines – and any form of shelter against public scrutiny excites
a confessional impulse. Even the doors of a taxi provoke, more
often than not, a collusive unburdening.

I had imagined, in those early days, that I might inch my way into the confidence of strangers, extracting, one day perhaps, some hushed intimation on matters political. But I had not counted on the loquacity of the nation's taxi drivers, or the universality of their grievances. They did not complain about the traffic or pollution, as one might expect; they complained relentlessly about everything else.

The state of the economy topped a baleful list. What kind of life was it, I was asked daily, when a man had to work two or three jobs just to earn enough to survive? One embittered driver claimed to earn more behind the wheel of his taxi than as a university professor. Prices were spiralling; there were no jobs for the young, and Iran, a country rich in natural resources, should not have to live with such poverty...

These dirges soon had a familiar ring. Blame was always generously apportioned upwards. The nation's wealth lay firmly in the grip of the regime, whose leaders grew fat while the nation starved. All talk of social and economic reform was hollow. Even the name of Khatami, Iran's most moderate and progressive president, twice elected with overwhelming margins, evoked disappointed sighs. Yes, he was a good man all right, and had meant well enough – no one disputed that. But he was powerless, and his promises amounted to nothing.

Among older men, these simmering plaints were welded into a bitter nostalgia, and tinged with conspiracy. 'In the Shah's time...' they would begin, pointing out the streets which, in their youth, had been lined with bars and nightclubs. No wonder, some said, the young were turning to drugs; worse, the government itself was making drugs more available and cheaper than ever, in the hope of stupefying an entire generation. These, one sensed, were ills of a new and entirely crueller order than those of the past. With wistful smiles, foreign friends from the old days were tenderly recalled; Mr John from London, Mr Mike from Texas; good and generous people who were 'gone, all gone now...'. But the government? Thieves and plunderers, the lot of them.

Such heresies as these, I had naively supposed, would be

uttered – if heard at all – in whispers, and only then between the best of friends. But they were a daily litany. My naive fear of informers, trained to evoke subversive sentiments from foreigners, was soon dispelled by the sustained tenor and range of local protest. The woes of the nation were not an open secret: they were not secret at all. A few times, emboldened by a vociferous ranting, I asked whether – if things were really so bad – anything might be done. Done? The response was always the same: 'Heech...' Nothing. Nothing? An answering finger, drawn silently across the throat, expressed the fate of transgressors.

Some boasted cynically of illicit vices to be had at home. One extolled the virtues of opium, another his preference in foreign whiskies, and another the ease with which women – old, young, fat, thin – could be procured by a single phone call. Younger men looked outward to distant and idealized worlds. What was my monthly salary? What amount could one comfortably live off in England? What were the prices of things there – an apartment, rent, bread, a haircut, a kilowatt of electricity, a dowry? – the answers to all these evoking gawping expressions of disbelief. How easy was it to get a British passport? Almost daily I was asked whether I knew someone at my embassy. The implication was obvious, and I found myself attempting to head it off. Even if I did know 'someone', I said, the rules for passports were the same for everyone; and was surprised to hear a note of righteousness creep into my own answers, a defensive impulse to quash extravagant misconceptions before they took flight. But my explanations – on passports and state benefits and profit margins always evoked the same tuttings of puzzled disappointment, the same expression of simmering disbelief.

Φ

Iran is vast. Three thousand miles of terrestrial border, and one and a half thousand miles of coastline, enclose a country of enormously varied geography. A determined and diagonally inclined visitor, walking from the border with Turkey in the north-west to the south-eastern coastline of the Sea of Oman, would cover the same distance as London to Athens, and encounter even greater contrasts in climate and landscape along the way. There is permanent snow and ice on the slopes of the highest mountains, and searingly hot and corrosive desert winds all across the lowest plains. Fertile and temperate valleys enclose their periphery, and encircling the southern shores of the Caspian Sea there are lush forests of tropical humidity.

The main body of the country is bounded by two lofty and extensive mountain ranges, and the coastlines of two oceans – the Caspian in the north and the Persian Gulf in the south. The northern mountains, called the Alburz, run from Iranian Azerbaijan in the west to the Afghan border just beyond Mashhad in the east, and confine the watery atmosphere of the Caspian to a lush and fertile rim of land along the country's upper border. One feels sorry for the land south of this range, which sees nothing of the life-giving deluges of the far side, and culminates, across the huge central swathe of the Dasht-e Kavir, in the bed of an extinct interior ocean – the most arid depression in the world.

The second major mountain range stretches for six hundred miles from the north-west to the south-east in multiplying parallel folds up to a hundred miles wide. The area thus enclosed is called the Iranian plateau; six hundred thousand square miles of land roughly triangular in shape or, as it occurs to me now – taking the north–south Afghan border as its rim – a Phrygian cap in a southerly wind, whose northern and southern edges roughly delineate the lines of the Alburz and the Zagros.

Only ten per cent of this vastness is today cultivable, though the figure may once have been much greater. Prior to the depredations of the Mongol armies in the thirteenth and fourteenth centuries, an extensive and ingenious system of irrigation allowed garden-ringed cities to flourish in desert regions where now only desiccated ruins remain. Even in their own time, the architects of these oases drew on an already ancient precedent; a system of underground channels known as *qanats*, first put to use three thousand years ago in the Assyrian territories of what is now northern Iran. The Achaemenid King Cyrus the Great, recognizing the transformative potential of widespread irrigation, ordered the system to be spread throughout his burgeoning empire in what has been called the greatest civil-engineering project in the history of the world. Ten million gallons of water a minute are estimated to have once flowed along these subterranean aqueducts of the east, enabling water from the snow-fed aquifers around mountain bases to be borne along gently sloping tunnels for as far as thirty miles. From the air these life-giving arteries resemble the meanderings of giant and restless moles, poking upwards every fifty feet or so through the mouths of shafts encircled by rubble.

They are a constant feature of the Iranian landscape and a reminder of the enduring marriage long ago consummated between water and survival and between its loveliest expression, the garden, and the soul's repose. All Persia's early god-kings were gardeners, and wherever its rulers built palaces they built gardens too, and boasted proudly of them. The walled gardens of the Achaemenids were called *pairidaeza*, the very meaning of which is preserved in our modern word for paradise; and in countless mythological, religious, and poetic allusions, the garden, as a place of physical welfare as well as of spiritual promise, an image of perfection and contemplation and symbol of the victory of life over the obliterating elements, penetrates all Persian culture.

The land itself celebrates this ancient pact. During the short-lived month of spring, the entire country bursts into momentary colour. Even the desert is transformed into a carpet of wild flowers, and the eye-punishing glare of abrasive alluvium is relieved by a radiant mantle of buttercups and anemones and narcissi and tulips and long-leafed wild hyacinths. 'I saw a garden pure as paradise,' says Nezami in his *Haft paykar*,

> A myriad different hues were mingled there
> A myriad scents drenched miles of perfumed air
> The rose lay in the hyacinth's embrace
> The jasmine nuzzled the carnation's face

Φ

Until recently, apart from those visitors making pilgrimages, nearly all foreign visitors to Iran had travelled in approved groups. The restrictions were gentler now, but it was still early days for independent wanderers. A lone Englishman, loose in the vicinity of troublesome borders with camera and notebooks, was bound, at some point, to excite the local authorities.

It seemed prudent to ask for advice. I called on the BBC's Tehran correspondent, who was kind enough to fill me in. The south-east was off limits to foreigners, he said; the border with Iraq was sensitive; and it was inadvisable to travel alone in Kurdistan. Recounting uncomfortable nights spent in police cells, he suggested I register with the authorities, obtain an identity card, and let them know my plans in advance. This seemed like good counsel: if I were to be followed by the secret police, they would at least know who they were following.

A day later I made my way through a warren of corridors at the disconcertingly named Ministry of Islamic Guidance. The Deputy Minister of Cultural Affairs received me at his desk, wearing on his face the national look of weariness and the three-day stubble that in Iran designates high office.

I had prepared a speech of the kind which elsewhere had worked quite well, and launched in. News from Iran was all too often coloured by politics, I proposed. But a great many people in my own country, who knew something of Iran's abundant heritage, were hungry for more than news alone. A personal account of travel through the country was the perfect means to introduce the richness and variety of Iranian culture to a generation of readers: it would be the first to appear for twenty years. This was the very opportunity which, with the kind assistance of the ministry, I was hoping to explore . . .

There was a silence which seemed very long. Then, with a look of tolerant perplexity, the minister spoke.

'How can we help you?' he asked in English.

I felt a ripple of panic: perhaps he had read quantum theory at Oxford or Harvard, and was unaccustomed to being talked to like a child. I said I had thought it a good idea to introduce myself and that, before travelling to the remoter parts of the country, I would alert the ministry to my intentions.

'It is unnecessary,' he said flatly. 'You can go anywhere.'

'Anywhere?'

'Anywhere.' He shuffled in a drawer and passed me a copy of the *Iran Media Guide*, suggesting it would help: I flicked through the pages, glimpsing extracts of the 1989 constitution, details of women's revolutionary organizations, and megawatts of electricity produced by region.

'Perhaps...' I extracted a copy of my previous book, and presented it with a reverent flourish. 'To give you a better idea of what I had in mind...'

He turned it over in his hands, glanced indifferently at the covers and put it aside, unopened, its dedication unread. Even the glowing jacket quote from a very-famous-English-travel-writer had failed to impress.

'Somebody has already done that,' he said, with a touch of irritation. 'A Frenchwoman.'

It seemed impudent to suggest that English-speaking people had in general stopped reading books in French after Voltaire, nearly two hundred years ago. There was another pause, and I sensed it was time for a tactical retreat. The telephone rang. The minister spoke for fifteen minutes. Then, after a concerted staring at the papers on his desk he looked up, as though surprised to see that I was still there.

'Is there anything else?'

I thought of the advice of the correspondent I had talked to, and asked whether an identity card might be possible to arrange. 'In case,' I suggested, 'of difficulties.' Vengefully, I pictured myself presenting it to the staff at the National Museum, and entering for the Iranian price.

The minister sighed, leaned back in his chair and looked vaguely at the ceiling as he spoke. 'If you want,' he said, 'you can make an application, which will be passed to the Minister of Foreign Affairs. It must be approved by your embassy. You must provide details of your project and letters from your organization.

Then it will be evaluated by the Ministry. If it is successful you can apply for an identity card. But for this you must have a press visa.'

'Where do I apply?'

'In your country of origin.'

Our meeting had ended. I thanked him for his time. Next door, his secretary gave me a few more official guides. As I left, I reached out instinctively to shake her hand, but she tucked it protectively into her lap.

'I am sorry,' she said meekly, 'it is the regulation.'

I went to Isfahan. No other city in Iran is associated more deeply with the charms and delights of Persia. For several years I had idly cherished a vision of sharing a water pipe with a native in a tea-house beneath the arches of one of the city's famous bridges, and whiling the day away to the murmur of the river.

It had at last materialized; although the native had lived most of his adult life in Amsterdam, the tea-house was nearly deserted, and the famous Zayandeh River, its murmur supplanted by the pneumatic drills of nearby roadworks, was dry. Its vacant bed was lined with a desiccated mat of water weed, and a child was batting an old tyre across the fracturing mud. On the opposite bank, a dozen stranded paddleboats were beached like stray fragments of brightly coloured driftwood.

'A punishment from God,' said Ramin. We had met on the

morning bus from Tehran, talked the whole way, and had decided on arriving to spend the afternoon together in the city of his youth. Ramin was in his late twenties and returning to Iran after a decade of study and travel in Europe, where he'd trained as a film-maker. He spoke fluent English, and his gentle manner was shot through with a dark vein of cynicism towards the plight of his country under its present rulers.

He had already argued with the taxi driver who brought us from the bus station to the bridge of thirty-three arches, and thrown the fare onto the dashboard as we got out with a protesting curse (so that was what one did when overcharged!). Now we were amply consoled with tea and garlanded in swirls of thick and fragrant smoke. Beside us was a tall and shapely water pipe producing a muffled and satisfying bubbling. At first sight, these apparatuses, looking like the offspring of a snake and an alchemist's alembic, evoke all the illicit pleasures of the East, a suggestion of the stupefaction of opium-den habitués, and Alice's enigmatic encounter with the caterpillar in Wonderland. Nothing could be unfairer. In their native home they are as ordinary as teacups in England and bear no comparison to their uncouth and self-centred relative, the cigarette. The tobacco that is smoked in them is infused in rosewater or honey and flavoured with apple, lemon, banana, or strawberry, the 'Frankish mulberry'. It produces smoke as mild as mist, and a small nugget shared between friends outlasts even the lengthiest Cohiba.

At a neighbouring table, a portly fellow pipe-smoker was explaining why the river had dried up. Divine retribution for the moral laxity of the city's populace was only one of the likely causes. Another theory held that too much of the water was being siphoned off upstream to irrigate the pistachio orchards belonging to the former President Rafsanjani; another, that the entire flow had been diverted under a secret and hugely lucrative government deal to sell water to the Kuwaitis. I asked Ramin, after we had thanked our neighbour for his news, whether it might have something to do with the recent lack of rain. He shook his head, as if I had failed to understand.

'This is Iran,' he said glumly. 'They prefer the conspiracy.'

He was as keen as I was to explore, so we took a few final puffs of our pipe, looped the slithering coils of the mouthpiece around the cooling stem, and got up to pay. A new argument now ensued, this time with the owner of the tea-house who, having heard us speaking English, had charged us above the going rate. Ramin launched into a long and vociferous tirade, heaping scorn on the conscienceless (and impassive) owner, to whom he turned his back with a snort of disgust and left only after a long stand-off, which I insisted on breaking by paying the difference – a minuscule sum – despite indignant gestures of refusal from both sides. This highly evolved sense of protest – seventy per cent theatre, twenty per cent a matter of principle, and ten per cent about the money – seemed a vital tool for survival, but I knew I would never fully acquire it.

We set off northward with the afternoon sun above our left shoulders, and wandered towards the monuments of the city centre along the Chahar Bagh. The name given to Isfahan's main thoroughfare means 'four-fold garden', and echoes an ancient prototype beloved in Iran for millennia. Geometrically ordered gardens, laid out on the symmetries of squares and rectangles, were built at least as early as the Achaemenid era; Cyrus the Great is recorded as having himself designed the vast park at conquered Sardis, and planted the trees there with his own hands. Later Sasanian palaces were often built at the intersecting axes of enclosed gardens whose perimeters stretched for miles.

Islamic artisans took up the theme of the garden as a re-creation of heaven on earth with simultaneously artistic and scientific relish, investing it with geometric sophistication and aesthetic grandeur. And in Isfahan, the idealized garden found one of its most exuberant expressions which stood in direct line to its most ancient Achaemenid antecedents. More than two thousand years earlier, at the royal capital of Pasargadae, Cyrus the Great had built a palace complex surrounded by a shimmering and fragrant expanse of gardens. From a throne set within the palace colonnade stretched a broad and tree-lined avenue three-quarters of a mile long, down the axis of which ran a limestone water channel set at intervals with reflecting pools made of stone.

Somehow, across this vast sweep of time, upheavals of dynasty and centuries of foreign domination, the underlying template was transmitted to Safavid Isfahan. Though conventional history offers us nothing as to how it was preserved, it became gloriously visible once again at the turn of the seventeenth century, along the very trajectory which we were now following.

The original Chahar Bagh was a mile-long promenade, bisected by a central canal built of onyx and interspersed with broad reflecting pools, fountains, and cascades. It was a hundred yards wide and, according to the indefatigable French explorer Chardin, three thousand paces long. Eight rows of cypress, juniper, plane, linden, and oriental-pine trees flanked the thoroughfare, which was scented along its length by rose hedges and jasmine-wreathed arcades; the Shah himself is recorded as having supervised their planting, scattering gold and silver coins among the roots. A late-seventeenth-century description by the English explorer Fryer evokes the Chahar Bagh in its heyday: a place 'as much frequented as our Hide Park, and for as little purpose', and where the city's nobility could be observed 'striving to outvie each other in pomp and chivalry ... only to see and be seen, though the whole pretence be to take the air.'

Beside it grew up the glittering pavilions of the court, each with its own expansive gardens, and the private homes of the royal ministers, high-ranking officials, magistrates, diplomats, and the Shah's favoured subjects. Even the court jester and the court astrologer had their own mansions. Each was a miniature kingdom, and surrounded by lesser buildings to house guards, staff, stables, baths, wine cellars, and personal harems. Among them once stood the homes of such colourful characters as Mirza Razi, the Shah's grandson, who had been blinded at birth by a clumsy eunuch, and wore a paper mask to conceal his disfigurement. His household numbered four hundred; his harem needed three walled pavilions; he was skilled in algebra and wrote books on mathematics, carried out astronomical calculations with an astrolabe he had made himself, and had a collection of two hundred clocks which he liked to take apart and reassemble to entertain his guests.

The Jahan-Nama, a royal pavilion of which no trace remains today, stood at the northern end.* At the southern end, beyond the prowling tigers of the imperial zoo and the imperial aviary, where such curiosities as featherless ostriches were confined, stretched the Hezar jerib, a vast ornamental orchard built on twelve ascending terraces and a grid of canals, where five hundred fountains danced. Doves cooed in the overhanging boughs, and at night, thousands of lanterns were lifted into the branches along the entire length.

To the east, enclosed by high walls, lay the heart of the imperial complex. It was three miles in circumference and contained the royal palaces, harem, and suppliers and workshops of every kind serving the imperial household: jewellers, carpetmakers, blacksmiths and metalworkers, the royal physicians and apothecaries, cotton-carders, shoemakers and saddlemakers, bookmakers and engravers, the royal kitchens and the royal syrup house, the royal wine cellars, tailors, armourers, tentmakers, saddlers, butchers, bakers, and, it seems very likely, candlestickmakers. A large portion of the enclosure was dedicated to the royal harem of nearly a thousand women, as well as the staff (and guards) that served them. There were residential apartments to house children, widows, and even women who had fallen from royal grace. An ornamental pool, large enough to row across, was constructed for their diversion outdoors. The Pleasure House stood nearby; its walls and ceilings were made of mirrors, and in its centre was a sunken chamber down whose gently sloping sides the Shah would slide, and frolic naked with fifty of his favourites.†

---

*   The name means 'world-revealing', and echoes the term used in mystical poetry to denote mystical insight.
†   The Lazzat-khaneh, a building added to the complex under Shah Sultan Husein. A man of specific tastes, it was under his rule that Isfahan fell to the Afghans in 1722.

The rest of the city stretched far beyond this royal microcosm: twelve gates pierced city walls; twelve bridges spanned the Zayandeh River, and in its heyday the city was home to half a million souls. Chardin, in 1666, counted 162 mosques, 48 madrassehs, 182 caravanserais, and 273 public baths. So verdant was the city that visitors likened it to a forest, a balm to eyes weary from the encircling glare of parched rock and sand. Even after its decline in the eighteenth century, Isfahan made an unforgettable impression on visitors.*

Such extravagance owed itself to the imperial vision of Iran's most celebrated monarch, the Safavid Shah Abbas I, who made Isfahan his capital in 1598. It had been a favourite city of earlier rulers, but none had glorified the place with such munificence. Under Abbas, Isfahan became not only the kingdom's political and cultural centre, but a showpiece to the world, whose grandeur and beauty hypnotized and beguiled its foreign visitors. Behind its creation was an ambitious, restless, and enormously energetic personality. In paintings of the era he looks lean and slightly built, and his bearing suggests the controlled poise of a tiger. He is said to have dressed plainly, gutted and cooked his own game, and personally performed the castration of his slaves. A hands-on sort of king; with a habit, according to the accounts of the time, of emulating the legendary Persian rulers of antiquity by moving among his subjects incognito, wandering the bazaars and chatting with shopkeepers to tease out rumour of corruption or oppression.

To a scandalized Augustinian delegation he remarked that 'to go about in this way is to be a king – not like yours, who are always sitting indoors'; and a Carmelite chronicler has him complaining to his attendants that he could never go anywhere

---

* 'Ce premier coup d'œil', wrote Gobineau in the late nineteenth century, 'est très beau. Ispahan se présent environné de jardins et tout rempli de bouqets d'arbres...' Pierre Loti, in 1904, waxes yet more lyrical: 'Et puis, avec un effet de rideau qui se léve au theatre, deux collines s'écartent devant nous et se separent; alors un Eden, qui était derrière, se révéle avec lenteur ... c'est un bois et c'est une ville.'

'without everyone else wanting to come too.' The descriptions from Pietro della Valle, a Roman patrician admitted to the court, are frequently, and irresistibly, poignant; one has the Shah, at the end of a long evening, leaning against a pillar of the palace, and listening to the gentle airs of his musicians in a posture and expression of immense melancholy. We also glimpse him leading a party of foreign diplomats, with proprietorial gusto, on foot through the seedy tumult of a night-time festival, chastising them for their prudishness, addressing the Spanish Ambassador as 'grandpa', tweaking the ears of the Indian Ambassador, and drinking hard till dawn.

He was only twenty-seven when he made Isfahan his capital, but had already ruled, albeit precariously, for ten years. Like his ancestors, who a century earlier burst from the south-western shore of the Caspian under the leadership of the charismatic adolescent Ismael I and within ten years conquered most of Persia, his reign was threatened by two persistent insecurities. Internally, the state was rent by powerful factions of the Qizilbash, a military aristocracy founded by Ismael, drawn from the zealous chieftains of Turkoman tribes. Rivalries between the tribes erupted whenever the issue of succession loomed, each advancing their own favourites for the position of shah and, at times, dragging the fragile state into periods of civil war. Frequently abundant offspring of the royal line, born to mothers of different nationalities, further exacerbated frictions between Turkish and Persian elements of government, never wholly resolved in the lifetime of the dynasty.

The second threat came from beyond Persia's frontiers: from the west, the powerful armies of Ottoman Turkey, who repeatedly attacked Azerbaijan and several times occupied Tabriz; and from the East, the Uzbeks, who persistently raided the provinces of Khorasan and Sistan, and at the time of young Shah's accession had laid siege to the Persian cities of Mashhad and Herat.

The young Abbas met these early challenges with both daring and determination. He appeased his enemies by massive territorial concessions, brought the unruly Qizilbash chieftains to heel by a series of ruthless purges, and created a new army from Circassian and Armenian prisoners loyal to the Shah alone. A little more than a decade later he had won back the lost territories in a series of celebrated campaigns, and the empire, rescued from the brink of fragmentation by the Shah's reformist zeal, was fast establishing its reputation as a world power.

From Isfahan, Abbas centralized the control of outlying provinces, created a single currency, drew up tax and land reforms, and strengthened Shi'ism as the religion of the state. Sensitive to their economic skills, he also settled thousands of Jewish and Armenian families in new colonies around the city, as well as artists and craftsmen from all over the kingdom, and encouraged the missions of Christian orders to found convents in the new capital. Diplomatic and commercial deputations shuttled to and from Russia, Moghul India, and all the leading nations of Europe. The Shah's reorganization of the army was even assisted by a team led by a pair of enterprising English brothers, Anthony and Robert Shirley, both of whom, bizarrely, became ambassadors for Persia abroad.*

We turned off the Chahar Bagh, where today the perfume of jasmine has yielded to diesel fumes and the once stately gardens have given way to shops full of all the cheerless paraphernalia of modern life, and headed east. Passing under a pointed arch, we entered the great maidan, the epic rectangle where, four hundred years earlier, Abbas had led his scandalized entourage. It is spectacularly large – nearly a mile in perimeter and twice the size of Red Square – and enclosed by a double-storeyed brick arcade.

---

*   The three celebrated Elizabethan adventurers – Thomas, Anthony, and Robert – were the diplomatic Marco Polos of their day, and moved in high circles across Europe, Turkey, and Persia. The younger pair, Anthony and Robert, arrived in Isfahan in 1598. Van Dyke's portraits of the Shirley brothers in extravagant Persian dress hang, I discovered by accident, in Petworth House. Denys Wright's *The English Amongst The Persians* (Heinemann, 1977) describes the ups and down of the Shirleys' careers as well as many other colourful incidents in early Anglo-Persian relations.

Today the arches are blind on the upper storey, and there are shops below. Their surface is white, and in bright sunlight, dazzles the eye.

The rhythm of the arcade is interrupted at key points by the city's most famous structures: at the southern end, by the portal of the immense Royal Mosque,* to the west by the smaller Lutfullah Mosque, and opposite it the Ali Qapu Palace, from which, in grander days, privileged audiences would watch military parades, polo matches, horse racing, and archery contests. At the northern end rises the monumental entrance to the bazaar, on whose walls today a fading mural depicts the Shah's victory over the Uzbeks. This grand architectural assemblage is still called, as it was at the time of its construction, the Naqsh-e Jahan, 'Design of the World'.

We walked towards the minarets and vast turquoise dome of the Royal Mosque. As we drew closer, it began to loom like a William Morris hot-air balloon straining at its moorings. But as we reached the soaring portal we discovered that, along with the other monuments, it was closed for the day in observance of Khomeini's birthday.

Ramin cursed, lit a cigarette, and heaped invective loudly on Khomeini's soul. I was very shocked, and looked around to see if anyone had heard. His blasphemy, thank goodness, had gone unnoticed; so we wandered, disconsolately, through a courtyard behind the nearby shops. There, in an open space behind the Lutfullah Mosque, we spotted a workman's ladder leading to the roof of the arcade that surrounded the square. It was too good to resist: Ramin was up it in a defiant flash, and I followed guiltily.

Scrambling through a network of dusty chambers, we emerged a minute later on top of the portal of the mosque, and looked out over the maidan from the base of the magnificent dome. The tendrils of its design, draped over a hemisphere almost feminine

---

* Since the revolution it has been called the Imam Mosque. As it was commissioned by a king, and built for a king, I will call it the Royal Mosque.

in shape, were close enough to touch. We were both thrilled. Its surface is unique among Persian mosques in both colour and texture; the former a pinkish shade of terracotta, the latter ingeniously varied by the use of glazed brick for the pattern itself and unglazed for its background. Around the base ran a band of dense and rhythmic calligraphy in blazing white against a deep blue field, like a magic foam of letters across a suspended corridor of ocean; and underneath, the floral swirls of the window grilles, made from woven curves of brick, faced with turquoise glaze and interspersed with panels of pixellated Kufic script.

Creeping down again, we found a long passage running the length of the upper storey of the arcade, where the open doorways ran into the distance like an image in opposing mirrors, compressing to a rectangular speck of blackness at the far end. The sound of voices sent us scurrying back into the sunlight. Brushing off the dust, we set off again from ground level, buoyed by the success of our act of trespass.

The twists and turns of the old bazaar were begging to be explored. Tunnel-like arcades, long burrowing passages and half-open doorways brought out the Theseus in both of us and we visited a dozen shrines, mosques, madrassehs, and caravanserais on our spree of discovery, greeted at times with the murmur of prayers, and at others by the thump of sacks and boxes being unloaded or, in the many tiny workshops which cling like limpets to the main body of the bazaar, choruses of tapping and hammering against wood and metal and tile. I was having too much fun to write down their names, much less how to find them again. Once, lured by a narrow upward spiral of stairs, we burst by mistake into the cluttered workshop of a man engraving pewter plates with fantastically minute calligraphy. He looked up and smiled and said he was happy to let us stay, and brewed a fresh pot of tea while we looked on.

Scattered around his workbench were bundles of thin wooden beads in different colours, reds and green mostly, and I asked what they were used for. They were the filaments, he explained, that were used to make the inlay, *khatam*, for which Isfahan is famous: pen cases, picture frames, mirrors, backgammon boards, ornamental boxes of all sizes, musical instruments, and even walking-sticks are decorated with its tiny tessellating triangles and hexagons in metal and different-coloured woods. But I couldn't connect the long and spaghetti-like strands with the obvious flatness and intricacy of the finished product; I'd wondered for years how it was made and begged for a crash course to reveal the basics.

Authentic inlay made by traditional methods was very rare nowadays, he said, and ten times more expensive than the modern kind, which made use of beads of wood which were artificially dyed.* But the essential method hadn't changed at all. The woods are first sawn into thin strips, then into long beads about a sixteenth of an inch thick, and given their final triangular profile by filing in pre-shaped grooves. Three light and three dark beads are first glued together to form the central hexagons and bound in string until they have dried. A second and third composite bundle is then constructed to form a star, and similarly glued; at this stage the resulting hexagon is, in better quality inlay, wrapped in thin metal foil. A second, smaller hexagon, calculated to fit between the larger ones, is then constructed and glued against the others to form a block, which is clamped into a vice. Once dried, the finished blocks are then cut into slices an eighth of an inch thick, glued onto a backing sheet, and cut again, yielding backed strips which are glued to the object to be decorated. They are sanded until the surface is completely smooth and painted with a final layer of transparent lacquer. In ordinary quality work there are up to seven hundred individual pieces in a square inch, and more in the better quality inlay. Designs vary; but the six-pointed

---

* Traditionally the different colours were provided by different types of woods: the red wood from the jujube tree, the lightest from orangewood, teak or rosewood for the darkest and, in the best work, ebony. Bleached camel-bone is still used for the white portions, and the green beads are made from bone pickled in a mixture of vinegar and copper filings for several months.

star enclosed in tessellating hexagons forms the basic theme of this ingenious method, and today I can never look at even the most ordinary examples without a sense of wonder at the effort and attention that goes into every inch of them.

Φ

Rahim and I took up our wandering again in the bazaar. It is hard to think of any urban structure which gives as much pleasure to explore. Walking along its vaulted tunnels is like being carried along by a complex and harmonious piece of music. The drone of activity is constant, but overlaid by the enclosing architecture into rhythmic, lyrical, and sometimes monumental themes. Coming from a passage crowded with people and stalls you reach an unexpectedly spacious junction and look up to see tier upon tier of intersecting vaults, as if a portion of a cathedral has suddenly descended, and where the noise, released now, billows upwards and fades and expires; or you turn from the monochrome gloom of a tunnel into a bright courtyard, where cypresses sway around a pool enclosed by a double arcade of friezes in glowing tilework.

Part of the thrill of this kind of wandering about is not knowing where you will end up next; but it is wrong to call the bazaar chaotic. In its conception it was carefully ordered to meet the exigencies of commerce, patronage, accommodation, public health, and religious observance. Water, light, space, ornament, and orientation were all taken into account in the original architectural scheme. In the caravanserais, where bales of supplies were unloaded and distributed at the end of their desert crossings, the donkeys, horses, and camels have of course all gone now, the stables are garages, and the bathhouses have been converted into restaurants; but even today the different portions of the bazaar retain a configuration based on the type of trade and continue to serve the city with a rigour undiminished after nearly half a millennium.

The very light – un-European in its intensity – is put to work here, variously and ingeniously fashioned along with its more tangible partners of shape and surface. It is not romantic to suggest that light, or its absence, defines much of the rhythm of the bazaar; and long after the smaller details of faces and shops and scents and sounds have begun to fade, it is the memory of moving between so many oases of luminosity which stubbornly remains. At midday, funnelled through octagonal crowning oculi, the light drives downwards like a incandescent whirlpool, into which anyone passing seems to momentarily ignite like a human filament before being extinguished on the far side. Entering lance-like at lesser angles, it strikes opposing parabolas in dazzling ovoids before being deflected earthward; and diffused through geometric lattices across the glaze of tiles, it is transformed into a buoyant and luminous mist. More spectacularly, when the receiving surfaces are calculated to respond to its touch, its brilliance is attenuated by degrees as it tumbles downward over concentric corrugations the shape of diamonds and trapezoid bat's wings, or falls across in raised patterns of chevrons or herringbone or spirals or dog's teeth.

One might expect this kind of architectural sophistication in a palace or royal complex, but in a marketplace it strikes an unfamiliar note. Its ampleness is, I think, a measure of the dignity traditionally associated with trade; and the spirit of the architecture that supports it here is both generous and humane. But there is another important feature. The buildings of the bazaar and the old city, and the walls and passages linking them, melt into each other and form an organic system through which you move like a cell in a body. It is the interiors you remember, rather than the surrounding structures; and you begin to realize that spaces exist on equal terms with the structures that define them. Everything about this architecture reflects a sensitivity to the qualitative aspect of space and its effect on the onlooker: it is – if there is such a word – participative. Even the most outstanding monuments do not stand alone, and from above it looks as if you might be able to cross the city by hopping between the rooftops.

In the late afternoon we broke off our exploring to rest in a small park. It was full of people strolling along the stone paths and lounging and picnicking on the lawns between rosebeds around a long reflecting pool. After the bustle of the bazaar it seemed deliciously tranquil. The sunlight had lost its earlier fierceness and was turning everything to gold. Misty diagonals of shadow fell from the tips of the cypresses, unfurling at their bases into long and tapering bands of coolness.

We lounged on the grass, eating ice cream. Ramin asked why I wore a beard. I confessed I preferred life without one, but that I'd let it grow in order to look less conspicuous while I was in Iran. It had worked in Afghanistan.

He chuckled at my naivety. 'Haven't you noticed?' he asked. 'Only fanatics and people who work for the government have beards.' I hadn't noticed; nothing like this had even occurred to me. 'When I saw you I thought you were a *basiji*' – he meant the kind of hard-line supporter of the revolution, for which I was often mistaken – 'and I didn't even want to sit next to you. If you want to make any friends – with normal people I mean – you should get rid of it.'

We were finishing our ice creams when two elegant young women, dressed not in the usual enveloping black but in light jackets which fell to their knees, passed us and perched on a nearby bench. I guessed they were students in their late teens; Ramin observed (correctly, as it turned out) that they were from Tehran, where the unwritten rules of comportment were less strict than those of Isfahan. The light and atmosphere were perfect for a picture and I asked Ramin if he thought they would let me photograph them. A moment later, with his usual impulsiveness, he was sitting next to them, coaxing them into conversation with the expert charm and inventiveness of a carpet dealer at the height of the tourist season. They were visibly nervous at first and, as we couldn't help noticing, very pretty. Ramin winked as his head turned away from them to translate for me. I was a foreign journalist, he explained, investigating the theme of social freedom among the youth of Iran.

A trace of eyeliner clung to the roots of long dark lashes of the face nearest to us, and a rosy shadow of blush spread over her cheeks. 'Freedom,' she repeated quietly. *Azadi*. The answer was easy, she said: it was the one thing that they longed for; especially – she nodded very slightly – the freedom to associate with the opposite sex without exciting scandal. Even here in Isfahan they felt uneasy, they said, with the looks they'd been getting for their Tehrani attire. But for the time being it was impossible: all they could do was wait and hope. The other girl nodded pensively. With demure expressions of regret they refused my request for a photograph, saying that their families, were they ever to see one taken by a stranger, might be given the wrong impression.

It was strange to encounter such timidity in a modern-day city. Not wanting to add to their embarrassment, we thanked them and sat back down on the grass nearby. Already our boldness had drawn the eyes of a dozen young men towards us, and was rippling through groups of others with electrical swiftness. A few minutes later, a boy in his late teens approached us and asked if he might borrow a pen from me. 'Don't give him your good one,' said Ramin quietly in English, 'he doesn't really want it. He just wants to find out if you're a foreigner.'

He never came back. Ramin offered to search the park for him, but I suggested we continue our exploring. 'Typical,' he muttered, half to himself. 'They're not so ready for their famous social freedoms as they'd like to think.'

As night fell we found ourselves in the great maidan. At least a hundred families had migrated there and were gathered on carpets and cushions along the whole length of the square. Children were everywhere and playing between the flowerbeds and borders while the adults were laying out platters of food and samovars and priming paraffin lamps and puffing on water pipes. It was an unexpected and to me touching sight and I asked Ramin what occasion had brought so many people into the city's main square. The answer had never occurred to me: they were having dinner.

We wandered down to the bridge where we had started. All along the grassy slopes of the riverbanks, families were laying out their dinners on carpets and tablecloths. Some had already rolled out their mattresses and were shrouded in sheets: every night hundreds of families spent the night under the stars.

Crossing to the south side we sat on the polished stone of the steps on the far bank, and looked back at the span of its thirty-three arches, lit now from within with orange floodlights. The stone was still warm from the day's sun, and from somewhere under the bridge came the sound of a man singing an other-worldly and plaintive lament, which echoed hauntingly through the darkness of the lower arches in long, slow, tremulous notes.

Ramin was looking intently in the direction of the sound, deep in thought.

'Beautiful, isn't it?' I said.

'Yes,' he agreed dreamily. 'I was just thinking ... how good it would be if they could put a whore in every one of those arches, just like Amsterdam. Then they could talk about their social freedom.'

Φ

We went back to the great maidan the following morning. The asphalt of the pavements was already sticky underfoot and we ducked gratefully into the shadow of the Royal Mosque at the southern end. It is the grandest of Iran's Safavid monuments and probably the most famous, though not everyone agrees it is the most beautiful. Byron, always quick to judge, is dismissive of its 'huge blue bulk'; André Godard, the French godfather of Iranian archaeology, rated it alongside Chartres. Construction, which took nearly twenty years, began in 1612. Several years were lost when, after the portal and the walls of the mosque had been completed, the architect disappeared. On his return – and facing a wrathful shah unused to being kept waiting – he explained that the delay had been to allow the foundations to settle. The Shah was unconvinced and ordered an inspection, which did indeed show that to have placed a fragile dome upon the walls any earlier would have been disastrous. Building was resumed and the architect duly rewarded for his sagacity.

The rectangular entrance portal, and the minarets which flank it, dominate the maidan, and loudly proclaim the centrality of religion in the scheme of things. The door, and the blind arch above it, are mirrored at three times the scale by the dimensions of the greater arch above, which soars to about eighty feet, and is hemmed with a triple, corkscrewing turquoise ceramic cable. A network of hanging niches clings to the half-dome behind it, and the entire surface is covered with brilliant mosaic tilework in blues and turquoise and tiny white flowers like stars of differing intensities. The entire facade is bordered by a gleaming band of calligraphy and flanked by a pair of slender minarets.

Ramin crossed the threshold with a lighted cigarette in a gesture of self-conscious impiety, and I followed.

Within, the world cools and quietens, and you are deflected from the axis of the maidan towards a massive interior arch, beyond which a light-filled courtyard beckons. The shift in orientation is needed to meet the required alignment of the mosque in the direction of Mecca, and along a sort of spiritual ley line of the faith. But there is more to it than that; the reorientation affirms an inner shift as well, from the domain of worldly things towards a place of tranquillity and abundance. The rectangular court, centred on a wide pool whose dimensions equal those of the four interior portals, follows the ancient theme of quaternity. The vast portals are linked by a double storey of arcades, and everywhere the lines of the combined structure signal each other in reciprocating symmetries.

The main dome rises with magnificent grace from the points of eight arches beneath, and seems to hover overhead, fairly miraculously, without support; eight airy vaults flank the dome on either side, and rest on widely spaced octagonal piers. The overall effect is both grand and rational, and the communicating spaces flow into one another without hindrance and all at a single level. There are no stairs or restricted areas, and nothing to suggest hierarchy or exclusion; there is no altar, choir, clerestory, or iconostasis, or any area of special sanctity, much less any of those depictions, universal to Western religious architecture, of either passion or pain. The emphasis is different here, falling towards interiority and the very absence of spiritual tension. The atmosphere nourished by all this is contemplative, rather than passionate, and nothing expresses this more clearly than the central sanctuary, which is a balanced, empty space – a space resembling an enchanted garden, I was thinking idly, when it stuck me that I was in the middle of one. Across almost every surface of the interior, the fecundity of the natural world is replicated in acres of gleaming tilework. The dome itself imitates a shimmering canopy of vegetation; the walls, vaults, and portals are draped in endlessly stylized variations of leaf, blossom, and tendril.

We wandered through the twin madrassehs which flank the central sanctuary. They are no longer active; the students' cells are empty and the few remaining trees in their courtyards sway above empty pools. But even these last dusty representatives from the natural world are a reminder of the intended resonance between nature and its representation on the enclosing walls. It is not hard to imagine the days when, viewed from a distance, a verdant frieze would span the intervening void to a living branch, or when a row of white ceramic flowers would merge into a creeping tendril of jasmine.

In the central courtyard, which spans more than two hundred feet, you become aware that the different elements of the structure are strangely mobile: minaret, arch, arcade, and dome realign themselves as you walk, alternately claiming and relinquishing their dominance of the whole; behind the lucid and harmonious formality of the design, there is a fluid quality. The symmetries are not only exquisite but subtly imperfect, and in the broad reflecting pool, which introduces a further geometric melody informing the whole, the giant facades are reflected in a virtual and shimmering axis of symmetry.

Despite these complexities, there is something approachable and humane about this architecture; freedom of movement and accessibility are central features and nothing intimidates or is intended to overwhelm. Something of the humaneness, unity, and doctrinal simplicity of Islam is expressed therein. It reflects too the mosque's historical evolution, not only as a place of worship but as a forum for all manner of human exchange. Important mosques, before civil institutions could provide an alternative, witnessed legal judgements, notarizations, and swearings-in; books were recited there and copied down by scribes; they were places of study and teaching as well as instruction in mysticism and, in the form of the Friday sermon, political expression. The mosque was also a place of sanctuary, and of shelter for travellers. Most of these functions have been superseded, but today there is nothing to inhibit passers-by, pilgrims, and those needing to catch up on a prayer or two or a quiet place to finish homework from wandering in and out; nothing, in fact, to stop a pair of heat-sapped visitors from stretching out on a carpet, caressed by a breeze deliciously cooled by the sheltering vaults, and sleeping until the fiercest glare of the day has passed — which, in the company of a few wheeling pigeons, is exactly what we did.

Φ

We were woken by a noise of echoing shouts, which gradually resolved into the laboured English of a local guide, towing in his wake a little shoal of European tourists. Struggling under the weight of cameras and oversized sunhats, they entered the sanctuary, eyeing the pair of indolent natives by their feet with compassionate smiles. They gathered under the dome, where the guide described the sevenfold echo returned from a point beneath the apex of the sanctuary dome,* and explained that the shape of the chamber had been designed to transmit the voice of the Imam to the most distant members of the congregation in the courtyard. Then by way of demonstration he climbed the marble steps of the *minbar* and gave the call to prayer in a high and sonorous voice. The sound took flight and whirled through the vaults and

---

* Forty-nine separate echoes have been measured; but the human ear can detect about a dozen.

arches like a presence. The little crowd stood there transfixed; then, as the silence returned, began to clap.

We wandered back to the entrance, where I lingered at the door and stepped out backwards, in the manner I had learned from Shi'ite pilgrims in Afghanistan. Ramin shot me a friendly scowl.

'Would you stop all that devotional stuff?' he said. 'People will think I'm with a fanatic.'

On the eastern side of the maidan, we stopped in front of the portal of the Sheikh Lutfullah Mosque. This was the first of the great structures to be built around the maidan; work began in 1602, a decade before the building of the Royal Mosque. It is said to have been a private oratory for Shah Abbas, named in honour of the Shah's father-in-law, a Shi'ite scholar originally from Lebanon.* An official leaflet has it as the Sheikh's place of teaching; a popular theory suggests it was a mosque for the women of the Shah's harem, and linked to the royal palace opposite by a tunnel. Unlike mosques throughout almost all the Islamic world, there is neither courtyard nor minaret. At only twenty paces square, the sanctuary is a fraction of the size of the Royal Mosque, making its closest architectural relative a single-chambered mausoleum. It is also said to have a lower storey, which may explain the raised level of the entrance. Its original function, like the building itself, has an enigmatic strain.

Five steps lead upwards from the maidan to the doorway. This leads not into the sanctuary itself, but to a tunnel. You move forward, between walls tiled in Neptunian greens and blues, and under the first of three elaborately vaulted ceilings. The brightness and noise of the maidan quickly fade. To one side, a door-like lattice, through which filters a suggestion of space and luminosity, provides an intimation of what is to come. But it is indistinct;

---

* Though in contemporary Safavid documents it is referred to as the Masjed-e Sadr or Masjed-e Fath-Allah. The original portal inscription names the builders as Muhammad Riza ibn Husein and Ali Reza al-Abbasi.

70

you move on. After forty feet there is a right-angled turn, and the tunnel grows even more dim. Then, after almost the same distance again, and just as you begin to feel you might be losing your way, a doorway opens to the right.

Beyond it, the sanctuary materializes in a shimmering incarnation of light. Eight pointed arches, outlined by corkscrewing ceramic cable glazed in brilliant turquoise, enclose the square chamber. Four are flat; four enclose the right-angled corners. Their bases are hemmed by a carpet design in tile which, as if draped from the walls, would once have merged with the carpeted floor. The flat walls display, in turn, the design of a flower-studded carpet panel, the intricately tiled mehrab or prayer-niche, the grille through which the chamber is first glimpsed from the entrance tunnel, and the entrance doors. Each is pierced above with an arched window, through which the light is softened as it filters through swirling arabesques. The surfaces of the right-angled walls are covered with complex repeating designs; these tease the eye, resolving at the very moment they are deciphered into an altered pattern. Wide bands of brilliant white calligraphy on a lapis field run everywhere, coursing like foaming torrents beside the abundant gardens of spiralling vines.

Above these reciprocating melodies of light and colour stretches the dome, some eighty feet high at its apex and resting effortlessly on the thirty-two smaller arches which encircle its base. Half of these are blind, studded with turquoise medallions; half are windows, which permit a further injection of light and disguise the magical fusing of the square beneath with the circle above. An extraordinary decoration covers the interior of the dome. At one moment it is a glittering web, whose parabolic traceries are defined by biscuit-coloured unglazed brick. Within lie lemon-shaped, flower-filled lozenges growing harmonically from the apex as they descend, spilling at the base of the collar over the supporting verticals. The next moment, as the medallions dominate, it displays the template of a peacock's fan, or the gleaming head of a sunflower of cosmic proportions.

I had seen pictures of the mosque — or rather, portions of it —

but the inadequacy of the camera is driven home here; the camera can only convey a surface. But here the resonance and counter-point of shape and colour and light all conspire together in an alchemy of exquisite balance. It has nothing of the monumental expanse of the Royal Mosque, but is jewel-like in its intensity.

Φ

Once more we emerged into the sunlight. I felt immensely gratified to have set eyes on one of the wonders of the architec-tural world. But the visit posed more questions than it answered, and left me with the feeling that I had encountered a riddle, a jigsaw without a picture to follow. I was troubled, firstly, by the business of the orientation. Like the Shah Mosque on the southern end of the maidan – like all mosques, in fact – the qiblah of the Lutfullah Mosque is oriented towards Mecca. The maidan is not; and since the mosque is joined to it, a correspond-ing reorientation is required. But the angle of this reorientation – forty-five degrees from the axis of the maidan – is, from the point of view of construction, impossibly propitious to assign to coincidence. If the design of the mosque was conceived with the forty-five-degree offset in mind, then the orientation of the mosque determined a priori that of the maidan, and of all of the buildings extending from it.

Above this exciting prospect loomed another question. Viewed from outside, the entrance portal and dome are not aligned; the dome is skewed to the right. Visually, this strikes a troubling note in a piazza of such grandeur and formality. It is widely assumed to be an awkward oversight; Byron describes the discrepancy in alignment as 'careless of symmetry to a grotesque degree'. But given the attention to delicate visual harmonies observed so fastid-iously elsewhere, given that Safavid Isfahan was home to the most skilled architects of the era, whose knowledge was the distil-lation of a thousand years of architectural evolution and given, too, the monarch's tendency to lop off the heads of those who failed to carry out his wishes, it is difficult – irresponsible even – to put the so-called oversight down to error. Architecturally, the failure in alignment could have been easily solved: only the length or angle of the tunnel leading to the sanctuary would have had to have been altered. It was impossible not to conclude that the alignment of portal and dome, so obviously attainable, was deliberately forsaken.

Questions rushed in like a tide ... if the alignment of the maidan was determined by the Lutfullah Mosque, perhaps its dimensions were too; perhaps the different buildings around the maidan were also held in some invisible relationship. But a sudden impulse of self-censure kept these speculations in check. Investigations into geometrical symbolism always end up sounding like hopeful explanations for the Nazca lines and the Bermuda Triangle; and I assumed, too, that after a little searching back home I would soon find an explanation for these puzzles. The architecture of Isfahan had been studied more than that of any other Iranian city, and some learned monograph would have long ago unclothed the secrets of both mosque and maidan. Soon, in any case, the line of enquiry was swallowed up by the momentum of travel.

At night I saw domes whirling above me at the edge of sleep. I see them, without much effort, now, like an after-image cast on the retina by a sunlit day. The city's monuments had left a deep and restless impression, and I knew I would have to make the effort to understand them better. Those hovering canopies of multiplying arabesques and torrents of turbulent calligraphies, those kaleidoscopic vaults and cloud-piercing minarets wrapped in spiralling wizardries of gleaming tilework, at once both exuberant and rational! I was troubled by the mysteries of their colours and magically resonating shapes, and at the insistence of their bright geometries, as if behind them pressed a language longing to be heard; and I wondered if I might ever learn it. These monuments and their decoration were, I realized, the first examples of Persian art I had properly seen (how these early impressions fall most freshly on the senses and, like a first kiss, linger with uneven fondness!). On earlier visits to Afghanistan I had glimpsed a few of the surviving Timurid monuments at

Herat and Balkh, but war had always forced brevity and furtiveness on these encounters: it was not the same.

Troubling too was a question which, looking at books about Persian art, had never occurred to me: why this plenitude of floral life? The primary decorative theme of two of Iran's — perhaps the world's — most famous mosques was drawn from the world of plants. Multiplying plant forms adorned the surfaces of nearly every monument I had seen: vines, leaves, tendrils, and flowers and, in fabrics everywhere, the cypress tree, whose wind-blown tip describes a spiral like an unfolding baby fern.

Up close, these natural shapes, subtly geometrized, convey a force no book can properly transmit. They suggest an artistic impulse deeper than the merely whimsical. Yet the usual explanation for their abundance — the explanation replicated in almost every Western account of Islamic art — is that, deprived of a truly naturalistic repertoire by religious injunction, Islamic artists turned to both geometric and stylized motifs from the natural world by way of compensation; corralled, in effect, into an artistic holding-ground, their natural creativity fettered by a religion intolerant of realism.

This shaky explanation has been so tirelessly invoked that it now passes for an axiom in any study of Islamic art. But once you have actually been there — once you have seen how deeply and pervasively the theme of the garden penetrates all of Persian culture — the conventional exegesis seems particularly inadequate. So too does the term 'decoration' to describe the inescapable presence of the garden theme in all of Persian art. Decoration suggests a surface, but the garden runs too deep, and the word does not serve its object well. The garden materializes in a thousand different mediums across the entire spectrum of the visual arts; it is the resounding motif associated with religious art; symbolically it is central to almost all Persian mystical poetry and, concretely, has its most famous expressions not only throughout present-day Iran but as far apart in the East as Kashmir, Agra, and Lahore, and in the West at the gardens of the Madinat al-Zahra in Cordoba and the Generalife in Granada.

Nor is it useful to invoke the ostensibly aniconic origins of Islamic art to appreciate the saturation of Persian culture with the imagery of the garden. More than a thousand years before the appearance of Islam, the most beloved creation of Persia's rulers was already the garden: the creative agency that made it central to Persian culture was at work long before the arrival of the Arabs. The garden was already a thing of sanctity in Persia, steeped from antiquity with connotations of the otherworldly. And the symbolic alliance between spiritual and natural plenitude, between the earthly garden and the paradisiacal version to which it alludes was, in other words, already there. Under the influence of Islam it has merely been re-expressed. Today the theme of the garden is still woven into the fabric of the culture, and re-expressed in countless ways by the individual souls into which its roots descend.

Persians, of course, already know all this; it is the outsider who needs a new terminology to understand it.

Φ

The heat had driven us back to Ramin's home for restorative doses of tea and watermelon. His brother, a gifted musician, gave private music lessons in the house. His student that afternoon was a tall, handsome, and confident woman who, after we had been introduced, asked lots of questions, and one I didn't catch. I turned to Ramin.

'She wants to know if she can take you somewhere tomorrow,' he translated. I was not sure what to make of this, and accepted out of politeness, but after she had left, asked Rahim how I should understand the invitation.

'I don't know,' he said, with the faintest of grins. 'You have to find out. By the end of the day you will know for yourself.'

But was it normal, I asked, for a married woman to entertain a foreign man for the day? I reminded him that we had barely been able to speak for more than a few minutes with the girls we had met in the park before attracting attention.

'I would think,' he said coolly, 'that afterwards she'll take you home to meet her husband.'

'*Afterwards?* Wouldn't that make me –' I was struggling to find the right word – 'visible?'

'By being visible,' he said, 'you would be invisible.' Then, as if surprised by the ingenuity of his own logic, added: 'It's Iran – it's complicated.'

He escorted me to the waiting car the following afternoon. In the front sat Roya and another younger woman, the two of them wearing dark glasses and wrapped from head to toe in black chadors. Ramin waved me off with a knowing wink, and we sped into the city.

I had failed completely to know what to expect from this excursion, and had a momentary vision of myself through the eyes of a friend from home who, seeing me racing through the streets in the company of two strange women draped voluminously in black, would wonder whether my predicament were sinister or comic.

To the newcomer, the sight of women wreathed in black, and robbed of both colour and contour, falls on an unfamiliar portion of the senses. At first sight, all manner of associations rise alongside in the outsider's mind – lewd, obscurely fearful, or indignant, but always heavy with political connotation – and are strengthened by the endless portrayal of chador-clad and burqa-enveloped women in every photograph and film connected to the Islamic world as if they held some meaningful clue to understanding the life of an entire culture. Such images are always evocative, but not particularly useful; because once you are over this early frisson, they become what they are: ordinary, like the sight of an Englishman with an umbrella.

Nothing, in the event, could have been more innocent or charming about our excursion. The younger woman, Maryam, was the daughter of a friend; she was demure and very beautiful – all the women I had met seemed to be beautiful – and said she was studying carpet design at the city's centre for traditional arts. Roya drove at speed through the streets, chatting volubly on her mobile telephone as the tyres squealed on the corners. She had wanted, I finally understood, to visit the site of a Zoroastrian fire temple on the outskirts of the city, but it was closed for the day, so we headed instead for the famous Mosque of the Shaking Minarets. By climbing to the top of one of the minarets and pushing vigorously against its walls, its nearby twin is said to sway visibly in a reciprocal motion. This description, and the hand signals needed to explain it to me, took up most of the journey there; but on arriving we found the mosque temporarily cordoned off for repairs, so we settled for small talk over ice cream nearby.

In the late afternoon we drove to the outskirts of the town where the houses began to thin, and turned into an unpaved alley between mud walls. An elderly labourer opened a metal gate in the wall; we stepped from the dust into a spacious and walled garden.

Roya's husband waved from the far side. He was watering in a final row of fruit trees around the border of the garden and came bounding across to greet us. He was a vigorous and back-slapping man in his fifties who had, he explained, laid out and planted the entire garden himself. There was no grass; the whole acre-sized plot had been given over to fruit and vegetables, though there'd be a small lawn around the house, he said, waving towards the half-built structure in one corner. He took me on an enthusiastic tour which wound like a maze between the neatly laid-out rectangles, all of them linked by tiny streams, and pointed out the varieties of melons and marrows and herbs, whose medicinal benefits we debated. He was never still; a tour of the unfinished house was next, then we were all summoned as he clambered up a tree to shake mulberries into a blanket which we held below like firemen, waltzing imperfectly beneath the branches to receive a pattering of fruit.

Some carpets were thrown over the dust where we sat to talk, and the husband built a small fire nearby. Then he summoned the old man to fetch a water pipe and, after balancing a nugget of glowing charcoal atop its slender neck, sucked so vigorously on the mouthpiece I thought he might implode. When the fire had died down, a handful of potatoes were extracted from the nearby beds and buried in the embers. Then a fiery kind of moonshine appeared from a stash, evoking grins of conspiracy all round. The sun fell behind the walls. We prodded the fire into life with fresh sticks; Roya tried her terrible English on me, and explained the history of an operation which prevented her from eating some kind of food; her husband followed with a lengthy and confident account of British complicity in the affair of the Bab; and the beautiful Maryam, resting her chin on her knees, the dark lustre of her eyes directed soulfully into the flames, resembled nothing so much as a love-stricken princess, conjured from a miniature painting of an enchanted garden.

As a broad flame of turquoise dimmed in the western sky, Roya drove me home. Passing the lower end of the Chahar Bagh Avenue, I glanced northwards between the artless silhouettes of the buildings stretching along its length, and acknowledged inwardly an unlovely impression of traffic and creeping neon. For a moment I wondered what the avenue must have looked like when, as dusk fell, the avenue was lit by thousands of lanterns suspended from the branches of its trees. I was late by about three hundred years.

I spent another day exploring with Ramin. We seemed no closer to exhausting the city's supply of discoveries, tracing several dusty circuits through the old city until, late in the afternoon, we stopped to sit on a bench to share a watermelon. On the far side of the road beyond hung a giant portrait of Khomeini, which glowered at us stubbornly between passing buses. Ramin observed that such portraits tended to be smaller nowadays. The implications of this steady diminishment amused him deeply. He stretched out an arm, and between finger and thumb compressed the Imam's offending gaze to invisibility.

I shuddered at his irreverence. Khomeini was a figure, to my mind at the time, as incomprehensible as he was terrifying. It seemed scarcely possible to link him to the extravagance and sophistication of Safavid Isfahan. I shared this thought with Ramin, and we tried to plot the main points in the intervening stretch of history. Our combined knowledge was sketchy and the resulting line only emerged much later. But it was obvious why the monuments of Isfahan had once attracted the admiration of the world, and still had the power to do so. They shelter the embers of a creative magma which has surfaced time and again through periods of upheaval and devastation, producing master-pieces to the world in nearly all branches of art and under all of the nation's most famous rulers: Achaemenid, Sasanian, Parthian, Arab, Seljuk, Mongol, Timurid, and Safavid. Even under lesser dynasties the contribution was often vigorous and original. On the shock waves of conquest, the creative flame was borne far beyond its territorial origins and transmitted its energy to the arts and architecture of the last great Islamic empires of the world – the Moghul and the Ottoman. And though perhaps not the greatest or most original, the Safavid contribution was refined, exquisite, delicate, and sophisticated, and drew on the successes of millennia.

It was also the final peak in this lofty creative range. Isfahan represents the high point, and nothing really comes close to it later on; no ruler, for that matter, approaches Shah Abbas for such restless benevolence towards the arts. We know little about the lives of the artists themselves, but Shah Abbas is rightly remembered as its most generous patron. In his long reign he had brought Persia the status of empire, overseen one of the world's great artistic flowerings, and established Persia's name as syn-onymous with both luxury and sophistication. His end, sadly, is incongruously morbid. The ageing ruler grew haunted and his final years were marked by irrational cruelty. Astrological warn-ings of assassination were appeased by the temporary appointment of a new shah, who was then duly murdered. Fearing a plot in which his eldest son was implicated, he had first the conspirators, then his own son, executed. When Abbas fell temporarily ill and his next son, Khodabanda, rather imprudently began to celebrate his father's death, he had him blinded; five years later his final son suffered the same fate. Shah Abbas died in 1629, after ruling for forty years.

None of his successors could match him as a leader. His grandson and successor, Safi, was debauched by the age of eighteen and spent more time hunting and drinking than on matters of state, and though under Abbas II the empire briefly regained a more sober course, subsequent rulers were pitifully dissolute. Suleyman, a drunk and a recluse, was said not to have emerged from his harem for seven years; his son Husayn insisted on travelling with an escort of sixty thousand.

Such royal excesses provoked outrage from the clergy, whose power grew in proportion to their doctrinal intolerance and puritanism. Under the powerful Mohammed Baqir Majlesi, the Jewish, Christian, and Zoroastrian populations of the country were broadly persecuted; the humanitarianism of the Sufis was denounced, and classical learning condemned as a curse of the infidel Greeks. The army was neglected, corruption spread, and, predictably, the empire began to fray at the seams.

At the turn of the eighteenth century, Baluch tribesmen were raiding Kerman towards the south; Herat in the north-east was captured by the Abdali Afghans, Mashhad was besieged, and a few years later the Ghilzai Afghans defeated the allied Georgian protector of Qandahar, Prince Georgi XI. To the Afghan's young leader Mahmud, Isfahan and the now teetering crown of Persia must have glittered irresistibly; and in March 1722, the Persian army was routed on the outskirts of Isfahan by an Afghan force less than half its size, and fled in disarray back to the city. As many as a hundred thousand died in the six-month siege that followed, during which the population was reduced to eating cats and dogs, and then, it is said, one other.

The Afghan occupation lasted seven years, and is not forgotten. When, a few months later, I was the guest of a family in Shiraz, and my host began to wax lyrical about the old days – bemoaning the country's demise as a world power which had once possessed Azerbaijan, parts of Turkey, Russia and Afghanistan, and which not been invaded for three hundred years – I reminded him of the Afghan interlude. 'That was aggression!' he shot back. 'They never held the country!' I had no idea that this might offend – any more than mention of the Viking occupation of England offends a native of Wiltshire – but a silence had fallen suddenly over the room and the whole family looked genuinely hurt.

The end of the Safavid dynasty is a grim story. The increasingly deranged Afghan leader – now Shah – Mahmud slaughtered thousands in Isfahan, including all the remaining members of the Safavid royal family, and was overthrown in turn by his cousin, whose inauguration brought a further round of slaughter of likely rivals.

A fugitive royal prince, Tahmasp, had meanwhile enlisted the services of a tribal leader of Turkish descent, who had presented himself at the head of an army to Tahmasp's court-in-exile. Nader Quli Afshar was a camel driver turned soldier who had earned his spurs fighting for the Governor of Khurasan, and was now a general looking for a campaign. In a matter of months, the resulting alliance had driven the invading Afghans from Isfahan; few of them, it is said, saw their homeland again.

Under Tahmasp, the ruling house briefly was restored in the ruins of its capital, but the ambition of his leading general remained unquenched. A few years later he crowned himself Nader Shah; Tahmasp and his children were imprisoned, and finally despatched in 1740, and the Safavid dynasty was now utterly extinguished. Rebellion had been silenced, the neighbouring great powers were on the retreat from Persia, and the lost territories in the north and west had been reclaimed. But instead of turning his efforts to rebuilding his empire, Nader indulged his talent for warfare on a spectacularly broader front. For ten years, infected by a dream of world conquest, he dragged the country through constant war. While portions of the country suffered famine, he threw his army against the Russians and the Ottoman Turks, captured Kabul and Qandahar, reduced the Uzbek khanates of Bokhara and Khiva, sacked Delhi,* and invaded Daghestan in the Caucasus. Parsimonious by nature, he locked up the stupendous loot from these campaigns in a mountain fortress. He was soon a hated man, and bouts of syphilitic madness hastened his inevitable assassination. The disintegration that followed was unstoppable.

When the dust of several years of turmoil had settled, the empire had fractured roughly into quarters. Nadir's blinded grandson Shah Rukh held sway in the north-east from Mashhad. In the east, one of Nadir's former generals, Ahmad Durrani, occupied Qandahar and later founded the kingdom of Afghanistan. The north fell under the tribal rule of the Turkomans. And in the south-west, centred on Shiraz, arose the first dynasty of Persian origin for nearly a thousand years. Under Karim Khan, the humane and tolerant leader of the Zand tribe, a rare interlude of peace was restored. He did not take the title of shah but that of *vakil*, meaning regent, and his rule was both humane and tolerant. It lasted nearly thirty years until 1779. After his death, wars soon erupted between rival family claimants, who succeeded one another like toppling dominoes. The ruling line was extinguished fifteen years later at the siege of Kerman by the notoriously brutal Agha Mohammad Khan, who personally counted the seventy thousand eyeballs extracted from the captured survivors. In 1796, two years later, he was crowned shah, and the dynasty of the Qajars – which carries us (at last) into the orbit of modern times – was born.

Qajar rule was imperfectly extended by ambitious and often unruly local princes. The empire's frontiers were more or less

---

* And, famously, looted the Peacock throne and the Koh-i noor diamond from the Moghul throne. When the British annexed the Punjab in 1849, it became Crown property, and was set in the coronation crown of George VI's consort, Queen Elizabeth.

fixed; a degree of centralization was achieved, and the new capital was established in Tehran. But the decadence of its rulers allowed extortion and nepotism to flourish in government while rural life was reduced to prehistoric poverty; local rebellions were frequent, banditry flourished, and taxes were imposed with a heavy hand, sometimes requiring military expeditions for their extraction. Intrigue, rivalry and rumour attended every political event, and the Shah's whim was law.

Persia entered the nineteenth century like a hobbled giant, pitifully diminished by misrule and increasingly subservient to the rival designs of external powers. The expansionist ideals of Tsarist Russia cast a deepening shadow over her northern frontiers, and a fearful government in Tehran looked increasingly to Europe for help in staying the Russian menace: first to France and then, after Napoleon's defeat at Waterloo, to England. Wary of Russian designs on India, the English reciprocated warmly, and established their first diplomatic presence in Tehran in 1809; a Persian envoy representing the Shah was received in Buckingham Palace later in the year. Thus began a relationship whose essential goal – Persia's independence from Russian encroachment and the protection of British interests in the region – was to last almost a hundred and fifty years. It was stormy and complicated, at times deeply poignant, and ultimately, uneven. The English cultivated their Persian alliances with boundless charm and ceremony when it suited them, and exacted withering punishments when their interests seemed threatened.

Educated Persians were nonetheless entranced by the liberties of English society and its institutions. When, in the early 1800s, the first accounts of life in Europe began to appear in Tehran, Persian society was shocked and intrigued to learn that royal succession in England was determined by law, and that the king himself had no power to kill anyone – even his own servants.*

---

* The first Persian to write about his first-hand experience of the English was Mirza Abu Taleb, who visited England at the turn of the century and stayed two and a half years. His dash and sharp wit endeared him to

But admiration was mixed with resentment at English high-handedness, and further tainted by a tendency – not unreasonably, looking back – to blame the nation's woes on the divisive scheming of external powers. In Tehran, opinion was frequently polarized over the benefits and dangers of Russian and British protection. Russia inflicted frequent territorial humiliations in the north, where its military and economic dominance was gradually extended; British power grew in the south, from where it could threaten invasion.

Pinioned by the giants of the Great Game, reform within Persia was slow and, in its early days, hampered by the indifference of a fatalistic and largely unlettered population. Resistance to the twin humiliations of foreign domination and an autocratic government percolated only at the level of the elite, who through contact with Europe grew ever more aware of their own nation's

---

London society, and he was feted widely by aristocratic friends. He was fascinated by the technologies of modern life, the liberalness of society in general, and, conspicuously, the independence and intelligence of the nation's women; he was deeply impressed by the constitution, but the Commons reminded him of 'two flocks of Indian paroqeets, sitting upon opposite mango trees scolding at each other.' Summarizing the admirable traits of his host nation, he praised the English people's high sense of honour, dread of offending the rules of propriety or the laws of the realm, passion for mechanization, plainness of manners, sound judgement, and hospitality. Their chief vices were, in order of diminishing severity: want of chastity; extravagance; want of faith in religion; pride; a passion for acquiring money; a desire of ease and a dislike of exertion; irritability of temper; throwing away their time in sleeping, eating, and dressing; a luxurious manner of living; vanity and arrogance in their scientific achievements; selfishness; and a contempt for the customs of other nations, 'although theirs,' he notes, 'may be much inferior.' The first official Persian envoy to arrive in London was Mirza Abul Hassan Shirazi in 1809. He was a hugely popular figure and retained a lifelong affection for the English, and was later appointed Persia's first Foreign Minister. He appears, thinly disguised as 'Mirza Firouz', in James Morier's famous books *The Adventures of Haji Baba of Ispahan* and *The Adventures of Haji Baba of Ispahan in England* – both deeply satirical accounts of the Persian character.

backwardness. Persia's Constitutional Movement climaxed in the summer of 1906, when Muzafferuddin Shah (known to the French as Mauvaise Affaire-uddin) conceded, a few days before his death, to the creation of a Parliament and written constitution. But his successor, Muhammad Ali, was an outspoken recidivist. 'I have nothing against the Parliament,' he said, 'so long as it does not interfere in politics.' The constitutional movement was crushed on the Shah's orders by a rain of artillery onto the Parliament building in Tehran, and its remnants rounded up in Tabriz on the points of Russian bayonets.

The British had at first supported the movement – giving frequent sanctuary to its members on legation and consulate grounds – exploiting all the while a useful anti-Russian streak. But after a joint treaty with Russia agreeing the formal division of Persia into spheres of control, British attention turned irresistibly to the south, where oil had been struck in 1908. Persia's experiment with democracy had been cruelly extinguished; the throne was held by an obese, juvenile shah with no interest in the affairs of state, his position sustained by a British allowance paid into the (British-owned) Imperial Bank of Persia. Only revolution in Russia and war in Europe saved the nation from complete dismemberment.

How far the empire had fallen from the era of Shah Abbas, when delegations made the perilous journey from Europe to glimpse the King of Kings, and waited a year to be admitted to his court! The final Qajar shah, Sultan Ahmad (who died childless in exile, at Neuilly in 1930), had to submit his very holiday arrangements for approval in Whitehall. The collapse of Tsarist Russia gave the British a free hand in Persia, bountiful oil was now flowing (virtually for free) from the Gulf, and the fate of Persia's future leaders could at last be comfortably decided over lunch in Belgravia.

We must look at the final run-up. Well into the twentieth century, Persia's poverty and illiteracy were endemic; higher education was non-existent; the Shah and his cohorts remained aloof and dissolute, and nepotism and corruption remained essential for survival. The democratic movement, comet-like, had gone from incandescence to cinders; and the clergy, hugely powerful, were still the country's kingmakers. Persia had virtually none of the infrastructure of a modern state, its economics were chaotic, and many outlying provinces functioned with virtual autonomy. The Russians remained a constant threat to the north, and the British, though not territorially acquisitive, were helping themselves generously to the country's most precious natural resource in the south.

Enter Reza Shah (I nearly said Marjoribanks),* one of the outstanding figures of modern Iranian history: six foot six of self-made, bullet-headed, hawk-nosed general, whose coup d'état in 1921 brought him first control of the armed forces, then Prime Ministership, and a few years later the throne itself. For fifteen years the country creaked, groaned, and cowed under his unyielding authority. He was deeply scornful of the social malaise of corruption and apathy, and his broad reforms were as much a campaign to restore Iran's physical integrity as its morale. He delivered rousing attacks on the character of his own people, discredited his Anglophile ministers, and was the first to insist that foreigners drop the anachronistic appellation 'Persia' and use 'Iran' instead when referring to the country – which is how it had always been known to Iranians. He smote his opponents – the obscurantist clergy, unruly tribal leaders, feudal landowners, and the apparatus of foreign interference – with soldierly vigour. With an admiring eye on Atatürk's recent successes to the west, he was particularly intolerant of the religious hierarchy. He personally horsewhipped a leading cleric for criticizing the immodesty of the Queen's dress, introduced military service for others, banned all but the senior clergy from wearing the traditional gown and turban, and created state schools to limit their educational rule. He also outlawed the veil. Resistance was frequently and bloodily suppressed.

Amid all this, he was the first to bring about substantial modernization (the construction of a trans-Iranian railway was a

---

* Byron's irreverent nickname for the Shah in *The Road to Oxiana*.

personal passion), and today his memory is even enjoying a quiet revival — but his methods were so brutal they were perhaps bound, sooner or later, to be politically fatal. Reza Shah's refusal, in 1941, to join the Allied cause led to a humiliating invasion by British and Soviet forces; his sympathies with Germany provoked the punitive hand of Whitehall to push him towards abdication in favour of his son, Mohammad Reza.

Indian independence after the war loosened the British grip, but the oil issue grew ever more contentious. As the young Shah's ties with America supplanted those of imperial Britain, anti-royalist sentiment ran high. Foreign help quashed the promisingly democratic Prime Minister* who had dared to nationalize the oil industry and wrest it from British control, and the Shah's hand was strengthened to the point of absolute might. He despised the nation's clerics as much his father had, and his recklessly ambitious reforms proved, to all but the most privileged, as offensive as those of a generation earlier. Oil revenues brought phenomenal wealth, and the purchase of massive quantities of American arms. American bases, listening posts, and thousands of military personnel appeared throughout the country. When, in 1964, Parliament passed a law to grant Americans stationed in Iran immunity from prosecution, a defiant voice rang out above the murmurs: 'If the Shah were to run over an American dog, he would be called to account; but if an American cook ran over the Shah, no one would have any claim against him.'

This incendiary cry came from a quarter of society tradition-ally averse to overtly adversarial politics: the clergy. Since the time of Shah Abbas, the nation had produced vociferous and defiant Shi'a clerics, but none had dared call for clerical rule. Crucially — and unlike the political theory of the earlier Constitutionalists — the call for change was delivered in a language accessible to all, and charged with universally familiar religious themes. Ruhollah Khomeini, a hitherto obscure cleric from Qom, thundered against

---

* We are already swimming in detail here, so I will try to infiltrate the important story of Mossadeq's downfall somewhere else.

the un-Islamic tyranny of the Shah, evoking, by contrast, the golden age of the first and universally revered Imam, Ali; he held out the promise of a golden age yet to come, led by men of piety and wisdom; and championed the martyrdom of Imam Hussain, cut down without mercy by the villainously worldly Umayyad Caliph Yazid on the burning plain of Kerbala, nearly thirteen hundred years earlier.

These were all heady themes, and touched on collective passions inculcated over the course of centuries. But the call for direct clerical rule over the nation was an unprecedented – and, as unrest grew, increasingly appealing – challenge to royal authority. Khomeini, was, to nobody's surprise, sent into exile in Iraq.

The Shah, meanwhile, aggressively promoted the glory and mystique of Iran's pre-Islamic kings, took for himself the ancient titles of 'King of Kings' and 'Light of the Aryans', championed the monarchic and xenophobic strains of Ferdowsi, and in 1971 celebrated two and a half millennia of Persian royalty at the Achaemenid capital, Persepolis. In nearby Shiraz, families were starving.

His reforms – which in a different light can be seen as tragically well intentioned – had fractured and brutalized the nation. They were too radical to succeed, and the hand that imposed them was too unforgiving. Clerics, intellectuals, merchants, students, landowners, nationalists, and communists gathered force in a broad coalition of resistance.

As Khomeini railed against the 'American lackey tyrant' – first from Turkey, then Iraq, and then Paris, where he got more attention than ever – the Shah's reforms seemed to border on megalomania. He decreed obligatory membership of a single political party, and abolished the Islamic calendar, reforming time itself to date from the accession of Cyrus the Great in 559 BC. Resistance had never been broader, or more violent, and as crackdowns hardened, the ugliness was inevitable.

The Shah saw the wave rising and, characteristically, fled. Ten days later, Khomeini returned from his seventeen-year exile to be greeted by rapturous millions on the streets of Tehran; and from that day, Iran has been linked irrevocably with the robes, turban, beard, and awesome visage of the Imam. It was 1979.

But hadn't Khomeini promised he would settle down quietly after the Shah had gone? I asked Ramin. That, at least, had been the prediction of the CIA. We were at home now, and stood on the balcony watching the profile of the city fade into darkness. Ramin had turned unusually gloomy.

'Everyone thought he would give way,' he said quietly, twirling the tip of his cigarette to a point against the lip of an ashtray, 'but the power was irresistible to him.' For a year or so, Iran enjoyed an extraordinary freedom. Khomeini was little more than a figurehead, a symbolic champion of the moderate nationalists who had reclaimed their nation from foreign manipulation. But they did not survive.

Groups opposed to Khomeini's autocratic style were dissolved or silenced by the Imam's decrees – notably the communists, without whose disciplined and well-organized networks the revolution itself would have been impossible. Even notable ayatollahs who opposed Khomeini's role as both illegal and un-Islamic were mysteriously silenced. 'He used the war,' said Ramin, 'as a cover to have them killed.' As overt political resistance to Khomeini's power became too dangerous, protest began to take the form of cultural resistance. But even Iranian writers and artists, both at home and abroad, became the target of Khomeini's implacable Revolutionary Police. A generation of the most prosperous families had fled, and the eight-year-long war with Iraq drew a bloody veil over the decade. Today the prospect of further conflict was abhorrent; it had to come, said Ramin, in a different form.

I had intended, before setting off to Iran, to give politics a wide berth; but it had quickly become a portion of my daily experience. So often did I encounter resentment at the regime's broken promises it was difficult not to suppose that the whole country was disillusioned and weary and resentful and simmering like a Vesuvius; and I often wondered along which hidden fault line the surface would eventually fracture.

Some friends of Ramin's family — a married couple, recently returned from America — visited the next day. Hearing I was planning to leave, they offered a lift to the bus station. I was sad to leave Ramin's kindly and mischievous company, but accepted.

The husband spoke fluent English. 'We lived for five years in LA,' he said, as we drove north along the Chahar Bagh. He had been an engineer. I wondered why he had given up the obvious benefits of life there and come back.

'For the children,' he said.

'You wanted an Iranian education for them.'

'It wasn't that,' he said. 'Every week someone would go crazy and start shooting kids in a playground. In LA people shoot each other for fun. At least here you know the worst that will happen in an argument is that someone will punch you in the face.' He shook his head. 'We couldn't live like that.'

A bus for Tehran was ready to leave. I ran to it to ask the driver to wait, then ran back to the terminal to say goodbye. My ticket had been covertly paid for in the meantime, and my protests were in vain. We parted hastily. The ancient bus was billowing diesel fumes and honking wildly. My bag was thrown into the hold and I heard my name called from a list as the driver checked the list of passengers and ticked them off like a school register. A few desperate-looking characters — widows and war veterans and the dispossessed — clambered on at the last minute with pleas for small change, extending withered hands and muttering benedictions at the appearance of a few tattered banknotes.

Then we lumbered from the square as the driver's sidekick hung from the door, yelling our destination as we pulled away, and scooping up last-minute passengers as we joined the main road. The trees began to thin. The city fell behind us and I drew a dusty curtain against the glare of the parched hills. The driver was splitting sunflower seeds between his teeth and muttering curses at oncoming trucks, and from time to time his mate topped up a glass of tea which trembled on the dashboard. Soon heads and necks were lolling against the seats like stringless puppets, tranquillized by the heat. I fell asleep and woke up later, wondering where we were. A few miles away, a keel of mountains rose from the land through bands of haze, the nearest in a long, ragged chain of summits, violet now in the declining sun.

Through bleary eyes I watched as the driver, keeping one hand on the wheel and a foot pressed against the accelerator, left his seat and deftly changed places with his mate. The bus had not even slowed. Then more mountains. Then darkness.

Three

Tehran · Gombad-e Qabus Gorgan · Eastern Alburz Golestan

Fatter is Better · Louise Firouz · Conspiracy Theory · Steppe Country Ranch Life · The Rescue of the Caspian Horse · Opium Dog-Hell A Day at the Races · Romans and Parthians · Mithra Myths Parabolas and Colonnades · A Forgotten Corner of Iran Golestan · The Sound of Eons

عاقلان نقطهٔ پرگار وجودند ولی   عشق داند که در این دایره سرگردانند

The men of reason may be the pointer of the compass of Existence,
But Love knows that in our circle, they are apt to lose their bearings

'YOU LOST WEIGHT,' said Sorush, when I reappeared on his doorstep in Tehran. I was not sure, at first, how to interpret this observation; it was not the compliment it usually is at home, and the tone was akin to mild reproach. But crossing and recrossing paths with friends over the coming months I heard the expression several times and began to understand that, among men at least, no Western stigma attaches to the subject of excess weight. The contrary, in fact, is true. To be fatter is an indication of prosperity; to lose weight, a symptom of self-neglect – hence, I eventually realized, Sorush's look of reproof. Leanness suggests privation, not prowess, and its inverse condition implies a liberation from slavish physical endeavour and the happy consequence of a mother's or wife's homely regimen. After a long separation, men will tug at each other's midriffs as a compliment and pat their own stomachs with rueful pride; and it is not unusual for the returning visitor to find his weight the topic of extensive but affectionate scrutiny, sometimes by entire households.

'His cheeks are fatter, but not the rest of him,' said the mother of one family when I joined them for dinner a year after we had first met. 'No,' observed the daughter, 'his face hasn't changed, just the rest.' 'Definitely fatter all over,' pronounced the father with final authority. This unaccustomed form of greeting was followed immediately by a hearty meal.

It was the middle of June. The reservoirs above the city, built thirty years earlier, were struggling to supply a city whose population had multiplied threefold since then. Water was being rationed and in daylight hours the taps produced a hollow gurgling. The well in the garden had sunk below the level of the pump, and a dusty sheen had settled over the plants in the garden. Sorush asked about my trip to Isfahan. I told him I had been surprised at how modern everything had seemed. The traditional ways of life of the Iran in my imagination remained curiously evasive; perhaps they didn't even exist.

'What you are looking for you will not find in the cities,' he said. 'Thirty years ago, perhaps. But now only in Kurdistan or Khorasan. You must go to the villages.'

Various neighbours, he told me, had visited while I was away, and asked all about me. Their curiosity, he brooded theatrically, was symptomatic of the cupidity of his compatriots.

'Ten years I live here and nobody ask questions – but one foreigner come and questions, questions! Always they think: he is foreigner, maybe can exploit!'

They had brought diplomatic gossip too, from the wife of a friend who worked at a foreign embassy, where the ambassador had died of a heart attack a few days earlier. The second secretary was on holiday, and could not be found, so the funerary protocols had been delayed. The Iranian authorities had meanwhile insisted that the body remain at the embassy; but no coffins could be found, and elsewhere the facilities did not exist.

I asked if there was a deep freeze at the embassy. They had tried that, he said with a chuckle: the ambassador wouldn't fit. Perhaps he had been too fat.

Φ

Each day the tide of smog lapped higher against the hills, and I began to plot the next stage of my journey. 'The problem with Tehran,' I had read in a guidebook, 'is not how to get there, but how to avoid it.' The heat and pollution made summer the worst time to be trapped in the capital, and I was beginning to sympathize with this uncharitable judgement. Escape routes beckoned in every direction, but around them loomed unavoidable difficulties. In the west stretched the mountainous enclaves of Kurdistan, as well as the early Christian sanctuaries of the north-west, but the storm clouds gathering in Iraq made me look elsewhere for the moment. The Persian Gulf was a thousand miles of coastline begging to be explored, but broiling in summer. In the east beckoned a long and virtually lawless frontier in a state of undeclared war with drug smugglers from Afghanistan; I would need a permit to travel there, or at least a good friend who knew the area.

Evenings spent poring over history books suggested an architectural route. Iran was full of world-famous monuments and I could, in the course of several journeys, cover the historical route backwards, as it were, from the Safavid splendours I had encountered in Isfahan. In the north lay the former capitals of Iran under the Mongol Ilkhanids at Soltaniyeh and Tabriz, and not far away, the famous Assassins' castles near Qazvin, dating from the era of the Seljuks. South of Shiraz, in the heartland of ancient Fars, were the pre-Islamic ruins of the first Sasanian palaces, and in the same region, the famous remains of the Achaemenid headquarters at Persepolis. Each route suggested a circuit of several months' travel, and the scale of the endeavour seemed suddenly daunting. Visions of mounting bills at home clouded over my outstretched map and all prospects turned momentarily gloomy. Then I remembered Louise Firouz.

I had heard of her in London: an American woman who had married an Iranian aristocrat, moved to Iran in the time of the Shah, and weathered the long and stormy years of the revolution. She bred horses somewhere up in the mountains, and a rare breed she was said to have rescued from extinction had become the favourite of royal houses around the world. All this was hard to picture, sounded improbably romantic, and I didn't believe she really existed. But by good luck I had been given her telephone number, and had managed not to lose it.

To my great surprise it answered on the first ring. It was Louise.

'Come to lunch,' she said, so I did.

An hour's taxi ride from the city took me to the sprawling satellite town of Karaj, where the range of hills that overlooks the capital begins to sink back into the land. On its outskirts we turned down a dusty track and followed it to its end.

'It was all green here before,' said the taxi driver mournfully, 'in the Shah's time.' Explaining that the journey had been further than he had predicted, he robbed me courteously and left me by a pair of tall green metal gates. A taciturn boy in working clothes answered the bell and led me to a house on the far side of a leafy compound. Half a dozen energetic but friendly dogs surrounded me as I walked to the open doors, and waved to their owner across a large and airy room. It was Louise: a tall woman in her sixties with kindly and faintly melancholic features and short silvery hair tucked loosely into a flowery scarf. She was talking in fluent Persian on the telephone and beckoned me inside with an answering wave and a welcoming flash of bright blue eyes.

I laid an offering of cherries and melons on the table and looked around. I was definitely in the right place: there were lots of framed photographs of horses on the walls, and on either side of a fireplace, big bookcases filled with handsome and glinting volumes of every size. A glance at the spines revealed all the best books on Persian art and history, all first editions by the look of it and all deliciously out of date: Herzfeldt, Ghirshman, Godard, Porada, Auriel Stein, E. G. Browne, Sykes, Tarn, Ackerman, Ettinghausen, and, I noticed with a pang, all fifteen volumes of Arthur Upham Pope's *Survey of Persian Art*, the Golden Fleece of Iranophiles.

When she had finished talking we walked outside and sat at a table under the shade of a cluster of tall silver birch. The dogs settled like odalisques in pools of shadow nearby. Over tea, a few mutual acquaintances were quickly established, and we were soon exchanging stories. But I couldn't resist asking how it had all started.

'Beirut,' she said, 'in the good old days.' She had gone there for a year as an exchange student from Cornell. It had opened her eyes to a greater world, and from one of the new friends she had made came an invitation to visit Tehran. There, a dashing young Iranian of Qajar descent, Narcy Firouz, had proposed to

98

her — it was a heady time — but she had turned him down; her whole life was ahead of her and she had her studies to finish. She returned to America to take up the life she had left behind, but an interview with a careers adviser in her final year had altered the trajectory of her ambitions.

'Can you imagine?' The recollection evoked a girlish laugh. 'He was deeply concerned that I wouldn't give more thought to a pension plan. A pension! My life had barely begun and I was being asked how I wanted to end it. The whole idea put me off so much I went straight back to Beirut to take up Narcy's offer. And here we are,' she smiled, 'forty years later!'

She had raised a family in the intervening years, founded a riding school near Shiraz in the south of the country and a successful breeding centre. But the revolution had changed everything. They had seen the wave rising, she said, and had decided to stay. But her husband's association with the former ruling family had earned them the enduring attention of the Revolutionary Police, and in the years that followed, a sustained and debilitating harassment from the authorities. Twice they had been deprived their livelihood by the confiscation of both land and horses, and found themselves starting from scratch. 'You can't take possessions with you,' she said, with an impressively philosophical evenness. 'I accept that it can all be taken from me again.' Then, musing, she added: 'But I would miss my books.'

A leisurely lunch guided us into the afternoon over a succession of good-humoured stories punctuated by ample jokes. After hearing of so many difficulties I wondered if she had ever been tempted to leave. 'Of course,' she said, 'who wouldn't have? But what would I do about the animals? We had to leave a sick dog behind when we moved here from Shiraz and I never forgave myself.' As if to demonstrate this deeply humane streak, a young magpie, which could only fly for short distances, had fallen into the paddock as we were talking and was being chased by one of the dogs. Louise got up at once and shooed the dog away as I fielded the bird into a hedge. She dismissed the dog with an affectionate scolding and we sat down again.

As the sun passed over the yardarm we moved on to a local moonshine mixed with cherry juice. Beneath the girlish manner I began to catch glimpses of the steeliness that had sustained her during more difficult times. Early one morning, during the darkest days of the revolution, when the obituaries of their friends were appearing daily in the newspapers, a trio of cars had pulled up outside the gates. Her husband had already been imprisoned; now a team of plain-clothes officials had come to arrest her.

They had burst into the house and started emptying cupboards and drawers and sweeping her possessions from shelves onto the floor. 'The usual routine,' she scoffed, 'and completely unnecessary. It was very early so I went back downstairs to go to sleep until they took me away. The one in charge was furious. He came down to find me, and started yelling: "Don't you know what's happening?" "Yes," I said, "you're smashing up my house. I'm going to have a rest until you've finished." He was astonished and thought it most rude.' She let out a girlish giggle. 'Here,' she added, 'you're nobody if you haven't been to prison at least *once*. In America, when my grandchildren ask me in a restaurant why I went to prison, people edge discreetly away. Here, they gather round...'

But why had I heard, I asked, that she lived 'in the hills'? It was true, she said; twenty-five years ago she had founded a second breeding centre in the far north-east of the country, near the border with Turkmenistan. It was there that her search for the Caspian horse, thought to be long extinct, had begun in the 1960s. It was also the traditional home of the Turkmen, a tribal people whom she admired not only for their traditional love of horses but also — acknowledging in herself a resonant stubborn streak — for their archaic pride. 'They have none of that Persian sycophancy. That's partly why I love it up there.'

Then, with words that fell like music, she said: 'I'm thinking of going up there in a couple of days. If you've got nothing better to do, why don't you come?'

I hadn't: so I did.

Φ

On the evening before we left, Louise had been invited to dinner with a family who owned a horse at her stables, and hearing she had a guest they asked if I would come too. In the evening we drove to their home in the nearby town and pulled up in a quiet street lined with modern-looking houses.

A woman's voice buzzed us through an outer door over an intercom. Inside we exchanged our shoes for slippers and entered a large room with a white marble floor. A raised dining area was surmounted by plaster Ionic columns with gilded capitals and triglyphs and, more incongruous still, framed and hung over the dining table, was a six-foot-wide rendition of da Vinci's *Last Supper*, woven in bright anilines. The centrepiece of the lower part of the room was a gigantesque and noisy television, around which we settled into faux Louis XIV chairs and were welcomed by our hosts.

Father, mother, son, son-in-law, daughter, and grandmother all greeted us warmly and began to ply us attentively with glasses of tea, pastries, nuts, and a succession of snacks. Louise did most of the talking; I was still very rusty and could hardly hear the conversation over the noise of the television, which was impossible not to look at from time to time. It was tuned to a Turkish channel: a slapstick comedy dominated by a parody of the American President. Booted and spurred and waving two silver six-shooters, he was riding across the floor of the Oval Office on the back of his Secretary of State, puffing on an absurdly oversized cigar and shooting at whatever took his fancy. It was shockingly and refreshingly irreverent, but no one else seemed to be paying any attention to it.

'You don't get that sort of programme at home,' I said to my host.

'No,' he replied, without irony, 'you have to adjust the dish.'

Soon we were being ushered to the table, where a prodigious array of dishes was assembling like ships steaming into a crowded port.

There was a big bowl of barley and noodle soup called *ash-e reshte*, a baked and puréed aubergine dish called *kashk-e bademjan*, a lamb and spinach *khoresht* or stew, verdant piles of fresh herbs, yoghurt with mint and cucumber, several supporting salads, platters of fragrant saffron rice, and seven-spice pickle; all exquisitely presented and each as delicious as the next.

Conversation was all about politics. I knew none of the names of the characters involved, but the general idea was clear enough. At the naming of an official post, there was a suggestion of political favour; at the resignation of another, a hint of covert pressure from above. Coincidences inevitably implied collusion, and to every manoeuvre in government policy there was talk of underhand goings-on.

There was scarcely any mention of more abstract things; conspiracy was as natural a theme as the weather is to the English. But as soon as these suppositions moved abroad, things began to look shakier. Somehow the conversation had turned to the police and their relative merits in different countries. At least the police in Iran could be trusted, someone said; foreign police forces weren't the same. Only the other day there had been a report in the news of an Iranian journalist in London – beaten up by the English police and hauled off to prison.

There were some gloomy nods of assent. I was surprised by this ready note of conspiracy, but there was more. The British government, everybody agreed, had approved of the mistreatment to appease the Israelis, outside whose embassy the journalist had been arrested. They had, after all, ordered the assassination of their own Princess of Wales; and it was obvious that royal approval had been given to the plan.

A cautious intervention seemed called for. I said that I didn't believe in the assassination theory, but that conspiracies always flourished when the fates unexpectedly claimed the lives of those who were broadly popular. It felt appropriate to add that our own future king, more than any European monarch, was not only controversially sympathetic towards Islamic culture, but had even, in the heart of London, established a foundation where the traditional arts of Islam could be studied.

There was a lull; no counter-argument was raised to this

revelation, only a brief exchange of looks full of mute sympathy, as if I had confessed to believing the earth was flat. '*Kar-e Inglisi!*' I joked, to lighten things, 'The hand of the English!' and added a self-censorious wink for good measure. There was a ripple of relieved laughter at this once-popular expression, which history had by now robbed of its seriousness, and the conversation turned to less controversial things: horses, I think, and the cost of living in Romania, where the son-in-law had trained as a dentist.

In all this talk of schemery and plot there was no trace of conscious criticism, much less ill-will towards a guest. The entire spirit of the occasion was too obviously good-natured, and talk of scheming royals and slippery police was rather, I think, an attempt to affirm the common fate of ordinary citizens everywhere; more of a pact between the oppressed than a veiled slight. But the readiness to assign such dark incentives to the unexplained betrayed a deep susceptibility to belief in hidden doings and high-up collaboration. I had already heard the explanations for the lack of water in Isfahan (none of which, I remembered, had anything to do with rainfall), and that the government was secretly drugging the entire youth of the nation; I had already met with plenty of knowing smiles at the mention that I was English and travelling the country in order to write; and, only a few days earlier, had heard the account of British support for the emergent Baha'i faith in the nineteenth century as a means to undermine Shi'ism, and Persia in general. It was not hard to join up the dots.

A belief in the spirit-like hand of colonial (and especially British) powers behind nearly every event of historical import was, at least until the Islamic revolution, almost universally held. Today, a wary streak still lingers among the older generation and, to be fair, it is not without reason. The weaknesses of the last three Qajar shahs were ingeniously exploited by outside powers, whose interference in Iranian affairs is frequently invoked as proof of international treachery in general. Topping the list are the British support for the Constitutional Movement at the turn of the century as a cynical countermeasure to Russian interests, the later Anglo-Russian convention dividing Persia into spheres of interest, the British disgracing of Reza Khan, and the simultaneous occupation of Persia by British, Russian, and Turkish forces during the First World War (and, during the Second, by the Americans as well) — all of which left deep feelings of powerlessness among Iranians against the designs of foreign governments. For a long time, the cunning of the British was seen to have repeatedly duped the Russians (who were too simple-minded to see through them) and the Americans (who were too naive). But after the overthrow of the government of Prime Minister Mossadeq in 1953, in which the CIA was deeply implicated, the dark accolade passed quickly — inevitably, perhaps — to America.

Opponents of the former Shah have since then produced ample literature to support the fancy that Iranian prime ministers were in fact vetted and selected in America, and that the controversial land reforms of the Shah's 'white revolution' of the 1970s were part of an American plot to force Iranian dependence on imported American food. But conspiracy is contagious and respects no ideological borders; and on all sides the arguments are equally and ingeniously convincing (or unconvincing). The very same foreign Imperialist–Zionist–Masonic devils suspected of having brought the Shah to power are also named as the engineers of the Islamic revolution which brought about his downfall; the plan having been to undermine a rapidly developing Iran with an unpopular and vulnerable regime which could be manipulated, puppet-like, from beyond.

Even Khomeini himself was considered, by his opponents, to be little more than a pawn in a grand foreign design (why else did the French give him refuge in Paris, or the BBC's World Service give him so much time on air?). Underneath the very beard of the Imam, went a popular joke of the 1980s, were stamped the words *Made in England* . . .

Unchecked by cool analysis, and generously abetted by history, all seedling intrigues share a tendency to luxuriate. It is tempting to see this as a national mania; the prerogative, perhaps, of a theology steeped in the themes of heterodoxy, persecution, and martyrdom, and the miraculous occultation of the Shi'ite messiah, the hidden Imam. To be fairer, a judicious sorting would probably find grains of truth in even the wilder suggestions. But in their raw state they are devious enough to make an oriental Le Carré blush and a no-win contest for common sense.

Unless, of course, they are all true...

Φ

After our sumptuous dinner was over, rounded off with meringues and profiteroles, the son, who was a handsome and slight man in his early twenties, took me aside with a solicitous tug of my hand and guided me to a comfortable chair across the room. In my lap he laid a heavy album. It was the record of his older sister's wedding; a grand event attended by four family generations, and captured by a professional photographer. The first album was dedicated to the happy couple who, embowered in a nuptial soft-focus haze, floated across the pages in multiplying vignettes. Then came the relatives; three more albums of them, photographed and re-photographed in exponential permutations. Nearly a thousand photographs later, my admiring murmurs began to wear thin ('lovely ... beautiful ... look, there's Grandma again – and again!'). Sensing perhaps that I was flagging, he led me to his room.

He sat next to me on his bed, pinching my cheek from time to time, intoning my name repeatedly and melodiously and with unconcealed affection. Then he summoned his brother to photograph us cheek to cheek and, after he had left, closed the door and produced from a small cupboard a bottle of ruby-coloured liqueur. It was deliciously alcoholic and was made, he explained, from the mulberries collected from the tree just outside. Lighting two cigarettes between his lips, he passed me one, and balanced the other on the edge of a cabinet from which a dreamy and vaguely flamenco melody began to sound. He asked if I liked it and what it made me think of; I didn't dare say it made me feel lonely. He tugged on my cheek again and chastised me for not relaxing enough.

I felt an excuse coming on, but just then looked over to a chest of drawers, and was glad to see several framed photographs of an elegant young woman. 'Who's this?' I asked, picking up the nearest one and passing it to him. 'She's very beautiful.'

'I know,' he said, and for a few moments his eyes fell adoringly over the photograph in his lap. 'That's Mum, when she was young.'

تاریخ آیه گذشته است درس حال

History is a mirror of the past and a lesson for the present – Sa'di

It was a day-long drive. We left after an early breakfast in Louise's loaded jeep, skirting the creeping greyness of the city before heading east beyond the sprawl of the outermost suburbs. Our route climbed slowly over the parched slopes of the Alburz, then turned gradually north, cresting the range in a series of passes at about seven thousand feet. The climate changes suddenly here: the glare and haze of the plateau fall unexpectedly behind and the northern air, held captive by the gates of the mountains, releases from bands of hovering mist a welcome and European humidity. There is thick forest on the far slopes, dense and deep green and hidden on the uppermost slopes by a tight cape of cloud.

Entering the province of Mazanderan, the road winds north-wards and steadily downwards through deep and twisting gorges scarred with gulleys like ritual sword wounds, where the raw and purple volcanic soil is exposed by torrents of seasonal meltwater. It emerges from the diminishing mountains on the Caspian littoral in the region of the province's capital, Sari. Here, twenty miles from the shore, the land flattens suddenly into a coastal band a hundred miles from east to west. Dust and dehydration are unseen and a new colour, a green of tropical, almost fluorescent intensity, strikes the eye from plantations of young rice.

As we turned east to skirt the base of the hills, even the

inhabitants were becoming more colourful. There were tall and swarthy Zabuli tribesmen wearing white turbans and shalwar kameez and walking with the confident gait of Pashtuns from the north-west frontier, and Turkmen women with the narrow eyes and high cheekbones of the steppe, dressed in bright floral shawls and swirling gowns. In the fields lining the roads were lines of both men and women in bright shirts bent double over hoes or the muddy embankments of rice plantations. Scarcely a trace remained of the eye-deadening black of the chador, or the fugitive moon-like faces of the women of Tehran.

In the early evening we reached Gombad-e Qabus, where the famous tower from which the town takes its name looms like a misplaced monument from the future. It had the unkempt air of a frontier town, and until a century ago was still prey to Turkmen raiders on horseback. Here we refilled the jeep with petrol for the equivalent of £2 and drove for a further hour north-east, then crossed the snaking ravine of the Gorgan River on a smooth meandering road. Beyond it, the land opened up as if a curtain had been lifted, and suddenly we were in an unbroken vastness which seemed to reach to the rim of the world. Fields of shorn wheat with no visible borders stretched on every side and in the final hour of light the entire landscape looked like an ocean of gold. We had entered steppe-country. Louise saw me looking, and turned her head towards me.

'I'm glad you noticed,' she said. 'People have been riding up here for three thousand years. That's why I love it. That's why the horses love it, too. I sometimes think they know this is their ancestral homeland.'

A few miles on we turned from the road onto a dusty track, where purple-bodied rollers swooped ahead of us like dolphins frolicking alongside a boat. To one side ran a low mound like an ancient barrow, on top of which I could make out tufts of reddish brickwork; the remains, said Louise, of 'Alexander's Wall'. It ran for more than a hundred miles from the south-east shore of the Caspian to the Kopet Dagh Mountains which separate today's Iran from Turkmenistan. Long ago it had served as a barrier against nomadic incursions from the north. But the Hellenistic attribution was spurious; it had almost certainly been built by the Parthians about two thousand years ago. The local Turkmen knew it as *qizil alam*, red snake, and villagers still pillaged its length for the ancient bricks, finding them stronger than modern ones. Louise had too, she confessed.

A final turn set us towards a cluster of buildings half a mile away, nestling among a scattering of eucalyptus, cypress, and pine trees. In a dusty courtyard beyond the gates, three men sprang from the buildings to help us unload. They were Turkmen with prominent cheekbones and deeply lined dark skin that told of a life spent in the sun. The friendliest of them, Khidr, had a round face which burst readily into a smile as he fussed over our bags and questioned us volubly; Ibrahim was sullen and gaunt, and murmured a husky greeting. A knife in a leather sheath hung from his belt, and he moved with the unhappy deliberateness of a man in constant pain. Ghorban sported a bright red shirt and a perpetual scowl. I liked them all at once, but was disappointed that they didn't carry automatic weapons, feeling that men with such features looked better with them.

We settled into a small house with terracotta floors and arched windows through which a warm breeze circulated over simple furniture and walls hung with Turkoman rugs. Louise showed me to an upstairs room which gave onto a small balcony, where she suggested I sleep if it got too hot. I unrolled a mattress there and took in the view. Two dozen horses roamed the corral below. Beyond the ranch, a few miles to the south, ran a wavering dark line of forested hills; to the north stretched the golden expanse of the steppe. It was then that I noticed how quiet the place was. There was no sound but the whisper of an encircling breeze, dancing through the leaves of the eucalyptus nearby, and the very land seemed held in an ancient and nourishing stillness. It was the first time I had felt such quietness since arriving in the country. I told Louise it was the perfect place to come to spend a year to write; a bare room, horses, hills, and yet another bookcase full of first-edition volumes on Persian and central Asian history.

'People come up here and complain that it's too far away from anywhere,' she mused. 'Just far enough, I say. Good thing the British stayed in the south,' she added with a grin. 'If they'd come up here they would have built roads everywhere and that would've been the end of the place.'

We ate lamb roasted in the embers of a fire outside, and played backgammon over a variation of locally made moonshine tasting somewhere between paraffin and nail varnish. My hostess was a fund of amusing and self-deprecating stories. She was probably the only person, she said, who'd met Salman Rushdie in London and not known who he was (though his notorious volume, *The Satanic Verses*, had actually won a literary prize in Iran before the even more famous fatwa); or who couldn't stand the sight of caviar after having eaten so much of it during the revolution, when it was issued as a daily ration.

I was never able to write down her stories quickly enough afterwards; in the best Persian fashion there were tales of treasure, corruption, plot, and high intrigue, and a few which were impossible to forget: the day an Iraqi Scud missile engine fell through the roof onto her kitchen table in Tehran (she moved out shortly afterwards), and the time she was propositioned by an enterprising mulla. Conversation, on this and other evenings, was delightful, eclectic, and always illuminating, ranging over traditional bone-setting techniques (she had broken nearly all of hers, she giggled), instances of animal telepathy, Model 'A' Ford repairs, different uses for porcupine quills (occasionally her dogs would be transformed by a night-time encounter into canine pin-cushions, noses and jowls perforated with long quills), Scythian art, fond recollections of the genteel and privileged lifestyle of her in-laws, now utterly extinguished ('I told Narcy if they kept calling me "Princess Firouz", I'd leave him'), the jubilation that followed the fall of the Shah and the gradual suffocation of the nationalists by Khomeini's henchmen, the sight of Iraqi missiles ('great big lighted cigarettes flying backwards') plunging day after day onto the capital, prison memories ('you get used to cockroaches – the baby ones are quite cute'), businesses which had disappeared from the region after the revolution (Armenian pig-breeders and local insect-gatherers),* much speculation over the consequences of American folly in Iraq, the challenges of meeting various financial hardships, and some romantic evocations of mounted jackal hunts meeting in the gardens of the British Embassy in Golhaq, when the surrounding area was scrub and woodland and not the jungle of apartment blocks and flyovers that it is today.

No trace of nostalgia clouded these recollections, and the years prior to the revolution were evoked with the detached affection of a farmer recalling an earlier harvest. But it *had* been fun, she admitted. In the fifties and sixties, when Iran had been a fashionable destination for well-heeled foreigners, the family home in the south had become an almost obligatory venue for visitors in the know.

'Everyone went through Shiraz in those days,' she said. 'We never had lunch for less than thirty – fifty usually – though people didn't seem to realize this was our *home*.' She recalled – with a cruel and very funny imitation – a visiting German diplomat who, as she was ushering him into her dining room for lunch, enquired of his hostess, 'And who iss ze owner of ziss restaurant?' The constant flow of visitors was too much for some, she said, and a relative of her husband's had actually burned down his own house in protest.

---

* Who would gather large quantities of the insect *Kermococcus vermilio* in order to extract the red dye formerly used to colour Campari. The ancient dye is called kermes (or *qermez* in Persian, meaning red); the name comes from the Persian for worm, *kerm*, from which our own 'crimson' and 'carmine' descend. The dye was produced from the female insect and harvested in early summer. An older term, *sakirlat*, became *scarlatum* in Latin, and has reached us as scarlet. Few worms can boast such far-reaching etymological connections.

She had got to know a great many of the explorers, authors, and diplomats of the day, and the spectrum of names went back further than I had expected. She was so peculiarly youthful and irreverent I was astonished to discover that Byron, travelling through Iran in 1933, had actually described meeting her mother and father-in-law in *The Road to Oxiana* ('not very flatteringly, as it happens').

Thesiger had passed through several times, spurning offers of pampered treks; David Stirling, of SAS fame, was a regular visitor, along with various Jellicoes and a Romanov or two; Freya Stark had become a good friend. Then there were the giants of Persian architecture and archaeology: Arthur Upham Pope, Phyllis Ackerman, and André Godard, and later on the scholarly teams from the British Institute for Persian Studies; all the British Ambassadors and their families from the time of Sir Denis Wright ('Denis was wonderful') to the most recent and newly arrived ('he'll grow into it...'); and many of the American ones until their demise in 1979 – notably Richard Helms, later director of the CIA; and of course there was Kermit – *Kermit?* 'Not the frog,' I interrupted, 'surely?'

'No, silly,' she said, 'Kermit Roosevelt' – grandson of the former President and (we now know) mastermind of the 1953 coup which drove the government of Mossadeq from power. 'He used to come for lunch,' she said. 'Short guy, but very confident. He was always going off for meetings with "HIM".'*

Once, after a Persian event at the Royal Geographical Society in London, an Englishwoman had struck up a conversation with her. Her mind had been elsewhere, and later she had asked a friend to remind her who she'd been talking to: it had been Byron's sister. 'You would have thought she'd have been more interesting.'

'You're very wicked,' I said.

'Of course I am,' she giggled.

When it was time to turn in, I confessed that I wasn't much

---

* His Imperial Majesty, Mohammad Reza Pahlavi.

of a horseman and hoped I wouldn't let her down. 'Don't worry,' she said, with another kindly flash of her big blue eyes. 'Take advantage of Ibrahim and Ghorban. Try the horses out one by one. Stay a week, a month, and learn how to ride.'

Φ

We rode at dawn and dusk to avoid the worst of the heat, taking in a four-mile circuit across the shorn wheat to the edge of the Gorgan ravine. Ibrahim would lead, singing to himself in a high, plaintive melody; Ghorban followed behind. Three dogs from the ranch ran eagerly at our sides. Dust devils pirouetted across the fields like miniature tornadoes, and in the distance rose half a dozen ancient burial mounds like inverted pudding bowls. From the lip of the steppe a network of narrow and twisting trails led downwards through an eerie maze of ravines, returning only the sound of our creaking saddles, the panting of the dogs, and the occasional knock of hoof against stone. Ibrahim and Ghorban were undemanding instructors and taught by glance and gesture alone, and quietly monitored the progress of their new apprentice. Returning on our first day to the ranch I realized I had lost a sheepskin saddle-cover during the ride, and Ghorban produced it from between his knees with a wink. He instructed me wordlessly in the business of washing down the horses and cleaning the tack and saddling up in the mornings, the importance of mounting without kicking the horse's rump, and how to read the semaphore of the horse's ears when riding. Over the next few days we took longer and more challenging routes, driving the horses at the end of a ride into the river and returning drenched and exhilarated, or cantering under the entrance arch and skidding to a halt in front of the stables in quadruple bursts of yellow dust.

Φ

Louise had lived horses. Her parents had kept several horses at their Virginia home, and she had even ridden to school as a child. Sixty years on, the memory of having to saddle up with numb fingers on dark winter mornings still evoked a shiver. Spontaneous and open-ended explorations with friends on horseback were the best part of this Tom Sawyeresque life; they would skirt the farmland of Fairfax County or the forest trails bordering the Potomac, living off the land and their wits until they were eventually missed either at home or at school. These were the days when parents began to worry about their children only after they had disappeared for several days; the resulting admonishments, it seems, were neither lasting nor — to judge from the manner of the recollection — meant, or taken, very seriously.

After she had moved to Iran with her husband, she founded, thirty-five years ago, Iran's first children's riding school. But the generally available hot-blooded horses were inappropriate for younger riders, and a search for smaller and gentler mounts led to a series of expeditions in pursuit of a miniature horse, rumoured to survive in the foothills above the southern Caspian region. A pony-sized horse, appearing on Mesopotamian relief plaques, vases, and jewellery, and widely portrayed in such Achaemenid artefacts as the trilingual seals of Darius and the Apadana reliefs at Persepolis, pointed to the existence in antiquity of a small but agile horse, native to Iran and selectively bred long before the existence of the Arab. But the miniature horse was thought to be long extinct, and its ancestral position relative to the Arab and all Oriental horses had never been fully investigated because of the difficulty of accurately identifying true horses from bone fragments alone. The discovery in 1908 of the remains of a small oriental horse in a Neolithic settlement of Turkmenistan had, in the absence of any living examples, been squarely discredited. Officially at least, the trail ran cold about two and a half millennia earlier.

In 1965, on a small expedition to the mountain villages above Amol ('it was all dirt roads then, not like now'), Louise encountered the first examples of the ancient, diminutive breed. They were pitifully neglected and mistreated, scarred and tick-covered, and their owners knew nothing of their illustrious ancestry. But the features were distinct: big bold eyes, prominent jaws and the high-set tails which so distinguished their larger cousin, the Arab.

They were on the brink of extinction. Louise rescued three, and made a survey of the area to discover how many might still exist. Only a few dozen were thought to survive. Seven mares and six stallions were eventually bought, and became the foundation stock for the world's first Caspian breeding centre.

The encounter would send tremors through equine gospel. For generations, it had been held that the Arab was the true ancestor of the thoroughbred, and the only pure-bred horse of oriental origin. Louise was not the first to posit the idea of a miniature horse ancestral to the Arab; but she was the only one stubborn enough to prove it. Its conformation had already been put forward, based on skeletal remains and the study of graphic artefacts, but as it was thought to be extinct, claims to any ancestral role remained speculative. The evidence, in the form of living examples, was now reviewed: the shared traits with the Arab were unmistakable.

Another native breed, the Turkoman (a slim, tall, elegant, and swift horse), was put forward by Louise as the other ancestral parent of all better European strains; a distant predecessor, in other words, of all points along the Heavenly Shabdaz–Buraq–Bucephalus–Beynard–Bayerly–Rosinante–Black Beauty line. The Turkoman had been much favoured by the Greek overlords of Persian territories more than two thousand years ago and Alexander, according to Herodotus, had sent fifty thousand back to Greece. Strabo, calling these horses Nicaean, wrote of them as 'the most elegant riding horse in the world'. Sheathed in glittering coats of chain mail, Turkoman horses bore the Parthian archers who ravaged the massed legionaries of Crassus and Mark Antony; the Han emperors of China sacrificed armies to obtain just a few.* Later they were given as gifts by the Parthian kings to

---

* The famous 'blood-sweating' horses of the Han; more specifically, the strain known as the Akhal-Tekke. The bleeding is thought to be caused by a water-borne parasite existing only in the general area of Ferghana and the Gorgan River in northern Iran. Many of these highly prized,

Roman emperors, and introduced into the Roman cavalry. They were the chosen mount for the guard of the Caliphs of Baghdad, were much sought after during the Crusades as trophies by the Western conquerors of the Holy Land, and in the sixteenth century it was the Turkoman that carried the ostrich-plumed janissaries of Sultan Suleiman and the billowing green banners of the Islamic faith on their fateful journey through the passes of the Carpathians and the penumbral forests of Transylvania all the way to the terrified and encinctured defenders of Vienna.

This did not all go down well in orthodox equestrian circles. It suggested an unacknowledged debt to Persia, the diversity of whose native breeds, selectively nurtured nearly three millennia earlier, had provided the raw material for the favoured horses of later civilizations. And though Iran was home to a fascinating range of native breeds, Western equine history, hypnotized by the beauty of the Arab, tended to come a halt at the Euphrates.

Louise's efforts to preserve the purity of these ancient breeds courted controversy within Iran too. Within a few years of her discovery she was breeding and exporting Caspians to foreign buyers: Prince Philip was presented with a stallion and mare on his visit to Iran; the Shah bought dozens. But as a private venture the breeding centre became financially impossible to maintain, and the Iranian Royal Horse Society took over her herd a few years later. She began another, rebuilding her stock from rescued animals, on the edge of the Caspian's original heartland (where we were now sitting on the veranda of her house). But its closure was ordered in 1977, after a ban on exports was declared by the government.

As the shadow of revolution fell over the country two years later, the Caspian's (as well as Louise's) association with royalty brought her into conflict with the nation's new rulers, who could not make up their minds whether to give her a medal or to put

---

'Heavenly' horses were said to have golden coats with a metallic sheen, just as they do today.

her in prison.* They chose the latter. She and her husband were repeatedly arrested: imprisoned with a broken ankle, she chose to starve herself in protest and was released several weeks later. ('What else could I do? I knew they didn't want to kill me, and I had the horses to feed.') But a subsequent and crueller edict threatened owners and breeders of the steppes in possession of more than one horse with the confiscation of their property. Forced to surrender all but one mare, her founding stock was again wiped out. The horses were auctioned as pack animals or for meat, and were never recovered.

Thirty years after her research had begun, the correspondence between the historical, graphic, and archaeological evidence was finally confirmed by genetic studies. Blood tested from a wide range of horses affirmed that the Caspian occupied the most ancestral position of all oriental horse breeds, followed closely by the Turkoman.† Along with Prezewalski's horse and the Tarpan, the rescue of the Caspian is one of the most exciting discoveries in equine history. It had come, I suggested, at a high price. 'That's not the point, really,' she replied. 'If I had to do the whole thing again, I would. The point is to have lived.'

We had talked for hours, but it had never occurred to me to ask: Did she have any Caspians at the ranch? Could I see

---

* The former, I think, is long overdue. Firstly for restoring Iran's primacy on the map of equine history; secondly for not allowing the relentless harassment of the authorities to cloud her judgement of true Iranian culture and values; and thirdly for not giving up. No foreigner living in Iran has done more to send a positive message about the country to the greater world, or been treated so poorly in return.

† I have made this story simpler than it is: the Turkoman breed, for example, embraces among others the Yamoud, Akhal-Tekke, Yabou, Jargalan, and Goklan; and it seemed better to skip the time spent defining allele frequencies, equine parafilariosis, the measurement of the epiphyses of distal metapodials and receding frogs as osteological diagnostic criteria, and the whole Pleistocene–Holocene debate over the survival of the true horse (as opposed to the equid) in the Zagros. But I hope I have got the main facts right.

one? She had rescued one quite recently, she said: a young mare which had been shot in the eye by a boy with an air rifle. We walked to the stables, where a dozen chestnut heads and twitching ears loomed over the doors of the stalls at shoulder height. To the upper straps of their bridles were attached headbands with long multicoloured tassels to keep flies off; and incongruously I thought of Haight–Ashbury girls dressed as squaws. At the far end in a lonely stall stood a dark and unexpectedly diminutive-looking and gentle creature with a cruelly scooped concavity where its left eye should have been. Its withers rose no higher than my waist and it looked like a pony; the kind of creature a hobbit might choose to ride. It did not seem an obvious contender for chief ancestor of the mighty Sons of the Desert who thunder over the home stretch at the Grand National and the Kentucky Derby; nor, indeed, one whose distant predecessors had carried the Achaemenid King of Kings from Pasargadae to Lydia, watched Croesus burn at Sardis, wheeled east along the Oxus as far as Bactria and, clattering under the gates of Nebuchadnezzar's conquered palace at Babylon, witnessed, with a snort and a swish of tail, the birth of the world's first empire.

Φ

It was very hot. For several days in a row the afternoon temperature crept to well over a hundred degrees, and held the land in a windless and shimmering embrace. The horses didn't seem to mind, but the dogs lay tranquillized by the heat in havens of shadow, and human activity slowed to a subsistence pace.

An Anglo-Saxon reluctance to sleep during the day prompted me to ask: was there anything I could do around the place to make myself useful? An outdoor table, said Louise, would be good; there was bound to be enough scrap wood around the property to make something. So with Khidr I foraged in the outbuildings for old planks. An exaggerated fear of snakes kept him at the door, peering nervously, and joking with a mirthful slap to his thigh that if I were first to be bitten he would be sure to suck out all the venom. We salvaged four old posts for legs and half a dozen of the least warped planks we could find, and piling them up in the courtyard, wondered what to do next.

The task became a magnet, and the men gathered and squatted on their haunches to study me expectantly. Not wishing to disappoint, I peered gravely along the lengths of the planks, and stroked the grain of the posts meaningfully. Khidr unearthed a rusty plane, a drill, and a saw so blunt we took turns to share the eventual crop of blisters it produced. Behind this endeavour lay a vague hope of showing that Westerners could apply themselves usefully to physical tasks, and I expected a measure of competition from men who, I idly assumed, could probably make tables blindfolded before breakfast. I had not purposefully meant to injure them all in the process. But they had never used tools before. Ghorban received at least two blackened fingernails from his own hammering, and Khidr drilled straight through one of the posts into the hand steadying it on the far side – his own – and collapsed onto the dust in a spasm of pain and laughter. A part-time helper on the ranch, abnormally cheerful, slightly deaf, and whose trousers were fastened with a length of knotted string, also insisted on being put to work. His helpfulness – sawing the planks too short, driving nails into the wrong places, removing them and hammering them straight again (we were short of nails) – doubled the time we spent on the project.

Only Ibrahim remained aloof. He would inspect our efforts, scowling vaguely, for a few moments each day, but passed by each time in silence. I told Louise I liked Ibrahim's sullenness; despite it, he could not disguise his devotion either to her or the welfare of the horses.

'He's quite a character,' she said fondly. 'If he trusts you, he'll probably want to have a friendly smoke.' I didn't grasp this fully until she added, matter-of-factly, 'You probably won't have time to get hooked.' Her words returned to me the following afternoon, when Ibrahim appeared at the door, inviting me to join him in his room.

'It's early,' I said, 'perhaps a bit later.'

'Later,' he repeated, without changing his expression; then turned and left. The following evening I stayed up late, writing on the porch. Louise had already turned in when I heard a gentle tapping on the doorframe. It was Ibrahim.

'You didn't come last night,' he said. 'I waited for you.'

I pictured him sitting alone, waiting, and immediately regretted the flippancy of my earlier and casual rebuff. Wanting to undo this act of neglect I agreed to come with him that moment, and followed him to his room near the stables. It was tiny and lit by a bare bulb and filled with indescribable clutter. Ghorban was already there, lying on an improvised bed of what looked like sacks and boxes. Every few minutes he would reach out to beat a cracked and dusty black-and-white television, which struggled to receive the snowy image of a Russian soap opera transmitted from across the border.

Ibrahim sank stiffly to the floor, brewed a small metal pot of tea on a paraffin stove, and spread an old newspaper in front of us for a tablecloth. From the sheath at his waist he drew his knife, its blade black and slightly concave near the hilt from countless sharpenings, and cut an apple into segments, laying them gently on the paper in front of us. Then, after ferreting about in an ancient trunk, he produced a pea-sized nugget of opium and began to soften it between his finger and thumb.

I didn't want to seem squeamish in front of the men who would be looking after me over the next few days and, giving my best impression of intimacy with the ritual, took turns to draw the nugget across a red-hot wire, watching the tiny eruption of smoke as it vaporized on contact with the metal. The room soon filled with the unmistakable smell of carbonized poppies. Ibrahim hunched intently over my hands with a cardboard tube the size of a pen-barrel for a pipe, filling his lungs with the snowy vapour before the wire cooled, then leaned back like a man listening to his favourite music, swaying slightly.

But for the conversation it was a pleasureless session; and I was soon feigning intoxication as a vicar declines more tea. Yet I have no recollection today of our conversation; only, over the course of the following hour, of the darkening tenor of the stories he told as the opium began its work of unloosening; my notes refer to horse injuries he had suffered over the years and, more obscurely, to the difficulty a man faces trying to rise once he has fallen. Ghorban fell asleep where he lay and a little later, as if in sympathy, the television subsided to a snowy haze.

I stayed with Ibrahim for a couple of hours; it was obvious that the drug had its talons in him, and as I had no wish to follow suit, was relieved when at last the third little pellet was exhausted, and he laid down his makeshift pipe as a weary soldier might his sword.* He acknowledged my request to leave with a heavy blink, and rose to his feet, a little unsteadily, to walk me back to the house. But I thanked him and left him, silhouetted and slightly stooped, in the doorway, and crept back past the silent stables in the starlight. On the balcony I unfolded a mattress and lay awake for a long time beneath an ocean of incandescent stars, feeling I might scoop up a handful of constellations from the heavens overhead, keep them captive awhile, and release them again on a dark night of need.

Far off, a dog was barking. Its voice broke the silence with an insistent and irregular cadence and, just when it seemed likely to subside, and I to fall asleep, would start up again. It was soon joined by another equally troublesome voice, and then a third which, each time it neared the end of a burst of barking, broke into a desperate and wolfish howling. Then the horrible chorus began to gain momentum and, as if a signal indecipherable by human ears was being passed to every dog within miles, began to rouse fellow malcontents from ever further afield until, along a

---

* In *A Year Among The Persians*, the scholarly Edward Browne describes not only the process leading to his addiction to opium but also the satisfaction by which his hosts greet the news, and notes that 'it is a curious fact that, although the opium-smoker will, as a rule, never tire of abusing his tyrant, he will almost always rejoice to see another led into the same bondage, and will take the new captive by the hand as a brother.'

thickening front to the south, a whole army of dogs seemed to be massing.

It was very strange. Other than docile pooches that belonged to Louise, I had not seen a single dog in the daytime. So many dogs could not have simply been hiding: they must have gathered for a purpose. I wrapped a pillow over my ears, then two; but nothing worked, and I tossed and turned resentfully until, for a moment, all was quiet. I stood up and looked into the blackness. There was neither light nor movement, nor anything to suggest the involvement of any human agency: it was dog thing. And, perhaps, *too quiet*. This happened several times. And each time I returned hopefully to sleep, the pandemonium flared up again with new and even more raucous vigour.

There must have been fifty dogs, or a hundred — perhaps a thousand. *What were they planning?* A revolution, or at the very least, a campaign to rid the surrounding villages of their human overlords. I pictured the messages passing between them, received at each end by cocky, brindled local commanders, gathering round in circles of stiffly wagging tails to discuss them under the starlight, before the elders, among them the one-eyed, three-legged, and scrofulous veterans of earlier campaigns, would despatch one of the more energetic messengers to a nearby hillock to relay their decision. Then a few staccato barks would ignite the chain of noise again, and the sound grew in waves now, borne on the overlapping tides of escaping heat, alternately muted to a vague and junglish murmur, or suddenly amplified into worrying closeness.

No dog could reach the balcony. The trellis, however, might conceivably give access to a canine mujahed agile enough to use his teeth. *When would they come?* By now anything seemed possible. Impatient to redress a lifetime of iniquities suffered under their biped tormentors, crack teams of house-clearing dog troops stood at the ready, wearing dog balaclavas and, looped like sagging collars between neck and rib, the coils of miniature grappling irons to reach even the highest of balconies. Others, ready to abseil down chimneys, tightened their harnesses between slobber-coated incisors; a volunteer unit from across the border in Turkmenistan, equipped with can-openers, would supervise the capture of foodstuffs; and a small team of Afghan mongrel mercenaries had agreed to do anything at all, in exchange for a guaranteed booty of cats. A thousand ebony-coloured claws glinted in a flurry of valedictory salutes, and soon the night was a battlefield of sound: the predatory yapping of rapid small-arms fire, the steady beat of medium-calibre woofing, and, from heavy chests wheezing between salvoes, the thump of dog cannon. Soon, over all this, and from every point along the spreading line, came the high-pitched baying of the wounded and the helpless.

It was bedlam. Even Louise's own dogs, I now felt certain, were colluding from the edge of the property nearby, and when their allies began to flag, roused them back into action with piercing howls. I am not sure how long all this lasted: it seemed like hours. Eventually, blurred by exhaustion, the din grew less distinct and, at last, faded into silence. Sleep fell moments afterwards like a much-needed balm – but not before a chilling thought that from the stillness there was worse to come: perhaps an Iranian Cerberus, himself garlanded in swirls of opium smoke, had ascended in dog-person from the underworld to steel the will of his officers, silencing all with his terrifying six-fold gaze, before uttering the dreadful command to *unleash dog hell*...

'Dogs?' repeated Louise the next morning at breakfast, with a look of puzzlement. 'What dogs?' A universe of dogs, I was about to explain, had surrounded the property the night before. Then her frown suddenly lifted, and in its place settled a knowing grin.

'You had a smoke with Ibrahim last night,' she said.

It was not a question. My canine cacophony had gone unheard.

Φ

In nearby Gombad-e Qabus,* I went to the races with Khidr. The Turkmen were passionate about horse racing, he explained,

---

*   Later on, we visited the Gombad itself (or kir-e Qabus, as Khidr liked to

and loved to gamble. The racecourse in Gombad had been shut down by the government after the revolution, to discourage the un-Islamic vice of gambling, but had reopened a few years ago. Officially there was no betting on the horses, but locals knew better.

The main building was a run-down place built in more prosperous times, and looked as though it hadn't been maintained for a generation. But the atmosphere was pure carnival, and thousands had gathered for the day. A local friend and racehorse-trainer had agreed to infiltrate us to the VIP balcony on the top floor. We were ushered upstairs past several guards, and in the uppermost room, introduced to half a dozen solemn-looking officials, unshaven and wearing suits and collarless shirts. I was reminded of Louise's irreverent observation that the higher the rank of an official, the scruffier his appearance. Then, after a perfunctory approval for our visit had been granted, we were shown out onto the balcony.

'Here,' whispered our friend, 'is where the Shah used to sit.'

We settled among a few rows of privileged guests. Their wives sat separately, wearing expensive sunglasses, cream slacks under their jackets, and Dior headscarves, and clutched at Louis Vuitton handbags. Beyond, a mile-long oval of racetrack enclosed a half-shorn field of wheat dotted with bales. A double line of plane trees encircled the track, and in the far distance a grey curtain of mountains shimmered in the haze.

Beneath us reigned a scene of medieval chaos. The tiers of seats were crammed, and a noisy crowd seethed all round the

---

call it). The hundred-and-sixty-foot brick tower stands atop a much more ancient artificial mound, and must once have served as a kind of lighthouse for miles around. Byron, among many other Western visitors, has described in detail this starkly beautiful eleventh-century monument, built for the Ziyarid ruler Qabus ibn Wushmgir. Yet I have read nothing that describes the building's extraordinary acoustic properties. Neither the astonishing precision with which the entrance reflects the approaching visitor's voice nor the phenomenal resonatory qualities of the interior seem to have been noticed.

building. Children were darting everywhere like ants, and clinging to the fences and poles like barnacles on an anchor. The grey-blue smoke from improvised grills filled the air, and picnickers were throwing blankets over the dust. A group of musicians, wearing the traditional dress of Cossack-like hats and long red gowns, was playing to a circle of a hundred men. Vendors jostled through the throng selling food and drink, and a wandering madman was waving his arms in a seamless repertoire of gestures, as if directing a flow of demonic traffic. Every few minutes, a miniature tornado would sweep unpredictably through the crowd, sending up columns of dust and litter and leaving a wake of men clutching at their eyes like the victims of tear-gas at a riot.

There was some electronic buzzing and squealing, and the echoing voice of a commentator started up over the loudspeakers. I could make out, at the far end of the track, a commotion of men and animals. It didn't look like the start of an ordinary race. There seemed to be far too many bodies gathering on the track, and I mentioned to Khidr that the horses looked very small.

'They're not horses,' he giggled, 'they're donkeys. And they're all on opium.' He laughed out loud at my expression of disbelief, and described how the donkeys were force-fed with opium, washed down with veterinary-strength alcohol. I never found out if he was joking or not; but the donkeys – at least fifty of them – were exceptionally energetic.

They passed below us in a dusty roar, while their riders – mostly teenage boys – bounced at an incredible rate, flailing at their animals' sides with little sticks. I had never seen a donkey gallop. How far could they go? A hundred yards seemed likely; but as the pack began to thin I realized they were heading for a full circuit. Then they passed the finish line and kept going, still bouncing at the same unbelievable pace, and led by a comet-like cluster of about a dozen animals, several of which had long since shed their riders. At last a roar went up, and the winning rider was lifted from the saddle by a jubilant mob of supporters and carried aloft into the crowds. I had never seen anything like it.

As the track was cleared of the final stragglers, a high-ranking cleric arrived in our midst. The nearby seats cleared like a parting sea at his approach. Trailing behind him was a shoal of parasitic and unshaven underlings, and a dramatic personal bodyguard of half a dozen soldiers, who positioned themselves menacingly around the balcony. This was the first time I had seen soldiers who really looked the part: nothing about them resembled the undernourished sad-looking conscripts to be seen in the streets. They were all nearly seven feet tall and had in their eyes a manic look suggesting an ample willingness to commit violence. Their neckscarves, belts, and spats were bright white, and their shoulders were draped in looping braids and red epaulettes. They were unarmed but long white truncheons dangled from their hips. The nearest, whose eye I was very careful not to catch, was blond and pale-skinned, and his eyes were a striking green; a genetic throwback, perhaps, to Alexander's royal guard – perhaps much further.

A mobile starting-gate had meanwhile been rolled onto the track, and the serious races began. We hadn't had time to look at the horses, but Khidr insisted I choose a winner from the list. An effort of transliteration revealed some incongruous names: *William Tell* and *Lucky Jim*. With exaggerated solemnity I picked a name; the horses galloped past in a thunderous cloud; the crowd erupted in a crescendo of shouts; and much to my surprise I found I had chosen the winner.

'I bet,' said Khidr, 'that you can't do that again.'

I chose another name, and the same thing happened.

'All right,' said Khidr, 'now it's my turn.' He snatched the list from my hand, pretending to be annoyed, and made a show of divining the next winner. The afternoon seemed blessed; Khidr's horse came in first. We laughed out loud and, as if by an initiation, our friendship was from that moment firmly cemented.

But they were not quite the races I had imagined. Children ran onto the track ahead of the horses for a dare, fleeing into the undergrowth at the last instant. Several times, ripples of horrified gasps echoed through the crowd; once, as a horse fell and rolled over its rider, and again as another horse, galloping on the final stretch, fell and snapped both front legs like matchsticks at the knee. Yet another broke a foot and hobbled to the finish with its hoof dangling horribly from a flap of skin.

The final race was the most disturbing of all. The riders were all disabled war veterans. I looked questioningly to Khidr, who shrugged his shoulders and made a slicing motion against an arm and then a leg, as if to indicate the rider's condition. The race was not a happy spectacle. The leading rider, unable to negotiate the first bend, ploughed straight on through the trees and disappeared into the field beyond; the rider behind him fell moments afterwards and was thrown into a deep ditch; and nearly all the others dropped from their horses at full gallop as if picked off by snipers from afar. By the end only a tiny quotient of the original riders were even visible, and most of the horses crossed the finish with empty saddles. But a few valiant survivors had survived the circuit, crossing the line in heroic states of collapse. Like rescuers to stricken fighter pilots, teams of helpers ran up to control the horses and free the riders from their saddles.

I looked at Khidr. A strange expression had come over his face, suggesting that he too was wondering whether to laugh or cry. Then the whole crowd stood as the national anthem was played over the loudspeakers.

Φ

Our ride into the hills was planned the following morning. A breeze had brought a welcome coolness, and wanting a walk I told Khidr we might find treasure at the nearby *tappeh*. A visiting English archaeologist had found Neolithic shards there, suggesting a settlement dating back seven thousand years. It was a natural mound poking up from the surrounding plain, but the summit had been artificially flattened to an acre-sized plateau. An eroded mesh of ancient walls covered the surface, where I poked about in the dust, finding delicate fragments with a turquoise and yellow glaze, and a thicker and much older-looking type of pottery from large-handled vessels with designs of sweeping black strokes across a deep red glaze. Khidr sat on his haunches nearby, asking, 'So where's the treasure?'

The plan was to load up a battered truck with the camp equipment; Khidr would drive ahead to meet us at the end of the day, in a tiny settlement in the hills to the south. He needed some supplies from his home a few miles away, and invited me to lunch. His wife, a beautiful and smiling woman who appeared only at moments from the kitchen, served us on the floor of his living room. Then after it was cleared away he produced two cushions; we tucked them under our heads, stretched out, and slept for an hour, after which his wife appeared again and brought tea and pastries. Khidr's two young sons joined us, and he turned on the television to watch the headline news.

It was not good. The commentary was too fast for me to follow, but the pictures told the story. All eyes fell on an apocalyptic street scene which I assumed was Tehran. It was night; smoke was billowing from a car that had been overturned and set alight, and a crowd of youthful silhouettes was confronting an advancing line of police with a shower of bottles and stones. The police bore down in black body-armour and helmets, flailing their truncheons at the young men in their path, who crossed their arms above their heads in desperate gestures of defence before being overpowered in headlocks and half-nelsons and hauled brutally away. I felt a pang of sympathy for the defiant spirit of the Iranian youth, and tried my best to show it with a friendly look of gravity.

At that moment one of Khidr's children interrupted with a question, but was silenced with a scowl from his father. The child persisted: something was obviously the matter, and Khidr stood up to extinguish the television in a gesture of frustration. I asked him what it was his son had wanted to know. He replied, uncharacteristically, with an embarrassed smile for an answer, and added that it was nothing important. Sensing it could not be too serious, I pressed him to tell me. He was visibly troubled, but in the end relented.

'My son wanted to know,' he said, nodding towards the television, 'whether everywhere in England is always as bad as that, or just that place called Brad-ford.'

Φ

Our small mounted convoy left at six, crunched over the stubble towards the river, then dipped in and out of the cutting and filed through the dusty lanes of the small village on the far side. I was secretly glad there was no one about. This new and lordly height brought with it guilty twinges of intrusiveness on my part as we passed shuttered windows at stirrup level. I was clearly out of practice.

The feeling left me after we had clattered across the asphalt of the road to Qabus and began to climb a beckoning slope. The horses soon settled into a steady pace and were all well behaved. Louise took the lead on a white Turkoman mare called Ahu Aq, 'White Gazelle'. Ibrahim wore a tired jacket and beret; he had even had his hair cut for the occasion but looked as worn out as his clothes and not at all well ('The opium,' muttered Louise, 'he's going to have to struggle for the next few days'); Ghorban, more obedient to equestrian fashion, wore a full-length oilskin coat over his favourite red shirt.

Buzzards were tracing lazy spirals in the clear air overhead and kestrels hovered above the edges of the track. The higher slopes, rising to the south in a trio of ridges several miles long and breaking at their summits into grey rocky outcrops, were thickly forested; the lower were covered by a jigsaw of interlocking fields, reaching upwards as far as the tilt of the hills would allow and divided by dark wavering lines of hedgerow. In the intervening sweep of valley, scattered plumes of smoke were slanting through the air above plots of burning stubble. Tractors had already reaped the main crop of wheat, but antlike teams of families had emerged to rake the fields below for a second gathering of the precious straw and were piling it onto matchbox-sized carts far below us. There was something unexpectedly familiar about this landscape: it made me think of Andalucía. A stage-set hoarding of an oversized black bull emblazoned 'Tio Pepe!' would not have seemed out of place; and we might have glimpsed, on a blustery knoll, the sails of an abandoned windmill; perhaps, even, a gaunt and inexplicably silvery figure, lanced and mounted on a skeletal nag with a rotund bearer labouring at his side . . .

It was stirring to think that a millennium earlier, when the Umayyad empire was at its greatest extent, one might have ridden all the way to Spain without leaving territory loyal to the Caliphate of Baghdad. But the historical thread ran back much further here — nearly another thousand years, in fact, before the Arabs received their fateful check at Poitiers.* It was 250 BC — the tallest structure in England was Stonehenge, the hills of Rome were still all green, Hannibal a belligerent toddler and Archimedes' watery footprints on the streets of Syracuse, barely dry — when the natives living between the Caspian and the Aral seas began to get restless. A branch of these Scythian tribesmen moved south to occupy the area at the foot of the Kopet Dagh range, but were beaten back by the ruler of neighbouring Bactria and, breaching the mountains, invaded instead the neighbouring region of Parthia. As they advanced over the Hyrcanian steppe, sun-blackened and saddle-weary, they beheld through the haze what must have been a dream-like vision: forest-draped hills, rising from the baking plain towards peaks garlanded with luminous clouds — just around the spot, it seemed quite likely, where we were now standing.

We had stopped on a gentle ridge at about three thousand feet, and tethered the horses on long leads in a grove below the summit. A pair of shepherds were dozing nearby, and a wisp of smoke curled upwards around a blackened kettle from the embers of their fire. We picnicked there, rested awhile, and after giving our melon skins to the horses, walked out of the trees to look at

---

* In AD 732. French schoolchildren are as familiar today with this famous date as English schoolchildren used to be with that of Marathon. I have just looked up Poitiers in an encyclopaedia, but there is no mention of that momentous turning-point in the heart of Europe. Could the omission suggest an unconscious willingness to forget? Speculating on the arrival of an Arabian fleet in the Thames, Gibbon is dour, but at least makes no attempt to dodge the issue: 'Perhaps the interpretation of the Koran would now be taught in the schools of Oxford, and her pupils might demonstrate to a circumcised people the sanctity and truth of the revelation of Mahomet'. *Decline & Fall*, v. IV, p. 25.

the view. To the north, far below and several miles away now, we could make out the meandering gash of the Gorgan River, and beyond it the village from which we'd set out. Miles beyond that, now that we were higher, I could see a thin dark line of hill stretching halfway across the horizon. But to the north-east, the land receded into a sun-drenched, cadmium-coloured flatness.

Louise pointed out the line of Alexander's Wall, an unnaturally straight ridge running like a fracture across the table of the landscape. Intersecting it was the faint outline of a square fort, one of many along its length from which the first Parthians sallied to protect the borders of their newly claimed Eden. The ridges we had seen on the slopes on the way up, said Louise, were all that was left of their country villas.

'They knew how to build walls,' I said.

'And recognized good real estate when they saw it,' said Louise.

Good qualities, we agreed, as we looked down over the very land where the Parthians had entered history. Then Louise said, almost wistfully: 'It's the one time I wish I could return to. Even for a week — just to see how they lived.'

It was an infectious longing, which I soon shared; the Parthians remain the least known of the great Persian ruling dynasties, and their legacy the most enigmatic. Against the sweep of Parthian achievements, our knowledge of their era is disproportionately small. Historically, it lies in dead ground. Virtually nothing of their own written records has reached us, and the fragmentary Greek and Roman sources through which the Parthians are best known adopt, even at their most charitable, a wary view. We do not even know what name they used for themselves. Our view is further eclipsed by the grandeur of their Achaemenid predecessors and the *damnatio memoriae* of the Sasanians who followed them, and whose policy, it seems likely, was one of deliberate obfuscation. By the eleventh century, there is little more than a plaintive echo of their existence in the *Shahnameh* of Ferdowsi: 'I have heard nothing but their names, and have not seen them in the chronicle of kings'.

Yet they were the most enduring of all the Persian dynasties, and the dominant power in western Asia for over four hundred years. They dismembered the post-Alexandrian empire of the Seleucids, supervised the world's first intercontinental trade route, held successive invasions at bay across multiple fronts, and raised Ctesiphon from a muddy village on the banks of the Euphrates to a capital coveted by East and West alike. In the process they restored a concept of Persian identity that had been diluted by centuries of Greek rule, and laid the foundations for the resurgence of Persian culture that would follow them. It is not a bad record for a people invariably referred to in Western histories as 'semi-nomadic tribesmen'. One pictures them rubbing sticks together and wrestling plundered virgins from their saddles into lightless tents sewn from mouse-skins; not founding empires.

By the second century BC the eastern empire founded by Alexander was disintegrating unstoppably; each Greek reverse became a Parthian gain, and a series of ambitious annexations brought the most famous of the early Parthian rulers, Mithradates,* as far west as the Tigris. The Achaemenid title of King of Kings was henceforth resurrected on Parthian coinage, and its statuary chiselled into walls and rock-faces beside that of its royal forebears. In the north-west a Parthian monarch was installed in Armenia; all the way over in the east Sistin was a compliant

---

* The Mithra-prefix, akin to Caesar or Augustus beside the names of Roman emperors, denotes a religious lineage after the Mithraic deity and protector. Probably the most famous Mithradates is Eupator, King of Pontus (now northern Turkey), who died in 63 BC. He is said to have murdered his mother and, as protection against reciprocal intrigue, to have been the first monarch to practise immunization by gradual poisonings; hence mithridatism. He was also an accomplished linguist, and spoke the two dozen languages of the nations he controlled. Cicero accords him the status of the world's greatest monarch, and for thirty years he was at war with Rome. When, humiliated by eventual defeat, he took poison to end his life, it had no effect, and a guard was ordered to complete the grisly task. After his death, twelve days of public thanksgiving were appointed in Rome.

vassal state, and a potentially catastrophic irruption of nomad tribes — the Kushans, who took over the Graeco-Bactrian kingdom — had been daringly contained. A little more than a century after the Parthians' first westward breach, Mithradates was negotiating with China to draw up international trade treaties. The sun had set definitively over Hellenism in the East; Seleucid power had been reduced to a tottering throne in Syrian Antioch, and was soon to be absorbed by the imperial Roman behemoth.

In 92 BC the armies of Rome reached the Euphrates, and the clouds began to gather. The Roman attitude towards the barbarian rulers of the East was one of contempt, and although an alliance with the Parthian king against the crumbling Seleucids was signed, Roman high-handedness caused frequent offence; they were untrustworthy allies, violated treaties, and launched undeclared wars all across the region.

A generation later, Roman arrogance appears personified in the high-ranking and ageing consul, Crassus. Fierce, defiant, and hot-tempered, he was perhaps the richest, and one of the most powerful, men of Rome. Dreaming of conquest and lured by the promise of Parthian gold, he prepared to subdue the eastern territories and outstrip the military glories of Caesar and Alexander. The following summer, at the head of an army of forty thousand, he confidently invaded Parthian Mesopotamia, believing that within a few weeks the East would be his.* A scanty Parthian opposition, which appeared to flee from his legionaries, inflamed the dream.

The whole catastrophe is recorded grippingly by Plutarch. Seven days' march beyond the Euphrates, rumour of a retreating Parthian force led the Romans in pursuit across open ground. Crassus had read nothing of Parthian history; but his opponent, the talented young general Suren, had studied Roman tactics well, and drilled his men accordingly. His light cavalry struck first, fast and mobile, wheeling, feinting, and striking repeatedly with

---

* This was in 53 BC, the same year that Caesar invaded Britain.

bewildering agility. The horsemen fired even as they retreated – the Parthian shot. A sky-darkening hail of arrows punched through the Roman armour, and the legionaries began to drop into the dust. Crassus, confident that his enemy's supply of ammunition would soon falter, held firm. But again the deadly bowmen returned, replenishing their arrows from a reserve supply of a thousand camels, each laden with giant quivers...

Then, to the terrifying roar of the Parthian kettledrums, the heavy cavalry advanced onto the ailing Roman square. 'Suddenly,' writes Plutarch, 'their enemies dropped the coverings of their armour, and were seen to be themselves blazing in helmets and breastplates, their Margianian steel glittering keen and bright, and their horses clad in plates of bronze and steel.'

Crassus' son, Publius, was ordered to counter-attack with a force of six thousand. The Parthian force withdrew before it, raising Roman hopes. The body of the Imperial army regrouped, and waited for the detachment under Publius to return. But after a wait of several bitter hours, only a Parthian rider was seen emerging from the haze, bearing on his lance the severed head of Publius. The retreat had been a well-rehearsed trap; Suren's cavalry had surrounded the isolated force, broken it utterly, and left his archers to do the rest.

A despairing Crassus retreated to the nearby town of Carrhae; next morning his diminished force was surrounded in a failed attempt to escape to the hills. Crassus himself was killed, and his head delivered to the Parthian king. Only a quarter of the original Roman army had managed to escape. Twenty thousand had been killed, and ten thousand were taken prisoner and settled as slaves in distant Merv.

The defeat of Crassus ranks – not only as a military humiliation but also as an international awakening to Parthian power – alongside such spectacular reverses as the Mongols' defeat by the Mamluks at 'Ayn Jalut, Sultan Bayazit's humiliation by Timur at Ankara, the Turkish thrashing of the Safavids at Chaldiran, and the disastrous British retreat from Kabul. But incredibly, we find the Romans still at war in Persia (against the Parthians' successors, the Sasanians) six hundred years after their first encounter. Seen from a historical distance, the centuries blur into a concatenated struggle of titanic stubbornness on both sides, and evoke a sense of spectacular futility. Successive Roman campaigns were always bloody, and at best Pyrrhic. Only twenty years after Crassus, Mark Antony drove a hundred thousand men — the largest Roman force ever assembled in the East — against the Parthians in a campaign which ended again in misery and humiliation. Thirty-five thousand of his soldiers died from wounds, cold, and starvation, forcing his eventual retreat to Egypt and the consoling arms of Cleopatra.

The Euphrates became the frontier between the two empires. For the first century of the Christian era, the Eastern hatchet was buried for a while; negotiation suited both sides. Young Parthians of noble birth were even sent to Rome to be educated (though their Romanized manners tended to make them unsuitable for state duties). But the legions were destined, through the agency of several ambitious and charismatic Roman generals, to fight again and again in Mesopotamia — roughly every fifty years. Trajan, infected by the dreams of his predecessors, wreaked havoc across Mesopotamia in 115; Lucius Verus, co-emperor to Marcus Aurelius, was next, but was forced to abandon his campaign when his army was struck by a plague of smallpox. At the turn of the second century, Septimius Severus sacked the Parthian capitol at Ctesiphon, slaughtered its men and enslaved its women, and occupied fabled Babylon; his troops were beaten back by volleys of flaming naphtha-bombs and jars of bloodsucking flies catapulted from behind the defenders' walls. For three centuries, Roman attempts to reduce Parthia to vassaldom failed, while the Parthians for their part proved incapable of extending their rule to the west. It is a grim record.

We see the royal Parthian house, meanwhile, increasingly struck by dynastic squabbling and all the corrosive symptoms of decline; murderous disputes of succession, intermarriage with foreign slave-girls, poisonings, fratricide (and its gentler alternative, the shearing-off of ears), harem-seizing, concubines-turned-queens and exiled kings; a good deal of incest in high circles; a number of debilitating invasions by marauding nomads from the north-east, and the usual quarrelling with the Romans over Armenia. Enfeebled by war, internal dissension, and the growing powers of rival lesser kingdoms, the dynastic heart was, by the third century, fatally sclerotic. In 224, the penultimate Parthian king, Artabanus V, was killed in battle by the upstart vassal Ardashir Sassan. The final Parthian coinage was struck a few years later. And from then on, of the descendants of these semi-nomadic tribes, who against the odds stayed the Roman juggernaut in the West, dammed the nomadic flood in the East, and forged the template on which Persian nationality is indelibly drawn, nothing more is heard.

All this, somehow, is rather unsatisfactory. Carnage and the clash of steel make for dramatic headlines, then as now, but the coherence of an empire rests on more than battles. Of less incendiary things, sadly, our knowledge is tantalizingly partial. We do know a little of what Parthians actually looked like. Perhaps the best-known statue of the era is a life-size bronze in the National Museum, presumed to be the likeness of a vassal ruler. I saw him during my first days in Tehran: he is tall and very fit-looking and wears a tunic like a judo gi, belted around a trim waist, and leggings of marvellously complex drapery. Handsome features boast a fastidiously trimmed moustache and goatee, and shoulder-length hair coiffed into elegant bulges over the ears. Kitted out for battle in conical headgear, Parthian warriors bear a strange resemblance to the Lewis chessmen, only with a more sophisticated dress sense.

We have glimpses of their women too, from perhaps the best collection of Parthian statuary in the National Museum of Iraq in Baghdad. The funerary busts are famously elegant; silken shawls fall from elaborately bejewelled tiaras and abundant necklaces, bangles, and rings. Traces of paint still remain, and betray the use of lipstick, rouge, and mascara; Pliny records the use among Parthian nobles of a skin ointment made from a decoction of helianthus in lion's fat and mixed with saffron and palm wine. Some exquisite jewellery also remains.

The artistic and architectural record is more confused. In religious art we find a number of Greek gods, dressed in Parthian uniform, conscripted into a complex trans-Iranian panoply. Excavated buildings and temples comprise a sort of cultural bouilla-baisse, incorporating an eclectic repertoire of classical elements which scholars are tempted to call Graeco-Iranian. But of the principles that informed and guided the spiritual and intellectual trajectory of the Parthian Empire, only hints and whispers remain. Of their sciences, poetry, and ideals, we are strangely bereft. There is little to help us explain the appearance of such innovations as the barrel-vaulted hall, open at one end to the elements, and later known as the *ivān*, which would become a central and distinctive feature of Sasanian and Islamic architecture; or the decorative geometrical patterns appearing in Parthian times which were later developed with such vigour by Islamic artisans; or – perhaps most puzzling of all – the earliest examples of the electric battery.* Nothing is known of the extinguished discipline that enabled our tribesmen to harness the restlessness of the electron, or what beliefs were really encrypted in their art. Such things are too fine; they leave no tangible remains, and slip invisibly through the historian's net.

Yet in Mithraism, the spiritual discipline of the Parthian elite, it is just possible to trace a thread leading from the occulted

---

* Two thousand years before Count Volta attached electrodes to his famously quivering frog's legs, the electric battery appears to have been in use in Parthian Mesopotamia. The 'Baghdad Batteries' were discovered by the Austrian archaeologist and director of the Baghdad Museum in 1940, and carbon-dated to 200 BC. They are constructed of an earthenware shell containing an iron rod, insulated by an asphalt plug from an outer copper sleeve. A modest electric current is produced when the housing is filled with an electrolytic solution such as lemon juice. Later experiments showed that the batteries could have been used for electroplating jewellery.

labyrinth of the era to our own; for gods are harder to extinguish permanently. Although the worship of the solar deity Mithra seems to have been widespread in Parthian times, it does not survive the increasingly authoritarian Zoroastrian priesthood of the later Sasanians, and is extirpated in its own heartland. Mithraism, like so many components of Parthian culture, thus disappears from the surface of Persian life after the end of Parthian rule.

But it has only slipped below the radar of history. As a popular mystery cult, especially strong in the Roman military, it resurfaces, albeit in a variant form, all over Europe as the pagan religion of choice. Late Roman emperors even underwent Mithraic baptismal rites supervised by members of the Parthian priesthood. Their Mithreaeums — dark subterranean sanctuaries, where the initiatic mysteries were gorily celebrated with the sacrifice of living bulls — are found as far apart as Armenia, Scotland, and the borders of the Sahara Desert, and abound in Rome (over the site of the last official sacrifice, St Peter's Basilica was raised by Constantine the Great at the end of the fourth century). Their dank limestone wall-carvings depict a haunting story: that of the celebrated sacrifice of the bull by Mithra himself. Intermediary between man and the Divine, a spiritual being of threefold nature, light-bearer of the world, born of a virgin mother Anahita on 25 December, it is Mithra himself who drives his sword into the neck of the beast he has subdued. By the redemptive power of blood, his twelve companions are spiritually reborn, and share in a final feast of sacred bread and wine before their master's ascent to heaven.

It is a long time before the same thread becomes visible again in the East, when Mithraism and its arcane doctrines reappear in the writings of the twelfth-century Persian mystic and martyr Sohravardi. Though scarcely known in the West, his works have been enormously influential in Iran and the Islamic world, and link the ancient and mythological priest-kings of Persia to the mystical philosophers of Greece and to the early saints of Islamic Sufism. In this compelling lineage, Mithra — far from having been extinguished, but, like the later Imams of Shi'ite belief, merely temporarily occulted – remains a divine intermediary and spiritual guardian, as well as bearer of the goblet that contains the Heavenly and transformative wine ... symbols that become central to all of Persian Sufi poetry and, through universally revered poets such as Hafez, come to permeate the spiritual ethos of Islamic Persia. The same compelling metaphysical allusion to wine and its Divine Envoy in both East and West has a distant but common origin ...

History, in our own time, has rendered it all but invisible. But what if Constantine's vision at the Milvian Bridge had never occurred,* Christianity had remained an outlawed cult, and the Sasanians taken a friendlier view of their predecessors' spiritual persuasions? Had not the stamp of state religions been so firmly impressed, the Mithraic link between East and West might have been preserved; and the besiegers and defenders of Aleppo and Acre and Antioch and Jerusalem and Istanbul might, glancing momentarily from the line of sight between trebuchet and crenellation, have recognized on one another's shields a common and reconciling insignia.

One can only play lightly with the thought. But, for a moment, both Grail and Saqi's goblet cast a shadow of transcendent similitude, and the fateful gulf between the turquoise parabolas of Isfahan and the encircling colonnades of the Vatican is suddenly reduced.

Φ

We were riding upwards now through a forest of tall and ancient beech, whose great trunks were dusted with a powdery coat of dark-green lichen. But for the porcupine quills scattered on the ground and the occasional snakeskin, the resemblance to any

---

* John Julius Norwich reminds us sensibly that if Constantine's celebrated vision of a cross emblazoned across the skies had indeed been witnessed by his entire army, '98,000 men kept the secret remarkably well'. *Byzantium* (Penguin, 1998).

sister-forest at home was uncanny. The air was filled with the scent of moss and bracken and humus, and from the south-west a long arcade of tilting shafts of yellowing light stretched through the weft of the trees ahead of us. Soon we were out in the open again, and recognized, creeping towards us along a dusty track by a field half a mile away, the battered blue pickup truck from the ranch. Eventually it pulled alongside and a sunburned arm reached up to pass us cans of beer. At its other end was Khidr's face. The beer was cruelly free of alcohol, but eagerly received all round.

'Not far to go!' he smiled, and wheeled cheerfully away ahead of us. Half an hour later we rode through a line of trees onto the flattened skirt of a shorn hillside dotted with hay bales, and our camp suddenly appeared as if by magic. A great green canvas tent had been planted over the flattened stubble, and was lined with felts and carpets. We could hear Khidr applying the finishing touches with the wooden thump of a mallet against peg, and in the fire he had already lit a trio of metal ewers were puffing energetically.

Nine hours had passed since we had left the ranch. We lifted hot and heavy saddles from the sweat-soaked flanks of the horses, and sank gratefully into the tent to massage our aching knees. Ibrahim and Ghorban began filling nosebags with handfuls of barley and tethered the horses in the field nearby. They looked very glad to be there; I was too. Word of our arrival had quickly spread and a celebratory flotilla of children was soon circling around the tent, followed by a more stately party of half a dozen villagers who had come from a tiny settlement nearby to welcome us.

'They're always happy when I come back,' said Louise with an affectionate grin as they walked up. 'They say I bring the rain.'

They all knew Louise well, and after we'd exchanged greetings over tea, a few of them stayed on, sitting cross-legged on our improvised canvas doorstep, to hear her news. Despite the heat the three men, who I guessed were in their fifties (the younger ones, they explained, were at work in the fields), wore dusty sweaters and jackets and one of them sported a tapering Turkoman hat made from tightly knotted black lambskin. Their wives, sturdy women in long skirts with loose and colourful scarves over their heads, sat beside them. They had all come with their families from their homes in the plain below to spend the month in the hills for the seasonal reaping. An unhurried and rustic goodwill radiated from their sun-burnished features. When they rose to leave, we turned down their invitation to dinner, pointing to our own blackened pots poised at the fire's edge.

Meanwhile, their children and grandchildren – about a dozen of them, from about six years old to sixteen – trailed in and out of the tent, playing and chattering and loosing a stream of questions. I took some photographs of them; one of the girls, hearing that I could read Persian, ran back to the village to fetch a book and put the claim to the test, and soon a circle of shining and expectant young faces was around me, giggling and nudging as I deciphered an Iranian version of Hansel and Gretel. Later we signed each other's notebooks, until at some signal they took flight through the trees again as gleefully as they had first appeared.

Louise mentioned a Scythian burial site at the top of the hillside, so I walked with Khidr to the ridge above the camp. We found it at the end of a rising trail through the woods on a natural promontory, the far side of which dropped over tall grey cliffs towards a sea of forest. A mound the height of a man had been three-quarters scooped out by looters long ago, and through the undergrowth we could see the prehistoric brickwork of the violated interior. But the place was still revered. In an old tree growing at the edge of the mound, I could see dozens of tiny strips of coloured fabric knotted around the more slender branches: each one told of a prayer and an offering in the manner of a votive candle in a church. But who, I wondered, had journeyed to this lonely place to offer prayers aside a grave whose name was lost three thousand years before? I found a fallen piece of tattered cloth and retied it to a branch, watching it flutter for a few moments in the breeze.

I told Louise I felt the site was one of great natural mystery.

She said she felt the same, and was pleased that I had felt it too: it was the very reason she returned there, year after year.

'Up here,' she said, 'you begin to get a feel for places that you can never have when you live indoors. I bring friends here who think I'm crazy when I mention it, but the locals know exactly what I mean.'

We agreed that this was probably the reason that the area's first inhabitants, to whom urban life was totally unknown, had buried their nobles in such places. I had felt the same thing a few times before, in landscapes whose natural conformation seemed to emit an indefinable sanctity, the memory of which acquires an added quality of vividness.

A little later I walked back up to the hill to look for a quiet spot to sit and write. I found a path which wound between banks of fern, bracken, and cow parsley, and wandered a little way into the woods until I came to a natural clearing where the air was alive with birdsong. From nearby came the rattle of a woodpecker against a hollow bough, and a few moments later an owl flew onto a branch just close enough for me to see its large dark eyes and the strange pirouetting of its head.

Above me towered an enormous tree with great buttressing roots and twisting boughs from which radiating canopies of horizontal foliage spread like giant's fans in every direction. The late afternoon light was tumbling through the layers of branches in translucent and overlapping vesicas of brightness, and from the palest lime of the uppermost leaves to the deep mossy hue of the leaves within arm's reach glowed an infinity of greens.

These sylvan moments, so intimately linked to a childhood in rural England, were unexpected, and I felt a stab of homesickness. A fat wood pigeon was calling from somewhere beyond the clearing, and I felt Robin Hood or a druid gathering mistletoe might appear at any moment. All that was missing was the reassuring call of the Greenwich pips.

Returning to the camp just as the sun was beginning to dip below the westernmost ridge, I saw one of the village children running towards the tent. 'The bread,' she cried breathlessly, 'the bread's ready for baking!' She was about twelve years old, enchantingly pretty, and beckoned me with a compelling wave. I skipped down with her through the bordering trees to a square earthen platform where a dozen villagers, mostly women, had gathered. The girl's mother, an archaic beauty enveloped in folds of black cotton, was sitting cross-legged by the mouth of a clay oven sunk into the ground like a buried amphora. She was snapping twigs from a pile beside her and feeding them into the fire below, to which all eyes were drawn with a shared feeling of awe. A few pointed tongues of flame were soon dancing like snakes below the rim. Then, as the temperature grew, the flames began to turn in on themselves with a strangely liquid motion and a deepening roar. Before long a column of black smoke was billowing from the mouth of the oven like the fumes of a smelter's crucible, and the circle of misty eyes first widened, then shrank again, as a carefully aimed pot of water reduced the flames to a glow of hissing embers.

Meanwhile a child had brought a tray piled with spheres of dough like pyramids of cannonballs. The old woman, in an expert flurry of slapping, stretched them between her palms into flattened ovals and laid them at her side, delivering over them a final sprinkling of water with a sorcerous flick of her fingers. Then, tipping forward across her folded legs and turning her face from the incandescence below, she stretched a leathery hand into the mouth of the oven and slapped the loaves one by one against the wall of the oven. Within a few minutes they were erupting in fragrant and darkening blisters. Then she scooped them off with a wooden paddle and piled them into the arms of several dutiful and expectant children.

As the steaming bread was being carried indoors, an elderly hajji with a magnificent white beard and turban loomed from the smoke into our midst. Big prayer beads of yellow amber were clicking between the forefinger and thumb of both hands as he glanced with grave affection over the assembly.

Then, after exchanging a few greetings, he raised an ancient finger and with solemn knowing said: 'Brown bread's better for you all! They take out the bran because they can get money for it, and then leave us with the white flour. Our children—' he began, but was drowned out by a parliamentary and affectionate scoffing from the women, and fell silent with a gently admonishing shake of his head. But they were all smiling, and even the hajji himself bore a rueful grin. No trace of anxiety disturbed their features around me and all eyes were aglow with kindness. For the child sitting beside me, who followed my gaze wherever I turned and whose light-filled expression had captivated me by its innocence, I felt a sudden tide of tenderness.

As the first bread was broken and passed approvingly from hand to hand, a new scent was added to air already rich with the smell of smoke and freshly cut wheat. While we ate, a solitary rider passed by in silence with a wave and a smile, and a fresh loaf was passed up to him along a line of hands. Beyond him the setting sun was throwing crimson and widening spokes into the sky, and drawing from the fields below us a luminous and encompassing atmosphere of gold. I had the feeling of having slipped for a few moments from the ordinary grasp of time and hoped deeply that this remote and elevated place of enchantment would never be obliged to submit to the slavery of haste and anxiety of the world below. Louise had called it her forgotten corner of Iran and just then it seemed possible that it always would be.

We were all sad to leave. But early the next morning we saddled the horses, tightened the straps of our saddlebags, and Khidr began dismantling and packing up the camp. The villagers gathered round to see us off.

'Don't go,' they said to Louise, 'we need the rain.'

We rode for an hour in delicious silence along a forest path made remote from the world by a secluding shroud of early morning mist. Our route trailed gently downward and later emerged above a small village of about fifty houses. Most of the homes were built from mud brick and rendered with adobe and their rounded profiles seemed in keeping with the gentle contours of the land, but a few, looking out of place but probably the pride of their owners, were raised from concrete blocks and painted a garish white. It was an unkempt-looking place. Wires like the filaments of broken spider's webs linked their roofs and gathered in confused tangles at the tops of leaning telegraph poles. The path between the houses was narrow and unpaved and ran downward between porches warped like outstretched harmoniums. The inhabitants, to judge from their reaction to us, were unaccustomed to mounted visitors – perhaps the memory of raiding horsemen still lingered in the local blood – and at fifty yards mothers were sweeping up their children in protecting arms or, if they were too large, shooing them inside on waves of high-pitched shrieks. Everywhere we were aware of faces peering at us from behind shutters and curtains and disappearing again like shadows as we passed. A conflagration of barking was spreading through every yard and alley and we were glad to reach the far side and begin the climb towards the sheltering trees beyond.

Wisps of dissolving cloud hung in the air above us and a hoopoe, its feathery crown flattened against it back, swooped above the path ahead of us as we paced upwards to another wooded spur. Halfway up, Louise spotted a grey Turkoman mare grazing in a cultivated field, and a little further on we found its owner, weeding the soil between neat rows of marrow-shoots. She asked him if he wanted to sell his horse. Resting an arm on the smooth wooden handle of a long hoe, he smiled and shook his head.

'I don't really blame him,' said Louise, slightly wistfully, 'it's a lovely looking horse.' I asked her whether by such chance encounters she had acquired many horses. That was exactly how, she said, and told the story of her favourite mare, Rohana. She had found the long-boned jet-black creature hauling overloaded carts of wood and in pitiful condition, but had patiently nursed her back to health at the ranch. After several years, during the darkest moments of the revolution, she was forced to sell her, and gave up hope of seeing her again. But by a stroke of immense luck she found her again a year later and bought her back. When the mare was released at the ranch she ran whinnying three times around the property, and Louise had vowed she would never sell her again. Soon afterwards she gave birth to a foal which went on to become the Turkoman national champion racer. The mare was thirty years old now, but still outpaced the other horses on a long trek.

My own horse, meanwhile, was quietly misbehaving. She refused to walk at the pace of the others and I lagged helplessly behind for long stretches. But her trot was too fast and, since I didn't know the route, I couldn't lead. We settled for an uncomfortable jog ('the Mongol Bounce', as Louise called it) which was somewhere in between, but my stirrups, which were slightly too short, made for a difficult stretch. When we dismounted five hours later I realized, as my feet touched the ground, that I couldn't straighten my legs. They felt as though they had been broken at the knees and, like the extruded limbs of a mounted toy cowboy, remoulded around the horse's ribs.

But the camp, again as if by magic, had already been set up in a cool clearing beside a small stream where the air was full of the sound of the water and a chorus of cicadas. Ample doses of anaesthetizing moonshine sent us gliding along a gentle trajectory towards an evening meal of lamb kebabs grilled on an open fire. The cicadas had fallen silent and only the watery whisper of the stream and the trilling of a solitary cricket competed for conversation, which had slipped downward towards a melancholy and indulgent note. It had begun with speculative talk of Scythian and Parthian gold still hidden in the mounds and tumuli we had seen over the past few days. Even the everyday things of these forgotten peoples had been beautiful, we agreed, and in their crafts was preserved a quality of humaneness of which in our own time we had lost both the standard, and the reward.

'You put your hands around one of those ancient cups and you actually feel better,' said Louise. 'What will future archaeologists think of us when they find what we've left for them?'

We pictured the tender caresses of a yet-unborn team of experts across the surfaces of cracked cathode-ray tubes and their soulful pondering over dusty rows of excavated mobile telephones. But what really shocked her, she added, taking our doleful theme a step lower, was the sight of so many obese women on her trips back to America. It wasn't just the tiered and encircling cornices of flesh that offended the eye; it was the complete loss of physical dignity that seemed to afflict their owners. She had never seen a fat Turkoman woman, she said; much less a fat, badly dressed one devoid of any vestige of self-consciousness.

Well ... we weren't far behind, I suggested: England now had fat-farms for teenagers run by deranged Marine Corps instructors, who bludgeoned their cadets psychologically to the point of breakdown, and captured the whole miserable process on television.

It wasn't such a new phenomenon, either. I recounted how during a spell at school in America at the age of twelve, I had been silently terrorized by an abnormally fat girl whose awesome stature and leering, porcine eyes had haunted me for years afterwards. Though she was only in her early teens, her girth was such that she was forced to turn sideways to negotiate the aisle of our school bus. Along the seats on either side, a perceptible ripple of cowering spread in advance of her wheezing bulk, followed by sighs of deliverance when at last she swung like a wrecking-ball onto the rearmost cushion, and wedged the first cigarette of the day between her bloated lips. Anyone bold or foolish enough to meet her belligerent gaze became the instant victim, at the quivering end of a pale and sausage-like finger, of a torrential outpouring of profanity and threat.

Nothing in early life had prepared me for this unnatural

KURDESTAN Iran's north-west border with Iraq.

GOMBAD-E QABUS The tower of Ziyarid ruler Qabus ibn Wushmgir, 1006.

ISFAHAN The north ivān from the Royal Mosque courtyard.

Calligraphy in mosaic tilework.

The kashgul or begging bowl in
the mehrab of the mosque.

The tripartite language of Islamic visual art: cursive, geometric, vegetal.

The spectacular interior of the dome. 'Al-Rahim'.

The mosque from the Naqsh-e Jahan Square, showing asymmetry of dome and entrance portal.

TABRIZ Iconography old and new.

TEHRAN Antique shop on Ferdowsi Street.

GOLESTAN PROVINCE Children of Khajah Saleh.

YAZD View from the Friday Mosque.

GOMBAD-E QABUS Louise Firouz's ranch near the Turkmenistan border.

worldliness and accelerated physical deterioration among children my own age. When I was later and more safely ensconced at public school back in England, even the sternest of punishments seemed quaint and almost comic beside the memory of my former schoolmate's terrible physiognomy; and from then on, even the most notorious or unshapely English girls were universally transformed, by this relative measure, into paragons of self-respect and quintessences of loveliness.

I was re-enacting a portion of this uncharitable recollection when — it was shortly after dusk — a trio of local men passed by and struck up a conversation with Khidr and Ghorban. They were hunters on the spoor of wild pigs, they said, which were causing havoc to their newly planted crops. Did we want to join them later? If they got any pigs, they said, we could have them if we wanted. The prospect conjured six months' supply of sweet and sour spare ribs, Knackwurst, sizzling chops, and stuffed tenderloin for Louise. I said I thought it was too good an opportunity to miss.

We agreed to meet them at midnight, and at the appointed hour, Khidr and I caught up with them in a sloping field a quarter of a mile away. Booted and dressed in army jackets and fatigues, they were gathered around a small fire, propped on their elbows and smoking and reminiscing. The smiles on their youthful faces were caught in the ring of firelight and the barrels of their shotguns returned a faint gleam of flame. Bandoliers stuffed with cartridges were buckled around their waists, and we were soon discussing the virtues of different types of shot. Lacking rifles, they were using wide-gauge pellets the size of dried peas; nothing else, they explained, would stop a charging boar.

The fire and the darkness and promise of pursuit, and above all the presence of guns had awoken a restless feeling. Looking at the youthful and smiling features of the hunters my mind kept turning to the men I had known of a similar age some years ago, but beside whom these hunters looked as gentle as pampered children. That was across the border fifty miles to the east, and their prey had walked on two limbs instead of four. Bearded and turbaned and recklessly brave, they had won their weapons from the corpses of Soviet soldiers in a ten-year-long war virtually unknown beyond its borders. Its full consequence was only now beginning to be known.

We split up into two groups. The others disappeared into the darkness while I followed one of the men, who carried a portable searchlight and a motorcycle battery, into a wide-open field where we took up position in a natural dip in the ground like an old shell-crater. The battery was connected and a hundred-yard-long beam of light shot like a comet's tail across the intervening slopes. For an hour we lay there, sweeping the fields and hedgerows with the beam in the hope of glimpsing a bundle of galloping shadow. But there were no pigs; only moths. We retreated back along our tracks and met up with the others, walked to their old truck, and drove along the track that bordered the field. One man probed the undergrowth with the searchlight from the back of the truck while another, advancing ahead of us with a shotgun at his shoulder, tramped loudly through the undergrowth.

It seemed a rather modern and unfair way to hunt – not to mention noisy – and I was relieved when, after having raked the length of the track with the searchlight, one of the men escorted me disconsolately back to the tent. It didn't seem likely they would catch anything. But I realized I had judged them wrongly when, in the middle of the night, I was pulled from a deep and dreamless sleep by a tug on my shoulder. One of the hunters had returned. It was too dark to see his face but I could make out his silhouette against the moon-silvered sky and the steamy vapour of his breath rising from it.

'Pigs!' he whispered urgently. 'We've got two! Big ones! What do you want us to do with them?' I was a bit bewildered; I hadn't heard the shots. Then dimly I remembered they would have no use for them themselves, and that if we wanted the pigs we would have to deal with them at once. Then I pictured disembowelling a still-warm pig by torchlight, and thought of the gore and the smell and then having to leave at dawn to ride all day long. It was too much and I caved in without a struggle.

'Perhaps you should ask Firouz *khanum*,' I suggested, hoping they wouldn't dare wake Louise. They didn't; the hunter disappeared and I fell instantly back to sleep. But as we were preparing to leave the next morning, Louise shot me a deeply wry glance from behind her steaming glass of tea.

'Perhaps you should ask Firouz *khanum*,' she said. She had heard every word! 'Don't feel bad,' she added, 'I wouldn't have fancied gutting a pig in the middle of the night, either.'

Φ

Our final destination was a site in the Golestan National Park, nearly four hundred square miles of forest, scrub, and steppe. It was protected land and a sanctuary for all kinds of rare animals, where bears and leopards were said to roam. The weather was much cooler and we rode for several hours, stopping en route to fish out our waterproof gear as a fine rain began to fall. The final two hours took us through a misty enclave of woods which rose to about five thousand feet. The beech and maple of the warmer slopes fell below and we were moving through the upper layer of hollyoak when there was a sudden crack of a branch in the trees to our side. My horse shied violently and someone shouted, 'Bear!' I thought I glimpsed a shadowy mass darting behind the trees, but it was difficult to see: I was lying on my back with my left foot in one stirrup and the other pinned underneath me.

Seeing I was more surprised than hurt, Ibrahim and Ghorban offered consoling grins, and said we didn't have far to go. And soon we were there, in a sweeping meadow up to our knees in alfalfa, vetch, hollyhocks, flowering timothy, and clover, where the horses – I think they must have sensed we had arrived – broke into a long canter, cleaving a passage like a parted sea through the grass and sending up a shower of tiny seeds and petals in our wake.

There was no track but Khidr had driven deep into the meadow to meet us, and was unloading the truck into the immersing grass. With him was a game warden who from a hut on a hillside nearby kept a lonely vigil against hunters. He had guided Khidr to our new campsite and remembered Louise from one of her earlier visits. Perching on an upturned crate and leaning his automatic rifle against a knee, he settled down for the ritual exchange of news. Over a pot of tea he confirmed that there was indeed a bear in the woods along the route we had taken. We were lucky, he said, that it didn't have cubs this year; it was a female and might have attacked us. Then, after we had shared a restorative pot of tea, he offered to accompany us to a village a few miles away where we could find running water.

A winding track snaked into the valley beyond the meadow and we began a long descent, weaving in unfinished loops over a long series of barren and intersecting spurs. We seemed in the process to have crossed some invisible climatic threshold; soon there was no trace of green or even grass and the landscape grew wilder and rockier and its features more stark at each passing mile. We pulled our scarves over our mouths against the dust and at about the halfway point spotted a dozen mouflon scampering effortlessly over the crags in the distance, and later on a flock of about thirty gazelle. Then came a third treat; a Turkoman fox, the same size as its European relative but with a bushier and creamy-coloured brush and much more rare. It fled down a slope and darted into the shadow of a gulley as we approached.

As the valley deepened, solemn and enclosing battlements of rock began to rise on either side, but ahead the land stretched to a bright and yellowish infinity, and once again I had the feeling that we were approaching the edge of the world. Fortunately, we stopped short of it: the road ended just above a tiny village of mud-brick homes sheltering under the shadow of a thousand-foot-high ridge. It was much remoter than the hamlet through which we'd passed the day before and seemed barely touched by the outside world. We pulled up and the warden agreed to wait for us and pointed to the spot where we could fetch water. The spring was no more than a pipe emerging from the earth above a muddy pool, and I walked down with Ghorban along a steep footpath. Four young women were already there, but took flight like butterflies as we approached, drawing their veils hastily across their faces and settling a few yards away to peer at us from behind an earthen wall.

The water flowed at a trickle and our plastic barrel took a long time to fill. As we waited a small boy walked past in silence with a cow tethered on a piece of string. Another boy, about ten years old and riding bareback on a tall chestnut mare, stopped nearby and slid deftly to the ground by the edge of the pool. Its withers were the height of the boy's head and, after his horse had drunk for a few minutes, he enlisted Ghorban with a wordless nod to help him remount.

When the barrel was full we each took one end, carried it up the slope to the truck, and lashed it to the canopy. We brushed ourselves off and paused to catch our breath. Then Ghorban, who had said nothing to me all day, spoke.

'What do you think of this place?' he asked. The women at the spring had disappeared now and the village looked utterly deserted. A brooding mass of grey cloud was advancing over the ridge in the distance and the sky was darkening by the minute. A storm was coming: at least the villagers we had left behind would be pleased. But it was a lonely place, suffused with an atmosphere of exile, where the ordinary bonds of time and space seemed to have found scarce purchase. The very earth seemed to emit a vibration of immeasurable antiquity.

'It's a bit quiet for me,' I said.

'Quiet,' he scoffed, 'you think this is quiet?' Then he lit a cigarette, and nodded vaguely towards the cluster of silent homes, the dusty hoof prints in the paths between them, and the vacant slopes of the encircling barrenness.

'This isn't quiet,' he said. 'This is *busy*.'

Four

Soltaniyeh · Tabriz
Sanandaj
Takht-e Suleyman

The Traveller's Ritual · Mongol Hoards · Dark Days for Islam

Pax Mongolica · Fantasy: the Persianization of the Mongols

Uljeitu and the Italian Connection · Sunni or Shi'a?

Ali, Prince of Martyrs · A House of Strength · An Irreverent Host

Muqarnas · Border Manoeuvres · Wine and Women

Daydream at Vanished Shiz

در ازل پرتو حسنت ز تجلّی دم زد   عشق پیدا شد و آتش به همه عالم زد

Before time was, a ray of Your beauty was breathed into existence
Love woke up; and set the universe alight

THE RITUAL unfolds predictably on both sides. It is usually midnight. The taxi has left you in a deserted side street, and the door to the hotel is locked. You knock hopefully, and the grizzled night manager rises like a ghost from his improvised bed and shuffles forward to the door. There is a rattle of keys. Above the reception desk hangs a portrait of the Ayatollah, under whose implacable gaze you ask if there is a room to be had for a solitary traveller.

'*Ya Ali,*' mutters the manager to himself, licks his thumb, and turns the pages of a Dickensian register dense with swirling script.

'Passport?' This he opens from the wrong end, fans through the pages, and with a look of exasperation, tosses aside. 'A single room? Ten thousand *tomans*. It's the government-regulated price.'

'No it's not,' you protest, 'that's the tourist price. Do I look like a tourist?'

'All right.' He sighs heavily, and scratches his chest under his open shirt. He is in no mood for the challenge. 'You speak Persian — seven thousand.'

'Seven thousand? Here, I'll fill out the form for you if it's too much effort.' This you do.

'I have never seen a foreigner do that,' he says, half to himself.

'And I have never paid so much for a room.'

'Six thousand, then. But you pay in dollars.'

'Dollars? What have I to do with dollars? I am English. My currency is the pound.'

A look of suspicion follows this revelation. He asks how much a pound is worth; a dollar and a half, you explain.

'If the pound is worth more, then you are even richer than an American.'

'If I were that rich,' you say, casting an exaggeratedly cynical glance around the place, 'then why would I stay *here*?'

'All right. Five thousand.' He hands you the key, and flings your passport into a drawer. 'England,' you hear him mutter as the register is slammed shut, 'the mother of all politics...'

Φ

Upstairs you realize the effort is not wasted: the room is worth even less. On the floor lies a plate with the remains of an unfinished meal. The door won't lock from the inside. The sheets have not been changed since the last occupant, merely shaken; and the pillow bears the unmistakable imprint of a head, and gives the impression of having been hurriedly abandoned. Overhead, a pair of fluorescent lights comes reluctantly to life; one blinks stubbornly, and its twin buzzes like an old fridge.

You don an undersized pair of plastic slippers to enter the bathroom, where the taps spit like demented cobras. Above the cracked mirror, tendrils of bare wire unfurl from a lamp-fitting that was stolen. And in a tiny adjoining chamber, where the light refuses to function, you approach with deep apprehension a dark and slippery vortex, from which issues an indescribable fragrance. None of the usual amenities accompany this unavoidable encounter. There is only a plastic tube grafted to the cold-water pipe which, when activated, writhes across the floor with unexpected force, spraying you icily where you least expect.

You wash your hands, and realize the drain from the sink trickles over your toes. The shower offers a different challenge: it shakes epileptically for a minute, coughs up a splash of tepid water, and expires. Then, as you experiment with the wrongly labelled taps, a boiling torrent descends on your back. You wash as a family of inconvenienced cockroaches takes refuge in a recess inches from your face. Only afterwards do you realize there is neither soap nor towel. Leaning against the sink to steady yourself back into the sandals, it detaches from the wall and slumps downwards like a bombed-out bridge.

For half an hour, all is silent. There is nothing for it but to read; but the cold glare of the fluorescent lights overhead soon gives you a headache. Meanwhile, the heating system has come to life and the radiator begins to pulse with metallic spasms, as though its pipes, somewhere deep in the building, are being violently snapped. You are grateful for the warmth. But soon it is producing more energy than a small power station, and is impossible to regulate. Opening the window to cool the room, you realize that the noise of heavily laden trucks, which have inexplicably begun to fill the little street below, will make it impossible to sleep. They roar past, billowing diesel fumes, shaking the building and detonating the night air with their triple-toned air-horns. The radiator leaks, too; in the morning, the book you have abandoned on the floor is a sodden pulp.

The door is paper-thin. The bed is too short. The pillow is like a sandbag, and the sheets are as rough as sandpaper. By one o'clock, the heating system and the trucks have quietened down, and your eyelids grow heavy. But at two, a battalion of conscripts arrives and begins to tramp up and down the corridor, shouting, laughing, smoking, and slamming doors. An hour later, it is almost silent, except for the sonorous drip of the cistern, like a Chinese torture ... but at last, as the sky begins to lighten in the east, sleep descends like a healing balm – until dawn, when a construction team begins demolishing the wall of the room opposite. But it would be wrong to suggest that rooms are always this bad. Some, to be fair, are worse.

Φ

It was November now. A plan to return in the early autumn had failed, and I had followed instead a contrary urge to see the country in winter, reasoning that the romance of the place, the dust, tourists, and insect life, would all be at a minimum. I could travel south, I reasoned, as the weather cooled. Already the season had begun to tighten like a grey noose around the landscape, and for a month I seemed to move beneath a canopy of brooding cloud. Only in the afternoons would the skies sometimes clear and release long pale drapes of yellow light, calling forth across the ever-barer hills an answering shade from the surrendering foliage; and to the eye at least, these were melancholy days. Evenings were long, lacked the solace of wine, and, though frequently softened by the hospitality of newly made friends, full of sentiments akin to homesickness. I was city-bound for this portion of the journey, and no moment fell more heavily than at sunset when, to the simultaneous clatter of a thousand grilles and shutters, every stall and shopfront would be battened for the night, and the streets would empty with practised suddenness as though the Mongols themselves had been sighted advancing from the enclosing hills.

I had Mongols on my mind; hordes of them. Three-quarters of a millennium earlier, thirteenth-century Persia had witnessed two terrible waves of Mongol invasions; their depredations are well known. The first was unleashed by Chingiz Khan's vengeful crossing of the Syr Darya in the summer of 1219. Transoxiana, Khwarazm, and Khorasan were mercilessly reduced in a tornado-like campaign directed by the Great Khan himself. Centres of learning and culture — among them the great cities of Samarqand, Bokhara, Herat, Merv, and Nishapur — were decimated; and the Mongol scourge, as Muslim chroniclers described their invaders, left much of northern and central Persia in ruins. An unstoppable force of these steppe warriors drove north-west, eviscerating the kingdoms of European monarchs and striking eventually as far as Poland and Moscow. Another branch conquered as far as northern China, and soon after the middle of the thirteenth century the Mongols ruled the greatest empire known to history. The momentous task of subduing Persia and the territories of the Middle East fell to Hulegu Khan, a grandson of Chingiz Khan. In 1258, his cavalry rode almost unopposed to Baghdad, snuffing out en route the Assassins in their hitherto impregnable mountain fortresses.

The fabled seat of Islamic power was sacked, and five hundred years of Muslim rule ended in flame and plunder. Only the Christian population of the city, at the intercession of Hulegu's Nestorian wife, was spared total humiliation. But the Abbasid caliphate had been extinguished, and the great capitals of Aleppo and Damascus looted and occupied. Islam faced its darkest hour: of the heartland of the Faith, only Egypt and Arabia remained unconquered. The threat of ultimate defeat, strengthened by alliances between Mongol and Crusader forces still occupying Syria and Palestine, hung momentarily over the Muslim world. Yet the fall of this epochal curtain was stayed by an extraordinary reverse. In a crisis of succession, Hulegu was recalled to central Asia, and his depleted army was decisively beaten in his absence by the Egyptian Mamluks.* The Mongol defeat at ʿAyn Jalut – 'Goliath's Spring' – in Palestine marked the limit of their advance; Egypt was never again seriously threatened, and Hulegu's efforts turned to consolidating the lands that remained under his control.

But in Persia itself, the calamitous character of these early Mongol campaigns has tended to obscure what came next. Returning to the conquered territories east of the Fertile crescent to rule as Il-Khan, or Viceroy to the Great Khan in China, Hulegu and his successors oversaw an empire nearly as large as that of the Sasanians a thousand years earlier. They also rebuilt it. Reconstruction began all over Persia under Hulegu; cities were restored to prosperity, and during the ensuing, century-long period that historians have called the Pax Mongolica, Persia witnessed an extraordinary cultural flourishing. Its Mongol inheritors were, it seems, proud, ambitious, and increasingly worldly.

---

* This was in 1260, the year in which Qubilai – Coleridge's famous Kubla Khan – was elected Great Khan. Military alliances with Mongol leaders against common Muslim enemies were frequently explored by the Christian occupiers of the Holy Land. The last great Mongol assault on Syria was in 1303, in a Euro-Mongol campaign organized jointly by Ghazan Khan and Pope Boniface VIII. More than a few Christian princes were subsequently excommunicated for allying themselves with the Mongols.

They also possessed phenomenal wealth, and were fond of indulging it on a conspicuous scale. Vast palaces, mosques, mausoleums, caravanserais, observatories, and gardens were commissioned to outstrip any structure that had gone before. At Tabriz, where the city walls quadrupled in length under Ilkhanid rule, fourteen thousand workmen were employed to build a mausoleum and complex to rival Persepolis itself; and the city's congregational mosque, explicitly designed to outdo the colossal arch at the Sasanian capitol of Ctesiphon, boasted a vault a hundred feet wide springing from walls of equal height. At Soltaniyeh, another imperial capital (the remains of which I was on my way to see), a mausoleum was built to surpass the largest rival of the time, that of the Seljuk Sultan Sanjar at Merv.

Even their books were magnificently large. Paper-making machines from China were used to produce sheets three feet across for giant Qur'āns, whose titanic script swelled the glowing verses to thirty volumes, and hundreds of artists and calligraphers were set to work at royal scriptoriums on manuscripts lavishly illustrated with epic scenes of battle, hunting, and supernatural encounters.

Trade flourished too under these internationally minded rulers, and for the first time since the end of the Roman Empire, the Mediterranean was linked to China along a thriving commercial corridor. It was the era of the world's first global wanderers – Ibn Battuta, Marco Polo, and the Flemish Franciscan monk, William of Rubric. European delegations even set up permanent communities at the Ilkhanid court; residential complexes were built for foreign scholars; and an entirely new discipline – world history – was initiated with the vizier Rashid ud-Din's *Jami'at at-Tawarikh*, or Universal History. Architecture grew increasingly innovative and refined, and a corresponding enrichment occurred in the iconography of the visual arts, where Far Eastern motifs – the peony and the lotus and the chrysanthemum, serpent-like dragons, clouds like swirling flames, and the enigmatic gaze of moon-faced, slant-eyed princes – all appear for the first time in Persia. Nowhere, to my eye, does the Chinese influence seem more at work than in those angular friezes of interlocking tilework, where the lithe and graceful ciphers of the Arabic script seem to have been melted down and recast in disused moulds for hexagrams, emerging metamorphosed and at the very limit of intelligibility into maze-like and eye-teasing patterns.

Yet the early Ilkhanid rulers were not themselves Muslims, and their eclecticism is a reminder of the heterogeneous character of the dynasty. Many were Buddhists, but held on to their native shamanistic beliefs; many had Nestorian Christian wives. They glorified the military traditions of their Turkish dynastic predecessors, wrote in a Persian version of Arabic script, and stamped their documents with Chinese royal seals. On matters religious, they seem to have kept an open house, inviting Buddhist teachers from India and Tibet to their capital in Tabriz, and showed particular respect towards Islam's own mystical discipline, Sufism. Despite the turmoil of the era — or perhaps indeed because of it — the early fourteenth century was a golden age for Sufism and its literature. The Ilkhanids commissioned dervish monasteries and hospices, protected communities dedicated to the study of Sufism, and raised shrines dedicated to Sufi saints. A number of prominent Sufis also served at the royal court, and it seems likely that their influence was at least partly responsible for drawing their rulers into the spiritual fold of Islam — the consequences of which can hardly be overstated. When, at the end of the thirteenth century, the Ilkhanid ruler Ghazan Khan embraced the religion of his subjects, the political tide turned decisively in favour of the faith. Henceforth the Ilkhanids declared themselves the Great Kings of Islam, all future rulers of Persia would be Muslims, and their dynastic relatives would carry Islam through most of south Asia and as far as the archipelagos of the Indonesian Sea. Having a few decades earlier been threatened with virtual extinction, Islam was restored to the status of a world religion.

The warriors from the north and the scourge of civilization, once universally feared as Godless and bloodthirsty predators, had been tamed; guided, educated, refined, and ultimately seduced by the very culture they had nearly destroyed. It is a momentous transformation. We need no longer picture them under the glare of the steppe, peering from a tent-flap to escape the fumes of steaming yak-meat, or pacing for weeks in the saddle across desert and mountain or the vaporous deltas of Eurasia to unleash their quivers against the cavalries of Teutonic knights ... for their homes are by now no longer made from felt, but columns of ornamented brick faced with panels of lustrous mosaic, and their inlaid bows lie idle on embroidered cushions. The Mongol nobles of Persia gaze, instead, through doors of chamfered alabaster and across courtyards of lustrous marble into gardens built on the template of Paradise itself, where dragon-headed fountains feed pools of milk and wine. Within, gold candlesticks the size of trees and chandeliers of lacquered glass spread light across their palace interiors, glittering across cascades of stalactitic vaults and the iridescent glaze of star-shaped turquoise and cobalt tiles. Giant palimpsests and codices rest in ivory stands. Gold and the opulent bloom of lapis are everywhere; their celestial hues cover every wall, which rise towards gilded bands of encircling stucco and, above them, hovering ceilings of honeycombed plaster or domes covered with kaleidoscopic mosaics of multiplying stars and trapezoids.

Cross-legged on carpets and velvet bolsters, the nobles sip from cups of translucent jade. They are dressed in snow-leopard trousers and shimmering multicoloured tunics woven from silver thread, caught at the waist with belts of solid gold and decorated with dragons coiled in silken roundels. Eagle feathers sprout from the bifurcated rims of their brocaded hats, and their Confucian moustaches glisten with wine from Shiraz and Herat ... but it is dawn now, and the call to prayer sounds through the inlaid window-grilles ... and glances of self-censure ripple momentarily through the assembly. With a final tilt of forefinger and thumb and a hasty dabbing of whiskers against sleeve, the party rises and files towards the mosque ... the Mongols have been Persianized.

Φ

Today, Soltaniyeh is a small village lying on a broad sweep of plain between two low mountain ranges. Some two hundred miles north-west of Tehran, it was chosen as a summer residence by Arghun Khan, Ghazan's predecessor, for its cool climate and abundant game and pasture. Scarcely a trace remains of the city it later became under Uljeitu, but the magnificent mausoleum he commissioned in 1305 still stands, and is rightly considered the finest surviving remnants of Ilkhanid grandeur and a masterpiece of medieval architecture. I had seen photographs of this lonely structure – half-ruined but serene, rising nobly from the mud-brick rooftops of hovels around its base, where peasant women loaded hay onto donkeys – and had looked out for it eagerly on the way. But I'd been sitting on the wrong side of the bus, and the few promising shapes in the distance had resolved in turn into a vast grain silo, a water tower, and a cement factory.

I reached it the next day from nearby Zanjan, and caught my first glimpse from the main road a few miles away. The glinting turquoise dome, whose profile resembles the pointed end of a tethered but floating egg, was enclosed in a faint grey bloom of scaffolding. It grew vaster at the approach, until its bulk was looming nearly overhead. A taxi dropped me at the coach-park that now replaces the dusty lanes I had imagined – they are all paved now, and there is not a donkey in sight – and I entered the grounds through a newly built ticket office, where a guard tried to charge me three times the cost of my room for the previous night.

'One thinks,' wrote Byron, who visited the site in 1933, 'of Brunelleschi'; I did, and of St Paul's too. But the association with Italy's renaissance *capomastro* may be more than simply visual. When Uljeitu made Soltaniyeh his new capital, it became a centre for international trade. In the summer months, caravans of camels laden with jewels, silks, and spices arrived from the Middle East, Crimea, Turkey, the Caucasus, and the Persian Gulf. Venetian and Genoese merchants also flocked there. Uljeitu corresponded with the Vatican, and an archbishopric was established in Solta-niyeh in 1318. Reports of city's spectacular skyline and its two-hundred-foot-high dome must have reached the Italy at around the same time, and Brunelleschi's masterpiece – the dome of the Santa Maria del Fiore in Florence, completed a hundred years later – does indeed bear a striking resemblance to its eastern antecedent. The latter, to my eyes, is the more beautiful and harmonious. It has none of the complicated devices of its Florentine rival – external masonry ribs or chains of iron and sandstone within – and its double-skinned dome is a technical marvel, buoyant and utterly free of strain. Eight slender and gleaming minarets once rose from its octagonal base, 'framing the dome,' says Pope, 'like a diadem'.

The interior, roughly a hundred feet across, is majestic; no other word quite describes it. Ample light pours through upper and lower tribunes and the plastered walls, though cracked and badly damaged, further lighten the space (though I was sad not to be able to see the dome above; almost the entire space was filled with a metallic forest of scaffolding from which the present restoration is being carried out). Eight giant arches soar towards a vaulted gallery, where I paced, entirely alone, taking inadequate notes. The walls are covered in a wide range of decoration in floral, geometric, and calligraphic designs, the latter framing the arches and binding the uppermost portion of the octagon, which fuses into the dome across a triple band of mediating shallow niches. Dark blue and wine and gold, though much faded now, are the predominant colours, and the overwhelming impression is one of a perfect marriage of structure with ornament which, centuries after its conception, still conveys an atmosphere of equilibrium and power.

A tiny stairway led me to the upper galleries, where a warm breeze circulated under the richly decorated vaults – twenty-four in all – faced with patterned brick-ends and fantastically elaborate strapwork in painted plaster. From this second storey I looked out over the village. All seemed squat and drab, except for a single antique monument poking above the rooftops to the north. I wondered at the forces that the laid the place so thoroughly to waste. Matrakchy, in 1534, records a fortified city bristling with domes and minarets, a crenellated citadel, and man-made canals lined with abundant fruit trees. Seventeenth-century European travellers like de Bruyn, Olearus, and Chardin evoke a similar though declining site; Flandin in the mid-nineteenth century shows the area half-ruined, but still dotted with lofty portals and crumbling minarets. Less than a century later, Byron reports only a single outlying shrine – perhaps the one I could now see. Earthquakes could no doubt account for the city's partial collapse; wars and neglect for more. But the destruction seemed cruelly thorough, and left a strange feeling. I would feel it many times again.

Φ

Tabriz lies a further two hundred miles to the north-west, in the province of East Azerbaijan. It is the northernmost of Iran's former capitals, and has been favoured as a regional seat by nearly every dynasty of the Islamic era. The Arabs, Turks, Mongols, and Safavids and Qajars all fought over it; in the past century it was repeatedly occupied by the Russians. Home now to a million and a half souls, it has succumbed more recently to those modern and ineluctable invaders, concrete and neon.

I arrived in the city at night, and caught sight as the bus descended from the hills of a vast and glittering lake of yellow street lights. A fellow passenger, diverting his taxi for the purpose, saw me to a hotel, which from a tiny map looked as though it might be close to the *arg* or citadel (and the last remaining Ilkhanid building in the city). In the morning I was delighted to see it towering above me nearby; a hundred-foot-long, brooding mass of cocoa-coloured brick bisected by a vast semicircular bastion. The whole area was fenced off for repairs, but I crept in and asked a dusty-looking workman mixing cement whether I could climb to the top. He shrugged amiably, and pointed towards the airy grid of scaffolding that clung to the interior wall.

I was halfway up the switchback of rickety planks fastened with wire and string when a human silhouette appeared over the parapet, waving furiously at me to descend. I waved a piece of paper at him with equal vigour and kept going. Nearly a hundred feet above the city, I introduced myself to a dark-skinned foreman, who was built like a bear and wore a woolly jumper and hat and dark green tartan trousers. My fictitious permission was forgotten and, hopping nimbly over cross-braces and piles of brick, he took me on a dizzying tour.

The platform at the top was only six feet across, crumbled uncomfortably at the edges, and as I walked along it the ground below seemed to be slithering in the wrong direction. The walls, he said, were solid, and confirmed that a massive arch had once sprung from end to end. It had collapsed only a few years after construction, but the building had been used for several centuries. We were standing on the final fragment of it, which now resembles a stranded intrusion from a different architectural age. A dervish hospice and a madrasa had once abutted from either end; in their place were a car park and the mounting steel girders of what could only be a bank. It was impossible to imagine the marble courtyard, a hundred and ten thousand square feet in area, that had once stretched from the base below us. Legend has it that the city's miscreants were thrown from the top; a sole woman, goes a story, survived the fall because of the parachute-like effect of her voluminous chador.

I took a few pictures of the skyline, where one or two domes bobbed in the surrounding sea of rectangles, then asked if I might take one of my guide. He leapt with terrifying agility onto a parapet and struck a solemn and martial pose in the sunlight. Then he offered to reciprocate and, directing me with an outstretched hand from behind the viewfinder, tilted the camera at every angle and fired off a dozen frames. Dizzier than any model, I fumbled for handholds on the upright poles. I asked where I could send a picture to him. His name was Salman, he said. 'Just put "The Arg, Tabriz".' He grinned. 'There's no one else up here.'

Φ

I wandered a great deal through the vaulted avenues of the bazaar, still one of the largest in the country. And at the site of the Masjed-e Kabud, or Blue Mosque, I found an intact building where I had expected to see a ruin. Its original patron was the daughter of Jahan Shah, the leader of the Qara Qoyunlu, or Black Sheep dynasty, which took over Azerbaijan after it had been sacked by Timur. It was built in 1465 and long ago ruined by earthquakes. But a recent restoration has united its amputated piers and roofed what is one of the few entirely covered mosques in Iran.

I wandered in, bought a ticket at the local price, and turned away before the caretaker could challenge me. He eyed me suspiciously from his kiosk as I toured beneath the nine domes, wondering how the original dimensions had been recalculated. A television crew were filming a team of girls restoring a calligraphic frieze. I watched them for a while, then slunk outside as the ticket seller, overcome by curiosity, came out of his kiosk to question me.

Scattered around the resurrected walls were huge translucent slabs of marble from Maragheh. The facade, though much restored now, is a masterpiece of Timurid refinement. Its decoration, in predominantly lapis-coloured tilework, is rich and intricate, and the spiralling turquoise of the portal cabling reminded me of a mosque I had visited in Afghanistan, that of Abu Nasr Parsa in Balkh, which I later found out was built at about the same time. This was a small discovery; but it was evidence that at last the jumble of names and styles I had been reading and thinking about was beginning to resolve into something coherent. Now the mention of Mongols meant more than piles of skulls; I saw instead the massive walls at Soltaniyeh and Tabriz, and thought of caravanserais and schools. For a long time, the word 'Safavid' had meant only another Persian dynasty; now I had seen their greatest monuments, and run my hands across their polished cornerstones.

Architecture was perhaps the most eloquent and accessible route into the personality of these various eras; what seemed extraordinary was that in each of them, creativity had been expressed at such an accomplished level. But there were common elements, I was beginning to realize, in all their different styles: a love of symbolism and visual metaphor; an irrepressible urge to exploit the technologies and materials of construction to the limits of their potential; a humaneness and sophistication to even the most utilitarian of structures; a profound sensitivity to the effect of space, light, and sound on the human organism; and, allied to this, a passion for geometrical harmony and precision. It was satisfying to be able to formulate all this without having to visit a library. I felt that, very slowly, I was actually learning something.

Φ

'Ya Ali!'

This muttered invocation, unheard in the nations of Sunni Islam, made me turn my head. It had come from the lips of a young man ranging kebabs over a bed of white-hot coals, above which a blinking neon sign read Ali Baba Restaurant. Despite the cold, the door to the place was open and, beckoned by a friendly smile from the cook, I went inside for an evening meal.

The owner, after I had eaten, invited me to join him at his table, where he was puffing on a small water pipe. His name was Khalil. He was a stocky, handsome man, with cropped black hair and watchful, dark eyes the shape of almonds. He must have been thirty, but his manner conveyed the calm and authority of an older man. We liked each other and settled into conversation. Then, after the last of the customers had left and the cook been despatched with a wad of notes from the day's takings, we were joined by Khalil's younger brother and one of the waiters.

There was the usual flurry of exploratory questions. They'd had an English visitor, one of them said, a year or two ago – perhaps I knew him? No, he wasn't English, a voice corrected him, he was French. But what was I doing here alone? What did I think of Iran? What would I be writing about? How much would I make from the book? Did I have a wife, and did she work? What was the pound worth? Where had I been, and where was the best place so far? Frequent refills of tea accompanied this gentle interrogation. By now I had had ample practice with the answers and, sensing my interlocutors were as good-natured as they were hospitable, and in such a way as to show I wasn't too serious, I said: 'I wasn't sure, mind you, about coming to Tabriz.'

There were some indignant cries of '*Why ever not?*'

'I've heard,' I said, 'in Tehran, that the people of Tabriz have a bad reputation.' The three heads tightened closer to hear the charge.

'What do they say about us?'

'That the people of Tabriz are unkind and fanatical.'

'That's *exactly* what makes us angry!' Khalil's brother, a younger and more passionate man, raised a protesting finger in front of me. 'What do they know?' Then, simmering down, added almost ruefully: 'We're not like the Persians, anyway. We're Azeris.'

'That's right,' said someone, 'we're Turks, like all the great families of Iran.'

At this point the door opened and a melancholy looking, white-haired man in a tired suit joined us at the table, and greeted us in Azeri. Then, realizing there was a Persian-speaking guest, he switched languages.

'Have you heard the one about the Christian and the Muslim?' he pulled up the sleeves of his jackets and, looking down to brush aside a few crumbs, set his elbows on the table and looked at us in turn, as if to say, 'Then I'll begin.'

'You'll like this,' said the brother, refilling my glass of tea with a complicitous wink. 'He's a doctor. And his speciality is jokes!' But the crux of the long and complicated tale that followed, and ended in eye-watering guffaws all round, evaded me. It had all hung on a word I didn't know, which was dutifully explained with a gesture from one of them resembling a bottle being opened. Jokes about circumcision, it occurred to me eventually, must have been circulating since the Crusades.

'Are you from London?' asked the doctor. There was a comic glint beneath his sad features. 'I've been there a few times,' he said wistfully. Then he lit a cigarette, gazed upwards through a curl of ascending smoke, and sighed. 'Paris once. Frankfurt, too. They used to be beautiful places before you let so many Arabs go and live there.'

Khalil, who had kept silent for most of the time, now put aside the mouthpiece of his pipe, exhaled a long and expanding plume, and recalled the time he had met an Arab from Kuwait one evening in a nearby street. He was looking for a place to eat, so he brought him to the restaurant. As they arrived, the Arab had looked up, seen the sign *Ali Baba*, shuddered, and fled into the darkness.

'The forty thieves!' he chuckled. '*Ali Baba and the forty thieves!* He thought we were going to rob him!'

'The Arabs don't understand us,' added the brother. 'They think we're all Hezbollahis or something.' (He meant the much-feared and hard-line Ansari-i Hezbollah, not the popular Palestinian resistance movement of the same name.)

'For one thing, they're Sunnis.'

At this, there were a few solemn nods of assent.

'If you were Muslim,' one of them turned to me suddenly, 'which would you be: Sunni or Shi'a?'

'Shi'a, of course!' interjected the brother.

I said I understood that there were different kinds of Shi'a: apart from the main body of Twelver Shi'ism there were the Ismaelis and the Zaidis and the Nizaris, the Ahmadiyya, the Druze too in the Lebanon, and some others I wasn't too sure about.

'Yes,' said the waiter, 'but they're not really Muslims.'

'They've made up their own religion!' With good-natured passion, Khalil's brother started up again. 'Look,' he went on, 'there's only one kind of Shi'a, and that's our kind. We believe—'

'There *are* others,' said Khalil gently. 'The Ismaelis—'

'I'll get to them. We believe,' he tapped his finger on the table, 'that Ali was the rightful successor of the Prophet, peace be upon him, and the first imam. But the Sunnis put their caliphs – you know about the caliphs, Abu Bakr — and the others? Good. They put the caliphs in his place — the place of Ali, who was chosen by the Prophet himself at Ghadir Kumm. We don't agree with that.'

'They said Ali was too young,' said the doctor gloomily.

'But Ali was himself the fourth caliph,' I said.

'Yes, but he was also the first Imam. It's — complicated. The Sunni have their caliphs, and we have our imams.'

'The Twelve Imams.'

'Yes, twelve. Ali's son Hassan was the second Imam, and his brother was the third Imam, Husein, who was murdered — murdered! — along with his whole family, by the Caliph Yazid, the Umayyad, at Kerbala — you know about Kerbala?'

I nodded.

'Good. After them . . . after them—'

'After them came Imam Zein al-Abedin,' said the doctor.

'And after Imam Zein al-Abedin came . . . came the fifth Imam . . .'

There was a pause; Khalil's brother was running out of steam. A few names were hurriedly proposed, put aside, and rearranged like a puzzle. It was slow going; but we got there in the end, and I wrote down the succession in my notebook at the table.

Muhammad Baqir was the fifth Imam. His brother, Zaid, became the founder of the so-called Five-Imam Shi'a, or Zaidis. The sixth was Imam Ja'far Sadiq, perhaps the most famous of the Imams — whose son, Ismael, was chosen as successor by the Ismaelis — the 'Seveners', so called — who founded the Fatimid caliphate in Cairo in the tenth century.

The seventh, the son of Imam Ja'far, was Imam Musa Kazim; the eighth, Imam Reza, who himself nearly became caliph, and whose famous shrine is today in Mashhad; the ninth, Imam Mohammad al-Taqi; the tenth, Imam Ali al-Naqi; the eleventh, Imam Hasan al-Askari, who married the daughter of a Byzantine emperor,* and whose son became the twelfth and final Imam,

---

* I discovered this much later. An account of the marriage of the

Mohammad — known also as the Mahdi, the Rightly Guided, Sahib az-Zaman, Lord of the Age, Sahib al-Amr, Lord of the Divine Command, al-Qat'm, He who will arise, al-Muntazar, the Awaited, and the Baqiyyat Allah, Remnant of God — and whose earthly disappearance in 940 marks the beginning of that enigmatic period known as the occultation, during which period the Imam is alive, but invisible.

By this time, the original question — Sunni or Shi'a? — had been forgotten. But the events of thirteen centuries ago had not. We had touched on one of the pivotal moments in the history of Islam, the repercussions of which, pulsing across time like the radiation of an extinguished galaxy, still inform the pattern of events in the Shi'a world, and especially Iran.* Outwardly at least,

---

penultimate Imam is told in detail by a number of Shi'a historians. According to them, Nargess Khatun, sometimes called Malikeh, was a Christian princess — granddaughter of the Emperor of Rüm and descended on her mother's side from the Apostle Simon. Her marriage was foretold (according to the monumental *Bihar al-Anwar* of Majlesi) by a dream. Perhaps even less known in this connection are the Christian ancestors of Ismael, later Shah Safavi (d. 1524), founder of the Safavid Empire. His grandmother, Theodora Komnene, was the Christian daughter of the Greek Emperor of Trabzon, John IV; his mother was baptized as Marta, and another grandmother belonged to a different branch of the same Greek royal family. It is not long, in tracing the line back wards, before the first Cantacuzenes and Paleologues begin to appear — evidence of the long reach of these two illustrious families! Further still (and a little more selectively, via the Burgundian kings and those of Saxony and Lorraine and Poland and Hungary) it takes us to Charlemagne himself ... It is an interesting genealogical bridge, even if, in the words of Paddy Leigh Fermor, 'the Cantacuzenes were always a bit hangdog about fourteenth-century intermarriage with Muslims.'

* Shi'ism was not, of course, always the state religion of Iran; and it was largely Persians, in fact, who were the early theological champions of Sunni Islam. In the ninth and tenth centuries, Shi'ism was dominant in Syrian and North Africa, and the shrines of all but one of the Imams lie outside Iran itself. The way was paved only gradually; and despite the early successes of the Buyids, the Turkish Ghaznavid and Seljuk rulers of Persia were staunch Sunnis. Shi'ism was temporarily legitimized by the

the great schism that divides Islam into Sunni and Shi'a camps arose over the question of a successor to the Prophet Mohammad, who died in 632, leaving no male heir. A consensus of the Prophet's closest companions elected Abu Bakr, his father-in-law and intimate friend, to lead the community of Muslims. The majority who supported this appointment of a successor, khalifa, became known as the People of Tradition, Sunnah; a small group of others believed that the role should remain in the Prophet's family, and supported Ali, his son-in-law and cousin. These later became known as the partisans, or Shi'a.

But the split in opinion was more than political. The very role of successor was perceived differently, with the Shi'a laying stress on the initiatic dimension of succession; only Ali, in Shi'a tradition, had been chosen by Islam's founder for the task of interpreting the mysteries of the Qur'ān, conveying the esoteric inheritance of the revelation, and serving as a channel of Divine Grace flowing from the family of the Prophet. The choice of Mohammad's successor was not without controversy – contention, even – but three times Ali was passed over in favour of the earliest caliphs, Abu Bakr, Omar, and Uthman, the latter from an aristocratic Meccan clan, the Umayyad, which had earlier strongly opposed the Prophet.

Uthman's assassination in 656 brought Ali at last to the caliphate, and for five years his follower's hopes were realized. But like his predecessor, Ali too fell victim to an assassin's blade, and a cousin of Uthman, Mu'awiya (and the first of the Umayyad caliphs, so called), rose to power. Power there was; in the early decades of Islam, the Arabs and their allies made extraordinarily rapid territorial conquests; their armies, by the time of the Prophet's grandson Hussein, had already penetrated into North Africa in the west, advanced through Persia as far as Khorasan, and laid siege to Constantinople.

---

penultimate Ilkhanid Sultan Uljeitu in the fourteenth century, but only in the sixteenth century did it become the official religion under Shah Ismael, the founder of the Safavid dynasty.

They ruled over an ever-vaster empire. As the new government grew wealthier and stronger, there was frequent opposition to its methods (and even its religious integrity); the question of succession was still controversial, and the worldliness of the caliphate brought accusations that it had become no more than a privileged autocracy – a hereditary kingdom, in other words – that had largely forsaken the theocratic spirit of Islam's earliest days. Resistance came to head in 680, when Ali's second son, Husein, agreed to put himself at the head of a revolt against Yazid, the second Umayyad caliph. He first planned a pilgrimage to Mecca, stopping en route in Kufa to discuss plans with his supporters. But word of his movements had reached the worldly and ambitious Yazid, and the advance of his caravan – followers, guards, and family, numbering seventy-two in all – was checked at Kerbala in Iraq. Then it was attacked.

Deserted by his Kufan allies, Hussein chose nonetheless to fight, knowing the certainty of defeat. His defiance against all odds informs the core of Shi'a psychology, and the tragedy of his martyrdom is commemorated to this day by Shi'a everywhere. 'He died to save his people, the Shi'a,' chant the mourners every year in the month of Moharram, remembering the burning afternoon on which Yazid's troops, ignoring their pleas for mercy, slaughtered even the women and children of Hussein's caravan, and finally the Imam himself.

Yet it is wrong to call Shi'ism a sect. Not only is its influence too vast, but on fundamental matters of doctrine it is not different from Sunnism, and in this sense belongs to the orthodox community of the faith. The dispute between Islam's two main bodies is nowhere near on a par with the schism between the Eastern and Western Church, and nothing in the division approaches the magnitude of such bitterly disputed theological conundrums as the nature of Christ or the Virgin, the filioque, Purgatory, or infallibility; it more resembles the divide between Anglicans and Methodists or, even more approximately, Russian and Greek Orthodox Churches.

In fact, the separation can be said to have borne unexpected and far-reaching intellectual fruits. After the occultation of the final imam, followers of Twelver Shi'ism – lacking an earthly heir – were largely diverted from politics towards religious and scholarly goals. Most of Islam's early educational institutions came to life under Shi'ite tutelage, and in both art and science it was Shi'ite scholars who were to be found at the intellectual vanguard of the era. During the tenth and eleventh centuries, when the disciplines from non-Islamic sources became available in Arabic for the first time, they were given a much warmer reception in Shi'ite circles than in their Sunni equivalents, where interest lay more in the orthodox pursuits of religious law, Hadith, jurisprudence, literature, and theology.

Perhaps a predisposition for the esoteric, as well as sustained periods of persecution and seclusion in the lives of its leading thinkers, had given Shi'ism a stronger intellectual stomach and a greater power of assimilation of ideas initially beyond the Islamic pale. It ingested entire philosophies, Hermetic, Pythagorean, and Aristotelian, as well as more arcane Alexandrian and Chaldaean traditions, metabolizing them, as it were, in accordance with its own psychological and spiritual needs. The process is one of the least known in Islamic history; but the results are manifest in such extraordinary documents as the encyclopaedic corpus of the Ikhwān al-Safa', or Brethren of Purity, whose treatises are saturated with neo-Pythagorean and Hermetic lore. In a particularly fertile marriage with Sufism, this philosophical–religious heritage blossoms anew in the visionary metaphysics of the twelfth-century mystic Sohrawardi, and is again reborn in the Safavid era with the Illuminationist teachings of Mulla Sadra and Mir Damad.

In the transmission (and subsequent legitimization) of this sapiential legacy, the role of Ali is again crucial. It is through the conduit of the first Imam that the Hermetic dimension enters into later Shi'ite thought and, like the life-giving channels that nourish the different quarters of the beloved Persian garden, flows into the adjoining oases of theology, metaphysics, and Sufism. It is through Ali, too, that the majority of Sufi orders – including those of the Sunni world – trace their lineage to the Prophet.

'*Ya Ali!*' How often I heard the name! It is uttered at the outset of countless undertakings, as a benediction on parting from company and, often with a deep sigh, as a self-fortifying invocation. The sanctity of the first Imam permeates the fabric of all the Shi'a world. He is both warrior and master of chivalry, champion of the poor, compassionate towards his enemies, and exemplar of both worldly and spiritual virtue – attributes which both glorify and redouble the iniquity of his demise. And it is this tragic hue, along with the semi-divine status of the imams and the theological paradox of the occultation, which loosens Shi'ism from the more pragmatic spiritual atmosphere of Sunni Islam and, I think, imparts to it a quality more akin to the bathos and mystery of the Christian Passion; the tragedy of Ali's murder and that of Hussein and his family; the generations of persecution by cruel and worldly rulers; the suggestion of a secret tradition imparted to a spiritual (and, implicitly, rightly guided) elite, as well as the promise of an Awaited One – all contribute to the personal intensity with which Ali is venerated throughout the Shi'ite world.

His Christ-like portrait – the very iconography of which suggests a syncretic inheritance – is everywhere in Iran. His face is dark and handsome and unlined, his beard is full and flows gracefully around unsmiling lips. A blazing nimbus radiates from behind his saintly head, which is wrapped in swirling folds of deep green, the colour of Islam and its saints; sometimes in larger portraits his whole body is enveloped by a supernal glow. But doom-filled shadows haunt his serene features and more often than not, tears brim in the seraphical eyes, which are turned heavenward with an almost reproachful gaze, and the whole tragic story seems to be compressed darkly behind them. The effect is almost gaudy; but the message is unmistakable: that of a man bearing, as only a saintly warrior can, the full burden of a wronging of cosmic proportions.

Φ

I saw Khalil again the following evening. After we had eaten and smoked a water pipe together, he asked whether I'd like to go somewhere — always this inexactitude! — so we left the restaurant and hailed a taxi outside. Khalil handed forward to the driver a cassette he had brought; it was the same music that had been playing inside, which I'd said I liked. Then the other side played; the sad and ancient-sounding strains of a violin-like *tar*, over which a young woman was reciting poetry in a voice of passionate melancholy. To these bewitching melodies we wound through the streets until, on the outskirts of the city, the car pulled up at the entrance to what looked like a park.

Walking up a winding flight of wide cobbled steps, we emerged at the edge of a lake bordered by poplar and willow trees. The lake was artificial; not excavated, but built by raising the level of the surrounding land. As we reached it I realized I recognized it from an old photograph, but hadn't known it was in Tabriz. I had often wondered about it. It was originally remote from the city, but now we could see the street lights glittering beyond the trees for miles. No one quite knows when it was built (it is probably eighteenth-century); it is the last of a number of famous gardens which once existed around Tabriz. The effect of the raised terraces which enclose the lake is to make it float above the landscape. We paced round it, our breath luminous in the freezing air; it was two hundred yards square, nearly ten acres in area, and a pedestrian causeway led to a two-storeyed pavilion in the centre. It was closing time, but the owner let us wander about, saying it was the most popular place in the area for wedding parties.

It was late and bitterly cold but we were far from alone. Whole families were gathered at tables among the trees, and a couple of samovars were puffing at kiosks selling tea and snacks. A few couples, arm in arm, passed us in the opposite direction as we walked, and Khalil mentioned how much he'd like to get married. He didn't want a wife to be approved for him by his family, he said; that was the traditional way, and fine for most people. But it led, he went on, to a problematic division which he had no wish to emulate: the distinction, among men, between wife and woman, and led in turn to dishonesties he wasn't prepared to engage in. Too many men looked on their wives solely as the means to family life – and honoured them as such – but looked to other women for intimacy of a different kind. This wasn't a moral dilemma, he said; it was normal for Iranian men, on account of the constraints of the culture. But it wasn't for him.

A private scepticism made me wonder whether he were leading up to a proposition: could I get him to England, where he would have a better chance of meeting English women? I had no right to discourage him; it was impossible to predict where he might find happiness. But the issue, like so many others close to the irresistible theme of freedom, threw into sudden relief the axioms of my own culture, and I was reminded not only of the privileges but also of the complex burdens that adhered to the liberties of home. I thought of the accompanying slings and arrows of outrageous freedoms, ex-wives, and the bewildering and largely illusory choices of daily life, and wondered how such a pure-hearted man would fare in the jungle called the West. So I said, cryptically, that every freedom brings with it a corresponding hazard, and to my surprise he nodded gravely. I had underestimated him. He had long ago worked through and discarded the faulty logic by which the West was set all aglitter by the promise of infinite liberty. It was a common mistake, to imagine that the freedoms of the elsewhere would bring happiness; a weakness, he said, of his own culture.

I was very pleased to have struck this common ground together, and for the first time was able to explain the conflict I experienced almost daily when, in the act of dampening one of his countrymen's enthusiasm for living in the West, I was discomfited by my own presumptuousness. He chuckled, and said he understood exactly what I meant; he had the same problem with his own friends.

As we walked back towards the road, he asked whether I still wanted to visit a *zurkhaneh*. I said I did, so we took a taxi back into the city and a few minutes later Khalil was ushering me into a building like a rural sports club. In a central hall, some men were gathering; we were just in time, said Khalil, and hurriedly introduced me to one or two of them. Then he explained what I should ask the taxi driver when I wanted to return to my hotel and, extracting a promise that I would visit him the next day, left me there.

Zurkhaneh means house of strength or force, and all over the country similar gatherings were underway at that same moment. The origins of the institution are almost certainly pre-Islamic, though today the *zurkhaneh* is akin to a national guild which emulates the martial traditions of the warrior-knights of Shi'ite Islam, whose champion is Ali. The *zurkhaneh* is a place of moral as well as physical endeavour; competitions are held between the *pahlevans*, champions, of different towns, and the ritualized training is open to spectators. But the visible aspect is unmistakably physical.

There was a line of chairs against one wall, where I took my place next to a silvery-haired bank manager. An injury, he said, had prevented him from participating that evening, and he rubbed his knee with a theatrical wince. Nearby us was a raised kiosk into which a bulky-looking man was climbing with a big drum. He saluted me with a grin and looked down on us as he shifted the drum onto his lap and began tapping at a microphone. His little chamber was decorated with framed photographs, calligraphic banners, and plastic flowers, above which hung a large portrait of the haloed Imam Ali. A bell shaped like an inverted pudding-bowl hung near his head, which when struck made me think of last orders in an English pub, only it was louder.

'Look,' said my neighbour with a nudge, 'here come the *pahlevan*.' Twenty barefooted men from the age of twelve to about seventy, wearing club T-shirts and breeches, some leather and richly embroidered, hopped in turn into the octagonal pit in the centre of the hall. It was three feet deep and thirty across; the men spread out across the space and began to flex, and from the

179

kiosk there was a ceremonial invocation of blessings on the house of the Prophet, Ali, the assembled members, and (I realized, hearing the word Inglestan) guests too.

The bell struck loudly; the drum began a rousing rhythm and the much-amplified voice of the one-man orchestra began to chant poetry over the beat; simultaneously, arms and legs began to stretch in a two-thousand-year-old ritual workout. There was much twisting and flexing of trunks, all in unison and to the rhythm of the drum; a gesture like the drawing of a bow, and a knee-to-chest routine, leg-stretching and swooping press-ups – I knew how quickly these left most men gasping – in a routine which lasted half an hour. Claps, shouts, yells, prayers, and chants punctuated the changing tempos of drum and bell. Then there was a pause, as each man picked up a pair of clubs made of wood like giant skittles. To a new rhythm they swung them at varying rates over their shoulders; though there were only inches between the forty whirling clubs, there were no collisions, nor any sign of overt effort. The youngest wielded clubs almost as wide as their own torsos. Yet they didn't look like obvious athletes. The man nearest to me, who was swinging two tree-trunk-sized clubs over his shoulders, was short and bow-legged and a quivering cornice of flesh overhung his belt. His white hair had slipped from its natural position to the sides of his head, and his left eye looked like the white of an egg. But his strength was obviously enormous and I pictured an unwitting mugger being picked up and tossed effortlessly into the gutter with a 'Ya Ali!' . . .

After the clubs had been lowered to the ground, the men took it in turn to whirl for several minutes, clockwise and anti-clockwise, on place in the centre of the pit and in circles around its perimeter. The rhythm of the drum adapted to the individual's pace; shouts and claps went up as the turning grew to a climax and face and arms became a blur. Most of these human gyro-scopes stopped dead on the final beat; a few of the older men tottered, swiftly supported by the outstretched arms of their companions. Then the strongest among them took a metal bow strung with heavy metal links and noisy iron discs and swung it rhythmically above their heads until the point of near-collapse; and then the ceremony drew to an end. The men melted unceremoniously away, and soon I was in a dark street looking for a taxi with the sound of the *zurkhaneh* bell still ringing my ears.

The next day, Khalil did his best to try and persuade me stay in Tabriz: there was much more to see and do, he said, and if I needed a place to stay ... but I had to move on, and he could see I meant it.* I told him there was a shrine I wanted to visit in nearby Shabestar, then to go to Orumiyeh on the shore of Iran's largest lake, and then round my way into Kurdistan, where a friend of Louise's I had made in Tehran had said he would meet

---

* Among the sites I missed was the museum dedicated to the struggle of the Constitutionalists, who were so brutally put down in the city in 1911. Tabriz played an important part in the history of the Constitutional Revolution and I feel sad to be unable to do justice to the tragic story of Howard Baskerville, the American who, in a refreshing reversal by today's measure, fought so bravely on the side of the underdogs. He makes a romantic appearance in Amin Ma'alouf's acclaimed novel, *Samarqand*. His grave is in Tabriz. Another American dedicated to assisting the Iran of the era was Morgan Shuster, a New York banker retained by Parliament to reform the country's financial system. His poignant memoir, *The Strangling of Persia*, describes the collapse of his hopes under British and Russian pressure and Iranian corruption.

me. We swapped gifts. He gave me a small blue *tasbeh* I had earlier admired and the cassette we had listened to in the car; I gave him a illustrated translation into Persian of *The Prophet* by his namesake, Khalil Gibran.* He gave a flurry of commands to his staff, and a few minutes later some fresh bread appeared, still warm, from a nearby baker; someone else brought a packet of soft cheese from the kitchen, and a boy returned with a bag of little cakes and a jar of honey on the comb. Another had gone outside to flag down a taxi for me. I would miss Khalil's calm and sensitivity and was sad to be leaving. His dark eyes met mine for the last time. 'You and I speak the same language,' he said. 'That's all that matters.' And then I was hurrying to the waiting car.

Φ

As I moved north, veils of poverty seemed to thicken over the route. The buses grew more dilapidated, the roadside restaurants more run-down, the passengers less friendly, and their manners marked by the sullen introspection of continual hardship. The very landscape looked increasingly bereft, and I felt quite homesick for the friends I had made in Tabriz. Narrowing roads pushed through the planetary bleakness. There were frequent military compounds on hilltops and passes – usually a single crenellated watchtower with gun-slits, enclosed in a quadrangle of rusty barbed wire – and checkpoints like frontier posts on the outskirts of towns. Here, among the carcasses of abandoned cars or derelict warehouses, the driver would disappear to have his

---

* Though his name is spelled Kahlil in Western versions of his works. I owe the story of this confusion to Cecil Hourani, who tells me that the author's name was misspelled by an American editor of *The Prophet* but that Gibran himself made no effort to correct the error. Kahlil stuck (though it means nothing in Arabic), and the misnamed Gibran went on to become the world's best-selling author of all time. He is most often thought of as the best-known Muslim author in the West, though he was in fact a Lebanese Christian, and lived most of his adult life in New York City.

documents checked; occasionally an armed soldier would board the bus and throw a brutish glance up and down the aisle.

I was circling the giant silver-grey expanse of Lake Orumiyeh, and soon moving south again on the strip of land between the lake and the nearby borders of first Turkey, then Iraq. Several times I arrived in towns late at night at a featureless crossroads, and would ask from the driver: 'Is this the bus stop? Is this the town of——?' My familiarity with the language worked against me here. I knew enough not to be taken for a foreigner, but my behaviour was not as confident as a local and the impression I gave was, I think, one of inexplicable slow-wittedness. My look of bewilderment would evoke an impatient grunt and a nod in the direction of the darkness. A few other passengers would hurry towards predatory taxis or scatter purposefully into the shadows; I would shoulder my bag and begin a long walk in the direction of what I hoped was the town centre.

Φ

Sanandaj, the capital of Kurdistan province, was not an obvious destination. The look of suspicion from the hotel manager – it was midnight again – seemed to tell the whole story. A friend I had made in Tehran had enchanted me with tales of hunting on horseback in the mountains near the Iraqi border, of a wilderness utterly untainted by modernity and scarcely visited by outsiders. These were springtime stories, and it was winter now, the month of Ramadan and of the daytime fast. But flushed with the excitement of having at last arrived, I telephoned him from the hotel, half-imagining he would appear a few minutes later. I had allowed myself, again, to forget the conventions of modern manners, and cursed my own naivety when a sleepy voice at the other end of the line said he would see me in the morning.

Things gathered pace. Early the next day a man I'd never met was asking for me in the lobby, and said he had come in place of our mutual friend. His car was waiting. He was about my age, stockily built with short jet-black hair and a neatly trimmed moustache, and wore big, baggy Kurdish trousers. He didn't smile much, and I wondered if he might be a secret policeman; but his eyes, large and clear like a boy's, suggested against it. I settled the bill and we drove through the town and along a winding road that skirted the western suburbs. The road began to climb and we followed it upwards to a public park on a high ridge which overlooked the town. He pulled up where we had the best view and after the engine had been silent for a few minutes, said: 'I'm Majid, Reza's friend. He's sorry he couldn't come.' We talked for a few minutes, then he reached into a compartment between the seats and took out a packet of cigarettes. He held it experimentally towards me.

'You don't fast,' I observed. The fast of Ramadan prescribes that nothing pass the lips from dawn to dusk, and I had been wondering how strictly it was observed in Iran. In many countries of the Islamic world, a sort of hibernatory sloth falls over the population for the month, as the diversions of ordinary life are subsumed into the daily struggle of restraint.* The physical benefits of fasting are well known; but the process of inner resolve, which brings to each hour both a burden and a purification, is more difficult to chart from the outside.

'My opinion,' said Majid, 'is that if you can't fast properly, you shouldn't fast at all.'

I agreed with this logic. It was the very reason I had already decided not to fast; to do so would have been a hollow and imitative gesture, and to fast is as much an interior undertaking as an outer one. But he expressed my thoughts before I could speak.

'What's fasting, anyway?' He took a cigarette from the packet, glanced furtively from the windows, then put it to his lips. 'Fasting is not speaking ill of people, not thinking bad thoughts, and not acting wrongly – not just not eating.' I agreed. 'But look at what people do. The first thing in their minds when they get

---

* Travellers, pregnant women, and the elderly are exempted.

184

up is a complaint. The moment they get to work, they have to lie and cheat just to scrape by. Fasting! What kind of fasting is that? Nobody fasts.'

'It should be a matter of choice,' I said.

'Like everything in religion, yes – a choice. What's the value of a choice if it isn't made freely?' He unwound the window a little and tapped the ash against the glass. 'We had that kind of freedom,' he said broodily, 'back then. It wasn't like your country, I know – but at least a grown man could have a drink if he wanted, and women could walk about without looking like crows.'

I was surprised and delighted by his frankness; yet the moment I registered these feelings, it occurred to me again that perhaps my new companion had been sent to probe my reactions, and to elicit some subversive agenda of my own. Perhaps he was an informer, and our next port of call would be the local police station, where my deportation would be initiated ... the unexpected encounter, the casual conversation, the admissions given in confidence over a friendly drink, perhaps only a cigarette ... I thought for a moment of the circumstances of our meeting; and was privately surprised to register in my own system the presence of that dark background sense of alarm which, once seeded under more perilous circumstances, is never wholly uprooted or assuaged. Then I dismissed the suspicion: I knew I already trusted Majid. Nothing in his demeanour betrayed the scent of duplicity; we were simply exploring the territory of each other's values. But to be quite sure, I let him do the talking.

He delivered his thoughts on a string of gloomy, if faintly didactic, grievances which were by now familiar themes to me; the economy had been ruined by corruption; there were no opportunities even for those who were qualified; religion had been manipulated to political ends by the authorities, who had kept none of their promises but made themselves rich; people everywhere were in a state of apathy, a condition exacerbated by the twin evils of poverty and drugs.

'So what's the solution?' I asked, 'What can people do?'

'Nothing,' he said, 'there isn't a solution. How can people do anything when their first thought is for food?' He stubbed out his cigarette, glanced around, and threw it from the window. Then a wide grin flashed from his face and he sighed deeply, as if having shed himself of a weighty load. He revved the engine defiantly.

'Shall we go?'

I felt as though we'd known each other for a long time. His mood lightened, and the conversation turned to lesser things. As we wound down into the town, he called Reza from his mobile phone and agreed to meet him at his home. We picked him up and he apologized profusely for not having been able to meet me, claiming family obligations, and we began to plan the next few days together. Our first stop was the home of another friend; a large and dilapidated series of buildings a century old, built around a large cruciform pool overhung by tall walnut and plane trees. The owner's father had been a wealthy Kurdish landowner, whose home and land had been confiscated during the tumult of the Shah's land reforms in the 1970s. At last his son had been able to buy it back, and had begun the long process of restoration. We walked around the leafy quadrangle, where the owner took pebbles and threw them into a great walnut tree overhead, gathered the fallen nuts and cracked them in his palm. A staff of twenty had once run the place, he said, and we inspected the stables and the kitchens and what had once been the family hammam where a pool still bubbled up through a melon-shaped marble nozzle.

On the second storey, supported by slender wooden columns encased in plaster with stalactitic capitals, we were served tea and raisins and walnuts from the garden; the owner cheerfully abstained. I said I had seen, in a neighbouring storeroom, a pair of clubs and shields like those used in the *zurkhaneh*, and wondered if I could look at them. The others confirmed that their friend was a great sportsman, and goaded him into a brief demonstration. He twirled the clubs solemnly, his body as straight as a tree and the veins on his arms swelling across ridges of stony muscle. Then he lay on the floor, picked up two heavy wooden shields made of walnut and began flexing and extending each arm in turn and with great intensity until we begged him to stop. Watching him it was possible to see what an ingeniously simple exercise had been bequeathed by the tradition; arms, chest, legs, and abdomen all received a thorough conditioning. But it was the clubs that interested me. As I half-hoped, half-feared, the owner offered them to me to try. They were smaller than the ones I had seen in Tabriz being whirled around the heads of teenage boys, but as I took hold of them, they sank to the ground like lead. I needed both hands just to lift one; and to swing it over my shoulder was impossible. Under the weight of the shields, I was unable to straighten my arm even once. The others chuckled good-naturedly at my performance.*

Φ

We drove later to a second house near the centre of town, another grand residence from the Qajar era, this time being restored as a museum. A team of men – all on empty stomachs, it occurred to me – was labouring with bricks and cement around a similar central pool and a garden enclosed by characteristically slender columns supporting both pointed and semicircular arches. Inside, the rooms were decorated with ornate floral plasterwork and mirrors and fireplaces and cornices wreathed in blossoming vines, all echoing an antique love of eye-teasing designs. The windows of the upper storeys were kaleidoscopic lattices of stained glass. In an uppermost chamber I clambered up a scaffold and met a plasterer applying the finishing touches to a domed ceiling, from which dangled a complex of shadowy vertices. Thin pencil lines traced the outlines of intersecting rhombuses and triangles; these, explained their plaster-flecked

---

*   This awoke a defiant streak and much later I acquired my own set of clubs and got quite good at twirling them myself. But with each club weighing only twenty pounds I remain, by *zurkhaneh* standards, in the featherweight class.

designer as he smoothed an edge with a finger, would eventually be painted.

This type of ceiling was based on the shape called the *muqarnas*, an enigmatic architectural creation that, perhaps more than any other, tells of a particularly Persian preoccupation with geometry and precision. I looked at it for a long time. The *muqarnas* is special, if hard to describe. It is generally agreed to have appeared in Seljuk Iran in the tenth century, becoming to the Islamic world as universal as the Corinthian order to antiquity. Its precursor is the squinch; the *muqarnas* is really a type of vault made up of lots of tiny squinches or niches – quarter domes with curving roofs. Their apices hang outwards into space, and form the base of the meeting point of the two niches above; built up in cell-like tiers, they rise towards the apex of the greater vault. But the genius of the form lies in its adaptability; being three-dimensional, it can fill a whole variety of spaces. *Muqarnas* can hang from a dome – like the one I was looking at – or wrap around a minaret, or fill the curve of a right-angled niche, or form an almost flat frieze. The different surfaces can be straight or curved, and linked by intervening elements of different shapes; the individual niches can be matchbox-sized or as big as a house, and executed in a vast variety of media.

The finest examples are staggeringly sophisticated; it is difficult to fathom how the cataract-like volumes could be transformed from two dimensions into three, and just how the interlocking modules were originally calculated is not really understood by modern architecture. In translucent stone, the *muqarnas* ceiling comes to resemble a hovering mass of geometricized cloud; in multicoloured mosaic faience, the deep blue arching tiers loom like gravity-defying waves. Elsewhere they can look like honeycombs or waterfalls, in which light and shadow joust and multiply in infinite gradations.

The images of some of the lovelier examples of these had been stamped in my mind's eye ever since I had been to Isfahan. But it was only now that I began to wonder what natural prototype could have possibly served for their inspiration. The closest natural phenomenon is the stalactite – the usual translation for the word *muqarnas* – but the resemblance is very approximate, and no cave has either the smooth curves of the *muqarnas* niche or the very geometric configuration of niches piled up on each other. Or so I thought.

I chatted with the plasterer for a few minutes, and said how impressed I was with the ongoing restoration. At the mention of my interest in architecture, he fixed me with a look of concern. Had I noticed the transitions between the different spaces? he asked. Yes, I said: passages and twisting corridors, though I hadn't thought more about them. They, he explained, were all designed to introduce an element of *timing* to the overall building. All spaces were made meaningful by what preceded and followed them; all the most important architecture of Iran incorporated this principle and I would never understand Persian architecture if I didn't understand it. I was grateful for this nugget of knowledge and wished we could have talked more, but the others were waving to me from below. I thanked him and he wrote down his address in Isfahan.

'What was all that about?' asked Reza when I had scrambled back down to the garden where they were waiting for me. I said one of the workmen had been telling me about architecture.

'Don't you believe it, he said. 'All he wants is a mention in your book. Let's get some lunch.'

A grand meal had been prepared for us by Reza's aunt, who lived nearby. A second aunt and several nephews and nieces were already gathered, and we all exchanged greetings and then tucked into great helpings of lasagne. His aunt, who had prepared the meal and waited on us throughout, observed the fast, as did his grandmother too, who sat nearby in silence passing the beads of a rosary between her fingers. Afterwards the women disappeared into the kitchen, and the men lounged and smoked. Reza's uncle, hearing I had been to Afghanistan, asked me whether I thought the long war against the Soviets had solved anything; I said that in general I thought it was much easier to wage war than to solve the challenges of peace, and that on both sides it created widows and orphans. He nodded with a sad smile. 'And Khomeini,' he said with quiet irony, 'told us that war is a blessing.'

He had the kindly, old-world courtesy and learning of an earlier generation. We played backgammon together. He looked up from the pieces from time to time to tell me that he was retired now, but had been a professor of sociology in the time of the Shah. They were good times, he mused with a sad grin, adding, 'Not perfect, but good.' He asked if I had a favourite Persian poet, and I said I thought Hafez was the greatest of them, remembering a couplet:

> *Salha del talab-e Jam-e Jam az ma mikard*
> *Va an che khod dasht zi bigane ta'na mikard*
>
> For years my heart sought out the Cup of Jamshid*
> Asking from strangers what it already had.

He smiled and, without a pause, recited the couplet that follows it:

> *Gohari ra ke beparvard besa dar hame omr*
> *Talab az gomshodegan-e lab-e darya mikard*
>
> Searching from the lost ones of the sea's edge
> For the pearl beyond the shell of time and space

Then, swept up in the momentum of the poem, he went on to the end:

> *Faiz-e ruh-al quds ar baz madad farmaid*
> *Digaran ham bekonand an che masiha mikard.*
>
> Were the Holy Spirit to extend its grace again
> Others might perform the miracles of Jesus.

'You know a little about our leaders?' he asked between the fall of dice. 'They are divided between the medieval and the modern.'

Feeling oddly guilty as I said so, I told him I thought it was

---

* The mythical cup in which all wisdom is contained; gnosis, in other words, or spiritual vision.

inevitable that the reformists would win in the end because Iran had a young population who hated the reputation that the regime had given their country. Reza pulled up a chair to watch the game. 'It is the saddest thing,' said the uncle thoughtfully, 'that they have given religion a bad name.'

'Religion and politics should be separate, the way they are in Europe,' said Reza.

'But that took us nearly two thousand years.'

'Exactly; it has to happen at the right speed. It'll happen, but not from the outside. That's what the Americans never understand.'

'Look at the Shah,' nodded the uncle, 'he went too fast. But these mullas . . .' he shook his head again, 'very sad.'

'Iranians are waiting for a strong dictator to get rid of the lot of them,' said Reza.

'And thus we wait,' said the uncle, looking up from the board with his sad smile. He had beaten me by a single piece.

Φ

Another relative, of Majid's this time, was having a party of sorts in the evening. There were about fifty people of all ages; endless kissing and hugging as we went inside suggested they were all related. I have forgotten what the occasion was. We sat on cushions around a long tablecloth spread over the carpet. Next to me was a pale and slender man in his twenties. He had thick glasses and staring eyes and an air of incorrigible sincerity. He was an English teacher, he explained, at the city's university, and asked what Persian books I had read when I had been studying the language.

'I read *The Blind Owl* by Sadeq Hedayat, and Jamalzade's *Yeki bud, Yeki nabud*.' The former was a novel of complex symbolism, the latter a quartet of deeply satirical socio-political essays.

He frowned a little, and thought intently for a moment.

'I think even Iranian peoples cannot understand these books.'

This was a comfort; they had not been easy at the time.

'And you,' I asked, wondering what their literary equivalents might be, 'what are the texts of English literature that you studied?

'*The Enchanted Castle,*' he said, 'and *Rebecca.*'

I had never heard of them, but didn't tell him.

'And what Persian books, I asked, would you recommend me to read, to increase my understanding of your language?'

He thought again, then looked up.

'I think that the best books,' he said 'are translations of English books.'

Majid broke out the whisky as soon as we were home. Commanding me to sit, he threw two big cushions on the carpet of the main room and brought in a tray of baby cucumbers, pickles, and pistachios. His two children played quietly in their room, and his wife sat cross-legged on the floor in an open space near the kitchen. She was a gentle, plump woman, shelling walnuts in silence and looking over to us from time to time with a kindly smile. Then came a bowl of ice cubes and a bottle, smuggled, said Majid, from across the nearby border from Iraq. The label carried a picture of a kilted piper; it was called Scotch Guard and celebrated the heroism of a fictitious regiment. It was horrible stuff, tasted like caramelized paraffin, and bore only the faintest resemblance to the real thing. We drank it with great relish.

A cavernous television was meanwhile brought to life, and for an hour we watched a recording of a musical show called *American Divas* in which four women took turns to wail soullessly to an enraptured Hollywood crowd; then an episode on a national channel about an undercover police unit, in which the heroine, a chador-clad female detective, dived spectacularly through windows, jumped out of helicopters, and shot at fleeing criminals; then a painfully slow hour of home movies. At some point I looked up and saw that Majid's wife was gone. A little later, four hours after our arrival, the demon television was finally silenced; and then we slept.

Reza joined us the next morning. They had decided on a journey for me: a drive along the mountainous border with Iraq, stopping en route at points of interest. The day was sunny and mild. We packed a picnic of fruit and biscuits and a big Thermos of tea, and set off in the direction of some recently discovered caves which they had never seen. The route snaked along broad valleys between sweeping yellowing hillsides and was very beautiful; much more so, the others sighed, in spring. To our west, a range of higher mountains began to loom and dodge between the summits of the intervening slopes.

An hour's drive brought us to the site of the caves, where a kiosk and a parking lot were being built. Here, went the story, a few years earlier, a shepherd searching for a lost sheep had discovered the partially blocked entrance to a cave, from which a spring appeared to flow. But the spring was an underground river; it led into the heart of the hillside, and he had followed it inside. A mile underground, he had discovered a fabulous hoard of Sasanian treasure: gold and silver coins and cups, weapons, and jewels. The army had come soon afterwards in a convoy of trucks, and over the course of several days, hauled the entire cache away. But none of it had reached the National Museum, and it had never been heard of since.

This brought up almost identical stories from both Majid and Reza, which they related at length and with deep conviction. I had heard others like them, and would hear many more. The very imagery of these tales bordered on the mythical, and I was always sceptical of them; they seemed to transmit an almost genetic preoccupation with the theme of theft, and their similarity suggested little more than a projection of a people disillusioned by the unscrupulousness of their leaders. But a year later I raised the topic with an art dealer in London, who confessed that for decades he had been offered an almost continual stream of treasures of inestimable beauty and value, all from Iran: gold armour from the era of the Achaemenids, Sasanian statuary, and priceless Islamic jewellery and ceramics, all of it too fabulous to sell openly and, having left its homeland, unlikely ever to return and even less likely to find its way to any museum.

Talk of treasure enlivened our visit. We bought tickets and headed in, and for nearly half a mile followed a dank path enclosed by bubonic stone embankments and globular columns of ochreous and gleaming minerals. At intervals the walls and ceiling would unexpectedly recede into cathedral-sized galleries of outlandish shapes; vast banks of melting organ pipes and frozen waterfalls of stone. A million stalactites dangled overhead like leprous chimes, the largest of them fusing with their likenesses below in embraces of unreckonable slowness. I had never seen such beautiful caves; but their beauty was perverse, and the shapes and contours of the light-filled world we had left behind seemed all the more beneficent against their freakish subterranean counterparts. Perhaps the action of light itself calls forth a greater harmony from the raw materials of the earth; perhaps nature requires a witness, and gives up beauty in return. We were a little relieved when the path came to end and was blocked by a wire barrier, though it went for miles, the others said. The implication was obvious: more treasure had been discovered further along, and they were probably bagging it up at that very moment.

Φ

We drove on through diminishing settlements whose main streets narrowed as we drove deeper into the hills. Soon the road lost its smooth surface and at times our way was blocked by herds of dusty sheep. In the hillside villages, concrete began to give way to adobe, and men wore chequered headscarves and pleated black trousers held with brightly coloured sashes.

Reza and Majid chatted in Kurdish together, sang for a while, and cracked jokes like a pair of schoolboys. They were a perfect comic duo: Reza was tall and gangly and had an air of melancholy about him; Majid was small, impulsive, and mischievously sharp-witted. They bickered affectionately and contradicted one another's questions to me, each claiming superior insight into my background and wishes. They were hungry too for knowledge of the society to which I belonged, especially with regard to money, immigration, and relations between the sexes; on these they were as ill informed as most Westerners about the Islamic world, and I told them so. Gradually, and tenderly, they began to defer to me for my opinion on everything – on the distance ahead, on the best foods for one's health, on weather patterns and the shapes of rocks, and how to deal with difficulties of various kinds – as though, like some strangely gifted alien, I might resolve the dilemmas of their own world. I was uncomfortable at having been invested with this spurious authority, but felt repeatedly touched by their humility.

'It's very strange,' said Reza, with a mixture of sadness and delight, after we had been talking for a while. 'I thought Westerners were only interested in things like money and science...'

There were a few checkpoints along the way: cigarettes were extinguished, the food was covered up, and, brushing crumbs from moustaches, the two of them assumed a solemn air. But as soon as we had passed, the jokes, and the cigarettes, would be renewed. They had been stopped in their student days at just such a checkpoint; Reza told the story. The military were full of revolutionary zeal, and it was a bad time to be caught drinking – which they had been. A high-ranking officer ('a big, arrogant son-of-a-bitch – you know the kind I mean?') had lowered himself to the driver's window and demanded Majid to breathe in his face. Majid, seeing a fellow student being manhandled by a pair of soldiers nearby and deciding it was no time to get caught, stuck his tongue out and blew loudly through his lips. The dumb-founded officer staggered backwards as they roared away.

Hadn't anyone chased them? Of course not, they replied. Only the son of an important mulla would have dared to defy a military officer; so they had never dreamed of pursuing them. It was all a matter of nerve and bluff. But they'd both been to prison at different times; it was the standard fare of the era, and I was reminded of Louise's claim that unless one had been to prison in Iran, one was nobody...

Φ

As night fell we reached Paveh, a small town where the homes clung the slopes of a ravine cut by a swiftly flowing river. Some more of Reza's relatives lived here in a recently built house at the foot of a steep hillside. The newer homes, explained the owner, were built of concrete and were more expensive to heat in winter and got too hot in summer. But the traditional homes had been full of poisonous snakes, which lived in the roofs and cellars. I asked if people were bitten. Not very often, he said matter-of-factly; they knew each other's ways, and unruly snakes were warded off with spells until they behaved.

Platters of fragrant saffron rice and meat stews cooked with apricots came steaming from the kitchen, followed by sweet rice pudding, pomegranate seeds, and nuts. We were drinking tea when two more friends arrived. One had brought a bag of seeds from which, during the war when flour was in short supply, the villagers would bake a bitter bread. The other had been a commando during the war with Iraq and lived and fought in the surrounding mountains. He explained that the same seed, mixed with walnuts and wild mulberries, was used to make an appetite-suppressing paste. His men, he said, would eat nothing more than a handful of the mixture for the entire day without suffering from hunger.

We watched the news on a Kurdish satellite channel from Iraq and, for my benefit, the news in English from the BBC. Our host's wife sat with us throughout; the wide-ranging conversation lasted until after midnight. There was much exchange of news of friends and relatives; I was instructed in how to sit like a khan, propped on a cushion with one's legs outstretched. We talked about the belief in reincarnation of the Ahl-e Haqq; how to gather a natural chewing gum called *peste-ye wakhshi*; the Swiss bank accounts of Rafsanjani; prospects of Kurdish independence in Iraq, and how the Americans had misjudged the extent of resistance to their occupation; the cost of mobile-phone calls; and the output of a sock-machine, recently bought by our host (he showed it to me later). He described a trip to France twenty years earlier, when he had taken his life savings to buy a new Peugeot. He had crashed in Yugoslavia on the way back and been forced to abandon it and hitchhike home.

Φ

Ours was the only vehicle heading north along the border road. A few battered pickup trucks coming in the opposite direction met us head-on, causing some perilous reversing; these were smugglers, explained the others, coming back from Iraq with alcohol and outlawed satellite televisions. In one, lashed with ropes like Ulysses to the mast, was an exhausted-looking donkey. Occasionally a track would fork downwards: these led to the villages below, said Reza, which were in Iraq. The families were intermarried on both sides; they were all Kurds, and the only difference between them was that the Iraqis spoke better Arabic.

We must have been at about seven thousand feet, and climbing steadily. A shifting but more or less quadruple line of more distant ranges had become the backdrop of this spectacular territory. The surrounding upper slopes were nearly bare now, and had turned to parched rock and scrub growing in the vee of gulleys filled with rocky debris. Steep ridges plunged all around towards their intersecting neighbours below, like opposing saw-blades; the floors of these valleys lay beneath our line of sight. In places where the incline was less severe, or where a natural plateau offered a chance of cultivation, there were olive and pistachio orchards and leafless poplar trees and ever-tinier villages clinging beside glittering braids of mountain streams. Many of these remote and tranquil settlements, said Reza, were sanctuaries and gathering places of the Ahl-e Haqq. I wrote down the names of them in the hope of returning one day and exploring the region at what seemed a more meaningful pace – on foot or on horseback – and to learn something of the fraternity whose secretive ways lived on there in such magnificent seclusion. One is cursed repeatedly on a long journey with this kind of yearning. The momentum of travel favours movement and only the most general observations; but at times the fabric of the journey is suddenly stretched, and the daily trickle of experience swells unaccountably into broadening pools in which promising and detailed worlds seems to glitter and beckon ... leaving only intimations and feelings of helplessness.

Gradually the last traces of habitation fell away and the road became a scar bulldozed from the face of the rock, worsening as it rose and at times no more than a narrow ledge of watery scree. We crept upwards; a tide of white cloud began to advance over the slopes, and soon the world below was obscured. The others were disappointed, claiming that in clear weather we could have seen deep into Iraq. Then, as Majid was negotiating a dangerous corner, the clouds lifted in the west.

'Look,' said Reza, 'that's Halabja.'

Several miles in the distance we could make out the little Iraqi town, huddling on a green plain at the base of the mountains. It had been an unextraordinary place until one morning in March 1988. At dawn it had been bombarded first by artillery, and then from the air with poison gas. Several thousand villagers had died horribly, choking as they fled. It was the most notorious event in a long period of persecution; and briefly, it had brought to the world's attention the plight of another people robbed of a homeland by international machinations.

But before this, there had been other, lesser but equally barbarous attacks, which had killed and wounded villagers on both sides of the border. And it wasn't just the villagers who had suffered, said Reza; Halabja had been recently occupied by Iranian forces at the time it was bombed, and hundreds of Iranians had died too in what was locally seen as an Iraqi effort to punish the Kurds for welcoming Iranian troops onto Iraqi soil; the foreign press had never mentioned this detail.

I felt suddenly implicated in this historical web; the very border along which we were driving had been drawn by the British after the end of the First World War, when the fate of the Kurdish population, perhaps the most ancient indigenous people of the region, first began to be shaped by teams of mapmakers four and a half thousand miles away in Whitehall. The 1920 Treaty of Sèvres had anticipated an independent Kurdish state on the dissolution of the Ottoman Empire, but Britain and France, with a little help from the Russians, divided Ottoman Kurdistan between Turkey, Syria, Iran, and Iraq, and ten million Kurds had found themselves straddling the frontiers of four newly demarcated countries. Disputes still arose from time to time as to the exact position of the border; these were solved only when teams were sent to dig up one of the original columns left by British surveyors nearly a century earlier. An argument over their exact positions had brought Iran and Iraq close to war in 1975, and the terrible decade-long conflict that began five years later was sparked over the border further south dividing the Shatt-al Arab.*

A distant band of water, sunk at the foot of yellowing slopes some ten miles distant, indicated the border town of Marivan. We had skirted the border for twenty miles and now began to creep downwards. Two ominous-looking military posts loomed along the descent; Majid and Reza joked about how they would explain the Englishman with his camera and notebook, and I wondered how I might explain maps marked *US Department of Defense*. To our great relief they were both abandoned. It was late afternoon and the town had fallen under a brief spell of golden light. Men were sauntering along the dusty central avenue with the distinctive gait of a people yet to be subdued; they wore tasselled headscarves and the black trousers that ballooned in multiplying pleats around the thigh, and a few had waistcoats of thick cream-coloured felt with shoulders that flared dramatically into space. Long twisted sashes tied these ensembles at the waist and curving daggers abounded. Many of their fathers, under the legendary command of Mustafa Borzani, had fought both the

---

* The waterway dividing Iraqi and Iranian waters in the Persian Gulf, called the Arvand Rūd by the Iranians.

Iraqis and the British in the campaigns of 1932 and 1945, and held up a joint British–Iraqi force in the very gorge through which we passed as we left the town; Reza motioned upwards towards its walls as we drove past.

'*Kar-e Inglisi*,' muttered Majid: the work of the English. But he was grinning.

Φ

The return journey sank into irreverence: partly from the unconscious relief of having left the treacherous mountain road, and partly from the beer that Majid bought illegally at a roadside shack. We drank with the cans wrapped in paper bags, like tramps in Central Park. I asked what the penalty would be if we were caught. We'd all go straight to prison the same evening, they said, and began grumbling (understandably, I felt) at the dangers involved simply to have a drink. It wasn't right that a grown man couldn't have a beer without risking imprisonment, and the prohibition led to more social ills than it prevented. Alcohol, said Majid, was the reason so many Iranians went on holiday to Dubai, where they could drink to excess.

'And do other things,' added Reza, with a nudge.

They had both been to Dubai.

'Remember that Russian woman we met in the hotel?'

'That one! What a slut she was!'

'No she wasn't,' said Majid, ruefully, 'she was very nice.'

'Yes, a nice slut! They all are. That's why they're there in the first place.'

Majid turned his head from the road for a moment and shrugged his shoulders with a mixed look of both mischief and pain.

'The thing is to get so drunk you don't care.'

Yet alcohol was not the traditional intoxicant of choice, and Iranian men unaccustomed to drinking tended to fare badly under its influence. Opium, on the other hand, had much deeper historical roots in the culture, and I couldn't resist asking Majid whether he'd made use of it on such an occasion.

'Oh God,' he said, turning his head towards me with an expression of deadly rapture, 'you wouldn't believe it.'

'Watch the road,' said Reza.

'I met this Arab woman once . . . she wasn't much to look at. Must have been about fifty. I invited her to my room, and we had a smoke together. One thing led to another, and I swear I had the best night of my life. My God, hour after hour, the pleasure! It was like being with an eighteen-year-old girl.' His hand came up form the steering wheel to wipe his brow at the recollection. 'But when I woke up the next morning and looked at her face—!' His features contorted as if he'd sucked on a lemon, and the two of them burst once again into fits of giggles.

But there was something I had to know.

'Forgive me for asking,' I said, 'but aren't you both married?'

There was a little lull, then Reza said, a little sheepishly: 'It's not like that in Europe, is it.'

'Well . . . the general idea is that if you agree to get married, Russian prostitutes aren't usually part of the agreement.'

They understood the virtue of that, they said, and nodded gravely. But it wasn't like that in Iran: it wouldn't work.

'Take Majid, for example,' said Reza earnestly. 'He never knew his wife before he married her. The whole thing was arranged by his relatives. How was anyone to know if they'd be right for one another? But a man like Majid,' his hand suggested a visceral stirring, 'has needs. That's how it is here. He'd never dream of leaving her . . .'

Majid threw me a sideways glance and chuckled. But a few moments later, a look of resignation settled over his face. 'It's hard here on our women,' he said, 'especially having to wear the chador. They can't exercise in public or do sports, and they get depressed – and fat. It's not right. Fat crows! And you know what happens? They start to hate themselves.'

The empty cans were flung from the windows. Reza rummaged in a bag and passed round pomegranates. They were small and red and firm. As I was about to cut one open, Reza stopped me and showed me the preferred technique. He massaged it all over until the seeds under the skin were a pulp, then cupped it with a suggestive flourish to his breast, and pinched the skin at its tip. It burst and sent a jet of crimson juice all over the car. Then he passed it forward to Majid, who sucked at it with lascivious relish until they were both in stitches.

It had been an educative journey, but not quite along the lines I had imagined. I had learned the words for brothel, depression, and addiction, and Majid had learned the English for constipation and diarrhoea. The latter gave him particular delight, and throughout the remainder of the journey he would chant it comically at unexpected moments.

My heart went out to them both; and to their wives. I enjoyed their rebelliousness and impious charm, and they, I think, enjoyed the opportunity of sharing it with an outsider. Once again I felt the familiar tug at the prospect of having to move on again. We dropped off Reza at his home, and headed back to Majid's apartment. When we arrived, his wife was sitting in the same spot, stripping a pile of tarragon leaves from their stalks. They greeted each other tenderly, and the children ran up and wrapped themselves around his knees. Then came the television; and then the whisky.

Φ

It was obvious that both Majid and Reza had adapted and changed their plans to keep me entertained, though they were much too polite to say so. The next day, I told them of my plan to move on alone to Kermanshah, a few hours away, but put in a plea for a final excursion to a site about a hundred miles to our north. This was Takht-e Suleyman, Solomon's Throne. It was less well known than other sites in the area, but its name alone was irresistibly heavy with mystery and conjecture, and I knew I wouldn't get there if I let the chance slip away. It was long way off but we calculated we could make it there and back in a day.

The weather was gloomy and the peaks of the surrounding hills were swallowed in cloud. There was very little traffic. On a deserted road we were flagged down at a checkpoint, where a policeman inspected Majid's documents. One of them was out of date and the policeman issued a token fine; he paid it dutifully with his eyes lowered. It was disturbing to see this habitually cheerful man looking so cowed. But as we pulled away he crunched the receipt into a ball and threw it from the window.

He got fines all the time, he said; they were never too serious. What was serious was the precariousness of the economy. Private initiative was non-existent, and all businesses were at the mercy of government monopolies and the whims of the regime. It hit young men the hardest because they could never save enough money even to get married; this and the strictness of social codes made prostitution rife.

'One thing's cheap here, though,' he mused wickedly. 'You know what?'

I shook my head.

'Death!!'

As we passed through a village, half a dozen women in black chadors scurried across the road ahead of us. 'Look at those crows,' grumbled Majid. 'This place must be paradise for a mulla, but hell for anyone else.'

By the side of a road was a giant sign bearing the portraits of three martyred soldiers and emblazoned with lofty maxims from the writings of the Ayatollah.

'Look at that. More Khomeini-vomit!'

Then, on the open road again, he began to sing gently in a high, mournful key:

> *Dokhtar daram shah nadare*
> *Surati dare mah nadare...*
> *Avaz dare tar nadare*
> *Be hichkas namidam...*
>
> I've got a girl the Shah hasn't got
> She's got a face the moon hasn't got
> She's got a voice the harp hasn't got
> I won't be giving her away
> I won't be giving her away.

And now the landscape was beginning to change, growing more primeval at each mile. We had moved away from the highest peaks and the terrain had opened up, and we could see for miles across long rounded hills like the backs of clustering whales. But from them rose the prehistoric contours of a hundred volcanoes of every size, from the giant pyramidal slopes interrupting the sweep of the horizon to house-sized cones sprouting like tubers from the underworld. The sun was lost. Dense folds of brooding cloud enclosed this antique land, and all was lit by a strange and disconcerting greenish light. Swooping pterodactyls, their wings luminous from the glow of creeping lava-flows, would not have seemed amiss, and we might have seen a family of brontosauruses grazing by the road...

It was a fitting atmosphere for our destination. For centuries, magical associations had hovered about its name. Fifteen hundred years ago the notoriety of Takht-e Suleyman – though it was known as Shiz and Ganzaca at the time – had spread to Europe, and entered medieval romance. Of its earliest history, we know only that the site was inhabited in Achaemenid and Parthian times; before this even, it may have been a Median settlement. What is certain is that to the Sasanians, from the third century onwards, it was home to the most sacred of the dynasty's shrines. Documents record a holy fire burning there continuously for seven hundred years; from it were kindled the flames at lesser temples around the empire. The sanctity of the place can be gauged by the decree that each Sasanian king, following his crowning in Mesopotamian Ctesiphon, make the journey there on foot to complete the process of royal investiture. Byzantine, Roman, and Arab armies had all plundered the fairy-tale settlement; the Mongols chose it for their summer palace. It is not known when or why it was abandoned.

Yet it had once enclosed one of the great buildings of the world: a temple pavilion of mythical extravagance built, some say, to house the portion of the True Cross captured in Jerusalem by King Khosrow II in 618. Its precise architecture is obscure; witnesses report it was built of precious woods – cedar and teak

— and surfaced throughout with gold and silver, of which the very nails were made. The dome, designed to replicate the heavens, was inlaid with lapis lazuli; constellations were mapped in jewels, and the sanctum was enclosed by a gold-embroidered curtain woven with astral hieroglyphs. The entire structure was set on a system of rollers that allowed it to turn like an observatory; there were machines too for the simulation of thunder and lightning, calculated to goad the very skies into a sympathetic response. A meeting-place, in short, between heaven and earth, and a cosmic listening post, tuned to the sacred whispering of the divine syllables. It was doomed by its own notoriety; and in 628, a decade after its construction, it was destroyed by the soldiers of the Byzantine emperor Heraclius.*

Φ

The skies had opened, and we reached the site in pouring rain. We waited in the car for the worst to pass, then, raising our collars to the wind, walked to the outer walls. They were built from imposing blocks of tough grey stone, fifty feet high in places and roughly half a mile in circumference. Thirty-eight crumbling bastions enclose the natural flanks of rock.

We walked in under the main arch, a passage of thirty feet, and entered a circular enclosure several hundred yards across. A solitary caretaker poked his head, mole-like, out of a hut near the entrance, then retreated. We had the place to ourselves. An oval-shaped lake, roughly a hundred yards across, dominated the centre. It was brimming with jade-coloured and oddly luminous water, over which danced an ectoplasmic mist. The crumbling masonry core of a ruined building lay beyond, and from it stretched a network of eroded mounds. We scrambled over them in the drizzle. An ugly warehouse had been thrown up nearby to protect the most recent finds; it was closed but we peeked inside

---

*   So enduring were the rumours of hidden Christian relics that in 1939, German archaeologists recruited to the Nazi cause by Himmler searched there for the Holy Grail.

and saw fragments of stone mouldings and amphora and tables covered in pottery shards. Barely a trace remains of the original surface of the monuments there, though digs have yielded some of the most beautiful Ilkhanid tiles: they are star- and cross-shaped, in turquoise and cobalt and over-painted in gold with dragons and cranes. A stone plaque, inscribed with a complex geometric pattern, was also found here. Its purpose was at first a mystery; now it is thought to be a plan for the *muqarnas* vault of Sultan Abaqa's audience hall.

Majid wandered about, kicking at pebbles and looking bored.

'Where do you think the bathroom was?' he asked. 'I really need it.'

I wanted to see the site from above, and scrambled up the nearby hillside to take a photograph. From a few hundred feet, it looked almost perfectly circular, like the sliced-open base of a volcanic cone. Its configuration was exceptionally fortunate: flat, watered, and with naturally vertical walls; the result, I supposed, of eons of trickling minerals. A mile and a half away, through swaying curtains of rain, I could see the giant cone of another volcanic hill known as Suleyman's Prison and, further off, lesser extinct cones dotted over the slopes.

Majid was sheltering under the eaves of the warehouse with his hands deep in his pockets. He looked at me questioningly, as if to ask whether the place was all that I had hoped. The rain was pouring over his eyebrows in little streams. I imagined myself taking an Iranian friend to see Stonehenge, and having to wait for him in the rain as he paced adoringly around the site.

It was freezing, and I knew we had to leave. Was it all I had hoped? I wasn't sure. I could feel the natural sanctity of the place in my very bones, but to make sense of it was another matter. You need time in such ruined places; their surfaces alone yield little, like an unexamined riddle, an aborted tryst. History takes one only to the outer doors; the atmosphere of places speaks a different language and addresses a different faculty, to which haste is poison.

I was drawn for a final moment to the jade-coloured lake, and walked over to the water's edge. There was no shore but a stony, moulded rim, smoothed by aeons of ripples. I peered downwards into the darkening greenness; the walls descended vertically. It looked bottomless.

Curious, I dipped my hands in and cupped them beneath the surface. I heard myself laugh in surprise: the water was *hot*. Suddenly the atmosphere of the place was transformed, and the air was thickening with echoes. It was easier now to understand the powerful allure of the place, and I stood by the water's edge wondering at all the royal oaths and thaumaturgic invocations that had once been uttered across the water from some long-since vanished pier ... murmuring priests appealing to panoplies of vanished Gods, and then the sound of lances clustering around a breach in the walls, and the tramping of reinforcements ... I felt a swell of fantasy coming on, and couldn't help myself now.

There was a crack of imperial sealing wax and a flurry of unrolling parchments sent from the nobles of Hecamtopylis, and the Sultan, dismissing his musicians, twirled his moustache at news of the rebellious Satrap of Hyrcania. At an archery contest, I saw a stray arrow pierce the shoulder of a Yemeni slave; heard a clatter of hooves announcing the arrival of a chariotful of hybrid watermelons from Babylon; and met the very potter requisitioned from Kashan who had discovered by accident the effect of an oxygen-depleted atmosphere on the firing of metallic glazes, and been rewarded by the Sultan with a mouthful of Badakhshani rubies; I saw a sun-blackened and bloodstained Arab veteran of Qadisiyya and Nihavand, oblivious to the clash of swords without, running his hand breathlessly over a quilt of multicoloured Chinese silk; and looking down again, watched a falsely accused concubine, her delicate feet bound to a sack of lava blocks, spiralling towards invisibility in a tragic wreath of bubbles; and could not surpass a chuckle as a Nazi archaeologist, in a fit of anger at Persian inefficiency, tripped over the leg of his theodolite and stumbled backwards into the water ...

I pictured, fathoms beneath my hands, all the treasures strewn over the silent bed of the lake, and all that had lodged in its warm magmatic fissures; lost chalices and amulets, Roman swords, jewelled Isfahanian astrolabes, a jarful of Soghdian coins, and an iridescent wine flask now home to families of sightless fish; perhaps the calcifying bones of a horse or two.

I blinked; and it was night. A Mongol queen and her party were at the water's edge, disrobing for a midnight bathe in winter. I hadn't heard them; their footsteps were hushed by snow. A sable wrap unfurled from her porcelain-coloured shoulders, but the clasp of her necklace caught on the fur; it swung for a moment, an attendant's hand reached out, but too late. There was a gasp and splash, a pale hand rose to cornelian lips, and the necklace – little turquoises from the Tien Shan, I think, set in woven gold – glinted for a final instant in the starlight, then disappeared forever into the amniotic deep.

Five

Kermanshah
Hamadan · Tehran
Shiraz

✡

Trouble with Herodotus · 'Weststruck'

The Sons of Adam · The Importance of Being Azerbaijani

The Virgin Castle · A Subterranean Discovery: What Byron Missed

The First Dome · Sasanian Rhapsody

Hafez and the Language of the Unseen · Blame the Greeks

Little Britain · Déjà Vu · Begging For It

از آن بدیر مغانم عزیز می‌دارند   که آتشی که نمیرد همیشه در دل ماست

Why, in the tavern of the fire-worshippers, am I held in such esteem?
For what is in my heart: a flame that cannot be extinguished

'THE TROUBLE with Herodotus,' said the sad-faced and silvery-haired man opposite me, 'is that he never knew enough about Iran to give a balanced picture.' Resting one hand protectively on my parcel, he slid a customs form across the counter to me with the other, and pointed out the spaces where I had to sign. Then he returned to his theme. 'You can tell from the way he talks about Cyrus and Darius,' he said, naming the Achaemenid kings of two and a half millennia ago, 'and it's the same with the other Greek authors: they never saw the things they described with their own eyes.'

I had come to the post office in Kermanshah to send home a few souvenirs, and the conversation had sprung up unexpectedly across the counter at my casual mention of an interest in history. For a few minutes the bustle of nearby customers faded into irrelevance; though our brief exchange set off trains of thought that would occupy me for much longer. 'I hope you won't rely on Greek sources alone for your book,' he said, looking serious. 'It would be an injustice.'

I assured him I wouldn't, and thanked him for his advice. He turned and put my parcel next to a pile of others nearby with a sort of reverential flourish, then returned and said how much he hoped I'd come back so that we could talk some more.

He was quite right about Herodotus. Classical Greek accounts of the Persians – the *Histories* of Herodotus being the most voluminous – were written in the context of long and problematic relations between the two powers and, crucially, against the backdrop of the astonishing Greek victories against the Persians at Marathon and Salamis in the fifth century BC. Greek histories of Persian motives and behaviour have tended, perhaps inevitably, to cast their erstwhile overlords in a grand but decadent light. To descriptions of Persian character, such as those on the pages of Aeschylus, there is always a scent of vanity and irrational brutality, a suggestion of perfidy; Xenophon calls them hysterical and effeminate.* It is only very recently that a more balanced reading of the Graeco-Persian drama has been made possible by closer, and generally more sympathetic, readings of Persian sources, as well as a cautious re-evaluation of the glorious conquests of Alexander, whose sacking of Persepolis in 324 BC signalled the death blow to Persian rule in the Near East.

Until virtually yesterday, Western scholarship has of necessity squinted at Persian history through the Greek prism; educated Iranians know this, and even today are sensitive to the two-and-a-half-thousand-year-old slights made by Greek authors as if they had been directed at family members a generation or two ago. Herodotus, Xenophon, and others were, from the Persian point of view, the world's first orientalists; their works allude to all the glorious barbarism of the East and are expressed in mixed tones of fascination and dread. Perhaps their parallel can be found in the romantic descriptions of the orient expressed in the pages of Washington Irving, Pierre Loti, Flecker, and Dulac, or in the paintings of Delacroix and Jean-Léon Gérome. All celebrate the terrible allure of the harem, the opium pipe, and the frenzied ecstasy of the dervish. But they do not take us much deeper.

There is, in fact, ample evidence that exchange between Greece and Persia was in fact more fruitful and constructive; formative, even, in the evolving Greek disciplines of the era. There is plenty of debate about just how much passed from Persia into Europe in the fields of architecture and administration, but in science the

---

* The Roman Pliny, by contrast, writing in the first century AD, records the ability of Cyrus the Great to remember the name of every soldier in his army, and that Mithradates Eupator administered law fluently in the two dozen languages of his empire.

Persian contribution is beyond dispute. In Achaemenid times Greek scientists are known to have studied in Babylon, where they reaped a rich crop of knowledge – too rich, at times, for the superstitious Greeks. Astronomy, perfected over the course of several thousand years in Babylon, was banned in Athens, where oriental science was considered too controversial.* The years spent by Democritus in the Persian Orient were vital in the evolution of later Greek science; Plato too studied Persian customs and religion; Plotinus travelled extensively there; and much later, Greek scholars fleeing persecution from the Romans gathered in the university city of Jundishapur in today's southern Iran. Between these luminaries it seems safe to presume there were many others. The historical emphasis on the military conflicts of the time, then as now, has tended to obscure the intellectual side of the encounter.

But my post-office tryst was also a reminder of the long reach of history in the Persian psyche, and that there is a far deeper side to the ancient Persian gripe of having been misrepresented to the world by the Greeks. It is hard to say how old it really is, but it permeates Iranian thought and, in various interpretations, most of the cultures of the East. In Iran itself it was given its most forceful expression in the twentieth century by such philosophically minded authors as Ahmad Fardid and the better-known Jalal al-e Ahmad.† On the whole, its central argument lies below

---

* Olmstead, in his redoubtable volume *The History of the Persian Empire*, proposes that Babylonian scientists would have been shocked to find that the Greeks in Plato's time believed the year to be only 360 days long, and cites the example of the astronomer Kidinnu (known to the Greeks as Cidenas), who in the fourth century BC calculated the length of year to within a second and the sidereal movement of the moon to the ten millionth place. Science was hardly new to Persia. When at last Alexander entered Babylon in 331 BC, the records of observations made by Babylonian astronomers were found to date back thirty-one thousand years . . .

† The most articulate modern expression of the idea is probably Jalal al-e Ahmad's famous work, *Gharbzadegi*, literally 'Weststruckness' or Occiden-

213

the dialectical radar of modernity, so problematic is its central premise.

It is this: Hellenistic rationalism, by cultivating the philosophical germ of secularization and the eventual triumph of objective science, has exercised a pernicious effect on the human soul and, through its modern extension, technology, on human culture in general. I must truncate the historical aspect of this idea brutally here because the implications cover too vast a sweep. Its underlying premise is that the Christian establishment of the Latin West, lacking its own organ of thought and formal logic, was obliged to integrate into its theology the teachings of Aristotle, whose philosophical principles came to dominate the intellectual development of the Middle Ages, and culminated in the celebration of human reason known as the Renaissance. The scholastic philosophers, as the overseers of this process have been called, thus triumphed over earlier Christian tradition, enshrining among other tenets the supremacy of logic and the idea of rational thought as the gateway to Ultimate Truth.

The Christian world, however, was not a unity; and in the Eastern Churches, represented by Byzantium, the effect was less definitive. Here the teachings of Aristotle were known not in translation from Arabic and Greek, but in their original language; and the intellectual atmosphere of the Christian East was suffused with the currents and vapours of a much wider range of

---

tosis. It is an impassioned critique of Iran's disastrous sycophancy towards Western technology and all that it implies, and a plea for the preservation of traditional culture. 'The Weststruck man', he writes, 'is a man totally without belief or conviction, to such an extent that he not only believes in nothing, but also does not actively disbelieve in anything – you might call him a syncretist. He is a timeserver. Once he gets across the bridge, he doesn't care if it stands or falls. He has no faith, no direction, no aim, no belief, neither in God nor in humanity. He cares neither whether society is transformed or not, nor whether religion or irreligion prevails. He is not even irreligious. He is indifferent. He even goes to the mosque at times, just as he goes to the club or the movies. But everywhere he is only a spectator. It is just as if he had gone to see a soccer game . . .'

philosophical and spiritual traditions, notably those of Plato and the Neoplatonists. Even today, a counterbalancing Platonic influence can still be found in Eastern Christianity, which has preserved a greater emphasis on the mystical and contemplative.* But the path followed by Western Christianity, that strange orphan of the Orient, troubled and talented in equal measure and later adopted by Greek and Roman parents, was unprecedented – and was bound, if it survived, to be extraordinary.

It did; and centuries on, the results are still with us. We may never have studied Aristotle, but we defer, axiomatically, to something called objective science and its visible, knowable proofs – and not to the notion of a divinely ordered universe. The outcome, from this ancient and problematic point of view, has been peculiarly disastrous for humankind. Gradually, the notion of human responsibility towards the natural world, implicit in all traditional religious – though not necessarily theistic – systems, was superseded by the hitherto unknown notion that nature was a thing to be controlled and dominated. Stripped of its participation with the Divine, nature (and the human passions associated with it) became a force to be overcome, rather than engaged with creatively. Man no longer stood in relation to higher and lower forms of life, but at the centre of things; and all sense of reciprocity with the natural order was lost.

The death blow was delivered by Descartes, whose forceful division of reality into thoughts on the one hand and things on the other elevated the human mind to the supreme instrument for the apprehension of reality, and the means by which human felicity could be achieved. The Eastern conviction that the mind

---

* I imagine the spokesmen of these traditions, consigned now to eternal felicity and diversion, assembled for a Heavenly episode of *Univers(al)ity Challenge*, adjudicated by King Solomon: RATIONALISTS: Aristotle, Epicurus, Barlaam of Calabria, Leibnitz, Newton, Descartes, Spinoza, Kant, Darwin, Hegel, Freud vs. MYSTICS: Pythagoras, Plato, the Three Magi, Dionysius the Areopagite, Clement and Origen and Palamas, Gemistus Plethon, Dante, Eckhart, Goethe, Blake, Gurdjieff; though one suspects there would be some argumentative seat-changing.

was the least well-equipped component of the human being for this task was forgotten. Uniquely in the history of human culture, fundamental notions common to all traditional ways of life – the sanctity of nature, harmony with a cosmic order and the rites and rituals by which it is supported, the idea of a purpose to human life, and to all life in fact – began to disappear from Western thought. Supplanting them came ideas of human progress, the immortal soul, and man as the master of his destiny.

We know, if we admit to it, the rest. In the overrational soil of empiricism, the roots of a more ancient, more mystical concept of religion began to wither; so that in today's West the very word mysticism is associated not as it has traditionally been with a rigorous and transformative experiential discipline, but with little more than Tarot cards and crystals. Reverence for nature evokes only the hugging of trees, the term 'spiritual' is used to mean little more than a dreamy emotion, and the mention of cosmic harmony, except perhaps among astrophysicists, is cause for acute intellectual embarrassment.

These are monumental indictments; yet they form the background against which so much of oriental culture perceives the apparent spiritual rootlessness of the West, its voracity for domination of so-called less advanced cultures, its consuming haste, and its violent divorce from the sacred world of nature. The resulting divide is much deeper than politics; deeper even than religion itself. Its legacy is what Blake called Newton's Sleep; it is Kipling's never-meeting twain, and the already widened gyre.

I was about to leave when I felt the gentle touch of outstretched fingers on my forearm. 'Tell me something,' said my friend in the post office, leaning forward towards me across the counter, 'is it the Iranian people that your country has got something against, or is it just our government?' Recent events had made this line of enquiry inevitable. I said I thought the English didn't have anything against Iranians, and meant it.

'Good,' he said with a nod of satisfaction, lifting his fingers gently from my sleeve, 'that's what I thought. I just wanted to be sure.'

'But people do sometimes get Iran mixed up with the Arab world,' I said.

'With the *Arabs*?' A look of incredulity fell over his features. His voice lowered. 'What have the Arabs ever done for us, except put our women behind the veil and tell us how to pray?' He sighed, and then brightened suddenly. 'Can you imagine if we all got along? If we didn't have all these wars? People say the Israelis are the problem, but that's just politics. Of all the peoples of the Middle East, I've always thought the ones most like us are the Jews. I expect we'd get along with them if it wasn't for that business with Palestine.' He sighed again. 'Cyrus was good to the Jews.' He put both hands on the counter, looked at them for a moment, then looked up again, and said: 'Well, we're all the sons of Adam, after all.'

'The sons of Adam?' I had never heard the expression.

'Yes: *bani adam a'aza-ye yek digarand.* Haven't you read Sa'di?'

I confessed I didn't know much of Sa'di. So he recited the verse:

> *Bani adam a'aza-ye yek digarand*
> *Ke dar aafrinesh ze yek goharand*
> *Chu °ozve bedard aavard ruzgaar*
> *Digar °ozveha ra namaanad qarar*
> *To kaz mohnat-e digaraan bighami*
> *Nashaayad ke naamat nehand aadami.*

> The Sons of Adam are the members of a whole
> Each is created from a greater, single soul
> Whenever Fate to one of them brings pain
> No other can without distress remain
> You who for others' torment do not care
> Cannot the name of 'human' rightly bear.

The word '*bani*', I realized, could mean 'sons', 'children', or 'family'; '*Adam*' could mean the name, a man, or humankind itself. There could scarcely be a more universal expression of the interrelatedness of human life or a more eloquent call for its recognition. Seven hundred years after its writing it was being recited to me in a post office in Kermanshah.

'The United Nations took it for their motto,' he said. 'It's carved somewhere on a stone – in Geneva, I think.' This was another revelation. I only half-believed him, but he was quite right again.

Φ

A few miles beyond the city loomed a jagged mountain, at the foot of which the seventh-century Sasanian king Khosrow II commissioned a garden and a palace, and carved his likeness into stone recesses aside the royal highway. The site is called Taq-e Bostan, and I wandered around it on a cold and cloudy afternoon. It was one of several royal sites commissioned in the region by the legendary monarch, and overlooked the route from Babylon to the Median capital Ecbatana, now Hamadan, and the eastern cities of the Silk Route. Passers-by would have marvelled at the giantesque reliefs of the king's investiture by the Goddess Anahita and Prophet Zoroaster and, underneath these divinely authorized credentials, a more worldly statement of royal power: a statue of the king astride a royal charger, visored and clad in chain mail, with a lance under one arm and a jewelled scabbard at his side.

The garden was built around a lake fed by a perpetual spring, and the palace, to judge from an old engraving I had seen where masonry columns poke out of the water, may have been built on the lake itself. Today the lake has been reduced to the size of a swimming pool by concrete borders. Fragments of marble pillars and the severed capitals of the vanished palace lay scattered like jetsam around its edges. It was obviously a popular place in warmer seasons, but was deserted now. Some pedal-boats were tethered to the poolside, filling with fallen leaves, and the tea-house chairs were stacked and chained on vacant terraces.

The site was yet another reminder of the ancient themes that later passed into the artistic and architectural universe of Islamic Iran. The semicircular arches I had seen in the Qajar-era houses in Sanandaj, and would later see elsewhere, echoed the barrel-vaults of the recesses, the form of which was adapted by early Islamic architects as the *ivān*, or monumental archway. Tree-of-life motifs sprang upwards on the flanking pilasters; and the two winged and ample-breasted deities flanking the crown of the arch above the main cave are replicated in countless later variations. There are haloes too, in the royal hunting scene carved on the wall where, attended by boatfuls of musicians, the king hunts wild boar in the reed-filled lake of his paradise-park. The haloes are thought to have entered Persian art from the West; but the images of wild boar, which are frequent in Sasanian art, did not survive the journey into Islam.

For several days I wandered about the city; after leaving behind friends, it seemed a lonely place, and my memories of the place are nearly all in grey. One afternoon, tired from walking, I watched the sunset from a park on a low hill near the centre of the city. The wrecked fuselage of a military jet, a relic of the long war with Iraq, was mounted on a concrete plinth nearby. It must have been a Friday, and the streets were nearly free of traffic, the way they used to be in London on a Sunday, and the air was clear. Several miles to the north I could see the giant silhouette of the mountain that gives the city its dramatic setting, but the intervening sweep of buildings was a depressing sight, and I was hit by a wave of gloom at the ugliness of the modern Iranian city. The only structures on which money was being spent were mosques and banks. Both tended to be ugly. I had heard it confidently predicted that the mosques would be empty within a generation. And if the banks, with their grand facades and marble floors, were turned into hotels, the traveller might have the opportunity to experience comfort.

Perhaps this cynicism is part of the inevitable let-down in encountering a country so rich in architectural history, and a history itself steeped in romance; and the Western traveller, especially the half-educated kind, is hard to please. When his destination lacks the comforts he anticipates, he does nothing but bemoan the primitive mentality and barbarous lack of hygiene of his hosts; when his surroundings are too modern, he is privately outraged at their indifference towards the priceless heritage of tradition. But in a country where skyscrapers appear overnight like deranged mushrooms, where giant warehouses and silos erupt like pustules across landscapes undisturbed since time began, where abundant farmland is swallowed up inexorably by tidal waves of substandard and half-built concrete developments, and belts of factories financed by the tax concessions of a corrupt government obliterate the charm of vernacular rural architecture, and all this in a country as potentially wealthy as Iran, he has, I think, a legitimate gripe.

One has to travel so far off the beaten track to find areas where traditional architecture remains unmolested that the ordinary visitor, moving between Iran's main cities, is likely, as I often did, to despair. Around them, and along the roads that link them, spreads what can only be likened to an architectural skin disease. This is a visually and socially debilitating mix of industry and shabby concrete housing, hastily built, perpetually unfinished, strewn with refuse and bulldozed rubble and utterly oblivious to the natural setting. It is one of the saddest consequences of today's development, so called, and in Iran one feels it acutely. In a few places, like Yazd in the south, and the village of Abiyaneh near Kashan, the beauty and uniqueness of the local structures has been respected, and limits placed on the type of development. Where the attempt has been made to replicate traditional architecture, the ugliness is checked, and proves that it is possible; but this occurs only in places where tourism is predicted to compensate the effort. All this is painful to observe in the country whose greatest visual contribution to world culture was architecture.*

---

* 'On the whole it is the painful fact that there has been practically nothing built in the last ten or even one hundred years that could command the respect or admiration of those who understand architecture as for example the average cultivated Persian understands literature. What has been built has alas been unworthy of a great people and especially a people that have proved themselves great builders in the past ... how incredible that one of the most proud and ancient nations of the earth, whose achievements in architecture have won the admiration of the whole world for more than two thousand years, whose skill, taste and imagination in

My gloom only deepened when I returned to my hotel. The manager was asleep behind the reception desk, and I woke him up to ask for the key to my room. His mood was even more morose than mine. He asked me why in God's name I had come to Kermanshah. What was there here for a foreigner? Though I was beginning to wonder myself, I trotted out my usual line that I was interested in the culture, and in meeting people who could help me to understand it better. He gave me a despairing look, and sank back heavily from the counter to the cushioned bench where most of his day was spent.

'You won't find any culture here,' he said. 'Or anyone to talk about it with.' Then he sat forward and said emphatically, 'Everyone who was anyone has left this place. Gone! *Gone!*'

I asked him why.

'Why else?' His hands flew open at the question. 'What's the one thing you need in life?'

'Contentment?'

His palm slapped theatrically against his forehead in a gesture of despair.

'Money! M-O-N-E-Y! Well, isn't it? Where would you go if you had an education? You'd go somewhere where you could make as much money as possible. What's an education for, if it isn't to make money?'

This line of thinking is always distasteful to an author already at the end of his advance, but I heard him out.

'You want culture? Where is Iranian culture? Not in Iran! It's in New York, Paris, London ... that's where you should look for Iranian culture. Look outside at the street: what do you see? Poverty, misery, drugs – and everyone lying and cheating for a scrap of bread. That's the only culture you'll find here!'

---

building have been demonstrated by a succession of great styles, should at the very moment when it is entering on a renewed life throw away these magnificent resources and deck itself out in the cast off and shabby finery of a discredited foreign mode.' This from a speech delivered by Arthur Upham Pope in Tehran – in 1934.

He unhooked my key from a board, tossed it onto the counter, and, shaking his head, retreated to his makeshift bed.

Φ

The next day, the sight of a silvery dome flashing from behind the intervening rooftops set me on a weaving course through the city. I found it eventually; a domed, square building flanked by courtyards and resembling a mosque. This was the *tekkiyeh* of Mo'aven al-Mulk, originally a gathering place of a Sufi fraternity and built, I guessed, a century ago. Above the arched entrance was a brightly coloured tiled rendition of the buxom angels I had seen at Taq-e Bostan; inside, the tilework was even more garish. All the lower walls around the central chamber were tiled, but the tilework was unlike any I had seen. The colours were dull and unharmonious, and the abstract patterns crude. The finesse and precision of earlier centuries had disappeared, as had the reverence for the abstract image; here nearly all the friezes were naturalistic depictions of historical and mythical characters and events. The main four panels, twenty feet across, portrayed a variety of battles and encounters between various holy personages of Islam and the Sasanian kings. These were surrounded by individual tiles, too many to remember in all, with the images of various idealized landscapes and some very European-looking castles, Noah's Ark, and a snake devouring an elephant and another a stag; portraits of Alexander and Pharaoh and Joseph; the Sasanian kings Shapur, Yazdegerd, Bahram, Khosrow Parviz, and Anushirvan; the celebrated heroes of Ferdowsi's *Shahnameh*, Taj, Sam, Tur, Iraj, and the Turanian king Afrasiab; the Sufis Nur Ali Shah and Baba Taher; the later kings Fath Ali Shah, Nader Shah Afshar, and Shah Muzaferrudin; Shahrazād; some vaguely holy looking dervishes in a marble-columned temple, surrounded by the paraphernalia of their calling: pointed hats and begging bowls and rosaries and crossed axes and knurled clubs and bells and deerskins and curved swords; and a truly gruesome panel entitled *The Punishment of the Unbelievers on the Day of Judgement*, where crowds of prisoners were being led to torture, decapitation, and dismemberment by sword and several were being boiled alive in a huge cauldron.

In contrast to this grim atmosphere, heavy with political connotation, I found a different kind of *tekkiyeh* in the village of Kerind, a few hours from Kermanshah towards the Iraqi border. It was named after Pir Benyamin, a saint of the brotherhood of the Ahl-e Haqq. I found it by accident in the narrow streets of the village, which huddles around the base of a dramatic wall of cliffs. Some talismanic insignia on the entrance gate caught my eye, and I wandered into the enclosure that contains the shrine, *tekkiya*, and cemetery for the members of the brotherhood. A hundred elaborately carved gravestones in dark and light stone were set in the ground. There was no one there but a boy playing a sad tune on a *setar*, and for a while there was no sound but the haunting music and the voice of the wind fluttering in the prayer flags above the dome of the shrine. An old woman appeared later with the key to the shrine and gestured me inside. The sarcophagus was black and draped in a green cloth. Carved on the wall were seven panels: O place of memorial – O Benjamin – O Sultan of Truth – O Bearer of Secrets – O King Abraham – O Pir Moses – O Daoud. I should come back, said the old woman as I gave her a few *tomans* for her trouble, later in the year when members of the brotherhood came from all over the area to gather there. It was a spectacular natural site and I was sad to leave. I walked to the road below, flagged down a van heading back to Kermanshah, and returned in the company of a dozen women in flapping black chadors.

After dusk I returned to the post office to make a phone call. As I was talking to a clerk across the long counter, there was a power cut, and the face in front of me disappeared into darkness. Did this happen often? I asked. 'All the time,' he said, his voice muffled as he poked about under the counter. A moment later his features reappeared in the phosphorous glare of a striking match, with which he lit a small paraffin stove. Then he ducked out of sight again to retrieve a small teapot, filled it from a plastic can, and sprinkled a handful of tea leaves on top.

We chatted for a while and warmed our hands above the flames. Another man joined us, and insisted on sharing the final cigarette in his packet. He was tall and lean and must once have been strikingly handsome, though his features carried the burden of some long melancholy. He told a sad story about his time in Frankfurt, years earlier. I have forgotten the conversation, but remember the hiss of the tiny stove and the cold and the glow of the flames across their downcast faces. They were both disturbed to learn I was staying in the poorest part of the town, and asked me why I didn't stay in the better part. I told them I wasn't aware there was any other part, and they described how to get there; it was only a few minutes' walk away.

Without knowing it I had confined myself to the poorest portion of Kermanshah, the experience of which had coloured my every feeling over the previous few days. Next door, virtually, was a parallel world I had failed to discover, its streets lined with hotels, cinemas, restaurants, and shopfronts stuffed with gleaming washing machines and computers and women's nightdresses. I walked up and down the main thoroughfare like a country oaf, looking timidly for a place to eat. But in the end I went back to the derelict-looking lanes with which I'd formed an inexplicable allegiance. I found a tiny *kebabi* and sat at a grubby metal bench aside a line of half a dozen grizzled-looking men wolfing down portions of rice and meat. Overhead, two industrially powerful bulbs threw a brutal glare over the room. The tiles on the walls, as thick with grease as a mechanic's pit, were almost as filthy as those on the floor. A shaven-headed boy of about ten, whose scalp bore a dozen scars of varying length, took my order and shouted it to the owner, who lifted a ragged haunch of meat from a hook above his head and began to carve it swiftly into morsels with a knife of black steel. An old woman, wrapped in folds of black cloth, hobbled in from the cold, croaking a plea for loose change. She leaned heavily on a walking stick painted the colour of lilac, and walked almost unseeing from the door to the other end of the room and back, then disappeared again into the dark. '*Befarmaid,*' said the man next to me, as I was about to eat. It was eight o'clock, and all around the shutters were beginning to fall. Within an hour the city was sleeping.

Φ

I moved north-east under gloomy skies to Hamadan, Iran's most ancient city. It has been inhabited since at least the second millennium BC; it became the Median capital in the sixth century BC, and later that of the Achaemenids. Herodotus describes Hamadan as a palace-filled metropolis, where the seven concentric walls of the citadel were each coated with a different precious metal. Its palaces are today anonymous mounds. The citadel remains largely unexcavated but has yielded a few treasures: column-bases resembling those at Persepolis, some exquisitely wrought jewellery, and a contentious sample of cuneiform text called the Gold Tablet of Ariaramnes. This is the oldest Achaemenid object ever found and bears the earliest Persian text, suggesting that the early Persians invented both their own language and the means to express it.

The city lies on a high plain, half enclosed by a crescent of mountaintops. My first glimpse of it was from one of the minarets of the Friday Mosque. A cheerful keeper with a jailer's bunch of keys dangling from his belt had taken me on an enthusiastic tour. We started at the top, climbing a pitch-black and dusty spiral to a kind of crow's nest at the summit of the minaret, from where, before loudspeakers became the norm, a dedicated muezzin would have given the call to prayer. Clambering through a small vertical hatch, I was then shown the interior of the main dome. I wasn't sure how we could be inside the dome, until I realized there were two, and that we were in the space between them. There was a resonant cooing of doves and, as we scrambled upwards, a soft clattering of wingtips. Upper and lower domes were separated by a twenty-foot-high grid of brick arches resembling an aqueduct on two levels. The upper dome, visible from the outside, had the more pointed profile of a four-centred arch, and the lower, to which we now descended, was semicircular. Around its base ran a frieze in black calligraphy against a field of autumnal gold and beautifully preserved. The mosque, said the keeper, was built on the site of a Sasanian fire temple.

The Gombad-i Alaviyan, famous for its stucco decoration, lay on the far side of a school playground off a tiny street. It has been variously described as a shrine, family mausoleum, and *khanagah*, a Sufi gathering place, and probably dates from the thirteenth century or Seljuk era. It was being restored; the interior was dark and filled with scaffolding and the smell of plaster dust. The stucco ornament, once covering nearly every inch of the interior, was badly damaged – photographs I had seen of the place were all more than fifty years old – but showed the degree of perfection this difficult medium had already reached nearly a thousand years ago. I had never before pondered just how problematic a technique it must have been. Stucco – a type of plaster that dries to stone-like hardness – has a history of nearly two thousand years in Iran, where the world's finest examples remain. There is much geometrical design in stucco elsewhere in the Islamic world, but the swirling world of plant motifs is taken to its loftiest artistic heights in Iran alone. Here it was possible to see that the patterns were built up in layers of incredible precision and in designs of abundance and baffling complexity. There were leaves and blossoms, creeping vines and spiralling tendrils; all subtly different but contained within a rhythmic and controlled unity.

When the technology of permanent colour appears on the scene, roughly speaking after the Ilkhanids in the thirteenth century, stucco is surpassed for obvious reasons. It is not extinguished; but it loses precedence to that extraordinary technology, mosaic tilework, sometimes called polychrome. At this point, another very Persian adaptation occurs in which the motifs and fundamental symbolic devices are preserved but re-expressed at the furthest creative frontier of the new medium. In the art of the tile mosaic, or faience, tiles of different colours – each fired at a different temperature to achieve maximum brilliance – are individually cut to a design and then covered on their unglazed side by a bed of plaster. Panels of manageable size can thus be built up to cover ever greater surfaces. Here too it is the precision of the operation that astounds. Every curve of every tendril and multicoloured petal must be individually cut and rasped and fitted to the design. Whole buildings are covered with this exquisite drapery, and much of it remains as brilliant as it was half a millennium ago. But the passion for meaningful shape, and for both concealing and revealing patterns at the same time, is still there. It overwhelms at first, as it is perhaps intended to do. The complexity of the different panels is too much to take in and the eye, rather like a first-year student of Persian poetry, wanders over the alien grammar of all those shapes in bewilderment. But with time moments of comprehension descend into the confusion; and the separate visual themes, full of paradox and allusion, begin as it were to communicate. Tiny variations in colour or symmetry acquire their own significance, lesser motifs can be heard echoing in greater ones, rhythm and direction begin to appear out of nowhere from separate parts and the effort of study and restraint is suddenly rewarded when the whole acquires a magical articulation; in short, life.

Φ

There are other tombs in Hamadan. Esther, the Jewish wife of the Achaemenid King Xerxes, is said to lie near the centre of the city, as is the much-loved poet Baba Taher, as well as the Khorasanian polymath Ibn Sina, better known as Avicenna. A natural history museum, I had also heard, boasts the most extensive collection of stuffed animals in the country; and there were some famous caves nearby.

But I was not up to my own itinerary. The hotel room I had found had been repainted recently, and when I returned there at dusk, the fumes were so strong my eyes watered. After half an hour, a splitting headache drove me to the manager, who was asleep at his desk. There were no other rooms, he said, and shook his head irritably. I wandered outside to search for an alternative. It was bitterly cold. Another hotel was full; another wanted dollars. I could bear the headache, I decided, and returned to my room, opening the balcony door to the freezing air. But that night, listening to the scuttling of cockroaches across the floor and the metallic clicking of their bodies as they slipped from the legs of my bed back onto the floor, I realized that my loathing of the species was more powerful than any worldly ambition; and that for leeches, tarantulas, snakes, scorpions, and bats I felt something close to affection. Tehran beckoned like a Siren, and visions of Sorush's whisky danced in my mind's eye. Luxury is entirely relative when travelling and the promise of an insect-free bedroom a few hours away acquired unrivalled allure; a second night was out of the question. A journey, I reminded myself, throws one's motives into doubt at every turn; whims and goals and prejudices are reassessed according to inner and outer exigencies at every turn, and in this complex process one's trajectory acquires both intensity and meaning. But I had already learned all that. I had learned too that it is equally possible to give up one's plans, and move on without regret.

A clean white shirt and a dinner party in Tehran with Sorush the next evening assuaged any lingering feelings of guilt. Cocktails were in our hands as soon as we were sitting down, and bowlfuls of walnuts and almonds baked with lime juice were distributed within easy reach. Tiny glasses of tea with wafers of saffron-flecked sugar followed, and then, while we were still in our chairs, delicate portions of fresh yoghurt with a creamy crust and garnished with shredded pistachios. Our hosts ushered us to a table lined with platters of three different types of delicious *khoresht* and three of rice, all steaming like fumaroles. Fresh fruit and home-made ice cream rounded off the feast, with customary apologies for the insufficiency of the meal.

On such occasions it is difficult for the Western visitor not to feel like a dolt. It is not only the exquisite good manners and attention to detail of his hosts. All is delicacy and sophistication. After dinner conversation moves gracefully from worldly matters and ascends towards the metaphysical sentiments of the great poets, whose lines are exchanged from memory with longing sighs and grave nods of appreciation. Implicit in this ritual deferment to poetry is the acknowledgement of an unseen world, called *ghayb* in Persian, from which the soul receives its most rarified nourishment. Everything existing in the visible world is the imperfect mirror of this hidden reality, into which the human being may occasionally glimpse. And it is strange, and a pity, that such an essential notion should be so obscured in contemporary portrayals of Iranian society.

Φ

Back home, Sorush poured two generous whiskies into cut-glass tumblers. I joked that I had been unable to decide whether the mother, our hostess, or her daughter had been more beautiful.

'Wife is coquette,' he chuckled. 'Daughter is coquette. All Iranian woman coquette.' He lit a cigarette. 'You will write about politics?' I said politics wasn't my thing, but that I wanted to write an honest book. 'Yes,' he said, 'I believe. You will write about corruption?'

'If I write what I have heard, they will not let me back.'

He thought for a while, then shook his head.

'They will allow. With foreigners they are soft. With their own people, they are strong. Only what they cannot deny, that is what makes them angry. They can each leave with a million dollars: they *believe* it is theirs. But one billion is not enough for them!'

I thought of the growing storm clouds in America, and asked him how he thought people would react to an American intervention in his country.

'Some, yes, will be happy. If they see American soldier in street, will *kiss* him. But for sure, if America attack, situation will be worse. I *afraid* people who want big change.' He made a pacing motion with his fingers across the surface of the table. 'Should be slow. If they force, will be worse. *Much* worse. Extremists will have right to do anything – the lowest people.' His sad eyes sparkled suddenly. 'For this, all fanatic will *love* America! What American cannot understand – Iran is democracy. Not like West, but democracy. For sure is more democratic than time of Shah. West took two thousand years – Iran, twenty-five. Now they begin to see what is necessary. Before, I did not believe. Now I understand: is better now. Even now begin some social guarantees. Not much, but for farmer twenty dollars is something – you have seen the conditions in Afghanistan.'

I told him my plans to visit Shiraz.

'So, another adventure,' he said. 'Travel is travel – I have not the force. Always has been Europeans who travel and discover: oriental is too lazy. You must tell what you find, so world will believe.' He pushed his glass forward on the table, and stood up. 'Remember this is your house,' he said. Then, with his flip-flops slapping on the tiles, he disappeared upstairs.

Φ

On the flight from Tehran to Shiraz, I sat next to a friendly and voluble man in his mid-forties. He spoke fluent English and we were soon deep in conversation. 'Have I heard of you?' he asked, when I said I was a writer. I told him I doubted it. 'Any relation to George Eliot?' I had to disappoint him, and explained that my ancestors had been cattle rustlers. 'You won't guess what I am,' he said cheerfully. 'I'm a forensic pathologist.' He was returning to Shiraz with his wife from a conference in Stockholm and a brief tour of some European capitals. He had enjoyed the trip, he said, but confessed that the encounter with his fellow pathologists from Europe and America had left him feeling depressed.

'When they heard I was from Iran, they bought phrase books and tried to speak to me in my language. But what did they say?

As-salaamu aleikum and *kaifa halek*. Arabic!' He rolled his eyes and described, with mixed expressions of sympathy and exasperation, having to explain that neither he nor the vast majority of his countrymen spoke a word of the language. 'Then they asked if in Iran we are allowed to do autopsies on dead bodies. Someone had told them autopsies were forbidden by Islam. I told them: "Doing autopsies is my *job*." Then they asked if it was true that in Iran we hang the mentally ill. *Hang them!* Educated men, asking me this! Where do they hear these things? I told them we have institutions for the mentally ill. We have a constitution that protects the rights of the criminally irresponsible. We have psychologists. We have hospitals. We have rehab. My wife is a psychiatric nurse.' His wife, a good-looking woman, leaned forward and smiled. 'We have addicts. We have AIDS. Designer drugs? We have them all. Where is the Iran these people imagine?' He sighed, then brightened. 'What's the line from that movie, *Casablanca*? Round up the usual suspects! That's how they think of us.'

He said he was glad someone would be writing about Iran. 'I shall say I met one of the sons of George Eliot. And you,' he thought for a moment, 'you will say you met one of the sons of Aresh, whose arrow flew for two and a half days and where it landed became the border between Turan and Iran.'

This unexpectedly poetic reference was from the great mythic masterpiece of Ferdowsi, the *Shahnameh*. As it happened I had some of his poetry in a small book I had brought with me, which I now fished out. It fell open on the immortal lines composed by the blind poet Rudaqi:

> The Ju-ye muliyan we call to mind
> Longing for those dear friends long left behind*

---

* The uttering of which prompted the Samanid Prince Nasr ibn Ahmad to jump straight onto his horse and ride bootless in the direction of his beloved Bokhara, followed by his homesick soldiers. The book was Nizami Samarqandi's famous *Chahar Maqale* (The Four Discourses), a text I had hated for more than ten years since I had struggled to translate it at university, and which only now I was learning to enjoy.

I read the first couplet in Persian but before I could reach the second he said 'No, no, it's like this,' and prised the book from my hands. 'I remember this,' he said, 'it's wonderful,' and read the entire poem. Then he flipped through the pages and began on a new poem. As he read, his left hand began to mark out the metre like a conductor, and soon his whole body was swaying to the rhythm of the lines. 'They sing this bit sometimes,' he said, 'with a man and a woman.' So saying, he began to sing, switching between keys at each line, and after a few more lines broke into that passionate ululating that is so difficult to describe.

'Poetry,' he said, almost breathlessly, as if emerging from a trance a few minutes later. 'It makes us very emotional.'

Φ

It was dark when we landed in Shiraz. I took a taxi to the centre of the town; the streets were busy and brightly lit and overlooked by outsized neon-trimmed banks and I was once again surprised, as I had been in Isfahan, at the modernity of the place. I settled in to a hotel, walked a long way through the streets, got lost, and returned with sore feet after failing to find a restaurant. On television, an overheated ayatollah was ranting about the recent student unrest in Tehran. 'We will break the limbs of those who work against Islam,' he yelled, while the youth was urged to 'maintain its vigilance against the enemy's plots'. It was not clear who the enemy was. I fell asleep thinking of the things for which Shiraz was historically famous, and endlessly celebrated in the lines of its most famous and much-loved poets, Hafez and Sa'di: nightingales, roses, and wine.

In the morning I was woken by the sound of sledgehammers and the scent of plaster dust creeping like a gas into the room. I escaped to the roof to find a quieter place to sleep: it was warm and bright. From the surrounding rooftops poked a few glittering domes and sheaves of cypress trees. The sky was clear and a deepening blue and the colours reminded me of Provence; with the sun on my face I realized I had felt cold for a month. A little later an elderly cook brought me a glass of tea, laying it wordlessly on a tray beside me, before ducking beneath a washing line and stretching out wearily on a nearby mattress. I watched as his forearm reached above his eyes, then settled over them as gently as a feather.

Many of the city's best-known monuments date from the era of the short-lived Zand dynasty, which flourished for thirty years between the Afghan incursion of the early eighteenth century and the rise of the Qajars towards its end. It had been spared by the Mongols after a very prudent submission by the ruler of the time, and by the armies of Timur two centuries later. And while much of Persia was being torn apart in the meantime, Shiraz had become one of the great cities of the Islamic world and a centre of artistic and literary refinement. Its scholars, painters, and architects travelled widely; craftsmen from Shiraz embellished Timur's imperial capital at Samarqand and many of the cities of Moghul India; in the seventeenth century a Shirazi architect designed the Taj Mahal.

The city's fortifications were long ago destroyed, but the centre is dominated by a citadel with four circular turrets like the crenellated rooks of a chessboard, and their surfaces are patterned in raised brick with diamonds and zigzags. The door was locked, so I wandered through the bazaar nearby and through the now-familiar shapes of its vaulted and winding tunnels and tumbling light. At the end of a satisfying ramble I found myself at the adjoining Vakil Mosque. In the airy southern chamber, forty-eight impressive spiralling columns turn in alternate directions from the entrance, supporting a canopy of keel-arched vaults. Mason's glyphs identify each flagstone underfoot. As I was drawing some of them in my notebook, a toothless eccentric claiming to speak five languages offered to be my guide and translator. He handed me a scrawled card:

Shiraz Iran
Gate of the Vakil Mosque

One Mohammad Mehdi.
The most internal

The security Talent Guide
38 years of Five The Languages
The currency over the worled
Unmarried
No smoked a cigarat life
No Holiday
By Walking
Price As You Like After

He studied me expectantly. I told him I couldn't afford a guide.

'Oh yes you can,' he grinned confidently. I suggested I would get by with my Farsi.

'True,' he said, 'your Farsi isn't bad. But you need about a year here for it to be really good.'

He was probably right. It was a goal worth achieving, I thought as I walked stubbornly away, if only to escape the summary judgement of taxi drivers. I was weary of the disadvantages that being identified as a millionaire foreigner instantly conferred, and decided for the rest of the day to pretend to be a visiting engineer from Azerbaijan. The result was excellent, and the price of my next taxi journey was halved in advance. But I had not bargained on the driver's curiosity.

'Azerbaijan?' he mused, one eye in the mirror as we weaved through the traffic. 'Did you cross at Nachivan or somewhere else?

'At Nachivan,' I said.

'So the border's open now?'

'Yes ... just recently.'

He asked me what the population was of my homeland. I took a wild guess.

'About fifteen million.'

'Fifteen million?' he repeated, 'I thought it was about half that.' What was the country's size, he then asked, relative to Iran? *Much smaller.* I wondered if was perhaps a geography professor earning extra cash by driving a taxi. What was the Christian to Muslim ratio? *About half and half.* What was my family name, and its derivation? *Bovinovitch,* I said; we used to be cattle rustlers. Main import? *Cars.* Main export? *Natural gas.* Rate of inflation relative to Iran? *Similar* ... I was flagging. Relations with Ukraine? Moscow? Chechnya? *Up and down.* Perhaps, it suddenly occurred to me, he was Azerbaijani himself, and having a huge joke at my expense. Immigration policy towards Iranians? *Pretty fair.* And what did I think of the recent assassination of that minister?

'A terrible business.'

'Who do you think did it?'

'Well ... he had a lot of enemies ...'

'It sounds just like here,' he agreed dolefully. 'They kill anyone who disagrees with them.' He sighed. 'In the Shah's time ...' he began, but it was time to pull over. My heart went out to the next genuine Azerbaijani passenger, whom he would think a terrible liar.

Φ

Evening falls ... and restaurants, it is easy to forget, are a relatively modern phenomenon. Only travellers, desperadoes, and businessmen eat out: sensible people eat at home, where the best food is produced. At dusk, shying from the fluorescent glare and clamour of cupboard-sized *kebabis*, I walked to the point of exhaustion in the hope of finding somewhere to eat where attention to space, order, and lighting held out the promise of superior fare. This, in the end, proved to be a deception.

I had made the same mistake before. At an expensive restaurant, ninety per cent of what appears on the menu is unavailable; so you eat the same as you would have at a wardrobe-sized *kebabi*, only the cost is five times greater. On this, you pay an unreasonable service charge. The waiters are surly and inattentive, as if in an opium-stupor, and men shout into their mobile telephones even more loudly than their English counterparts on trains. The atmosphere is diminished in inverse proportion to the price, and the food, having been prepared in advance, is tepid.

By nightfall, the streets are deserted and shuttered as if the city has been struck by some silent catastrophe, empty of all life but fugitive cats and a few desperate souls burning cardboard boxes in the gutter for warmth. The television shows an international weightlifting contest and a depressing film about the war in which children scavenge for unexploded Iraqi munitions, and the hero is killed by a stray rocket.

But I had not come to Shiraz to see roses and nightingales. I wanted more than anything to visit the sites of two unique ruined buildings, which lay about fifty miles south of the city. I had first read about them in Byron's *Road to Oxiana* years earlier, and was rereading about them now in my own dog-eared copy, which I had retrieved in Tehran. Byron's description of these seldom-visited monuments remains, I think, one of the best observed, and is characteristically full of unexpected delights and mishaps. And although I didn't yet know it, it is also astonishingly accurate. This is interesting in a book whose many spirited conversations and encounters must be allowed a certain licence, since the author spoke hardly a word of Persian. To record and preserve the account of a visit to a virtually inaccessible site — especially at a time when few others would have been able or likely to challenge its veracity — suggests an uncommon discipline. To do so accurately suggests a motive resilient enough to withstand all the diverting influences of heat, fatigue, appetite, impatient guides, and the natural laziness of the eye. To make sense of one's notes a year later is another skill; to reproduce them faithfully, and then to disguise the entire endeavour as if it had occurred naturally and without effort, is rarer still. As a faithful chronicler of dozens of such encounters, he shows exceptional mettle; as a companion, he must have been intolerable. It is strange to think that, had his life not been cut so unnaturally short, he might have lived until a few years ago.*

---

* Byron was killed in 1941 just two days short of his thirty-seventh birthday, when the ship he was travelling on to the Middle East was torpedoed off the Scottish coast. Officially he was serving as a Special Correspondent for an English newspaper, but as his close companion Christopher Sykes later noted, 'Various departments were anxious to

The two buildings, one a ruined castle perched on a high cliff and the other a crumbling palace in the valley below, date from the early third century AD. They are the royal remnants of the first Sasanian King, Ardashir I, who ruled from an entirely circular city in the heartland of the province of Fars. They are not beautiful: 'only archaeologists', Byron tells us, 'see beauty in Sasanian architecture. The interest here is historical.' Both castle and palace are architectural mileposts, and demonstrate the earliest examples of two distinct architectural innovations: the *ivān*, or vaulted monumental entrance, which later became a ubiquitous feature of Persian architecture, and the squinch.* The latter is an arch built across a right-angled corner and its appearance solved the age-old problem, which for centuries baffled Roman engineers, of how to build a circular dome above a square base. Without it, we are reminded, 'architecture as we know it would be different, and many objects most familiar to the eye, such as St. Peter's, the Capitol, and the Taj Mahal, would not exist.' The prospect of visiting the birthplace of this venerable device, and of following in such distinguished footsteps to a little-known destination, gave my plan the faint thrill of a treasure hunt.

Times had changed since Byron's visit in 1934. He had made most of the journey from Shiraz on horseback, and with an escort of five armed soldiers and a devoted partridge-baking personal servant, Ali Asgar ('without a servant, one spends half every day packing and unpacking'). The expedition is full of alcoholic picnics, characteristically acerbic asides, botanical observations, and a sustained and purposeful iconoclasm towards the opinions of his forebears; hospitality is at the home of the local governor. In this, as with other expeditions he describes, there is always just the right balance between peril and resolution: cars are offered by

---

enlist his services ... there was no reason why he should not be a Special Correspondent and hold other appointments as well.' Syke's unique essay on Byron is recorded in his *Four Studies in Loyalty* (Collins, 1946).

* A square, pinched? It is a tempting etymology for this strange word; but it is more likely to come from 'scutcheon'.

high officials, but never work for very long, and though the various journeys usually begin in one, they end on foot or bartered and recalcitrant horses. Cigars and a half-full bottle of whisky are always to hand and, though he makes light of all the physical challenges, it is easy to forget too that his rare photographs from the journey were obtained with a great boxlike camera mounted on a heavy tripod: one pictures him studying the inverted and grainy image of his subject, sweating and cursing under the black vampire's cape. I reread the account of his journey to Firuzabad, discovering, with a pang of envy, that he had discovered three types of local wine on his visit to the region: '...a very dry golden wine, which I prefer to any sherry, though its taste is not so storied; a dry red claret, nondescript at first but acceptable with meals; and a sweeter vin rose, which induces a delicious well-being...'

Φ

The next morning I squeezed into the front of a shared taxi and was driven at terrifying speed out of the city. We passed the immense cooling towers of a power station to the south and, further on, a vast concrete factory resembling a military base. A crippled tank, stranded by the roadside for at least a decade, evoked fond recollections of Afghanistan, and I took the sight of it as a good omen.

Then at last the dreadful advance of half-built concrete boxes and the debris of construction was ordered invisibly to a halt, and the countryside grew more sparse. Though it was November, a hot wind blew up from the baking asphalt beneath us and I was reminded what heavenly respite the parks and gardens in the country's cities must have given in their heyday. Dust-devils were spinning across the stunted shrubbery and the hillsides returned the sun's glare to the unaccustomed eye with a tangible pressure. We reached a broad plain dotted with the ragged-looking black tents of nomads, each surrounded by a loose constellation of goats. Beyond it, several miles ahead of us, loomed a ridge of barren hills lined with dark and swirling strata interrupted by the vee of a narrow cleft, towards which we climbed steadily. As we climbed I could make out the old unsurfaced road which zigzagged through the base of the gorge, and beside it, the river. Three tunnels now abbreviate the old route; after the third, I caught sight of the castle on the crown of the high ridge to the left.

Around the bend where this ridge sinks down towards the road, I signalled to the driver to let me out. He asked how I would get back, and the other passengers stared as I walked away. A metal footbridge crossed the road here and joined a track leading upwards. I followed it and halfway up disturbed a shepherd sleeping under some bushes. At about five hundred feet above the road I came to a ruined watchtower and could make out the remains of a long perimeter wall, now reduced to a line of rubble snaking around the crest of the ridge. The castle was a little higher, but there seemed to be no path leading to it directly and I found myself scrambling across the fallen masonry on the steepest side, looking down to the shining braid of the river several hundred feet below. There was an unpleasant wind, and clutching at tufts of grass I realized I must have followed exactly the same path as had Byron. I heard myself muttering the words: 'Creeping gingerly round the edge of the wall, for there was a high wind,' – which there was – 'I attained the central chamber.' Which I did, and introduced myself to a pair of astonished workmen. They were mixing mud and straw for an adobe rendering of the walls and offered me tea, while politely endeavouring to conceal their disbelief and at the appearance from a cliff-face of a breathless foreigner who had come three thousand miles to look at a ruin.

A broad courtyard, which may have once been vaulted across its forty-foot span, was in the process of being restored. Round-topped niches were built into the main wall, which was over-looked by an upper chamber with turrets at its corners. On three sides this chamber is open to the elements through tall round arches; the fourth was long ago filled in but still displays the dead-end tunnels that Byron noticed had been driven into the wall by looters. A great dome, open at its apex, surmounts the whole structure.

A gentle, white-haired foreman offered to take me onto the roof, so I followed as he guided me up a narrow spiral of stairs inside one of the turrets. The dust from his footsteps curled upwards into slanting volleys of sunlight within, igniting momentarily in incandescent swirls before surrendering to the shadow again; and for a moment I felt that inexplicable loosening of the grip of ordinary time, and with it, the feeling that the goal of the trip had already been fulfilled. We scrambled out at the top, and I peered in gingerly over the aperture of the dome, which resembled the lip of an extinct volcano. This layer of crumbling stones, coated with mud and straw, had survived nearly two thousand years.

I asked him why the place was called Qala-e Dokhtar, forgetting that *dokhtar* (from which our word 'daughter' derives) could also mean virgin.

'Because no one could take her,' he said. 'She was impregnable.'

He gestured towards the crumbling walls where they dropped towards the cliffs and pointed out that there had been no way into the castle except from one side. It was a dramatic site, from which a threat could have been spotted in any direction. About a mile away and a thousand feet below us I could see the black line of the road disappearing into the tunnel at the base of the ridge, like a snake into a mouse hole. I mentioned the looter's tunnels. There wasn't any treasure in the room behind the arch, he said, matter-of-factly. It had simply been blocked off in order to buttress the wall, which had probably been weakened by an earthquake. The outer turrets had been similarly damaged, and over the coming year would be braced and repaired.

Just as I was about to leave, I remembered that Byron had described an impromptu visit, in the vicinity of the castle, to a bat-filled and sulphurous cave. He had followed his guide there from the castle, and the thought occurred that I might be able rediscover it myself. I asked the foreman if he had heard of such a place.

'Yes,' he said, without expression, 'I know where it is.' He waved a hand vaguely towards the bare and stony flank of the ridge behind us. 'But you won't find it,' he added. '*Dur ast*, it's a long way.' This had the opposite of the intended effect.

'Oh yes I will,' I said.

'Oh no you won't,' he replied.

Seeing I was set on the idea, he offered to take me. I refused, not wishing to interrupt his work more than I already had, and because I wanted to scramble over the mountainside on my own and in silence. But with a slight tut of admonition he clambered back down the turret and began walking away. A few yards on, he turned towards me and waved me forward without a word.

A barely visible track led south from the castle, crossed a shallow dry ravine, and led towards the edge of the cliffs above the river: Byron calls the path he took 'devious', so this was probably the same one. My new guide walked in silence and without looking back; I had expected the usual plague of questions and the lack of them filled me with affection for him. From time to time he stooped to pick up sticks and small branches; vaguely I assumed these were for firewood which he would use back at the castle. We passed under an arch in the perimeter wall, crossed a second ravine, and continued some way until the track had disappeared completely. Then without warning we turned abruptly towards the cliffs and began to scramble downwards. The cave lay beneath the crest of the ridge above a platform just wide enough to feel comfortable on, and we stopped at the entrance. There was a faint smell of sulphur, which increased as we entered. The shape and the length of the tunnel leading from the entrance was exactly as Byron had described, and I knew we must be in the same spot: this was very satisfying. Seventy years earlier, a cloud of bats had caused the English visitor to flee in terror. But I have often wondered since what might have happened had he stayed.

We squeezed past a large boulder and stepped into the blackness of a suddenly enlarged space. The floor was spongy and looked black too; it wasn't mud, but a soft crust that threatened to give way under our feet. The air was warm and humid and alive with the electric twittering of bats. We could hear the beat of their wings near our ears and see their darting silhouettes against the receding glare of the entrance. Then I understood the sticks and branches, which my guide began to pile carefully at our feet. Moments later, a riot of tiny sparks was spiralling upwards from the crackling pyramid, and the walls were suddenly dancing around us in concert with the rhythm of the flames. When the roar of flames had died down we each took a flaming stick and crept further inside.

There was just enough light to make out the walls. Flapping like ghostly fabric in the unsteady light, they expanded to a width of about sixty feet and then drew in again; the roof, barely visible, was about the same height above us. At the widest point we were just able to make out four sticks driven into the ground and, tied to them, some strips of green cloth; these and the telltale rectangle they marked out betrayed a lonely grave. 'A holy man,' said my guide, with a grin of surprise, 'who must have spent his days there in prayer.' Several paces beyond the walls began to close in again and the ground became too soft to go any further.

And then we turned, and I looked back towards the entrance. Raising the flaming stick as high as I could above my head I took in the secret architecture of the place with a mixture of wonder and unadulterated delight. It was strangest cave I had ever seen. The walls were not dark and gnarled like other caves but pale, dry, and smooth. Perhaps the sulphurous vapour had, over time, a bleaching effect. But it was its shape that astonished me. The walls resembled the ribs of a whale; Jonah-like, we wheeled our guttering torches over their surface, and could just make out the almost regular spacing between each stony ripple and the thin bands of white, calciferous trim at the apex of each one. They curved upwards into blackness; not in a smooth arc but in a series of shadow-filled crescent-like hollows. These lesser curves, replicated in a watery geometry, were improbably regular and nearly symmetrical on both sides of the cave, so that the void they described was outlined by a series of pyramidal stalactites, repeating in diminishing profiles towards the entrance.

These were seized moments, made doubly precious by the brief life of our improvised lanterns, and must have lasted no more than a couple of minutes. But so enigmatic was the configuration of the place I promised myself I would return. I wasn't sure why or to what purpose; but I was already convinced I had encountered something unusual.

'*Khub bud?*' asked my guide, as we squeezed past the boulder again and found ourselves squinting against the afternoon sun. Was it good? It felt as though we had been inside the cave for a very long time; and then the world began to reconfigure. It occurred to me I needed to get back down and walk the few miles to the ruins of the palace below, but he anticipated my question.

'You'll be wanting to get down to the river,' he said. 'I'll show you the way.'

And in silence again we walked along the edge of the cliff as it curved round towards the north and fell into the cool embrace of shadow. He stopped ahead of me and pointed to the floor of the gorge. 'Follow the river, walk until the narrowest point, and cross it there.' We walked on a little further and he pointed over the ledge to a tangle of boulders and decapitated piers of rock and said simply: 'Try here.' It would be a scramble, but it looked quite manageable.

'*Khoda hafez,*' he said; we embraced and I lowered myself over the ledge. Losing height quickly as I jumped from one boulder to the next, I looked back from time to time to see his diminishing face still peering, with catlike intensity, over the edge, and each time a hand would wave me to the left or right. Fifteen minutes later I was at the base of the cliff, walked along the road for a quarter of a mile, and stopped where there was a track which forked and I wasn't sure which one to take. I glanced back at the cliff, and caught sight of the now-microscopic figure which had reappeared standing at the spot where he had first pointed out the route to the palace. I wondered whether he could see me; but just as the question took shape, an arm the width of a thread went suddenly up, signalling me to take the right-hand track. I waved back in thanks, and about a mile further on, took a last glimpse of the cliffs as they sank into shadow and hopped across a line of glistening stones to the far side of the river.

Φ

Five and a half centuries after the destruction of Persepolis by Alexander, a new royal line was born in the original heartland of the Persians, the province of Fars. Within three years its leader was crowned in Ctesiphon, and in the span of his fifty-year reign a new Iranian empire was established whose influence would spread wider than ever before. It became so powerful over the next few generations that virtually all of Europe and Asia submitted to the rule of either Rome or Iran, and for several centuries the fate of most of the civilized world was determined by the momentous clashing orbits of the two empires.

Ardashir's claim to the Achaemenid inheritance must have been a heady, not to mention provocative, undertaking. 'You wretched Kurd,' wrote the outraged Parthian ruler Artabanus V to his rebellious subject, 'how did you dare to build such a royal residence?' This was the palace of Firuzabad. Ardashir, so the story goes, revolted against his sovereign and slew him with his own hand.

Today the efforts of the early Sasanians to emulate the Persian kings of antiquity are visible in the scale and iconography of their architecture, which was both heroic and sumptuous. Giant domes and colossal facades set the tone, while within, lavish heraldic ornamentation, panels of gilded and whorling stucco, and poly-chromatic murals and mosaics drove home the royal message. Over time, the influence of these bold and vigorous innovations spread beyond the frontiers of the empire and can be traced in the later designs of Christian churches (particularly in Armenia, which lay at the heart of the Romano-Persian tug of war), in India, and T'ang China in the east; their inventive constructional methods prefigure the techniques later brought to their fullest realization in Gothic Europe.

Given all this, most Sasanian ruins disappoint: much of the effort to decode their architectural voice is down to the detective work of archaeologists. But the palace at Firuzabad still whispers...

A dusty road, along which a small boy was driving a flock of goats, led me to the entrance. A sleepy-looking guardian waved me past the gate, beyond which the site was deserted. It was late afternoon and a warm breeze circulated gently through the tunnels and arches, and I walked in and out of them in the delicious silence. It was all much bigger than I had thought: the length of the outer walls was about three hundred and fifty feet, and that of the facade a hundred and fifty; this, dominated by the central arch and rows of flanking niches, does indeed resemble a modest prototype for Ctesiphon; the germ of universal grandeur. After leaving me to scribble a while, the guard appeared at my side and asked if I wanted to go up; I didn't know one could go up. But he unlocked a gate near the entrance and we emerged on a parapet above the three main domed chambers. He scratched at a portion of the exposed wall and explained that the original mortar was mixed with stone crushed by hand, and added to some other component I wasn't sure of; I think he meant the tiny quartz-like fragments embedded in the whitish matrix of the mortar. It was as hard as the stone itself, he said, and much stronger than cement.

From here we could see that the walls supporting the enormous barrel vault were fifteen feet thick, and those of the transverse vaults slightly less: a phenomenal mass of stone. Against them the two surviving domes seemed as thin and insubstantial as eggshells, and it seemed incredible that these domes, so apparently fragile, and spanning a volume greater than anything previously attempted in the history of architecture, should have survived in a country where earthquakes have levelled far more substantial buildings. Its foundations must have been tremendous.

'It has no foundations,' said the guard. That's why it survived.'

Elaborate hand gestures accompanied the explanation that followed. There was some horizontal crisscrossing of palms like two trains passing at different levels, fists in opposition like colliding ram's heads, and double undulations fit for a story about migrating dolphins; this must have been the quaking earth. Sometimes a hand would fly in the direction of the lake outside, and at others plunge earthward. I never understood the details but did eventually grasp that instead of being built on conventional foundations, the entire palace was somehow afloat on a watery bed, which acted as a buffer against the movements of the earth.*

There were originally three domes, the central one a few feet proud of the others. The outer wall which once supported the southernmost dome has collapsed, and the chamber is open to the plain. The rooms beneath them are fourteen metres square, said the guide; and the length of the main barrel vault was twenty-eight metres. The walls are made everywhere of roughly hewn stone, which must have once been plastered; all of a sudden the sight of a dog's tooth cornice in brick running along a section of wall above me gave the feeling that the place had once been inhabited, and the knowledge, so abstract at first, that the walls had once contained the life of a palace, became suddenly more real.

The dome above the main chamber is about sixty feet high, resting at its corners on the ten-foot-high arched structures which transfer the weight of the dome onto the walls. This was called a *fil-poosh*, said the keeper, or elephant-mantle: it was a strange name for the squinch. More plasterwork, this time around the arched recesses in the walls, made the place seem more believable,

---

* Just as Salisbury Cathedral, the highest spire in medieval Europe, is said to have been built, a thousand years later, on the unlikely site of a water-meadow, with foundations of straw and gravel only five feet deep. Perhaps I can add the technology of hydropneumatic substructures to my list of Persian contributions to the West...

transforming the rude spaces into stately niches where, for a moment, one could picture a gilded statue or urn or a high-backed inlaid chair; perhaps a slave. The cornice above the main niche is decorated with tiers of scalloped feathers – cavetto so called – or, as Byron has it, 'bastard Egyptian, copied from Persepolis'. He is cruel about the design, but at the time it must have claimed for the youthful dynasty a vital link with the divinely sanctioned heritage of the Achaemenids, rather as Americans are wont to claim a distant relative on the *Mayflower*.

It was the middle of the third century, and a heady time. A vigorous king, ably assisted by the crown prince, extended the fledgling empire's borders to Kerman and Isfahan; soon Roman, Scythian, and Kushan opponents were all on the defensive. At its peak, Sasanian art would reach the Atlantic; the organization of its army would foreshadow medieval chivalry, and its administrative system, the court of Charlemagne; it was an age, in short, of burgeoning and undreamed-of power. For a few moments I allowed myself to imagine what the place might have looked like in its heyday, and let the plaster creep anew over the stonework . . . the rough surfaces were soon smoothed into stately verticals, the cornices and mouldings trimmed in bands of crimson and gold, and the soffits above the marble floor, polished to glass-like smoothness, were sprouting lines of geometrically patterned borders . . . the dome was all of a sudden metamorphosing into an ethereal similitude of the heavens, painted in deep lapis and inlaid with a thousand stars.

Tapestries heavy with gold and silver thread multiplied across the walls, depicting the king in triply heroic poses of combat, hunting at the gallop, and on a throne supported by winged horses, suspended in a magical world of *simorghs* and collared leopards in acanthus roundels. Layered and perfumed candles, calculated to release a different perfume at each hour, burned behind rock-crystal housings, gilded and mirrored at their backs and throwing a seductive glow over the gathering assembly, as the guests gasp at the sparkling constellations above their heads. There is a clatter of carriages and a scurrying of bearers through the corridors as some late arrivals descend beneath the cypresses outside, barking instructions for the safekeeping of their jewellery boxes ... fingers a-glitter with bulbous rubies clutch goblets of spiced and steaming wine; there are diplomats and dignitaries, a city planner rumoured to have won the king's favour for the design of an entirely circular city; a military commander with a face disfigured by a Roman sword and his following of officers, sweating uncomfortably under their gold piping and tassels; a dishevelled court poet smoothing down his hair in a silver mirror in the entrance hall; a princess or two, each with a pet leopard and flanked by tall and very fit-looking men wearing the equivalent of black turtlenecks ...*

We walked outside. Shallow tiers of excavated steps led towards a pool of crystalline water. A solitary man was fishing in it. It was fifty feet deep, said the guard, and was fed by a spring which had flowed at least since the time of Ardashir. He pointed out a partially excavated tree, preserved by the wet soil, and evoked with gestures and looks of delight and longing the ancient garden which eighteen centuries ago had surrounded the palace.

It was dusk when I walked back to the main road. A local

---

*   Two officials are talking ... For a moment the eye of one of them is caught by the bare-breasted dancers engraved on a silver ewer; the other's is held by the dark and lowered eyes of a slave-boy in a belted frock, who dabs the ewer's lip. 'By Anahita! Haven't seen you since ... when was it ... ages!' 'Ctesiphon, wasn't it? The polo championships in '28!' 'Of course! With your sons — mine are both serving in you-know-where. I can't understand why we invaded in the first place ... I wonder if we shall ever get our troops out now.' 'Sign of the times ... we got stuck behind a military convoy just outside Babylon. Nothing but traffic the whole way ... I blame all those horrible Roman prisoners.' 'Well, all roads lead to Fars!' 'We've got a little place on the Euphrates — why not come up for some hunting. We'll send an elephant and it'll only take a week to get there. Have you ever had flamingo? I'll lay on a dozen of those naughty Syrian girls — forgive me, boys — what is that little sect they all seem to belong to nowadays?' 'Christian? The ones who worship a pigeon?' 'I thought it was a fish — more mead?' 'Thank you ... what do you make of the roof? It's called a *dome*...'

248

farmer in a battered Land Rover took me to the outskirts of the village, where I found a shared taxi to Shiraz with two girls who sat in the back and giggled the whole way. At the hotel I returned to my copy of Byron's *Oxiana*, which I had deliberately left behind. Rereading the account of his visit to Firuzabad, my eyes fell on a line I had never noticed:

> Today has been the perfect day, the one day which, even if there is no other like it, makes the whole journey from England worth while.

I felt exactly the same. All that was lacking was the dry red claret, acceptable with meals.

Φ

The shrine of Khajeh Shamsuddin Mohammed Hafez Shirazi, better known as Hafez, lies in a small and carefully tended park north of the river in a quiet portion of Shiraz. It is called the Arāmgāh, meaning place of rest, and of all the city's shrines and monuments it is the most frequently visited. Among Iranians themselves, it is probably the most celebrated shrine in the entire country. Exactly why this is so is hard to say; there are other Persian poets whose works are far more widely read. Sa'di, who lived for most of the thirteenth century and was a fellow citizen of Shiraz, is probably the most widely read author in Iran, India, and Turkey put together; and Jelalludin Balkhi, known as Rumi, is even today known and revered the world over. But no other poetry reaches into the Iranian soul quite so intimately as the *ghazals* – the short, sonnet-like poems – of Hafez. None is so loved or cherished, or has decided the fate of so many dynasties, kings, and ordinary people.

His tomb is a single slab of creamy marble, intricately carved with his verses. It lies in the open air, protected by a roof on eight tall columns. I circled it and sat nearby. A few young couples were sheltering in the surrounding alcoves, unlocking hands furtively as I passed. I watched as people came and went, standing or kneeling at the tomb, and pressing their fingers against it as they offered prayers. I wished I had devoted more time to his poetry, recalling the lines:

> For years my heart sought out the Cup of Jamshid*
> Asking from strangers what it already had.
> Searching from the lost ones of the sea's edge
> For the pearl beyond the shell of time and space

Hafez was born in about 1320, in the aftermath of the first Mongol onslaught under Chingiz Khan, and lived until the second great Mongol invasions of Iran launched by Timur in the final decade of the century. Shiraz, though not unaffected by the upheavals of the era, remained relatively peaceful during the period, and the poet enjoyed the patronage of a number of local rulers. He showed an early talent for poetry and his *takhallus*, or pen name, Hafez, reminds us that at a young age he had committed the entire Qur'ān to memory, and received a classical religious education. He is also believed to have followed the mystical discipline known as Sufism.

The poetry of his youth, in keeping with the poetic conventions of the age, addresses the burning themes of love, human longing, and the dilemmas and transitoriness of life. A well-recognized stock of characters populate his verse, each conforming to a role with which his reader is assumed to be familiar, rather as today one knows how to tell villains and heroes apart in films, and predict how each will behave. Thus in almost all classical Persian poetry, but especially in Hafez, we encounter the lover and the beloved, the wine-seller, the drunkard, the bigoted cleric, the ascetic, the biased judge, the mythical phoenix called *simorgh*, real and false Sufis, the moon-faced maiden, the beautiful but cold-hearted Turk, and the Magian high priest.

A single overwhelming theme runs through nearly all his verse: that of the spurned and heartbroken lover, tormented by the cruelty of fate and the indifference of a distant beloved. Shunning

---

* The mythical cup in which all wisdom is contained; gnosis, in other words, or spiritual vision.

the world, he seeks consolation among the outcasts of the wine tavern, longing for his own extinction. It is a theme already well established by Hafez' day, and closely allied with the repertoire of classical imagery; the cypress that represents the slender body of a beloved maiden, the heart-piercing arrows of her eyelashes, ruby-like lips, and musk-scented locks that ensnare the lover's gaze. Only wine can release the lover from his incessant desire; reduced to indigence by his addiction, each new day brings a glimmer of hope, and new disillusion.

Hafez is wise, tender, and deeply humane. A recognition of the frailty of human endeavour, the inconstancy of the heart, and transience of worldly things informs all of his work.

> Even if the flood of materialism
> Drowns everything, do not sink into
> Sadness, because Noah is your captain
> Don't expect this rotten world to be faithful
> To you. The world we know is a hag
> Who has known a thousand husbands

As his poetry matures — the majority of his *ghazals* were written in the final two decades of his life — his verse becomes suffused with an exquisite quality of universality, expressed in a language rich in symbolism and so delicately refined that a faraway look comes into the eyes of grown men whenever a line is read ... because as any sensible Persian knows, Hafez was divinely inspired.

All the more surprising, perhaps, that such universality should have arisen from a medium strictly controlled by the canons of poetic tradition. No poet, wrote Nizami in the *Chahar Maqale*, 'can attain to high rank unless in his youth he commits to memory twenty thousand lines of the poetry of the ancients and ten thousand of the works of the moderns, perusing continually the *divāns* of the masters and observing how they have got themselves in and out of the poetic straits.' From its beginning, the poetic craft was a technical business, built on orderly foundations understood by both poet and audience. Refinement, rather than innovation, was the criterion of excellence. And since most of the great poets of the roughly thousand-year period that constitutes the era of classical Persian poetry were professionals, they were held, culturally speaking, in enormous esteem. Poetry was seldom a matter of light entertainment: kings and rulers went to war and dismembered entire nations on the basis of poetic prognostications; they rewarded timely couplets with trunkfuls of gold – or banishment, for an inappropriate one – and lifted the death sentence from miscreants. Poetry, and especially the poetry of Hafez, is still used seriously as a divinatory tool. Not because Persians are whimsical, but because his lines were trusted to convey the voice of the invisible realm, or *ghayb*.

> If you wish like Jamshid to reach the secrets of the Unseen
> Come, and befriend his world-revealing Cup

Part of the esteem for the poet's discipline came, of course, from respect for his technical achievements. Mastery was perfected over the course of years of training. A professional poet would have been familiar with a whole range of rhetorical devices in order to be competent, since every hemistich had to balance with an almost algebraic precision on both sides of a line. A variety of conventional rhetorical devices could be enlisted towards the goal: simile, hyperbole, allusion, and antithesis were among the most widely used, as well as subtler techniques such as exploiting words with ambiguous meanings, and the use of words which look identical but are read differently, and which only a knowledge of the metre of the poetry can clarify. A poet would know the seventy basic meters and their variations, the strophic forms and types of rhyme, as well as the themes associated with them. There were – and still are – times of day associated with different types of poetic melodies; these remain closely allied to the musical art.

The *ghazal*, a lyrical verse form akin to the sonnet in length and the one brought to such perfection by Hafez, can explore several different ideas while the overall theme tends towards unity; the gaps, as it were, are filled in by the reader familiar with the greater traditional picture. A *ghazal* by Hafez moves forward 'somewhat like a Bach prelude', writes the American poet Robert Bly, which 'reaches into the invisible world with its first note, and the low notes bring up the endless sorrow of life on Earth. The left hand goes on talking of failure and repentance, and the light, quick right hand talks about the magnificence of poetry and religion, of the side-glances given to us by God'.

Here we touch on the essential notion. Technical skill alone cannot account for the awe in which Hafez and other great Persian poets are held across such a wide sweep of culture. The reason is in a way simple, though scholars tend to start backing out of the room at this point. Hafez, and the great poets like him, are representatives of what is sometimes called the *lesan al ghayb*, the Language of the Unseen, or Invisible Realm. This ineffable language is the poet's raw material, fashioned with preternatural skill into arrows of meaning that simultaneously strike both heart and mind. To the philosopher the result is complex and profound; to the theologian, inspired; to the ordinary reader, it transmits the power of proverbial wisdom. It speaks to all; it has a paradoxically universal quality.

The poetry of Hafez is also saturated with the mystical symbolism of Sufi tradition, which is necessarily cryptic – partly because the ideas expressed by mysticism were dangerously at odds with orthodox theology, and partly because such ideas were meant to be understood intuitively, rather than with the intellect alone. All traditional Persian poetry, together with art and music, alludes in some fashion to mysticism, and it is to mysticism one must turn to decode their expressions most fully. Part of the difficulty of this, for the Westerner at least, is one of vocabulary: our own word, mysticism, tends from the outset to drag us closer to the Ouija board and the snake charmer than the Illuminative wisdom of the saints. The term 'spiritual' does not help us here much, either. We are stuck until someone comes up with a better word.*

---

* We have much more choice in Persian when it comes to modes of

To Sufis themselves, nearly every line of the poetry of Hafez affirms his spiritual immersion in the mystical path, and his poetry is an encyclopaedia of the spiritual way. It charts, for the benefit of fellow-wayfarers, the topography of the reality that Sufism seeks to unveil. Seen in this light, the theme of the lover's longing becomes none other than longing of the human soul, separated from its divine origin, to be reunited with its source. Wine becomes the substance of spiritual intoxication, and the beloved, God. Debates about whether Hafez was a nihilist, a Marxist, or an alcoholic tend to fall wide of the mark.

His *ghazals* can of course be read as valid social commentaries, and his satirical asides at the false piety of the cleric (and even the would-be Sufi) are as pertinent today as they were six hundred years ago. But they are no less the work of a great Sufi because they are also valid in their more worldly sense.

Worldly and mystical endeavour are, in any case, by no means antithetical in Sufi tradition. Many Sufis composed outstanding scientific works, and many – perhaps most – composed poetry too. In their work we find less trace of antagonism between the rational and the artistic, the logical and the poetic. Scholars in both East and West are on the whole reluctant to acknowledge this marriage of the analytical and the intuitive – it all suggests a problematically unifying dialectic at work – and prefer on the whole to deal with one or the other.* But in Sufism they have yet to diverge as they have elsewhere; they are the fruit of a singular

---

'mystical' experience: *ma'rifat* and *'erfan*, both meaning mystical knowledge, and derived from the Arabic verb, 'to know'; *Kashf*, 'unveiling', *shuhud*, 'witnessing' or mystical intuition, *jazba*, mystical 'attraction', *vahi*, revelation, *ishraq*, illumination, *ilham*, spiritual inspiration, *ittisal*, spiritual connection, *nida*, the divine call, etc.

* Though we have come a long way from the days when Sufism was thought of as an extremist sect, and its poetry a nihilistic celebration of drunkenness and the brevity of existence. For an indication of the breadth of contemporary scholarship in connection with Sufism in Iran, see *The Heritage of Persian Sufism*, ed. Professor Leonard Lewisohn (3 vols: One World, 1999).

vision. All later confusion, as we know, is the fault of the Greeks...

This is difficult to express and imprecise, but it would have been wrong, I think, to ignore. The predilection for mystical thought runs deeply through all the cultures of Islam, and Sufism has left its mark on all of them, cutting across all worldly frontiers. I well remember my own feelings of bewilderment when, the very first time I was invited to a gathering of Sufis, it was explained that one of the leading participants was the head of air-traffic control at the international airport. Another was a lawyer who, during a conversation about tackling gangsters, sprinkled his views with quotations from the great Persian mystic, Shams of Tabriz. And coming back to Hafez, I have a fond memory of a musical recitation of the poet's *ghazals* at a private home in Kabul. Only afterwards was I introduced to the man who had been sitting opposite me, swaying gently with his eyes closed and a look of beatific transport on his face: this was the Foreign Minister.

Much more recently – a few chapters ago, in fact – I had gone to visit the chief of immigration police in Isfahan. Between teetering piles of folders on his desk was a single, small volume from which he was quietly reciting – the *divān* of Hafez, I realized, as I went to shake his hand. I must have interrupted him mid-hemistich; because the final syllables, as he stood up with an unmistakably distant look on his face, were still fading visibly from his lips.

Φ

On the way back from the shrine, I stopped for a cup of hot milk in a street near the hotel and sat a table outside to watch life go by on the pavement. A slim young man with a dashing air, exaggerated by his jet-black hair and white jacket, walked past me and, a little further on, lingered as if he was trying to make his mind up about something. A few minutes later, as I thought he might, he came back and introduced himself. He had been trying, I supposed, to figure out whether I was a foreigner or not, and as he spoke I wondered cynically how much money I would be prepared to lend him when he asked.

The question never came; there were lots of others, but the thing he really wanted was for me to come to his home for a quick visit. Elsewhere this kind of invitation could be safely ignored, but he begged me with such earnestness that I gave in, reasoning that if there were anything untoward in the encounter, it would make entertaining reading one day. We took a taxi to his home. His parents, a transparently kind-hearted couple in their sixties, were watching a banned music video, and shuffled embarrassedly to their feet as we entered. The mother roused a teenage daughter to come and help in the kitchen, and the father offered cigarettes. Tea and pastries appeared; the father explained that he was retired now, but had been a customs officer for thirty years. A leather wallet, its edges pale and frayed, opened to reveal a black-and-white photograph of the younger man, half-obscured by an official-looking insignia. From the days, he chuckled cynically, when Iran had been a world power.

His son disappeared for a few minutes and re-emerged with a photograph album, which he laid reverently in my lap. In it was a collection devoted to an absent son, whose face smiled stiffly from a hundred poses in a very European-looking setting. He was in Leeds, they said; the government had provided him with a home, and he called every week; but they weren't entirely sure, said the mother, whether he was really happy. 'He misses his family,' she said gloomily. 'We don't know what it's really like for him there.'

Then came the burning questions, hard on one another and posed in such general and passionate terms that I was at a loss to know how to answer them: marriage and the business of dowries, parental authority, work and money, the cost of a home, the availability of state benefits, health insurance, the cost of a haircut (why this, particularly? I had been asked before), and how often one's family came to visit ... For the next three hours I was subjected to a good-natured grilling. I felt a familiar sense of inadequacy to all my replies; and on this and so many other similar occasions I felt almost as though I were an impostor, inventing comparable norms on issues which, if answered honestly, seemed too brutal for these gentle people; and hoped that my answers wouldn't disappoint. But I was always touched by this hunger for knowledge. The son, in particular, seemed to me like a drowning person clutching for purchase on a world that held out infinite promise and allure. 'Don't leave your world,' I wanted to say...

The usual opening to this kind of exchange – 'What do you think of Iran?' – is not merely small talk. It is the expression of an unquenchable desire to know how the country is perceived from outside; and the answer, not being a very happy one, always seemed better to disguise.

The father, who was as intrigued to hear the answers as the son, played the devil's advocate. His questions were more pragmatic; he asked about cars and fruits.

'Here,' he said, 'they export the best of everything. The lowest-quality things are what they keep for us.' Then his son would interject: could a man and a woman dance together in a public place?

'Women wouldn't talk to you! You'd be a refugee!'

But would a woman agree to marry an Iranian for the sake of a passport? No artificial diffidence hindered the question: it was a practical matter. Again the father scoffed. 'Europeans don't do that sort of thing. It's not like here – they don't lie! That's why they're ahead of us...'

But behind all these questions loomed a single overreaching issue: that of personal liberty. And I felt again a twinge of shame that I hardly ever dwelled on such liberties myself.

'It depends,' I heard myself saying a lot. One was free to choose many things; one lived with both the responsibility and the consequences ... but I was aware that I was censoring my own account of things. There was a lull in the conversation and the mother spoke up. They had all been shocked and saddened to hear, she said, that when an English friend of their son's had fallen ill, not a single member of his family had come to visit. Only their son had gone to his side.

But what were people really like in England? asked the daughter, who was sitting opposite me with her hands wrapped around her knees like a child listening to a bedtime story. What did they do? What sort of things were English?

For a moment I was stumped: it was like being asked to think of a word. What was English?

Stonehenge? Or the Costa del Sol? I thought suddenly of the sight of patchwork fields seen from above in interlocking shades of tended green, and of cow parsley and woodpigeons; then of the heartless rustle of *Evening Standards* on the rush-hour Tube. Nobody knew Rupert Brooke's 'Soldier' any more, or the words to 'Jerusalem'; not that I ever had myself. It depended which England. There was Berry Brothers and the Kray brothers; Turnbull & Asser and Manchester United; Irish wolfhounds and pit-bulls. On Friday nights, a minute's walk from the serene protectedness of one's club, gangs of vomiting receptionists roamed Piccadilly. Which was more English? I didn't know. Aspidistra and the twitch of lace curtains, a thin red line and a white feather, unarmed police and an enduring mistrust of authoritarianism, warm beer, football hooliganism, ever-lonelier and ever-more pornographic telephone boxes, Rotten Row, Mr Speaker and Squirrel Nutkin ... Little Britain?

'English people like long walks in the rain,' I heard myself say, 'and we talk about the weather a lot.'

It was ten o'clock when I left. Mahmoud came with me, lighting a cigarette as soon as were out of the door, and thanking me profusely for my patience. A taxi dropped me at the corner by my hotel, and I walked a little in the cool air. It was good to be outside. About a hundred yards ahead of me, walking between the intervening pools of light on the pavement, I could make out a couple; something about their manner held my attention, and I watched as they drew closer. Suddenly the man pulled the woman towards him and kissed her on the lips. She resisted and pirouetted away, but he repeated his effort and this time, for a

KERMAN Symbolical plasterwork in the ceiling of a shrine.

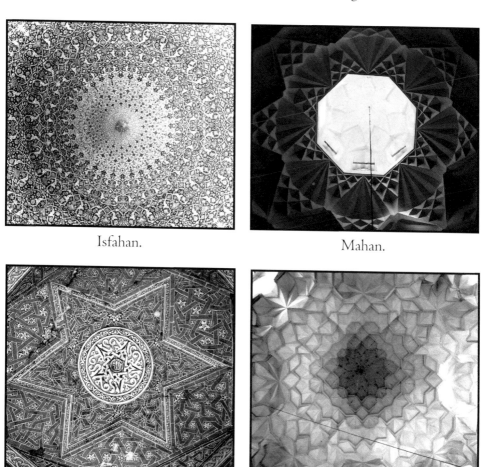

Isfahan.

Mahan.

Sultaniyya.

Natanz.

MAHAN
The shrine of the sufi Shah
Nim'atullah Wali, 1447.

ORUMIYEH
The church of Maryam-e Quddus,
probably the oldest church in Iran.

ISFAHAN
The Safavid Chehel Sutun Pavilion,
early seventeenth century.

SHIRAZ
Prayer-hall of the Vakil Mosque,
late eighteenth century.

SANANDAJ Muqarnas design in
newly built ceiling.

TABRIZ Salman atop the
Ilkhanid Arg, thirteenth century.

FIRUZABAD Foreman at the Qala-e Dokhtar, the Virgin Castle,
third century AD.

SHIRAZ The Aramgah of Khwaja Hafez, Spokesman of the Unseen.

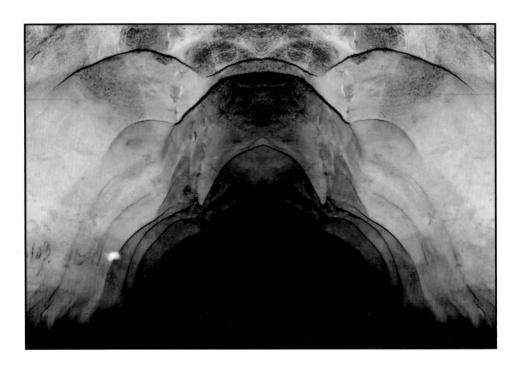

An Unexpected Discovery: the interior of the bat-filled cave near Firuzabad.

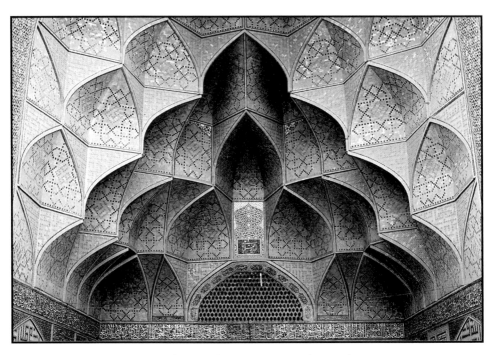

ISFAHAN The north-west ivān in the Friday mosque,
begun eighth century AD.

PERSEPOLIS
The Achaemenid Royal
Guard, fifth century BC.

Fallen bull-headed
capital from the
Apadana.

PERSEPOLIS (Takht-e Jamshid) from the Mountain of Mercy.
YAZD The Zoroastrian Towers of Silence.

few moments, their bodies formed a single silhouette. In public this was unthinkable and hugely risky; I had witnessed nothing like it on the entire journey.

I felt the shock and indignation of a mulla. As they approached I tried to glimpse their faces, to see what fearless social revolutionaries really looked like. But as they passed I heard them speaking. They were English tourists.

Φ

I spent a few days in and around Shiraz, visiting its gardens and monuments and discovering with a feeling akin to despair that for each site, another seemed to beckon. I had neither the time nor money to stay for much longer and, calculating how long it would take to get back to Tehran and see to some remaining details, realized I was coming to the end of my journey. From then on, the knowledge pressed against the remaining days like a hand, pushing me stubbornly in the direction of home. I didn't want to leave. I had a familiar feeling that I had learned nearly nothing meaningful about the country I had come to explore, and certainly not enough worth writing about.

Things I had at first thought strange – the sight of women with pink toenails, daily battles with unscrupulous taxi drivers, or the lack of religious observance among ordinary people – no longer seemed like novelties worth recording, and I was asking myself questions about things that hadn't caught my attention before; abstract things, like the notion of social liberty, what Islamic art was really all about, and why Iranian banks were so incredibly inefficient. You can report from a foreign country as a newcomer, and people will share your delight or surprise or disbelief. But familiarity blunts the impact of these first impressions. And the more time you spend in a different culture, the more your reactions and judgements begin to shift and accommodate; and soon, like a man asked to describe his home town, you can think of nothing to say. It's home that seems strange.

Early one morning I took a bus to Isfahan, having decided to break the journey there for a day before going on to Tehran. A big man in the robes of a cleric swept up the aisle, smelling powerfully of sweat. He glanced in my direction and, as I feared he might, sat down beside me, complaining about some minor discomfort. Dreading a theological debate, I pretended to be asleep for as much of the way as possible. But he never looked at me again, and spent the journey muttering prayers to himself. This would have been impressive but for the aggressive and wholly uncharitable manner in which he shooed beggars from the bus whenever they came aboard to plead for alms.

We reached Isfahan in the late afternoon. As I made my way into the centre of town, passing some of the sites I had explored with Ramin months earlier, I felt a comforting sense of familiarity. But one's experience of a revisiting a place without a friend is always different, and I found myself missing his mischief and spirit of enquiry. I found a hotel popular with foreign tourists and checked in. The house rules had conceded to the strange habits of the clientele, and the women shed their scarves and long coats as soon as they were inside. This, at first, is a novelty to the eye that has grown accustomed to the complete absence of the feminine outline in public. A woman wrapped in a long towel passed me in the corridor, combing her fingers through her wet hair as she passed, and I caught myself staring. An answering scowl brought me to my senses.

A little later, wanting to write some letters over a pot of tea, I found a table in the courtyard outside. Watching the other guests come and go, I registered, with a shock, the severity of my own eye. Opposite me a pink-faced and shaven-headed blonde woman emerged from her room and joined a group of friends sitting at a table. Another woman, sitting nearby and wearing military-style fatigues and hiking boots, barked a comradely greeting. It seems an uncharitable admission, but against the Iranian women I had met, their European counterparts looked curiously graceless. Even barefoot they seemed to shuffle like convicts, slumping into chairs with their legs splayed like the trunks of waterlogged trees, or heaving on cigarettes like navvies between batches of cement.

Their fellow travellers, clustering like revolutionaries at nearby tables, were conquering the world armed with nothing but their Lonely Planet guidebooks, and ticking off entire continents like vaccinations. At one a dapper young Italian was sharing his stupendous itinerary with a few others. From Iran he was planning to go to Pakistan, then along the Karakoram highway into China; Mongolia after that, and then on the Trans-Siberian Express back to Moscow; although he thought Sri Lanka might be an option at this point, for a bit of a break. A friend with a yacht had offered him passage from Africa round the Cape, so the idea was to get to Egypt by the end of spring, go south by camel to Somalia, and meet in Mozambique. They would end up in Chile: he'd never been to Chile, he said.

I wondered how far he would get; probably all the way, alas. But it seemed unlikely he would notice very much: the speed of today's traveller is against it. One can travel more and more now and, relieved of nearly all the inconveniences and hazards of one's predecessors, engage less and less with one's surroundings. Every kind of guidebook is available to lessen the burden of having to observe anything for oneself, much less make the effort of describing it afterwards. Soon perhaps, the entire world could be described in a few monosyllabic adjectives of boxed text.*

My own journey seemed very ordinary by contrast, and very timid. Beside the momentous trajectory of my neighbours, a guilty pang that I had seen scarcely anything of Isfahan's pre-Safavid architecture felt suddenly and absurdly introspective. But it was true: I had not even visited the Friday Mosque (although technically there were four Friday Mosques, as well as over a hundred others) and decided dutifully that I should go at once.

I was glad I did. After the clamour and congestion of the

---

* Later on I rediscovered Byron's rebellious musings on the same theme: 'I wish I were rich enough', he writes, 'to endow a prize for the sensible traveller: £10,000 for the first man to cover Marco Polo's outward route reading three fresh books a week, and another £10,000 if he drinks a bottle of wine a day as well. That man might tell one something about the journey.'

bazaar which you wind through to get there, the central courtyard of the mosque provides a feeling of relief and expansion. It is about two hundred feet square and surrounded by four great *ivāns*, all blazing with elaborate tilework. It has none of the formal coherence of the Imam Mosque on the great maidan, but possesses a tremendous and antique power. The overall structure covers nearly a square mile, and has been frequently built onto, damaged, and reconstructed at different times; the whole represents a sort of compendium of architectural styles spanning more than a thousand years. The greater part belong to the era of the Seljuks, that is, the eleventh century, though the original plan is thought to be ʿAbbasid, and there are even some columns which are thought to be Sasanian, suggesting a pre-Islamic origin for the site.

I found myself in the winter prayer room, which was so warm I wondered how it was heated. I asked an elderly man who had just finished his prayers and sat down nearby me. It wasn't, he said: the walls were so thick they provided a nearly even temperature all year round. Near its entrance stood a dramatic stucco mehrab built for the Ilkhanid Sultan Uljeitu: a twenty-foot-high rectangle with a central arched prayer-niche, enclosed by a greater arch and bands of intricate carving in at least three planes. A panel above the niche, which at first looked like an abstract pattern of arabesques, was in fact a highly geometricized writing; more bands of calligraphy of various sizes stretched with extraordinary fluidity against a field of leaves and spiralling tendrils.

I looked at it for what seemed like a long time. Here again, three distinct worlds had been given voice: nature, order, and the word. The abundance and vitality of nature is nearly everywhere in Islamic art, and in Persian art is nearly overwhelming; though reading about Islamic art you never get this impression. This, I think, is worth repeating. The tendency is to reduce the almost primordial presence of nature's pulse to the exigencies of mere design, and hugely undermines its significance. Then there is the ordering logic of geometry: profoundly rational, ingenious, and intellectually puzzling and stimulating at the same time. Here too, in most accounts of Islamic art, geometry is seen as scarcely more than prettification, the result of a scriptural constraint against naturalism. But one has only to look a little to see that it is too creative, too exuberant, and too purposefully lucid to be the result of a frustrated artistic impulse. Finally, sanctifying these two great rivers of expression, are the verses of the sacred text, which celebrate the divine origin of all things and remind the believer that he too has a place within them.

Without really knowing it, I had been looking at versions of this great triadic configuration nearly every day. Each, it struck me then, appeals to a different fundamental human function: instinct, intellect, and emotion. It is perhaps this combination that helps to explain the appeal of Islamic art to such a wide audience, even to people for whom the majestic swirls of the Arabic script are nothing more than fantastic and enigmatic shapes. The intimacy of this triple repertoire of motifs – I am not sure what the word should be – is interesting. It exists in nearly all the finest Islamic art, but especially in Persian decoration – though this word, now more than ever, seemed utterly inadequate.

Always there are the opposing forces of the geometric and the cursive. I realized now they were never far apart, and the way they interacted seemed to be becoming more intelligible by the moment. I felt as though my eyes were being slowly retrained to this unfamiliar language, and experienced the momentary thrill of unexpected comprehension.

Geometric patterns, in near-infinite variations of pattern and scale, are combined with floral and vegetal patterns for a *reason* that exceeds any aesthetic directive: they express something about the shape of the world itself. The crystalline and the fluid, the angular and the spiral – these are poles of meaning to be found in the very structure of both matter and events. They express the yin and yang of Islamic art, the immutable aspect of things and the changeable, the spin of the atom and the lattice in which it is held, the mathematical and the incalculable, the time-bound and the eternal. And between these a kind of reconciling element is almost always at work: that of calligraphy, itself composed in strict geometrical ratios but, overtly, cursive; and containing a portion of both elements. Of all the visual arts it is calligraphy that is the most sacred, the most visible and widespread; it binds together the logical and intuitive components of art and relates the whole to the revelation central to all of Islam's most sacred visual expressions. To the believer its very curves are impregnated with whispers of the divine.

You need know nothing of Islamic art in the formal sense, or anything about its history, to arrive at this: you just need to *look* at it. It was designed for the mind willing to contemplate it, and this provision alone yields ample reward. The more I read of contemporary scholarship on Islamic art and its meaning, the more I believed that looking, and contemplating, was the saner and more worthwhile option.

Suddenly I remembered my fellow passenger on the flight to Shiraz and the final comment he had made about his visit to Europe. A brief tour of several cathedrals had convinced him quickly of their beauty, 'but,' he'd said, almost apologetically, 'there's just one problem with them. They haven't got any details. You've seen Iran so you know how much we love the details. It's the details that count.'

At the northern and southern ends of the courtyard rise the two main domes, the larger dating from the time of Nizam al-Mulk, the famous Seljuk minister. An inscription records the year of its construction as 1072. A forest of thick stone columns, covering several thousand square feet, surrounds both the domes. But it is the north chamber, built in 1088 and called the Gombad-e Khirqa or Taj al-Molk, that steals the architectural show here. Byron and Pope — two of the most critical architectural minds of the twentieth century — are both, for once, unable to raise any objection whatever to the structure, and it is satisfying to observe them clutching at superlatives to describe their wonder and admiration. All others are unanimous. The exquisite architectural harmonies are indeed a marvel; it is only in the past decade or so that analyses of the building by computational mechanics have confirmed its structural perfection. But it is more than just a shape that has endured nearly a thousand years in an earthquake-ridden country without a crack: it is also a masterpiece of intellection, the rendering of a whole compendium of underlying ideas.

There was no one about. The sunlight broke into the dimness from an aperture in the south-west, driving an incandescent beam through the dusty atmosphere. I photographed the enigmatic pentagonal design built into the dome, wondering if anyone had ever tried to decipher the meaning of the shapes. Then I lay on the floor under the apex of the dome. It was all smaller than I had pictured. I was struck by the continuous echo sounded by the profile of the arches which, in their many different sizes, retain the same proportions; all are magnetically absorbed and finally overcome by the same encompassing profile expressed by the dome overhead. Gradually I began to have an inkling of why such a fuss had been made of the place by those who had taken the time to study it. A quality of balance pervades the space created by all those colluding arches, which no single component is allowed to usurp. It made me think of the mosque of Sheikh Lutfullah, where a similarly perfect marriage is achieved between the quadrilateral and circular, although there the surface decoration seems designed to conceal the structural elements and overwhelm the mind with symphonies of colour and light.

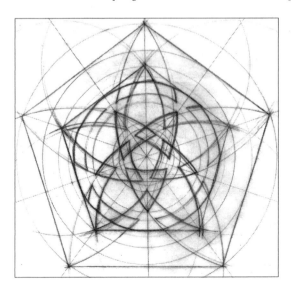

A little group of advancing Japanese tourists interrupted this line of thought, and I brushed myself off and wandered outside. In the sunlight again, I passed under the towering north-west *ivān* with its extraordinary scooped-out layers of giant squinch-like *muqarnas*. I photographed it, and was about to move on when a dim feeling of recognition began to work its way into my mind. I had the feeling I had seen it somewhere before, and wondered which mosque or monument it was reminding me of. It was a puzzling feeling, like trying to recall a familiar but momentarily forgotten name. Then I realized: it wasn't another building I'd seen at all: *it was the cave!* That brief and shadowy imprint I had glimpsed in the belly of the mountain above Firuzabad came suddenly to life, as if the same curtains of stone had been transported whole to Isfahan, delicately geometricized, and mounted into the walls of the mosque.

It wasn't only in the north-west *ivān* that the cave had magically reappeared. A variation of the design was built into the opposite *ivān* on a smaller scale; and it appeared again in the uppermost portion of the northern mehrab wall. Here the shadow-filled folds were divided into the same diamond-shaped recesses that had made such an impression when I had first seen their natural versions by the light of a flaming branch. Could the repetition of shapes all be coincidence? Or had the inspiration of the *muqarnas* vault – that stalactitic marvel pioneered in Seljuk times and transmitted in a thousand variations to the borders of China in the east and to Spain in the west – come from an entirely natural source: the very cave I had seen, or one like it? I had read nothing that suggested the role of natural shapes in architecture had ever been investigated. Or perhaps the architect's design was modelled on a form inherent in nature itself, and the prototypes for both resided in a single cosmic archetype, from whose occulted source nature and architect drew alike? Perhaps this was the meaning of nature imitating art after all ... it seemed a weighty proposition. I knew at once I would have to return on a later trip to photograph the cave, and find out if I had imagined the whole thing.

I could have no idea yet, but this puzzle had entered me like a barbed harpoon. It was not about to let me go easily.

Φ

Tehran was sunny and cool. Once again, Sorush greeted me with characteristic imperturbability, and I felt as though I had come home. Our evenings were spent in long discussions. He was keen to know about my travels, and sad to hear that I would be leaving in a few days' time. I told him there was much more I wanted to see and do, and that I hoped to come back in the spring.

'Spring is best time,' he said.

I told him about my brief encounter in Qom and that, with some regret, I had turned down an offer of apprenticeship as a mulla.

We had stopped on the outskirts of Qom, the country's centre of theological learning and the site of a famous shrine, that of Hazrat-e Massumeh, the sister of Imam Reza. Filing from the bus, we lined up at a roadside cafe for cupfuls of hot sweet milk, served from a huge saucepan. A cleric and fellow passenger was beside me, and asked if I had come to visit Qom. How did I find Iran? Was I a Muslim? This was a line of questioning I nowadays preferred to keep short.

'God knows,' I replied, 'you'd have to ask Him.'

A few people heard this exchange, and grinned wickedly. But the cleric smiled gently at this slight, and immediately I regretted my impertinence. He invited me, sincerely I think, to come back to Qom one day and stay. If I was interested in learning more about religious matters, he would arrange my accommodation himself, for a month or a year, if need be. I was touched by this disarming openness, by which my own opinionatedness seemed all the more misplaced.

As he walked away, the man ahead of me turned to face me, and gave me a collusive nudge. 'You did the right thing,' he said, 'putting him in his place like that. It's none of his business – he ought to have shown you a bit more respect.' I had scored a point for ordinary people, who revel in the humiliation of clerics.

'Before Islam – Iran had own religion!' said Sorush. 'Zoroastrianism was last good religion of Iran. Good words, good thoughts, good acts – simple! That is real religion – should be simple for ordinary people.'

I was surprised to hear of a belief which had been officially extinguished more than thirteen centuries earlier recalled with such affection: this was yet another example of the long reach of history in the Iranian psyche. It is hard to imagine thirty thousand druids living in Tunbridge Wells; but there were still thriving Zoroastrian communities in Iran.*

'Sunni religion is simpler,' he went on. 'One God, Prophet, then ordinary man. But Shi'ite!' He tapped his forehead with pursed fingers. 'How can mind focus on God with so many Holy Ones? God, Prophet, Ali, Fatima, Hassan, Husein – then twelve Imam, *how* many saint, *how* many ayatollah? Worse than Church!' Then, with characteristic wickedness, added: 'You can be much more than mulla – if you have idea, you can be prophet here, if you want. People will listen. After two, three years – maybe have ten thousand followers!'

Φ

On the day before I was due to leave, I decided on a final trip into the city centre for some last-minute errands and to buy souvenirs. I telephoned for a taxi from the house, and a few minutes later a giant thirty-year-old white Chevrolet was outside, its engine thudding like a barge. I jumped into the passenger seat and wondered if I hadn't got into the wrong car by mistake: the driver was a young woman in dark glasses and dressed not in black but a light-coloured scarf and jacket which fell open above

---

* Among many other religious groups, sects, and communities, of which the Christians, Zoroastrians, Baha'i, Yezidis, and the Ahl-e Haqq are the best known. Outside Israel, Iran has the largest population of Jews in the Middle East. The shrine raised over the Jewish prophet Daniel in Susa is much revered by local Muslims, though it is hard to imagine a reciprocal phenomenon in Israel.

her knees. This was another surprise; but by now I was used to surprises. We drove in silence for a while, but I couldn't resist asking: wasn't she ever afraid to drive a taxi alone?

'Not really,' she said, with a shrug. She had only once had a problem with a male passenger, but had managed quickly to dissuade him.

I asked her how.

'Seven years of tae-kwon-do.'

She wrote her mobile number on a business card ('in case you can't get through to the agency') and dropped me near the post office.

I had forgotten it was Friday, and a holiday. The post office was closed. The streets were quieter than usual and I decided to cut south towards the centre of the city. Roughly midway I came to what looked like the entrance to a park. A road led up a slope lined with dusty pine and acacia trees and a little further on a man was dozing in the shade of his car. I kept walking and soon heard the sound of children playing, then saw more cars and, beside them, men in twos and threes smoking water pipes beneath the trees. At the top of the hill, ranged over an acre of grassy banks, hundreds of people lay sprawling in the unseasonable warmth. Some had put up windbreaks for their portable cookers and were hauling sets of pots and picnic coolers from the boots of their cars. The sweet smoke of the pipes mingled with the smell of sizzling kebabs where families spanning three generations had laid out their afternoon meal. I ducked as a stray shuttlecock sailed over my head. Father and daughter had set up a net between two trees and were both giggling at the near-miss. I knew I would be sad to see this kind of sight disappear from daily life; it reminded me of a world of greater innocence. I knew that this place of innocence was within me, and wasn't a place at all. But I knew I'd miss it all the same.

I kept walking; down into the city, south of Ferdowsi Square near the British Embassy, where the antique shops cluster. I had bought a few things here before, but wondered if my eye had grown more discriminating, and hoped some affordable trinket I had never noticed might present itself from behind one of the windowpanes. The displays were stuffed with trays of rings, old Russian medals and samovars, miniature paintings, gaudy porcelain vases and oil lamps, entaglioed clocks, sparkling geodes, prayer beads of every colour and size, mouthpieces for water pipes with great bulbous amber collars, inlaid boxes and chess sets and walking sticks, ancient cameras, antique cigarette lighters and watches. But it was Friday and they were mostly closed; the only shops that were open were run by Jews.

In one, behind a dusty window, half a dozen painted penboxes caught my eye. They were unmistakably Persian. I guessed they were about fifty years old. My heart set on one of them. It was eight inches long, an inch and a half wide, and delicately painted with scrolling flowers and birds set in tiny cartouches on a black lacquer background. I wondered how much it might cost: there couldn't be that many foreign buyers in Tehran to drive up the prices, and it was only papier mâché, after all. It would make a lovely present, and with a crisp hundred-dollar bill in my pocket I was feeling quite rich.

'That one,' said the owner without ceremony as I pointed out the one I liked, 'is three thousand dollars. But I have much better quality if you'd like to see.'

A second attempt in another shop to buy a chess set, and then a Russian jewellery box, ended in similar humiliation. I retreated to a third. I had visited it a few months before and met the owner, an incorrigible and silvery-haired character with a faintly obsequious manner. His shop was full of clutter, most of it worthless, but hoping I might uncover some dusty treasure, I went in.

'Shalom!'

His sad features lit up with theatrical delight and a chorus of nasal and reciprocating shaloms!

'Where have you been all this time? Tea! Tea! Sit!' He rummaged beneath the shop counter and fussed over a stove and pot of tea. We chatted for a while as it came to the boil, until a pair of Dutch women came in. I watched as he slithered behind the counter and, carefully gauging his customers' every glance, launched gently into a shameless routine. 'Holland? ... *Very* nice.' The two women admitted reluctantly they were from the embassy; it was their day off. From under the counter he unwrapped a 'thousand-year-old' Seljuk bowl, caressing it before their eyes with a honeyed '*Very* special ... antique, antique.' When their attention began to waver, he produced a sheaf of painted miniatures, fanning them before their eyes with an expert flourish; then rosaries made from the finest *shah maqsud*, and finally a selection of solid silver tribal jewellery, which he stroked as he lay on the counter in front of them. '*Very nice, very nice ... special price for ladies...*' The ceramics were no older than his grandchildren; the miniatures grotesque, and the rosaries made from coloured glass.

The women fled; he returned to me with a look of resignation, and we chatted over tea. I had no money, I said; I just came to say hello. He was undeterred. Perhaps I needed a loan? He could send anything I wanted directly to England, and I could pay another time. Why, the British Ambassador himself was his old friend, and had that very week spent five hundred dollars in the shop ...

As we were talking, a young man entered, dismissed the owner's petitions in brusque Persian, and stood nearby, fingering a trinket. I had the impression he was listening to our conversation. A few minutes later he left, but lingered outside, and from time to time I could see his sunglasses bobbing inquisitively beyond the window. A little later, after I had bought a few small souvenirs, I went out.

'No offence,' said an American voice, 'but I could tell you were a foreigner.' He had been waiting for me. There was a friendly smile on his youthful features as I shook his hand, observing my own reflection in the black and bulbous lenses of his sunglasses.

'I was looking out for you in there,' he said gravely. He glanced over his shoulder and back again. 'You never know.' I thanked him for his concern and, a little mystified, told him he needn't have worried. We walked north together towards Ferdowsi Square, and talked a little. He was from Los Angeles, he said; this was his first trip to Iran, to visit family, and he was loving it. But his affection was heavily taxed by a sense of threat.

'The first thing you've gotta know is the price of things,' he said, peering over his shoulder once more like a bodyguard. 'These people are like *wolves*. They'll tear you apart if you don't know how to deal with them.' I hadn't actually asked him for this advice, but nodded appreciatively. 'Me,' he tapped his chest confidently, 'I look Iranian, so they know not to mess with me.'

He was in his early twenties. A narrow goatee, fastidiously trimmed, ran from his lower lip to a tapering point under his chin. He wore absurdly baggy jeans, expensive running shoes, and a watch as big as a computer, and carried a complicated-looking backpack. On his head sat that icon of sartorial impenitence, a baseball cap, worn backwards. I never saw his eyes; he never took his RayBans off. Only a large American flag could have made him more conspicuous.

We reached a crossroads, where he put a protective hand onto my shoulder. 'Watch out. They'll run you down and won't even look back.' A little further on, we stopped at a corner, where our conversation began to founder. 'This country,' he said, 'I tell you, is like ... going through something big.' His hands searched for gestures to convey this momentous insight. 'Know what I'm saying?'

'Perhaps you mean a transition?'

'Yeah — a transition. You can feel it. Being here is like ... like ...'

'Like surfing ...?'

'Yeah, surfing!'

'... the crest of a wave, just before it breaks?'

'*Exactly!* That's *exactly* right.' He looked serious again. 'It's an incredible opportunity for investment — but you gotta have the contacts. Listen,' he glanced at his watch, and for a moment I thought he would suggest an investor's meeting, or a dinner, 'I gotta get going.'

I realized then how accustomed I had grown to the civility of ordinary Iranians; the greetings, the ritualized enquiries, and all the assurances and invitations that adhere to the moment of human encounter. Suddenly I felt myself pitching in the wake of an alien culture, and for a moment recognized the distance I had come in my own habits, the way a familiar landmark, hidden awhile before returning into view, reminds the traveller of his own shifting trajectory. Now this unbidden familiarity seemed shockingly abrasive.

Perhaps I was judging him too harshly; but his manner reminded me of an old enemy and I had begun involuntarily to dislike him. No doubt or contradiction breached the sheltering certainty of his vision. He saw only allies and threats, between which no human frailty or ordinariness was allowed to intervene. His Iran was a child's montage, constructed hastily with all the confidence of the privileged outsider, but untempered by the complexities of the life he presumed to comprehend.

'Have you seen the women?' he asked suddenly. 'They're so, so ...'

'Feminine?'

'*Exactly!* Guys at home have no idea what they're missing. And they treat you like a *king* here.' Given the fate of Iranian royalty, this was not the most felicitous allusion. 'Listen,' he said, with a knowing look, 'I know all the places where they hang out.'

He asked if I had pen and paper and, squatting with my notebook on his knee, wrote down the names of a few restaurants in Tajrish. 'You have *got* to go,' he said. 'Know what I'm saying?' An opium-stricken beggar, swaying on his feet, stood nearby, watching us dumbly.

'I'm telling you,' he looked up, 'they're the most beautiful women in the world. Tall, slim, flat stomachs, great asses.'

Such were the defining assets of the culture, reduced now to anatomical portions on the third floor of the Alburz restaurant.

'And you know what the best thing is?'

I shook my head.

'They're all so damn *horny!* I swear to God: every single one of them.' He grinned with emphatic relish. 'Absolutely *begging* for it.'

Six

Aups · Isfahan
Shiraz · Firuzabad

An Unbeautiful Instrument · Phi, Fie ... · Lines Visible and Invisible

The Riddle of the Maidan · Clues and Discoveries · Zizou's Honour

More non-Euclidean Speleology · Caveat Lector: Nasruddin's Pigeon

Aspects of Islamic Art · Epistemological Conundrums

The Problem of Meaning · All Roads Lead to Metaphysics

Dissolving Snowflakes

گدائی در میخانه طرفه اکسیریست   گر این عمل بکنی خاک زر توانی کرد

Begging at the door of the wine tavern is a marvellous elixir
If you perform this work, you may turn dust into gold

SEVERAL MONTHS later, I had begun the long process of sorting through the raw material from which the book would be distilled. This was a longer process than I had foreseen, and a more solitary one. A friend had offered a lonely place to write, where my only visitor was a white cat with an unsteady gait and tragic air, yellow eyes and dusty-looking ears. It was winter and a wood stove crackled in a corner of the small kitchen. A little wine softened the approach of nightfall. There, late one evening, I made a small discovery.

Since my first visit to Isfahan I had often puzzled over the configuration of the famous monuments built around the great Naqsh-e Jahan Square, and wondered about its most curious feature: the glaring lack of alignment between the dome of the Sheikh Lutfullah Mosque and its entrance portal. Everyone who goes to Isfahan sees this curiosity. Now, with architectural plans of the square and the mosque spread across the table in front of me, I wondered if the puzzle might yield some answers.

The first thing was to ask whether the conventional explanations really made sense. Byron's observation – that 'the outside of the mosque is careless of symmetry to a grotesque degree', and that the discrepancy is a 'deformity' – sets the tone for nearly all later explanations. And in all but one of the descriptions I had read over the previous months, the reason given is the same: that the orientation of the mosque to the qiblah, the direction of Mecca, required an adjustment relative to the orientation of the maidan to which it is attached.*

---

* The exception is that of Professor Robert Hillenbrand, who notes in *The*

The diagnosis is only half-convincing. In the case of the Royal Mosque, which is similarly skewed, it is valid enough. But it is insufficient to explain the 'deformity' of the Lutfullah Mosque. There is no obvious reason why the dome could not have been constructed in a slightly different position, by extending the length of the entrance tunnel a few yards, in order to satisfy the conventional demands of symmetry. Had the mosque been built a little further to the north, both portal and dome could have been perfectly aligned.

Nor does it help to understand why, in a public setting so obviously attentive elsewhere to symmetry and harmonious proportions, the most talented architects of the era would have been so inept as to allow such a prominent error. Nor, finally, does it take any account of a highly fortunate coincidence from the point of view of construction: that the difference between the qiblah orientation and that of the maidan is precisely forty-five degrees.

It seemed fair to throw it out for the time being and look for a more satisfying reason; to assume that the mistake was both deliberate and precise. Professor Hillenbrand's suggestion – that the architects had chosen deliberately to draw attention to the misalignment – was intriguing. One could take the deviation not as a mistake but as a clue; to what, I didn't know. But it was possible, in this spirit, to look at the deviation between dome and portal as an *alignment*, instead of a misalignment, and I wondered what might happen if I joined up the point of the dome on my plan with the apex of the arched portal beneath it.

Perhaps the lines themselves might speak ... bisecting the square of the dome chamber, I found the centre, and put one end

---

Cambridge History of Iran that 'it is only when one analyses the relationship between the aivan (portal) and the dome that a discord is apparent, and it is highly significant that this discord is unnecessary.' However, he interprets the conflicting axes of mosque and maidan as an effort on the part of the architect 'to reveal, not to conceal, that the dues of Caesar conflicted with those of God.' Vol. 6, *The Timurid and Safavid Periods* (Cambridge University Press, 1986).

of a ruler on the point. A few inches away, I lined up the ruler with the mid-point of the portal, and began to draw. I pictured the line, four thousand miles away, creeping from the magic gloom beneath the dome, and heading west. Out it went: through the corner of the western wall and under the apex of the portal, out into the blazing sunlight, bumping down the steps, and creeping towards the far side of the maidan, until it reached the western wall about fifty yards north of the Ali Qapu Palace. I cleared off the paper and leaned back to look.

The point of arrival looked suspiciously like the halfway point of the maidan. Measuring the distances either side, I found that it was exactly halfway. This was more than I had hoped for. The maidan was now neatly bisected into two rectangles; perhaps there was something about their dimensions worth investigating. It was then that I wondered whether they might be constructed on the famous ratio known as the Golden Mean.

I hoped they might be: the Golden Mean was the only geometric ratio used in architecture I had ever heard of. The pervasiveness of this enigmatic relationship in nature was discovered in antiquity, pre-history perhaps. It is found replicated in Egyptian architecture, in that of the Greeks (who called it the Divine Proportion), and in the art and architecture of countless Renaissance artists, who knew it as the Golden Section. As a template for harmonious composition, it is ubiquitous in European art until about fifty years ago, and persists in unexpected places.* In nature itself it can be found in everything from the dimensions of plankton to those of the human body; an enterprising scientist has

---

* Though perhaps not as distantly as is usually thought. Seurat, Signac, Gauguin, Serusier, and Chagall all made use of mathematical proportions based around the Golden Section and were much influenced by the mystical symbolism written about by such authors as Josephin Peladin and Edouard Schuré. The first obviously visible use of mystical geometry appears in the later Russian school of Suprematism, headed by such artists as Malevitch, Goncharova, and Larionov. The UN headquarters in New York, designed by Le Corbusier, conforms to 'golden' proportions.

made a study of the Golden Ratio as it pertains to female navels. The claws of a lion conform to a spiral generated from the ratio; hurricanes, whirlpools, and breaking waves and galaxies similarly abide.

But I wasn't sure yet how a golden rectangle was constructed, and hunted for a description in an encyclopaedia. This took time. Midnight struck by the time I had found what I was looking for. A straight line (I read) divided by the golden section takes on an interesting property, whereby the ratio of the smaller to the larger portion is the same as the ratio of the larger portion to the whole. The mathematics are at once simple and forbidding: numerically, the golden ratio, called Φ or *phi*, is an irrational and ultimately incalculable quantity in the region of 1.618, and has many surprising and paradoxical qualities. But the beauty of this unique quantity is that it can be expressed geometrically. All that is needed is a straight edge and a compass or, for greater distances, a length of string or rope.

I had neither, for the moment. It was too late to buy anything; I would have to improvise. After some frustrated ransacking, I found, in a kitchen drawer, a packet of wooden sticks resembling childhood spillikins. They were sharply pointed at one end and must have been for making miniature brochettes or kebabs. I took two of them, spliced the ends together with a penknife, and held them in place with a rusty bulldog clip. This became my compass for the next few hours. It was an effective but unbeautiful instrument with which to penetrate the mysteries of one of the architectural wonders of the world.

A diagram in the encyclopaedia showed what to do, and I followed it as a first-time chef follows a recipe. Taking the short edge at the southern end of the maidan, I halved it, and drew the diagonal across the resulting rectangle. Then, with one point of the kebab-compass in the corner and the other at the far end of the diagonal, I began to swing the other towards the west. I marked it where it struck the wall, and added the half square by twirling the sticks like a pair of dividers. The final length was precisely the midway point of the maidan, the very point to which I had been led by the 'deformity' of the Lutfullah Mosque. The result was inescapable: the layout of the entire maidan was an expression — whatever else it was — of the formula

$$\frac{\sqrt{5} + 1}{2}$$

or Φ, *phi*.

After this, things began to happen quickly. If the configuration of the Lutfullah Mosque was, as now seemed likely, deliberately precise, then its position, and that of the Ali Qapu Palace opposite, might be related in another way to the overall layout of the maidan.

The usual explanation was that both mosque and palace were built a third of the way along the length of the maidan. But this measure is inexact, and unconvincing; the architects of the era not only required a precise and meaningful starting point for important monuments, but even employed astrologers to calculate the most auspicious *moment* to begin building them.

Taking the overall length of the maidan, I found that the entrance to the Ali Qapu Palace opened precisely on the golden section of the length of the maidan. The distance between the domes of both mosques also gave a significant distance, repeated between several other key points. The various openings onto the square could also be derived from arcs generated by the positions of the buildings. The entire layout of the place seemed to be singing in a chorus of geometries. My ground plan was soon darkening with intersecting lines and arcs, and eventually was too punctured by my improvised compass to be accurate any longer.

It was getting late, but this flurry of discovery had given me another idea. I moved on to a different map, on a larger scale this time, of the town as it had looked in the seventeenth century. Its outstanding feature is the Chahar Bagh Avenue, which runs north–south. But the great maidan nearby does not, and I wondered what the difference in orientation might be. It was nineteen degrees; the same deviation as the maidan from the cardinal direction, and, I now discovered, also the same as the discrepancy between the

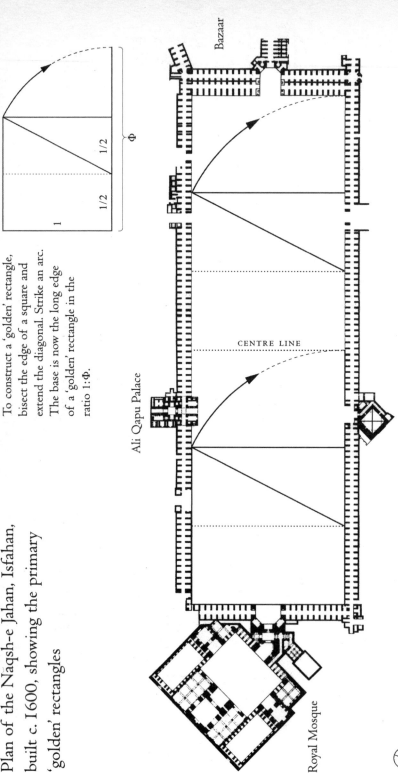

Plan of the Naqsh-e Jahan, Isfahan, built c. 1600, showing the primary 'golden' rectangles

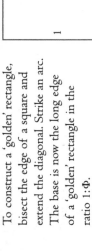

To construct a 'golden' rectangle, bisect the edge of a square and extend the diagonal. Strike an arc. The base is now the long edge of a 'golden' rectangle in the ratio 1:Φ.

1

1/2

1/2

Φ

Bazaar

Ali Qapu Palace

CENTRE LINE

Sheikh Lutfullah Mosque

Royal Mosque

20 40 60 80 100m

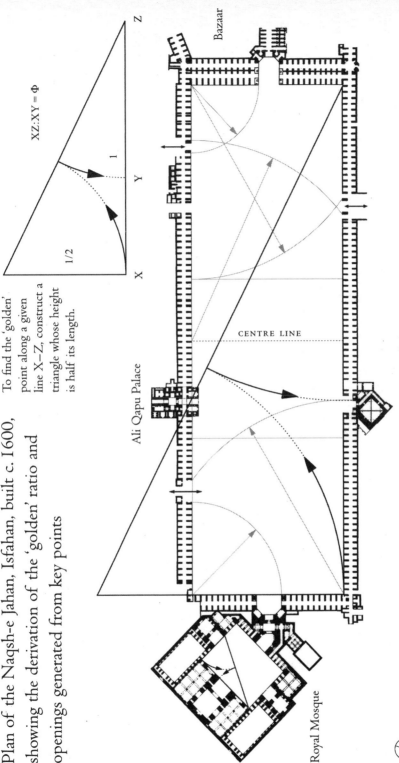

Plan of the Naqsh-e Jahan, Isfahan, built c. 1600, showing the derivation of the 'golden' ratio and openings generated from key points

To find the 'golden' point along a given line X–Z, construct a triangle whose height is half its length.

XZ:XY = Φ

Z

Y

1

X

1/2

Bazaar

CENTRE LINE

Ali Qapu Palace

Sheikh Lutfullah Mosque

Royal Mosque

20 40 60 80 100m

dome and portal of the Lutfullah Mosque. Were these coincidences too, or was the maidan linked with the Chahar Bagh Avenue in some similar way?

In the seventeenth century, the Chahar Bagh was a tree-lined promenade with a canal running down its centre. At its northern end stood the Jahan-Nama, the World-Viewing Pavilion, and at the southern end the bridge of Allahverdi Khan, also called the Si o Se Bridge after its thirty-three arches. Along its length were seven differently shaped pools, at uneven distances; these were marked on my map. I looked at them and began to wonder if their positions had been governed by some forgotten relationship. Could the length of the Chahar Bagh have been related to the proportions of the maidan? I experimented with the numbers using a scale and, with the same mixture of astonishment and delight I had felt earlier, found that the length of the maidan, multiplied by the golden ratio, gave me its midpoint, marked in its day by a large pool. With one point of the compass over the pool, and the other on the northern end, I traced another arc towards the maidan, which it struck on the western side, also in the middle. These two links – the one proportionate, using straight lines, and the other geometric, generated by an arc, suggested that the two were indeed connected.

There was much more. Using them as my point of departure, nearly all the pools generated arcs which struck the centres of significant buildings around the city: the Chehel Sutun Pavilion, the Hakim Mosque, the New Mosque, the Mosque of Ali, and, at the end of another which whirled across the city like one of the rings of Saturn, the famous Friday Mosque, all the way at the far end of the bazaar. I knew that these might just be coincidences. But even more improbably, the same technique yielded correspondences from the southern end too: arcs swung from the pools struck the very points from which the bridges were thrown across the river. I had seen old prints of other monuments and lesser palaces near the banks of the river. They did not appear on my map, but perhaps they too might have succumbed to a few of these roving arcs. We cannot know.

By now it was nearly dawn, and my punctured maps were streaked with multicoloured arcs and the triple furrows of redrawn lines. As magical as these elementary discoveries seemed, I was only too aware that wishful thinking and lack of sleep made for dubious geometry. I kept them to myself, but bought a proper compass a few days later, and decided to look for more accurate plans.

Several months later, hunting the shelves in dusty corners of the School of Oriental Studies in London, I eventually found smaller-scale plans of both the maidan and the city as it had appeared in the seventeenth century. In lulls between writing, I traced and re-traced the path of my earlier foray into the geometry of Isfahan, wondering all the while whether the measurements I was making were either accurate or significant enough to be worth writing about. A plan of the old city, based on a contemporary map, was bound to be less than perfectly accurate, but working from it I could claim an accuracy of a few metres – the thickness of a line – in two thousand, or more than 99 per cent. A modern architectural drawing of the maidan brought the figure for my calculations there even higher.

I found myself hoping, in the meantime, to find a scholarly analysis of the maidan, written by an architect with a knowledge of traditional geometric principles. Even without reference to its geometric subtleties, the maidan is recognized as an architectural wonder; each of the buildings built on it is a masterpiece in itself. But its geometric foundations, based on perhaps the most ancient of sciences, seemed not to have caught the attention of contemporary scholarship. I hoped too, in part, to be relieved of the task of suggesting that behind the architectural splendour of the maidan lay a marvellous and antique form of learning, and I longed to encounter the findings of somebody better equipped than me who could bring it properly to life. But I found nothing on the subject; realizing, eventually, that to modern ears the music of geometry is largely unheard.

My maps and plans of Isfahan became constant companions, and their cold lines, brought to life under the spell of compass and ruler, increasingly articulate. A sense that until now I had looked at architecture in terms of history alone strengthened into a feeling of neglect. So I studied the rudiments of geometry, and learned something of the sanctity in which number and shape were held in earlier eras. To those who gave themselves most fully to the science, all of creation, from the very humblest of natural structures to the shape of the solar system itself, resounded with the syllables of a geometric voice, impregnated into all matter from its birth. It was inevitable that civilizations conscious of the qualitative aspect of shape should express the principles of their science in architecture. Their monuments were built up from such elementary units as the circle, universally symbolic of the infinite, and its earthly counterpart, the square. Shapes derived from this most primordial of geometric relationships possessed personalities and communicated ideas – mysteries, rather, guarded by such influential schools as those associated with the name of Pythagoras and, closer to our own time, those of Vitruvius, Palladio, da Vinci, and Bruno.

Islamic civilization inherited this sense of wonder for the singleness of creation, and the Islamic fascination for mathematics invested geometry with special significance.* In Persia, especially, the centrality of mathematics to learning, combined with an ancient attachment to visual symbolism, brought geometrical art to a high level of refinement. Persian artists, shying from the uncertainties of representational art, chose to continue earlier traditions of geometric art, eventually making it the central device of their most sacred works. With characteristic genius, the best of this art was imbued with the principles of the Islamic revelation: the oneness of the Divine, and its reflection in all

---

* Our own 'Arabic' numerals are indicative of the European debt to Islamic scientific learning. Fibonacci, the most influential mathematician of the Middle Ages, received his formative training from an Arab teacher in North Africa. It is with his name that the famous numerical series in which each number is the sum of the two preceding numbers is most closely associated.

creation. This became allied with an entirely new kind of art form — that of calligraphy — which reinforced the transcendence of artistic themes and universalized the message of the new religion. The vigour and beauty of this combination proved contagious, and was taken up across vast blocs of culture.

I had not intended, when I began to trespass on the borders of the world of this art, to go deeply into it; much less to entrap the reader into my own haphazard investigation. Nor had I realized the extent to which Islamic art as a whole is seen by the great majority of art historians as essentially decorative, and lacking in any underlying principles. This and the puzzle of the maidan seemed a valid reason to continue the line of enquiry; the mystery of the cave, another. But a third finding, at home this time, convinced me that it was worth taking the risk.

This was the encounter one day with an article on the tomb of the Achaemenid King Cyrus, the founder of the Persian Empire. Cyrus died in 529 BC, having established at Pasargadae, not far from Persepolis, the earliest imperial Achaemenid head-quarters. A palace, pavilions, and a royal park were built on the once-fertile plain; contemporary Greek authors described such complexes as *pairidaeza*, from which our own 'paradise' derives.

His lonely mausoleum survives there today; the only building at the site to have weathered the intervening two and a half millennia relatively intact. At about thirty feet high, it has nothing of the epic scale of later Achaemenid structures, though the lowest course is the height of a man. In shape it resembles a gabled Greek temple atop a miniature ziggurat. An arcade-like structure once surrounded the mausoleum, and in old photographs one can see its broken columns and a collapsing stone portal.

There were lots of detailed plans and elevations, and I read the article in the hope of finding some mention of the geometry behind the most ancient surviving monument of Iran. There was none. I went to work on it with my compass, and was fascinated to see that the principal elevations could all be easily derived from the dimensions of the steps.

But it also became clear that the dimensions were built up on a series of golden proportions, and that some of the clues to finding these distances were even indicated by the joints in the courses of the steps. More than two thousand years later, the same underlying principles of number and harmony, as well as the tree and blossom-flanked canal of sparkling water, had been replicated in Safavid Isfahan. The line that links them is dimensionless to conventional history. But it is there; it can be traced — even with a pair of kebab sticks. Doing so had been an unexpected adventure. It was strange to think that the whole thing had started with the sight, on a summer's afternoon more than a year earlier, of a misaligned dome.

Φ

Credit histories wither, unopened bills gather in mutely scowling piles, and friends cease out of politeness to ask the obvious. Loved ones adapt to growing doses of saffron, pomegranate sauce, fresh herbs, and the sweet smoke of the water pipe; dinner conversations border on the arcane. Mention of the Taj Mahal serves as a reminder that the architect was in fact Persian; a passing reference to another approaching Christmas evokes the Zoroastrian tradition of venerating the cypress tree with gifts and candles; and an offer of a game of chess invites a guess at the solution to al-Biruni's exponential rice-grain puzzle.*

'I suppose the Persians discovered America too,' says a sceptic.
'As a matter of fact, there is some evidence . . .' you begin.

Φ

---

* The ancient chessboard problem is cited in al-Biruni's *Chronology of Ancient Nations*. The inventor of the game of chess is offered by his grateful ruler a favour, and appears to request nothing more than a few bags of rice: a single grain for the first square of the chessboard, two for the second, four for the next, and so on for each square. Guesses for the final figure run into thousands, occasionally millions. Al-Biruni's solution is:

$$\sum^{64} 2^i - 1 = 2^{64} - 1 \text{ or } 18,446,744,073,709,551,615$$

a number greater than all the grains of rice ever consumed . . .

I decided on a final journey to Iran, and returned to Tehran in late spring. My irreplaceable host, Sorush, had been called away, and a sad telephone conversation from the airport reoriented my plans to the south of the country. I headed for Isfahan the same day, to see if I could make any more sense of my pet discoveries, and arrived late and exhausted. It was a balmy evening and I strolled the length of the Chahar Bagh looking for a restaurant that was still open. In a small side street I found the Shahrazād, an unexpectedly grand establishment with Qajar-style stained-glass windows, where a dozen jacketed waiters circulated among the clientele.

The manager, who spoke a curiously colloquial English, fussed over me attentively and asked if we should speak in English or Persian.

'Your English,' I said, 'is better than my Persian.' He thought for a moment, then said: 'Yes, but *your* English is better than *my* Persian.'

'How do I get out of that?' I asked.

'You don't,' he said, with a smile, 'you just roll on . . .'

After the meal we shared a glass of tea in his office, where we chatted for a while. Years before, he had lived in America and married there, but things had changed. We exchanged some improvised gifts – a pen, and a box of nougat – and as the last of the guests were leaving, he saw me downstairs to the door.

'Hang loose,' he said, as we parted, and I felt as though I had made another friend.

It was after midnight. The streets were deserted as I walked back to the hotel, and I realized I was very happy to be back. Images of seventeenth-century engravings of the Chahar Bagh came floating into my mind. I remembered one in particular, dominated by the dome of the madrasseh hovering above the trees, pools, and fountains nearby, and the sauntering nobles and idling dervishes puffing at their water pipes.

I looked up, as if on cue, and there was the very dome: I was in almost the same spot where the artist had stood nearly four hundred years earlier. I was struck by the graceful buoyancy of its shape, its unearthly colour, and the lyricism of its decoration, and had a sudden feeling for the mystery of the invisibility of the past. I had noticed how prone I had been over the course of all these journeys to imagining the vanished sights and sounds of certain places I had visited, and wondered again whether such moments were the products of fancy alone or whether indeed the past exists, and whispers more audibly in certain places. Perhaps it was a little of both.

Further north, there was an opening between the buildings lining the road and beyond them I could see trees and neat hedgerows in what looked like a park. I wandered in, and walked across the grass under tall oriental pines. In the centre of the park was the beautiful pavilion called the Hasht Behesht or Eight Paradises. I sat on a nearby bench and looked at it for a while, admiring the slender columns of its porches, its symmetries, and the intricate mirror work in the lattices of its ceiling.

Then from somewhere across the trees I hear the voice of a man, singing. It was a beautiful and deeply stirring melody and I wished I had known enough of Persian music at the time to recognize the style of the *gūshe* or melodic form. I listened for a while as the voice grew magically closer, then caught sight of the solitary figure walking alone on one of the paths nearby. I walked up, casually, and the singing stopped. He was young and smartly dressed with a leather purse under one arm. We talked for a few minutes about the different types of melodies of traditional music; he was still learning but he knew most of them, he said. A *gūshe* might be named after a particular town or region, a specific emotion, or name; these were in turn associated with different times of day or night, seasons and colours.

I begged him to allow me to record his voice but he refused, gently and very firmly. We parted and he disappeared among the trees. Then, a little while later and from a different direction, I heard his voice start up again, and listened until it faded away beyond the trees as magically and unexpectedly as it had first begun.

Φ

For months I had wondered if there might be any visible correspondence between the position of the now-disappeared pools along the Chahar Bagh and the other remaining Safavid monuments around the city. I wasn't sure what one might look for; an architectural anomaly of some kind, which might indicate a particular spot was significant. A clue, in essence, bequeathed by the original architects. So for several days of delicious leisure I walked to and fro between them, keeping an eye open for anything unusual. Regular stops at an ice-cream stall and tea breaks with voluble carpet-dealers broke up the hours of pacing into easy stages.

I wanted first to plot the sites of the original seven pools and decided to start at the southern end, where the Bridge of Thirty-Three Arches joined the far bank of the river. It was from here that my improvised compass had traced so many intriguing relations with the monuments scattered about the town. I walked south along the Chahar Bagh and crossed the bridge. A steady flow of pedestrians swept along its length, and children were playing in the arches and in the shallow water around the piers. The river was full and multicoloured pedal-boats were circling nearby like windblown petals. On the grassy banks on the far side families were picnicking between fountains under the trees, and I felt once again as though I had stumbled into a protected realm, where a portion of the world's innocence had managed to survive.*
Some men were men playing chess on the benches. There were couples deep in conversation, and a girl sped past me on roller-blades. I walked along the paths by the water's edge, peered along the diminishing arches under the bridge, and looked around for

---

* So I cannot resist quoting Byron's first visit to the bridge at dusk, where he writes: 'The lights came out. A little breeze stirred ... I smelt the spring, and the rising sap. One of those rare moments of absolute peace, when the body is loose, the mind asks no questions, and the world is a triumph, was mine.' Later on he writes: 'The beauty of Isfahan steals on the mind unawares ... and before you know how, Isfahan has become indelible, has insinuated its image into that gallery of places which everyone privately treasures.'

anything that might be construed as significant and, finding nothing, began to think how improbable the prospect really was.

But walking back I made my first discovery. Along the axis of the bridge on the southern ramp was a dark shape I hadn't noticed on the way. Set into the surface of the bridge was a thick slab of glass about three feet square. There was no indication as to its purpose. Under the scratched surface I could just make out an earlier layer of stonework; a tiny portion, it seemed likely, of the original surface of the bridge before it had been restored.

A little crowd began to gather around me as I studied it. Soon there were about twenty people peering at the square beneath them, all of them speculating intently. Extricating myself, I sat down at the edge of the bridge to watch the scene I had inadvertently created. After a few minutes they dispersed and the flow of passers-by returned to normal. I went back to the mysterious plate of glass for another look, and within moments another crowd had formed. I thought how differently things happened in England. When a man kneels down in the middle of a street, people will diligently avoid him, fearing a lunatic; in Iran, they gathered around. It was odd, and very satisfying, to find it in the very position to which I'd devoted so much attention with my kebab-stick back home.

Today, a traffic roundabout marks the southern end of the Chahar Bagh. Shops line the remaining length, and no trace remains of the pools which once marked the entrance to the vanished palaces and gardens. But as I walked north to the mid-point, at the level of the Hasht Behesht Pavilion, I noticed a statue in the very place where the middle pool must have once been built. It was made of grey stone and depicted a tall and bearded man in a long robe with a volume under his arm. At its base I read the inscription: Sheikh Baha'uddin Mohammad 'Amili. 1546–1621. Sheikh Baha'i, as he was also known, was appointed the Sheikh al-Islam or leader of religious affairs of Isfahan by Shah Abbas. His popular title was Bahr-e al-Olum, Ocean of Knowledge; and his immense learning hints at the intellectual richness of seventeenth-century Isfahan. He wrote authoritative books on grammar, algebra, and astronomy, and was the leading architect of the Royal Mosque and, it is said, a public baths heated by natural gas. He was also one of the leading poets of the age, and his poetry is saturated with the lore and wisdom of Sufism.

It was very hot. I walked east and passed under one of the arches of the Naqsh-e Jahan Square. At the far end towered the minarets of the Royal Mosque and on the far side the rosy hemisphere of the Lutfullah Mosque, glinting serenely from its broken highlights. I had forgotten how dramatic the site of the maidan was; two hundred gleaming arches looked onto it, receding along lines as straight as railway tracks. Between them rose the monumental portals of the city's most famous buildings in a configuration that is indescribably impressive.

Two weary-looking opportunists approached me in turn, offering their services as guides; one recounting wistfully his whisky-drinking days in Stockholm and the promise of showing me Safavid friezes of naked women, the other complaining that events in Iraq had reduced the usual flow of foreign tourists to a trickle. I let them down as politely as I could, and sat in the shade of an archway to study my architectural plan of the maidan.

To first make sure that the plan was accurate I checked the positions of the main features and paced the length of the maidan, counting my steps. At the far end a young man was waiting for me with a knowing smile, and said: 'Five hundred and twenty-five!' 'I make it five hundred and two,' I said, so we walked back to the far end together, counting again. He'd seen me from a distance, and asked if I was an architect. He had a carpet shop and made tours around the city for foreigners, and confirmed that business was quieter this year. We walked a little around the central pool and past the cooling mist from the fountains, chatting about life and work.

'Will you write about our real problem?' he asked. 'You do know what our real problem is, don't you?'

'Money?'

'No, worse.'

'Job opportunities?'

He shook his head with an exasperated tutting and said: 'It's nothing like that. It's *that*,' and nodded straight ahead. Walking towards us was a trio of attractive girls, whose eyes met ours firmly as they drew near. He muttered something as they passed; there was a brief scent of perfume, and a slightly bawdy rejoinder from one of the girls, followed by a ripple of giggles.

'That's the problem,' he said, as he looked back at them with longing grin. 'Look at their jackets! They used to hang straight. Now they tighten them in.' His hands described the narrowing curves of a waist. 'It's the same with the tight trousers they all wear underneath. They only do it to show off their . . .' and his hands lowered into a lascivious cupping motion.

'I've noticed that,' I said.

'They know it drives us mad. You're a man — you have needs. It's only natural. Write about that!' He pointed out his shop in a street leading from the square. 'When you get tired of your research,' he said, 'come and see us.' Then he winked and added: 'Or if you need anything else.'

Returning to my plan, and comparing it to what was visible on the ground, I felt very pleased to find that the alignment of the dome of the Lutfullah Mosque with its portal did indeed lead to the halfway point of the maidan. Thus divided, the maidan as a whole becomes two precise golden rectangles. And dividing the greater length by the golden ratio gives the opening of the Ali Qapu Palace, and hence the Lutfullah Mosque opposite it. There were other correspondences too. On the west side of the entrance to the bazaar, I noticed a brick panel with the same spinning square pattern that is visible at the entrance of the Lutfullah Mosque. Plotting the distance between the two on my plan, I saw it was the same as the distance between the two main domes, the line of which passes precisely through the centre of the entrance to the Royal Mosque; it was also the same as the distance between the dome of the Royal Mosque and the Towhid-Khaneh, the octagonal building behind the Ali Qapu Palace, which in its day had been a Sufi *khanagah*. The various entrances around the maidan could also be calculated from key points.

These were exciting discoveries; each time I studied the plan there seemed to be more, though I was aware of the danger of looking for relationships that didn't exist, and spent a long time checking them. But all these fundamental melodies of angle and distance can be revealed by traditional geometry; that is, with a compass and ruler alone, by which the uncertainty of measurement is eliminated. Nothing more need be evoked to verify them.

I had been pacing up and down all through the nationally proscribed period of rest, and now felt the effect of so many hours in the sunshine. The maidan was nearly deserted and all the monuments were closed. A few soporific-looking horses, yoked to brightly decorated buggies, sniffed at their woven nosebags. I had hardly noticed that human activity wisely followed the temperature of the day. At lunchtime, shutters descend everywhere over shop fronts like knight's visors, and inert bodies multiply in shady doorways. On the grassy verges between the streets, countless eyes sink shut under sheltering forearms. For a few hours, while the heat is at its highest, the city hibernates, and its pulse slows to a hibernatory pace until late afternoon when it creeps back to life again. At eight o'clock it beats its fastest, when thousands of people begin to swarm on the pavements and traffic fills the streets. Police in gleaming white Mercedes appear in the flow of cars like sheepdogs, barking orders through loudhailers and fielding strays back into the flow. In the maidan, hundreds gather for an evening meal under the sky; children are everywhere. Down by the river, the banks and bridges are soon lined with families as if in preparation for a public spectacle. But they have only come to sit and talk, and watch the sunset.

The next day I returned to the mosque of Sheikh Lutfullah. At the entrance kiosk, as I was preparing to resist paying the tenfold price for foreigners, I was given a ticket at the Iranian rate. This was an unexpected reversal.

'But I'm a foreigner,' I said.

'Makes no difference,' came the reply. 'It's all the same now.' Ticket in hand, I headed for the steps, wondering whether my determined protests over the previous two years had actually contributed to this happy result.

Two girls in dark chadors hovered about the doorway, working as guides, they explained, for the Office of Cultural Heritage. They ushered me forward with friendly smiles and I followed the twisting passage to the main chamber. There was no one else inside. It was as lovely and serene as I remembered, and I sat for a while on the floor, noticing new details that I had missed on earlier visits.

The lower tilework panels, which depict carpets, were made of painted tiles in the *haft-rang* style, but the upper walls were all made from mosaic and astonishingly intricate. Within the swirling lapis-coloured vines ran secondary trails of tiny flowers with yellow and white petals and red centres, each fragment individually cut; and another thinner interweaving tendril swirled gently behind the dominant pattern, linking more flowers in complementary colours. For the first time I noticed how many of the shapes complement and resonate with each other and lead the eye into ever deeper levels of enquiry. Then, with a feeling of disbelief, I realized I had failed to register the shape depicted in the heart of the sanctuary arch, the mehrab: it was a dervish *kashgul* in turquoise, suspended from a diamond-shaped lozenge studded with flowers. I pointed it out to one of the girls, who had come in to offer me tea.

'What's a *kashgul*?' she asked. 'I'll look it up.' She opened a book on the history of Isfahan and soon found several photographs of the boat-shaped begging bowls used by dervishes for the collection of alms. The similarity of shape was unmistakable, as was the symbolic intent. Here, at the sacred focal point of the city's most sublime place of worship was the hallmark of the dervish, the aspirant of the Sufi path; not only an allusion to the dervish's abandonment of worldliness, but a reminder of the poverty of man in front of the Divine.

It soon seemed obvious there were many more symbolic devices at work in the Lutfullah Mosque, some of them unique to the place itself and others common to many other mosques. The very emptiness of the chamber, calculated to express its maximum effect after the confinement and darkness of the entrance tunnel, serves as a reminder of the importance of emptiness in the spiritual tradition of Islam; a placeness-ness, if such a word exists, where the materiality of the world is dissolved and the way cleared for a greater Presence. The life-affirming visual motifs – abundant flowers and plants, and in particular the ubiquitous depiction of the vase, bursting with floriated tendrils – belong perhaps to the most primordial category of visual symbolism.* The overwhelming effect of the designs on the walls, which defeat the mind by their complexity, is one of harmonious encompassment, by which the empty space is invested with greater potency, both as a void – a place where the invisible is felt most strongly – and as an idea.

Even a cryptic form of numerology has been put to work in the tilework to affirm notions expressed elsewhere by shape and symbol. On the southern wall, a panel depicting a carpet contains sixty-six floral rosettes. The number is significant: it is one of the most common numerical symbols derived from the *abjad* notation, whereby each letter of the Arabic alphabet is assigned a number. Sixty-six is the number derived from the letters comprising *Allah*, God. It seemed sensible to allow room for coincidence, until I

---

* I didn't know it at the time, but the extraordinarily beautiful tilework of the dome, so reminiscent of the head of a sunflower, has an antique precedent in Mithraic iconography, where it is presumed to express the solar principle. Pope notices these symbols at Persepolis, where 'on the underside of the pivot stones of doors is carved a large open sunflower placed face down . . .'

counted several other features, finding that each could be transposed by the numerical shorthand of the *abjad* system to concepts central to Islamic metaphysics.* Shape, space, colour, and number had all been combined with dizzying ingenuity, each with the aim of evoking allied meanings within the sensitive onlooker.

The girls had returned with a tray bearing glasses of tea and saffron-flavoured sugar formed into slivers, and sat down on the cool tiles nearby. They were exquisitely polite but unable to contain their inquisitiveness, and took turns to leaf through my notebook page by page, puzzling admiringly over my handwriting.

'Would you like to see the *shabestan*?' one of them asked suddenly. 'I've got the key if you want to.' This was the winter prayer room; I had heard of it but imagined it was off limits, and accepted gratefully. She led me back towards the entrance and unlocked a little door. We walked down a shallow flight of steps and emerged into a vaulted and white-walled chamber, the dimensions of which mirrored the floor of the mosque above. I looked hopefully for evidence of a tunnel which was said to have once linked the mosque with the Ali Qapu Palace on the opposite

---

* The intricate design covering the interior of the dome, itself a geometrical masterpiece, is made up of 9 levels of 32 lozenges and a single uppermost shape, giving a total number of 289 shapes, representing *al-rahim*, the divine characteristic or attribute of universal mercy. 289 is also the numerological equivalent of the *takbir*, *Allahu Akbar*. At the base of the dome, 256 white flowers represent *nur*, or light, the most universal symbol of divinity. It is also here that the visible light of the outer world enters the mosque by the grilles that encircle the base. There are other alliances of number and design in the mosque which I do not feel equipped to comment on; I hope someone better qualified will take up the challenge of bringing them to greater notice. The use of *abjad* to indicate dates chronomatically is well known, but its use in architecture and art is scarcely recognized by scholarship. Certain Sufi poets have used *abjad* to emphasize or clarify ideas expressed in their poetry, as well as in their pen-names (*takhallus*). Better-known *abjad* denotations (such as the 786 of the *basmala*) can be seen in more everyday contexts of the Islamic world such as on letterheads, or the vinyl sunshields above the windscreens of Afghan taxis.

side of the maidan; we looked in a little storeroom for signs of an underground entrance, but if there ever had been one, it had been long ago concealed. On the way out again, I pointed out the stone aperture with the spinning-square motif that is visible from the exterior of the mosque; the same pattern which, a few minutes later, I noticed was also carved on the door to the upper chamber.

'Oh yes,' she said, matter-of-factly. 'But it's not really a surprise. The whole mosque is very *ramzi*.' It meant 'full of secrets'.

Φ

Fear of reproof and the momentum of preconception had made me assume that the efforts of a foreigner to poke about the city's monuments would evoke only reluctance and suspicion. But my enquiries had met everywhere with nothing but courtesy and helpfulness; a taxi driver had even given me the correct change. I soon felt confident enough to visit the Office for Cultural Heritage, to see if I could find anything more about the layout of the city in its Safavid heyday. Its headquarters were in a beautifully restored Qajar home, and the afternoon found me at a table with half a dozen members of staff, poring over old maps. A woman brought me a bowl of delicious noodle soup as I worked, and a young archaeologist confided, sotto voce, that he was working on an excavation near the Khadjou Bridge. He had discovered an ancient subterranean piping system suggesting a higher degree of urban infrastructure than anyone had dared believe, and other things he was too excited to talk about. He asked if I had climbed the minaret of the Royal Mosque and when I said I hadn't, arranged my permission.

I went back to the Royal Mosque. 'Wait under the dome,' said the man in charge. So I wandered in to the mosque and lingered a while, sitting cross-legged on the floor in a corner of the magnificent sanctuary, until a little man with a squeaky voice waved me towards him. I followed him into the western hypo-style, where he unlocked a tiny door. We stepped in.

The stairs were entirely unlit, so we felt our way upwards in

299

darkness, then clambered from a hatch a few minutes later at the level of the enormous dome, and stepped onto the surrounding platform. I circled the base of the dome, and seeing it so close for the first time felt stunned at the immensity of the endeavour. A few other domes, all much smaller, peeked out above the sprawl of the city, and at last I had a sense of how the city fitted together in its natural environment, with lines of ragged mountains to the south and east, and in the west a strange and solitary pyramid of stone atop which there is said to stand an ancient fire temple.

Then we began to climb the minaret, which grew narrower as it rose. It was pitch black, and the spiralling turns made us both a little dizzy. Every so often I could hear the muffled voice of the guide ahead and above me, muttering encouragement to himself. My heart went out to the poor mulla whose job it had been to give the call to prayer from the top of the minaret, five times a day. After what seemed like a long time we scrambled out onto the tiny parapet, ringed with a very insubstantial-looking wooden lattice. But the view was worth everything. The Naqsh-e Jahan resembled a carpet spread far below us, and I had a better view than ever of the other famous monuments dotted around the city.

My guide pointed to some of them in the distance, and I took out my plan of Isfahan as it had looked in the seventeenth century. He eyed it as a hungry lion might a passing gazelle. It fluttered in the wind as we looked back and forth over the city below. I mentioned, to try and gauge his interest, that I believed the orientation of the two mosques was not only to do with the qiblah, and that the angle of forty-five degrees between the mosque and the maidan seemed too lucky to be coincidence.

'I know,' he said, much to my surprise.

'So what's the reason, then?' I asked him.

'You tell me,' he said, rather coyly, as if he knew more than he was letting on. 'Do you know?'

'I've got my ideas,' I said.

'Go on, then.'

I took the risk, unfolded a similar plan with my lines and arcs on it, and pointed out the distances between the domes, the golden rectangles in the maidan, its relation with Chahar Bagh Avenue, and the idea that, if they had really wanted, the architects of the era could have just as easily built the mosques to be aligned with the maidan, and not crookedly, as they are. I put forward the idea that the construction of the maidan and the mosques must have been conceived of jointly, unless one accepted the orientations as coincidence. Finally I said I thought none of it was a mistake, and that all the usual explanations I had read seemed to missing the point.

His eyes never left the page, and I watched as an expression of awe and delight passed over his face and culminated in look of complete astonishment.

'I don't believe it!' he squeaked. 'For five years the very same questions have been going round my head! People never believe me when I tell them that none of it was a mistake and has nothing to do with the qiblah orientation! And now you, a foreigner, come along and explain it for me!'

I hadn't really explained anything; only that the conventional reasons for the positions and orientations of the mosques were insufficient. But I did have my first convert.

Φ

A little later, after we had agreed to meet again, I walked alone around the mosque. The sound of tapping drew me to the western courtyard that had once been a madrasseh. At the far end a man was working beside a mound of brightly glazed tiles. He was sitting on one leg with the other tucked in front of him in exactly the same manner as the brickcutter in a fifteenth-century miniature I had seen, and wielding an identical tool.* His eight-year-old son hovered about him nearby.

Without stopping, he explained that he was cutting the tiles

---

* Behzad's rendition of the building of the castle of Khawarnaq, from Nizami's *Khamsa* [1492].

for a portion of the dome that was under repair. These tiles – in lapis blue, turquoise, yellow, brown, and white – were not the shape of ordinary tiles, but narrow oblongs about three inches wide and equally thick. Each had a numbered piece of paper glued to its surface, indicating where the cut was to be made. 'I've got a few more to go,' he mused cheerfully. He calculated the number; it came out to about seven thousand. Then he asked if I had seen the section of the dome under repair and led me, massaging his legs as we walked, to a corner of the mosque where a sixteenth-portion of the outer skin of the dome lay supported on a scaffold like a supernatural upturned melon-slice. It was nearly a foot thick and must have weighed several tons, and was being re-surfaced inch by inch. I thought suddenly how, from its exterior, the colourful surface of the dome expressed a buoyant and almost whimsical quality, disguising like the sky-craving ribs of cathedral ceilings any trace of gravity. But here its immense and palpable weight disclosed the achievement of the architect who had enabled half a million tiles to float so effortlessly above the earth.

Outside, I met Zizou, a wiry, keen-eyed young man from Luristan who had painted his name on his baseball cap and spent his days hunting for foreign quarry in the maidan. He tried first to engage me with the exaggerated gestures and rapid banter of an expert hustler. I didn't need a guide, I said, and he grinned sceptically. Then he changed his tactic.

'Do you know any poetry?' he asked.

I thought of the line from Saʿdi that had been on my mind for so long:

'*The sons of Adam...*' I began. He shook his head and grimaced, interrupting me.

'I know a much better version,' he said, reciting:

> '*Bani adam aʾazayeh yek digarand*
> *Ke sar-e panj riyal beham miparand.*'
>
> (The Sons of Adam are the members of a whole
> They'll fly into a riot when a sixpence is their goal.)

He asked if I had pen and paper. At lightning speed he wrote down his favourite lines from Sa'di, Ferdowsi, Khayyām, Rumi, and a later poet I didn't know, Fereydun Moshiri. He was restless and intense and talked nonstop, trying to find a way through my resistance. He tested my knowledge of the monuments around the maidan, and promised to show me things I hadn't seen. I was taken by his wily look and ready smile, and proposed that for every thing he showed me that I didn't know about, I'd show one that he didn't know about, but that money wouldn't come into it. He was silent for a few instants and weighed up the offer before agreeing. By dusk we had revisited every detail of interest. I knew about the sunken mehrabs in the Royal Mosque, the sundial, the echo under the dome, and the tiled friezes of birds and animals; but I hadn't seen the portion of the marble soffits in the mosque that had been left unpolished as a measure of the mason's work, or the asymmetrical details of the column bases in the portal. Nor had I noticed the striking resemblance between the floral shape appearing in countless tiled panels and the traditional Zoroastrian representation of Ahura Mazda. The floriated anvil shape, which Zizou called *farouhar*,* was almost identical in outline to the winged god of the pre-Islamic era.

In turn I pointed out the spinning squares, the arcs thrown out from the courtyard of the Royal Mosque that form the borders of the central pool, and the cruciform outline of the facade that is reflected in it. He had long puzzled, he confessed, over the exact positions of the Lutfullah Mosque and the Ali Qapu Palace opposite, so I showed him on my plan how to calculate the golden section of the length of the maidan, and watched his jaw drop as the arcs struck home. He told me that he'd once asked a religious scholar about the maidan, who'd said that the maidan and its monuments were *por az jafr* – full of the mysteries of number.

---

*   The Avestan *Xvaranah*. A more recent interpretation of the winged disc links it to the quality of divinity or celestial authority associated with kingship, and not representing the deity itself.

We ended up smoking a water pipe in the tea-house that overlooks the maidan, and agreed to meet the following day.

Φ

I had avoided visiting the Ali Qapu Palace. From the outside it has none of the spectacular curves or colours of the mosques with which it competes, and seemed likely to disappoint. I had perhaps been influenced by Byron, who called the building a 'brick boot-box', and mentions nothing more of it. But I regretted I had waited so long. Like the other monuments it is a structure of great precision and full of reciprocating architectural melodies. Unlike the mosques it was designed to be lived in: its fifty-two rooms on seven storeys comprised the headquarters of Safavid government. Every inch of the interior is decorated; not in tile this time, but with delicate murals resembling luxurious fabrics, whose pigments have weathered the centuries with astonishing resilience. Though they are damaged in places the arcs and divisions are picked out in dusty blue and rose and the panels depict an idyllic universe of enchanted gardens, populated with birds and gazelles and scenes of romance and the hunt.

From the first-floor balcony, the great square below assumes a new resonance. The roofline of the arcade sinks to just below eye-level like an ornamental plinth, beyond which the domes and minarets of the city seem to float as if on water. The profile of the city today has more concrete in it than mosaic tilework, but the impression is still that one is hovering just above the rest of life.

Eighteen tall octagonal columns support the roof, tapering as they rise towards stalactitic capitals. Their slenderness evokes the airy facades of other Safavid palaces such as the Chehel Sutun, and recalls a prototype of great antiquity reaching, perhaps, as far back as Persepolis. Under a ceiling inlaid with elaborate geometric panels, the court, seated around a lead-lined pool and fountain, would have watched the polo matches and parades and firework displays below, and looked across to the Shah's favourite mosque, which lies directly opposite. The failure, so called, in alignment between its dome and portal is even more striking from this height, and the usual explanations for the misalignment seemed to me more insufficient than ever: the royal eye, accustomed to precision and refinement in everything he commissioned, would have scarcely tolerated such a flagrant error.[*]

The uppermost storey of the Ali Qapu is generally considered to be a marvel in itself. It is called the Talar-e Musiqi, or Music Chamber, and follows a design unseen, I think, anywhere outside Iran. The coves, squinches, and vaults of all the top-floor rooms are honeycombed with countless recesses, and the effect, at first, is one of fantasy. But the shapes resolve into long-necked flasks and perfume-jars of varying sizes and resemble the shelves of an apothecary, only the ceilings carry these enigmatic patterns too. All are painted in meticulous detail. The hollow recesses behind them are said be miniature resonating chambers, the function of which, according to the latest theories, was to magically transform the soloist's notes into those of an orchestra.[†]

As I was writing a few notes on the balcony, one of the girls working as a guide approached me and, a little hesitantly, asked me in English whether there was anything she could help me with. She was captivatingly pretty, and as we spoke a line of poetry I had not read for more than ten years began to sound in my mind:

> Lips coral-red, eyes bright and black as jet
> With teeth like stars across the Heavens set
> Your eyebrows curve and flex like hunter's bows
> Your cheeks are softer than a budding rose

---

[*] Later on, it was possible to measure that the base of the dome of the mosque sits above the portal at the very point of the Golden Section along the length of the maidan. The king's view was one not of imperfection, but of precision . . .

[†] The clue to their function is perhaps announced in the entrance chamber of the palace, where a whisper, inaudible when projected across the open space, is transmitted from one corner to the other by some acoustic wizardry built into its design.

'I'm not bothering you, am I?' she asked in English.

'*Bar aks*,' I said, 'on the contrary,' savouring the moment of enchantment. She looked about thirteen and her eyes were sparklingly clear. She wanted only to practise her English a little, she said, and as she thought of questions to ask her body wavered slightly like a flower in a breeze. A hint of perfume breached the air between us. She asked me how old I was; suddenly I felt very old, and heard myself lie unexpectedly. She was eighteen, she said.

'Did you see the murals?' she asked. 'Many have been destroyed, but there are some which are still –' she looked upwards and back again and bit her lower lip as she searched for the word, then found it – 'untouched.'

'The only thing *she* wanted,' said Zizou with a cynical twinkle when I bumped into him afterwards in the maidan, 'was a British passport.'

We wandered together through the bazaar, noticing details that were new to both of us, like the geometric patterns carved into doors, and the variously shaped apertures that crowned the vaults above us, sending luminous circles, squares, diamonds, octagons, and stars into the dust at our feet. I became aware of yet another device at work in the tiled designs of the portals and ceilings: reciprocal patterns, which shift as you observe them, and where the voids become as significant as the lines that contain them, like the magically mutating creations drawn by Escher.

Occasionally we would bump into a friend of Zizou's and spend an idle hour in conversation over tea. He introduced me to a few useful shopkeepers he felt I should know, a handful of carpet dealers, as well as an immensely talented miniature-painter, in whose atelier a dozen chador-clad girls were cheerfully painting in exquisite detail. I had never met so many people in a single day, and he tried earnestly to arrange meetings with two local professors and was as disappointed as I was when we discovered that one was away in Tehran, and another attending a funeral.

Passing foreigners were his weakness: he could detect them at an incredible distance, and would introduce himself with a mixture of genuine charm and steely ingenuity. He could strike up conversations in more than half a dozen languages: he knew the names and merits of football players from teams across the world. Jokes scattered spontaneously from his lips and his natural talent as a mimic was put to immediate use to tranquillize a stranger's fears. I sensed all the same that there was always an eye open in the back of his head for any sign of authority, and had the impression that he might have to duck into a side alley at any minute.

He had left his village several years before, he said, and had ended up in Isfahan after a prolonged and difficult displacement, hustling for odd jobs and living on his wits to survive. His arms hugged his sides as the memory returned of nights spent sleeping rough. One day, a foreigner had asked him to guide him round an archaeological site, and had paid him handsomely for it. He saw his chance, and began to read everything he could about the country's ancient sites. He had learned so much since then he could now hold his own with any of the professional guides, and confessed he had managed to pass himself off on occasion as an archaeologist. But he didn't have the background to do it for a living, he said: and his English wasn't good enough.

We had spent a rewarding few days together. Finding ourselves once again at the entrance of the Royal Mosque, I explained it was time to for me to move on, and that I had to go back to my hotel.

'I'll come with you,' he said, then added: 'just to walk you there,' and I knew what that meant. He seemed preoccupied as we walked. He asked when I'd be back; perhaps by then he would have saved up for some English courses at the college ... he didn't have the money at the moment. He began to sing as we walked, almost to himself, a song about the joys of being penniless.

I was happy to give him money, but wished nonetheless that the convention were different; it is apt to spoil things for the outsider, who feels uncomfortable with the ambiguity, and dis-torts, retrospectively as it were, the spirit in which apparently altruistic gestures are made. So we sat down on the grass at the edge of the maidan, and I thanked him for all the time we'd spent together. From a crumpled packet Zizou offered me his last cigarette. I had very little Iranian cash, but had brought with me a ten-pound note in my wallet, which I now took out and handed it to him with a flourish.

'Her Majesty the Queen of England wishes to express her thanks.' It wasn't much, I told him, but it might be useful. For a few moments he stared at me with an expression of incomprehension, and I wondered if I had been too generous or too mean. Then he spoke.

'Are you out of your mind?' A reproachful and almost fierce look had come into his eyes. 'Put it away.' I didn't need it, I insisted, still feeling the need to overcome his resistance with an equal show of force. I wanted to give it to him, I said; I was a foreigner and I wouldn't need it; it wasn't that much in any case ... resorting to all the excuses, in fact, used by taxi drivers to cheat me out of my own money. But he didn't waver for instant. His expression of disappointment made it clear it was I who had failed to grasp the significance of the moment.

'What we did,' he said, with an earnestness that was impossible to counter, 'was for learning, not for money. We shared what we knew and we shared freely. You can't pay for that kind of knowledge, and not between friends. That was our agreement. Money would ruin the whole thing.'

Taking my hand in his, he folded it gently around the note and pushed it firmly back towards me.

Φ

It was time now to return to my cave. My subterranean tryst of a year earlier had acquired a private gravity inexplicable by logic alone, and I could hardly wait to return. I wanted above all to photograph it and discover at last whether I had represented the place fairly to myself, and had brought my camera and flash unit from England for the purpose.

I left Isfahan and returned to Shiraz by bus, found the same hotel where I had stayed the year before, negotiated with the same irritable manager, and ordered tea from the same elderly chef. Everything was easier this time; I knew the prices for things and the time they would take; I knew better than to pretend to be from Azerbaijan; and I knew that the taxi station for journeys to the south lay just beyond the imitation Persepolis pillar on the outskirts of the city.

I had taken a shared taxi to Firuzabad the last time, but had had to hitchhike in the darkness for the ride back. Now a gleaming new Peugeot caught my eye, awakening a lustful craving for comfort, and I wondered what it might cost to hire for half the day. Making a pest of myself I bargained with the owner until the price came down, and soon we were speeding towards Firuzabad.

The driver's name was Parviz. I liked him for his gentle manner and lack of questions, and we talked just enough to satisfy each other's curiosity. This and the freedom from the usual contortions of a shared taxi gave the journey a quality of luxury. I didn't mention the cave; I am not sure why. I said instead that I wanted to take a photograph of the Qala-e Dokhtar, the ruined Sasanian fortress on the top of the hill; he was not very interested.

The city soon trailed behind us, and the land grew barer. The hills appeared on the horizon through a haze, and we neared them through a succession of watery mirages above the pencil-line of asphalt. Then the road began to climb, and we passed through the first tunnel. After the third, we pulled over at the foot of the hill beneath the fort.

The sun was unexpectedly intense. 'Haven't you got a hat?' asked Parviz as I got out. I explained about mad dogs and Englishmen, and headed for the steps. They had been rebuilt since I had last been there, and the route up was quicker than I'd expected; this was a worrying development. All over Iran, I had seen ruined and abandoned monuments being restored and rebuilt and reinforced in preparation for new hordes of foreigners; not Mongols this time but tourists, the effects of whose invasions was arguably more destructive. I felt confident that the time was not far away. For a thousand years the site of Qala-e Dokhtar had been utterly abandoned, a place where no one but shepherds, treasure-hunters, and a few determined foreigners had really explored. Within a few more, the steps I was walking up would be thick with jostling and pink-faced Scandinavians, tramping unstoppably up and down from their air-conditioned buses. The ancient embankments at the foot of the hill would soon be a coach-park, and the riverbanks a rubbish dump; a stall run by cynical locals would serve food fit for dogs as authentic Persian cuisine, and opportunists from Shiraz dressed as Bakhtiari tribesmen would sell unusable carpet fragments as priceless traditional treasures.

But not quite yet. I circled the base of the castle, let the memory of the route filter back into my body, and soon found the track. I was happy and hot. There wasn't a soul about; only foot-long stone-coloured lizards, scurrying into crevices as I passed. I found the arched doorway in the perimeter wall and remembered the black mouth of the first cave, above me to the left. Then I kept going until I found the gulley leading to the cliff edge, and scrambled downwards.

I was very happy to have found the place again without difficulty. I had waited nearly a year for the opportunity to return and the prospect of the reunion filled me with a tender excitement. I crept into the mouth of the tunnel and went as far as the boulder that nearly blocks the entrance of the cave. Then I dug out my torch and camera from my bag. I could smell the sulphurous and humid air again and hear the electric squeak of bats. But as I looked for the flash unit, the very thing I needed to photograph the cave, I realized it wasn't there. I had left it at the hotel.

I wanted all the same to see the interior, to see if it matched the vision of the place I had held in my memory since I first glimpsed it by the light of a flaming branch. I squeezed past the boulder and stepped forward. But the floor of the cave, which had been dry when I was last there, was flooded with black and fetid water. I couldn't photograph the cave; I couldn't even get in.

With mixed thoughts I made my way into the sunshine again and back towards the path, cursing my neglect. There was nothing else to do but return to Shiraz. I walked down again.

There was a hut at the bottom. As I approached, the elderly keeper emerged and waved me inside. 'When I saw you coming down, I went specially to get water for you,' he wheezed, pouring a glass for me. There was a dog-eared visitors' book, which I signed. The old man watched me attentively and, to make quite sure I had grasped his point, poured me a second glass, adding, 'What with it being so hot, and you having come so far...' I produced the appropriate contribution, which he looked at with barely concealed disappointment.

Parviz was waiting patiently by the car, and asked if I had been successful. I was too upset to go into detail, and mumbled an evasive reply. I felt very let down, hot, and tired of all the effort involved in simple operations which elsewhere would have been easily achieved. We drove in silence for a while as I wrestled with the decision to return or not. I could always come back another year ... the cave would always be there. But I would have nothing to show for the trip in the meantime, and heard myself muttering apologies for the lack of photographs. Without them, the account of the cave would seem fanciful.

It was oppressively hot and the walk had taken the strength out of me. The thought of a further two hours' drive, and then another to return, seemed too much to contemplate. Then I thought of the Afghan driver I'd met and how he'd driven with me for fifteen hours on unspeakable Afghan roads and set out the next day on only a few hours' sleep in the back of his truck without a blanket in midwinter; and how he'd laughed out loud when I asked whether he was tired. I was being weak; I had to go back.

So I proposed that we return later in the day, and told him the whole story of the cave and how I had forgotten the flash unit, and that I wanted to have a second try; and he agreed as sympathetically and graciously as I'd hoped he might. He took me to the door of my hotel and, in the lull after the engine fell silent, invited me to return to his home, where his wife, he said, would cook us lunch. I was tired and refused as gently as I could, and we agreed that in the afternoon we'd meet in the same place.

At half-past five he pulled up at the doorstep of the hotel, and we greeted each other with a knowing grin. I had bought a big bag of cherries and something to drink, and Parviz had brought a bowl with some cheese and cucumbers, a bottle of water and more fruit. We had hardly spoken on the first trip; but a feeling of complicity in the absurdity of events had broken the ice between us.

'I didn't expect to go Firuzabad twice in one day,' he said with a smile, as we set off.

'At least you'll have a funny story to tell,' I said, 'about a crazy foreigner who went to Firuzabad twice, just to take a photograph of a cave.'

He turned to me for a moment with a serious look and said: 'It's not like that at all. I knew this was important to you. I could see how troubled you were by what happened this morning, and I was thinking about it all day. Insha'allah all your efforts will be repaid.'

On the outskirts of Shiraz we passed the scene of an accident. The road was scattered with broken glass and on the verge like a slaughtered dinosaur was an overturned truck. Two wrecked cars had been pushed from the tarmac and nearby lay half a dozen inert bodies, draped in sheets.

'Makes you think,' said Parviz quietly as we drove past. 'The line between life and death — it's so thin. And there isn't even a war on.'

He was a few years older than me and I wondered if he'd fought in the long conflict with Iraq. He'd been conscripted twenty years earlier, he said, but he hadn't done any serious fighting and was glad he hadn't: he'd been assigned as a cook. Then he told a story I couldn't quite follow about trying to prepare a meal during a bombardment by Iraqi artillery.

'All the bloodshed,' he murmured. 'And now there's another war over there. We haven't learned anything in all these thousands of years. It's still the *qanun-e jangal!*' The law of the jungle: I'd never heard the expression in Persian.

He was too polite to contest that the English hadn't wanted to go to war in Iraq, but I could see he didn't really believe me when I said the decision hadn't been a popular one. I mentioned I'd been to Afghanistan while the country had been at war with the Soviets, and he asked me what I thought of Afghanistan and the Afghans. I told him the Afghans took their independence, and their religion, very seriously; they didn't talk about religion as much as Iranians, I said, they lived it.

He nodded thoughtfully. 'That's what I've heard,' he said, as if Afghanistan were a far-off continent and not a neighbouring country. 'Not like us,' he grinned, 'we just talk about it. Not that we're not religious. But who wants anything to do with religion when it's *those ones*' — he meant the government — 'who represent it?' He quoted a well-known saying of the Prophet: *In religion, no compulsion.* 'We have a saying too,' he added: '*Musa be mazhab-e khish, Isa be mazhab-e khish.*' Moses to his own faith, and Jesus to his.

There were lots of jokes about *them*, he said, and told the story of a lustful mulla who tricks a God-fearing husband into sharing his wife; and then another, bawdier still, apologizing as he told it for the vivid terminology. Soon we were covering everything that came into our minds: the cost of car insurance, school fees, different types of military service, and the usual, overriding plaint I had so often heard before: that Iran was a country rich in oil, natural resources, and labour, and could be as prosperous as Dubai if only *they* didn't take all the wealth for themselves . . .

Then we were through the tunnels again and the castle was a silhouette perched on the ragged rim high above us. We pulled up once more at the same spot and parked at the foot of the hillside. I had brought my boots this time so as to be able to wade into the flooded cave, and changed into them. Parviz asked if I had enough water, then wished me luck. There wasn't much time before the light would begin to fade, and I hurried up the path.

I retraced my steps and, for the second time that day, reached the mouth of the cave. The sun was low and golden. I went in, squeezed past the boulder at the end of the tunnel, and waited a few minutes for the glare to recede from my eyes. My camera was ready this time, and I edged forward, feeling my way along the wall. The black water, I soon realized, grew quickly deeper towards the middle of the cave. I ventured in several places towards the centre, but it was too deep and the floor too soft. I remembered the grave that we had seen and wondered if I might bump against a floating limb, or get stuck in the mud; it would have been a lonely place to get trapped beside a rotting corpse. In the circular recesses above my head there were grape-like clusters of bats. I could see the pinkish web of their wings as they darted in front of the light thrown from the entrance; deeper inside I could hear the throb of wingbeats near my ears.

It was impossible to reach the middle of the cave for the view that I had hoped to capture, so I skirted it on both sides and took a dozen photographs. I couldn't see what I was photographing; the torch wasn't powerful enough to light anything but the nearest portion of the wall. I could see the cave only at the instant it was lit up by the flash, when for a fraction of a second its liquid corrugations leaped forward from the blackness.

Yet I felt much surer now. Not that this particular cave had been used a physical prototype for the famous *ivāns* I had seen in Isfahan, but that it was possible, and meaningful, to look at the structure of the cave — all caves, in fact — as a symbolic device that had been put work in religious architecture. It was no accident that Islamic artists chose those Neptunian shades and stalagtitic *muqarnas* for the entrances to their mosques and shrines; for the cave was a place of initiation — perhaps the most archetypal place of initiation of all — bearing in its very shape the antique language by which such ideas were once transmitted.

I couldn't afford to linger; it would be dark outside soon. So I apologized to the bats for disturbing their peace and slithered out. I pocketed the film and wondered if it would ever really reach home. Then for a few minutes I looked for traces of the artificial path which Byron claimed to have seen leading to the cave. I skirted along the edge of the cliff to see if there was another cave fitting his description, but found no evidence of either a cave or a path.

The light was fading now. I rejoined the track on the slope above and headed back towards the castle. Near the perimeter wall I noticed a natural curve just at the lip of the cliff where the rocks had fractured into portions resembling a row of cushions. It was hard not to imagine members of the royal retinue sitting there behind a wooden railing, sipping wine and watching the sunset. A little further on I saw a stone where someone had carved the words 'the Pain of Love'.

Soon I was nearing the castle, where a final look was irresist-ible. I scrambled up a collapsed rampart and, breathless and pouring sweat, reached the central chamber. The sun had just sunk behind the western cliffs on the far side of the river and a warm wind was stirring through the arches. Dusk is the time to see such places, when for a few moments the timeless draws near and breathes its stillness into things.

I had forgotten how large the space beneath the dome was. I thought of all the parties; the wine and the music, the oaths and decrees, and all the dreams that had been hatched in this mountain-ringed eyrie of empire.

It was nearly dark when I reached the bottom of the hill. Just before I did, I made out a figure coming up the path. It was a boy of about fifteen; he'd come to look for me, he said. Wondering who he was, I followed him along a shortcut down to the road, and crossed it to join a group of people sitting beside a car. The scene was lit by a small electric lantern attached to the car battery. Parviz was among them and stood up as I arrived.

'We were so worried,' he said, shaking his head slowly with a grave expression.

'There's snakes,' said the boy, 'and wild animals.'

'Worse,' said a man's voice, with a theatrical note. It was the boy's father. He was sitting cross-legged at the far end of a carpet that had been thrown across the dust. Around it sat two other women, another man, and at its edge, a much younger woman, sitting in a wheelchair. Despite the hour, this was a family picnic. Parviz explained that the family had arrived more than an hour earlier, and as it got dark had decided to send the son up the hill to look for me.

'Leaving your driver all alone like that!' said the father. His dark eyes and skin gleamed in the light. 'Poor man didn't know what to do!'

The women took turns to fuss over me as if I was an old family friend, and they all joked about how worried they'd been. A glass of tea appeared by my side and one of the women prepared me a sandwich. The father introduced me in turn to his wife, sister-in-law, and her husband.

'That's my son, Ihsan – you've already met him. And that's my daughter, Zohra.' He pointed towards the forlorn-looking but attractive girl of about seventeen who was sitting in the wheel-chair. I wondered what affliction had touched her life at such a young age.

'There's nothing wrong with her,' he said, answering my unspoken question. 'That's my chair she's in. I'm the one who hasn't got any legs,' he added with a chuckle, patting his knees where his legs, I now realized, ended. 'I'm a war veteran. Zohra!' He pointed to my empty glass. 'Use yours and give the man something to drink.' The daughter rose swiftly from the chair and refilled my glass.

'So, how's Iran then . . . ?'

I said I was enjoying Iran very much, then made my usual joke; the biggest problem, I said, putting an arm on Parviz's shoulder, was taxi drivers. There were laughs all round.

'You want to watch their sort. How much did you pay for the ride here?'

I told him, and he feigned outrage.

'How much? I'll take you back for half that . . .' He pretended

to make the effort to stand up. Then he returned to the theme
of how unwise I had been to go into the hills alone.

'Our biggest worry,' he said, 'was that you might have ended
up in one of those caves up there.' His expression had turned
serious. 'Dangerous places.'

'Dangerous?'

'*W'allah.* By God, yes! You know what lives in them?'

I said I had no idea.

'*Khafash-ha! Bats!* Blind things! Flying rats!' A shudder of
aversion rippled through the others. 'They hang from the walls
and wait for their prey there. They'll attack whatever passes by.
They've got eyes, mind you, but they don't use them – they hunt
with radar, just like a missile.' With outstretched fingers his hand
fluttered through the air in imitation of the creatures which, not
much earlier, had been wheeling in just the same manner a few
inches away from my face.

'Woe betide any man who ventures into one of those terrible
caves.' He paused for effect. His hand came forward from the
darkness, and a raised finger, gleaming at the periphery of the
lantern's reach, passed theatrically over us in turn. 'People have
gone in those caves and never come out.' He shook his head
gravely, and the others fell silent, spellbound at his description.
'No trace was ever found of them.' He paused again, then
widened his eyes in mock terror, and his hand went up, the
fingers pursed this time. 'If one of those bats gets the scent of
you,' his voice dropped to a whisper of light-hearted menace as
the hand began to waver like a cobra, 'one bite is all it takes!'
Then it made a sudden reverse and struck his own forehead with
an audible slap. The children jumped visibly.

He asked me what my plans were. 'When you're back in
Shiraz,' he said, 'you'll stay with us.' He was adamant I be his
guest, and wrote down his name and phone numbers. 'Call the
mobile if I'm not at home,' he said, tapping the phone on his
belt, 'and I'll come and get you.'

'You shouldn't stay in a hotel,' said his wife.

'Terrible places,' said the husband, shaking his head disapprovingly. 'And lonely.'

'We'll feed you properly,' said his wife.

'Once you've tasted my wife's cooking you won't want to leave. *Fahmidid?* Understood? That's settled, then . . .'

Φ

Long before I had ever been to Iran, I had often sensed the importance and centrality of art to Persian culture. I had even read somewhere that Persian culture could only be really understood through its art. The meaning of this had seemed obvious at the time, and just as valid for any other culture. But I had hardly guessed, until the jigsaw of a thousand glimpses and encounters took on a proper life of its own, just how intimately its various expressions were linked, or that I would come across some aspect of them almost daily.

Between travelling, I turned to scholarly accounts of Islamic art in the hope of shoring up my own instinctive suppositions, acquired by a sort of osmosis in the course of long journeys. The outstanding impression from these was one of the immense sweep of history, beneath which a core of underlying beliefs had somehow been preserved and expressed in a sublime repertoire of artistic forms. Empires and dynasties had come and gone; but art had survived.

The principles of such an enduring art, I supposed, would be intimately researched and well understood. But my own definition of art had begun, under the loosening effect of travel, to change and broaden. 'Art' was no longer quite the right word. And the more I searched the academic world for a better understanding of the meaning of Persian or Islamic art, it became clear I would never find it in the obvious places. Firstly, because of the way we divide up the idea of art, books about 'Persian art' are about miniature paintings. Secondly because 'Islamic art' does not, for scholarship at least, exist; and thirdly because of a reluctance to assign meaning to so-called abstract shapes or forms without some sort of written evidence as to how to interpret them. I had also supposed that studies of Islamic art would take as their point of departure those accounts written by or on behalf of the traditional artisan, whose job it was to create the art in question. But a gulf stretches between these worlds, and the bridge that links them is a narrow one; it is an uncomfortable place for an argument.

CAVEAT LECTOR

Readers uninterested in the origins and history of Islamic art, metaphysics, or pigeons, should skip to the next chapter, on page 337.

This is strange. It is not as though Islamic art has only just reached the West. Throughout the Middle Ages, countless Islamic artefacts found their way — often through trade, but more often as booty — into the palaces and aristocratic homes of Europe. They were much prized for their level of craftsmanship, which was seldom rivalled in Christendom. European monarchs were crowned wearing robes woven in Muslim Sicily, silk fabrics from Central Asia cradled the bones of Christian saints, and Turkish and Persian carpets were widely favoured as royal wedding presents (much of our knowledge of early Turkish carpets comes through their appearance in paintings by court artists such as Holbein and Lorenzo Lotto, whose names have been given to the styles of carpet they painted. Cardinal Wolsey ordered his own collection directly from Venice). Islamic silks and wall-hangings are a precious part of church and cathedral treasuries, along with iridescent rock-crystal ewers and reliquaries carved in Fatimid Egypt. Glassware, ceramics, and metalwork were particularly admired, and spawned their own imitative schools in Europe. Mamluk brassware helped carry the arabesque as a decorative motif into Tudor and Elizabethan bookbinding, and the widespread importation of Middle Eastern textiles brought new names into the languages of their destinations: in English we have damask (Damascus), fustian (Fustat), and muslin (Mosul).

A later era, of more peaceful exchange, saw a growing fascination for Islamic arts, first in architecture and later extending to the applied arts. In 1750 the Prince of Wales commissioned both a mosque and an 'Alhambra' for Kew Gardens. They have not survived. But the better-known Royal Pavilion at Brighton, designed by Nash in 1815 and based on Fischer von Erlach's famous *History of Architecture*, betrays the widespread European fascination for the recently visited monuments of the East, and gave royal approval to the oriental mode. Ottoman- and Moorish-style cafes, smoking-rooms, bathhouses, kiosks, and bandstands soon appeared in European parks and streets. Arabesques bridged the cast-iron spandrels of billiard rooms and exhibition halls, and in the homes of wealthy Englishmen, Turkish rooms, Moorish conservatories, Arab ceilings, and geometric floor patterns breathed eastern luxury into many a stronghold of Victorian rectitude.

Artists and designers of the nineteenth century were at the forefront of this transfusion, and the paintings of John Frederick Lewis, Gérome, and Delacroix typify the era's fascination with the Islamic east. Owen Jones' influential *Grammar of Ornament*, which appeared in 1856, was the first serious European study of Islamic design. By the turn of the twentieth century, Persian geometries had found their way into the fabric designs of William Morris, and echoes of the arabesque into the tiles of de Morgan;* the Persian *boteh* motif was renamed as paisley. Le Corbusier studied architecture in Turkey, and Gropius (of Bauhaus fame), the Moorish art of Spain. Turkish designs inspired the ornate glassware of Philippe Brocard; Villeroy and Bosch imitated Ottoman Iznik tilework. Matisse, Kandinsky, Gauguin, and Klimt all admitted a fascination for Islamic artistic techniques. In Potsdam, Herbert Gutmann's Arab Room exemplified European

---

* William Morris, many of whose designs were adapted unchanged to the ceramic medium by de Morgan, wrote: 'to us pattern-designers, Persia has become a holy land.' Years after de Morgan had achieved international fame, an admirer saw imitations of his tiles selling for inflated prices in a shop window, and wrote an indignant letter to the artist. 'Imitation,' came the reply, 'is the sincerest form of pottery.'

fascination with the exotic; in England Leighton House, its walls draped with original tiles from Syria, gave Victorian society dinners one of their most sensuous venues.* Damascus decorated Holland Park and museum collections multiplied.

Yet this fascination went scarcely deeper than a preoccupation with the most visible and formal aspects of the art. Islamic designs in Europe sought less to faithfully reproduce their originals than to explore the modes and fashions of the day. Architecture inspired by Islam was scarcely more than imitative, and about as faithful to its origins as was Coleridge's *Xanadu* to the distant palace of the Mongol King Kublai. Not surprisingly; Western and Islamic arts grew up and matured in cultures where different artistic principles were at work. But the West has always been fascinated by Islamic art, and the world's finest collections are almost all in European museums. Its appeal is not in dispute.

The dazzling variety among its works and a high level of execution across huge measures of time and space invite obvious questions about its significance and informing principles. But conceptual pickings on the meaning of this art and its inspiration remain fairly slim, and leave a hollow feeling in anyone who from time to time ponders – me, I admit, in this case – over whether there is anything more to this art than its aesthetic appeal alone. Modern analyses of Islamic art by historians – both Muslim and non-Muslim – are by no means agreed.

The obvious characteristics of Islamic art are not difficult to identify. The most immediate – at least to Western sensibilities, nurtured by naturalism – is the absence of those figurative forms through which European art has traditionally found its highest expressions. It is precisely the abstract designs of Islamic art which lend it such paradoxical allure. Paradoxical, because the appeal is hard to quantify beyond its purely formal aspects. But this appeal is indisputably enhanced by a second feature: the

---

* Though the keen and impudent visitor will notice the transposition of two of the calligraphic tiles on the main frieze of the Arab Room which renders the central inscription nonsensical.

mysterious resonance between its hugely varied expressions. Through all its diverse forms, there seems to run a single aesthetic language, to be heard from the banks of the Guadalquivir to the fringes of the Gobi Desert.

One can think of a few of these treasures — miniature versions of the Qur'ān, smaller than matchboxes and exquisitely illuminated in inks made from gold and pulverized lapis lazuli and etched with microscopic precision onto dried leaves thinner than paper; the majestically sombre column-forest of the Great Mosque of Cordoba, and the numinous spaces of the Taj Mahal; the gravity-defying stonework of the Hall of the Abencerrajes in the Alhambra; the swirling, triple-layered stucco mehrab of Uljeitu in Isfahan's Friday Mosque; sapphire- and ruby-studded Moghul daggers and scimitars; Ottoman battle headgear encrusted with liquid gold calligraphy; the geometrical marvels of mosaic faience, whose colours enliven half the ancient buildings of the Persian world; the architectural and acoustic mysteries of the Gombad-e Qabus, the engraved coco-de-mer *kashguls* of Persian dervishes; the intricate star-maps of bejewelled astrolabes; the copper, gold, and silver inlay on bronze ewers and pitchers and flasks and pen-boxes and candlesticks and monumental incense-burners; and the thirty million knots woven across the silken wefts of the Ardabil carpets — each is unmistakably Islamic, each representative of an artistic genius bridging fifteen centuries and half the landmass of the planet.

Universal to all these — even to someone for whom the majestic swirls of Arabic calligraphy are no more than fantastic shapes — is their beauty. One feels instinctively that the spirit of their art can be traced to a single creative source. But beyond their mysterious 'Islamicness', and the fact that they are all undeniably beautiful, does anything unite them conceptually? What explains their near-universal appeal to the human eye and senses? And can one find meaning in such diverse expressions of artistic excellence?

Not really, comes the doleful reply from the scholarly orthodoxy: because there is no such thing as Islamic art. There are different kinds of Islamic arts, there are periods of Islamic arts, there are the artistic expressions of various nations influenced by Islam; but to use the term Islamic would suggest a transcendent aesthetic directive for all art produced in different Islamic countries — for which no known evidence exists.*

So to ponder and contemplate the visible expressions of this art — to sit before them, as it were, and listen for their language — is wholly unscientific, a sort of betrayal of contemporary intellectual morals. To do so is to assume that we may know the mind of the artist, and that his mission was to speak to the onlooker across time and space — a problematic supposition.

To speak of Islamic art as possessing a 'spirit' is exactly the sort of sentiment that is anathema to art historians, and considered far too vague to be useful. Such a spirit would have to have been conceptualized in advance of its execution, as would its method of transmission across vast distances; and since no such mechanism is known to exist, it can hardly serve as a basis for the arguments of our naive onlooker.

In the absence of any conceptual foundation, any aesthetic or spiritual directive, the primary characteristic of Islamic art — its unity — is explained by most scholars as the product of the strict decrees of the Islamic religion, its insecurity in relation to the Christian world, its autocratic styles of government, and the monotony of harsh physical environments. Mobility across the frontiers of the expanding Islamic empires and a unique place of pilgrimage for all Muslims further encouraged the widespread diffusion of artistic repertoires, as did the whim of tyrannical rulers who shipped artists and craftsmen between their capitals.

Almost all the artistic motifs, designs, and methods of the early Islamic world can furthermore be traced to pre-existing traditions: there is nothing new, in other words, to the raw material of the art itself. Hellenistic, Byzantine, and Sasanian artistic styles were simply adapted to the strictures of the fledgling

---

* The methodological conundrums associated with assigning meaning to abstract forms are dealt with in frightening detail in such spectacularly inconclusive works as Oleg Grabar's *Formation of Islamic Art*.

religion. This rather stern premise has of necessity led to almost heroic investigations into degrees of historical borrowings, as well as the most intricate studies of the morphologies of artistic repertoires across the domains of early Islam; even though the vexing question as to how and when the art of the region became 'Islamic' remains.

The explanation for the non-figurative basis of Islamic art is well known. Here too, we are assured by the Western art historian that abstract and geometrical expressions – the other outstanding characteristics of Islamic art – have no real significance beyond their originality. Religious injunctions against representation, formulated to discourage idolatry among the newly converted, quashed the temptation to imitate the rich naturalistic traditions of Christendom. There is a suggestion of having to make do; of compensation rather than inspiration. Well suited to the celebrated *horror vacuii* of the Islamic mind, calligraphy and abstract designs covered every available surface, from the monumental to the microscopic.

But deprived of any definitive symbolism, any fundamental meaning, the appeal of geometrical and vegetal forms must, by all these subtly damning criteria, remain at the level of the purely sensuous. Western descriptions of Islamic designs are filled with a corresponding aesthetic language: 'splendid', 'proficient', 'charming', 'playful', 'remarkable', 'rich', 'bewildering', 'gracious', 'exuberant', 'vivacious', 'ingenious', 'elegant', 'distinctive', 'imaginative', 'evocative', 'enchanting', 'interesting', 'daring', 'peculiarly original', 'strangely imaginative', 'a hint of William Morris', 'almost Matisse-like . . . .'.

The irrational arabesque seems to embody all the ambiguity of Islamic patterns. Its arbitrariness and ambiguity lead nowhere. Its enigmatic twin, geometrical abstraction, is a kind of artistic idiot savant, hovering on the periphery of admission to real art. Over time, the broad appeal of the freedom and ambivalence allowed by these forms gave them, so the theory goes – primacy as a civilization's artistic medium. But no spiritual prerogative informs their existence; and if art in its most exalted sense can be said to be a transmitter of spiritual values, they remain largely mute — conscripted, assassin-like, to more worldly tasks: the expression of power, prestige, opulence, and sensuous diversion.

We are back, in a sense, to the harem and the opium pipe. The measure of this art is its aesthetic appeal. No intellectual content can be found in it: its function is simply that of beautification. And since no concrete evidence exists to justify claims of symbolic meanings in abstract art, the attempt to do so is methodologically unsound. Those who find religious, spiritual, or cosmological allusions in them are guilty of the most unrigorous universalism.

At best, therefore, Islamic art is what it appears to be: beautiful and creative — ingenious certainly. It remains, however, an essentially normative art, a reaction to restraints. At worst, it is wholly lacking in ontological significance; a styptic for an insecure civilization. Its flawed artistic universe, deprived by its own dogma of true creative expression, limps like Tamerlane: grandly indeed, but to no ultimate purpose. Its artists, corralled by circumstance into almost deviant forms of expression, became obsessed by ornament. Form reigns supreme over content and all notion of a higher guiding principle is assiduously disarmed.

All this is a gloomy verdict, on which nearly all contemporary studies of Islamic art converge. And having failed to find a rational backdrop to Islamic art, mainstream analyses remain rooted in the descriptive and historical approach. Every brick, gate, moulding, pier, buttress, squinch, and interlocking voussoir of every mosque and mausoleum has been meticulously measured. The dates and designs of every stuccoed bud and tendril have been traced from continent to continent by the finest minds of a veritable academic Interpol. Geographical, taxonomic, chronological, morphological, semantic, paleographic, lexical, syntactic, and phonetic analyses reveal all. From Seville to Samarqand, the arts of Islam have submitted their secrets to the overwhelming methodological cavalry of academia. All, says a nagging and impudent voice, except one: their meaning.

To return to the pondering of our hypothetical observer —

could a vast and dynamic civilization, inheritor of the intellectual treasuries of Greece and Babylon and Chaldaea and Egypt and Persia and India, really have been satisfied for the expression of its loftiest intellectual and spiritual ideals with an art that was no more than decorative? It is a strange indictment for a civilization whose medieval scientists were centuries in advance of their European counterparts. Can the high level of its art really be explained by a prohibition, a sort of artistic road-block, around which its most talented artists were forced to divert their creative efforts? One wonders. The conventional argument that Islamic art was shaped by social and political forces alone fails to explain how an art whose primary characteristic is unity could have arisen among cultures – as anyone who has actually visited them will observe – which are so very diverse.

A modern methodological lacuna might also be pointed out. The interpretation of contemporary abstract art, which is supposed to be pregnant with meaning, is considered a legitimate intellectual field; but is scarcely admitted into the study of an art embracing fifteen centuries and reaching across half the world. Volumes are disgorged about works of art barely distinguishable from cruel accidents of paint against canvas, but the masterpiece of an Islamic craftsman, whose very way of life has been surrendered to the study of his art and the perfection of its execution, is no more than a way to fill space.

One could argue too, that to try to understand a fundamentally abstract art by quantifying its external characteristics alone is to assess the meaning of a book by the shape of its printed characters. For much of Western art, this may be a valid enough approach. But to employ the methodologies based on Western aesthetic principles to fathom a fundamentally aniconic art seems at best insufficient: we come to Nasruddin's pigeon.

One day, Nasruddin found a wounded falcon and nursed it back to health. But its appearance troubled him. So he clipped its beak, claws, and magnificent feathers, and stood back to admire the result. 'There,' he said, 'that's much better. Now you look like a *proper* pigeon.'

326

At this point, the more generous among the scholarly do in fact concede a sigh of epistemological despair. How can a causal basis for this art really ever be formulated? they ask. Where is the evidence? If it indeed possesses a language, how could it be learned?

We must put forward a few ideas. They are not new, but scurry, as it were, like mammals between the feet of dinosaurs in the field. A small number of scholars have turned to the aesthetic theories of Islamic philosophers to investigate their possible influence on art and its expressions. Eleventh-century Persian and Arabic authors such as Ibn Sina, Ibn Rushd, and ibn al-Haytham – the West's Avicenna, Averroës, and Alhazen – all wrote on aesthetics, but largely in the context of cognition and perception, drawing heavily from Aristotelian models. Yet such discussions form only a small portion of their enormous works, and do not attempt to propose a doctrine sufficiently extensive to inform the visual arts of an entire civilization.

Others have turned to Islam's revelationary text, the Qur'ān, to search for evidence of underlying principles in art. Given the centrality of the Qur'ān to the life and history of the Muslim world, it seems a more judicious point of departure than the morphology of vine-scrolls at Mshatta.* The lack of an overt doctrine on art or aesthetics in the pages of the Qur'ān makes linking the art of Islam to the religion of Islam a methodologically troublesome endeavour in the eyes of the art historian. But the

---

* The fortified Umayyad palaces of Mshatta, Khirbat al-Mafjar, and Qusayr ʿAmra, among others, are the earliest surviving monuments of Islam. The most elaborate among them, at Mshatta in Jordan, bore an elaborately carved stone facade (now in the Pergammon Museum of Berlin) in the decoration of which some have found evidence of an emergent 'Islamic' art. But does the geometricization of vegetal ornament depicted in the facade represent a prototypical arabesque original to Islam, or is the juxtaposition of geometric with vegetal only a substyle of Late Antique compositional tradition? Arguments on both sides abound; it seems unfair to impose any greater detail on the (already) patient reader.

rich symbolism of Islam's most sacred text make it impossible to ignore.

The Qur'ān, like all the founding texts of the monotheistic religions, resonates with the twin imagery of catastrophe and bliss, but with a particular emphasis. The refinements of hell are no less grim than those of its Christian equivalent – it is noticeably hot, and is described as a place of fetid water that fails to quench, and poisoned foods that render the wicked as helpless as diseased camels. But on the day of Sorting Out, when the sun will fold up and the stars fall into darkness, when the seas boil over and the blazing fire is kindled, a Garden is brought near.

The delights of this refuge for the righteous are depicted with far greater detail than the other place. Here the souls of the faithful find infinite repose; tranquillity, luxury, and bliss await those of the patient and the constant. Cool streams nourish thornless trees bearing abundant fruit, which hangs humbly within reach of the believer. Neither slander nor idle chatter are heard. Peace reigns. There are rivers of milk which never sours, and wine which uplifts and never intoxicates, borne in silver and crystal goblets. Seated on cushions and carpets, tended by chaste maidens with lustrous eyes, here the righteous receive the bounty of God's garden, to which His Presence lends infinite contentment.

Hardly surprising that this powerful imagery, particularly among a desert-dwelling people, should have entered into the artistic repertoire of its artisans. Echoes of Paradise and its themes found their way not only into a doctrinal promise of the rewards of the righteous life, but into literature, architecture, and a wide variety of artistic media. The intricate design of gardens – one of the outstanding aesthetic features of the Islamic world – expressed an earthly foretaste of the Garden on High. The famous gardens of the Alhambra known as the Generalife take their name from the original Arabic Jennat al-Arefa, the Paradise of the Enlightened.

The ubiquitous depiction of gardens in Persian carpets,

frequently containing images of streams and fountains, and always expressing bounty and harmony, evoke irresistibly a Paradise to come. Prayer carpets in particular, whose central motifs are a mehrab or prayer-niche framing a garden scene or fruit-laden tree, demonstrate an inescapable symbolic alliance between prayer, the sanctum of the mehrab, and the reward of the world beyond. And for those to whom the idea of symbolic content is not in itself a leap of faith, the stylized vegetal and floral forms to be seen not only in the religious architecture of Islam but also in the traditional decoration, so called, of everyday objects – these too resonate with the tranquillity and abundance of the bountiful world beyond, promised by the Qur'ān.

One has only to glance at the imagery of Persian literature to see how extensively this imagery was adopted. In poetry, and especially mystical poetry, the theme of the garden as a destination of the spirit was developed into a pervasive metaphysical motif. Seen in these symbolic terms, earthly beauty is a reflection of the beauty of paradise, an invisible world mirrored in the concrete, and a reminder of Man's divine origin.

Yet these partial interpretations take us only so far; the philosophers of Islam never attempted to describe a universal hermeneutics of aesthetics, and the Qur'ān is more than a guidebook to symbolism. To understand Islamic art, it should not seem strange to suggest that we must enter the world of the traditional Islamic artist, whose mission is inextricable from the Islamic message as set forth in the Qur'ān.

No other notion is more central to the message of the Qur'ān than the reality of God. His transcendent Unity is the corner-stone of Islam. Man was created in God's image and is a servant of the divine purpose, but also, in the ordering of his life,

God's representative and deputy. Human life, consequently, is not divided into the realms of God and Caesar; the voice of the divine can be heard in all of creation, in which Man occupies a unique position of both privilege and responsibility. In Man alone the qualities of the Creator may be most comprehensively expressed. Everything else in the Qur'ān can be seen as a refinement and amplification of these momentous premises.

The traditional Muslim artist, today as much as a thousand years ago, is the anonymous spokesman of this vision. His art is the reflection of a life spent in close association with the Qur'ān, the traditional sayings of the Prophet, and prayer. Its philosophy – though this is not quite the right word – is best summarized by one of the shortest and most widely portrayed verses of the Qur'ān, *al-Ikhlas* –

> Say: He is God, the Unique
> God the Eternal and Absolute
> neither begetter nor begotten
> And there is none like unto Him

– from which much about Islamic art can be unharboured. To recall these principles in the midst of daily life is the prerogative of the faithful; to evoke them, the mission of the artist. Nothing is greater, says the Qur'ān, than the remembrance of God; and the artist's quest is no more, and no less, than to create visible reminders of the Divine Presence. The aesthetic basis of his art is founded on the famous Hadiths: 'God is beautiful and he loves beauty', and 'God desires if you do something you perfect it'. In the midst of this, the artist remains invisible, a humble translator of the Inexpressible.

All this is viewed warily from the intellectual redoubt of the art scholar. But it does, I hope, go some way towards penetrating much that at first appears enigmatic about Islamic art. It helps to explain its abstract nature – not negatively in terms of a prohibition, but as a positive affirmation of definite principles – as well as the universality of motifs and range of materials exploited by the artist. No doctrinal injunctions separate the secular from the religious, or pure from applied art. All of creation is the artist's canvas, and art ennobles everything from towering minarets to kitchen utensils.*

This idea of the artist as intermediary, rather than a Promethean imitator of divine ingenuity, helps also to explain his traditional anonymity and apparent slavishness to artistic modes. By taking fidelity to a central idea, rather than aesthetic appeal, as the measure of artistic success, the artist is not the pioneer of creative self-expression in the sense most commonly understood. He is expressive and indisputably creative. But the principles of his art do not provide a platform for the private torments,

---

* I think irresistibly of the tenth-century Samanid potteries produced in Iran and Transoxiana, which for me outstrip even the Iznik marvels produced five centuries later in Ottoman Turkey. The most striking are the white-glazed plates and bowls whose rims bear short quotations from the Qur'ān or blessings addressed to the user in black or purplish Kufic writing. They are both beautiful and functional. But life is not so simple for the art historian, who must assess both the visual import of the script and its textual semantics. The relationship between them must then be examined. The epigraphic content must be analysed in terms of its social setting; this may offer clues as to the true function of the artefact. If the epigraphic content is lacking in significance, it may be deduced that the aesthetic import of the artefact lies elsewhere; perhaps in the script's exploitation of the morphology of the bowl itself, in order to draw attention to its identity. It may, alternatively, suggest a figurative modality for the linguistic units themselves, thereby emphasizing the iconographic, rather than semantic, import of the script. The overall stylistic composition may also serve as a cultural marker, and provide clues to the social and moral values of the maker or user and their preferred mode of transmission for such values. The materials used and the technical competence with which they are exploited by the artisan may likewise serve as indicators of either a courtly or mercantile patronage. An emphasis on two-dimensional composition over the sculptural indicates a departure from Greek or Chinese models, and may reflect a regional or cultural trend explainable in terms of political climate ... But the last thing to be revealed through such ingenious methodologies is that a plate is a plate, and its decoration a celebration of the Divine through beauty.

longings, or existential angst of the personality, and are incompatible with art designed to shock or repel.* If this art's apparent resistance to historical pressure is seen as a sort of stagnation of modes and forms which are reluctant to change, it is precisely because man's relationship to the divine, even in the era of interplanetary exploration, has not itself changed.

We have come this far: there is not much further to go. The motifs and designs of the Islamic artist did not, of course, spring from nowhere. They drew upon the broad repertoire of Late Antique art as well as Byzantine, Sasanian, and Hellenistic tradition. But these were selectively nurtured in accordance with the vision of the Islamic message and developed into a supercultural art of universal appeal. Its sophistication deepened as Islam encountered and added to its cultural treasures the intellectual heritages of Greece, Persia, and India. The privileged position of mathematics in Islamic learning nourished a fascination for geometry, number, and their symbolic potentials, as well as a branch of science entirely dedicated to the numerical symbolism of the Arabic alphabet.† Across a civilization which had already

---

* In a rare moment of humility, Picasso wrote: "By amusing myself with all these games, with all these absurdities, with all these puzzles, rebuses, and arabesques, I became famous, and that very quickly. And fame for a painter means sales, gains, fortunes, riches. And today, as you know, I am celebrated, I am rich. But when I am alone with myself I have not the courage to think of myself as an artist in the great and ancient sense of the term. Giotto, Titian, Rembrandt, and Goya were great painters; I am only a public entertainer who has understood his times and has exhausted as best he could the imbecility, the vanity, the cupidity of his contemporaries. Mine is a bitter confession, more painful than may appear, but it has the merit of being sincere.' *Libro Vero*, 1952.

† The ʿelm al-jafr, said to have been codified by the fourth caliph and cousin of the Prophet, Ali ibn Ali Talib. Even the earliest monuments of Islam show evidence of an extraordinarily precise geometric configuration. At Mshatta the dimensions of the portal facade motif relate to those of its overall plan through numerically significant proportions. The column decoration of the great mosques of Kairouan and Damascus are similarly related through symbolic geometries virtually unknown to contemporary

rejected the hazards implicit in anthropomorphic art, pattern and symbolism entered into a ready and vigorous alliance. And in its finest and most developed expressions, the visual language of Islamic art became saturated with symbolic depth.

Yet it is metaphysics, rather than religion, that unites all these ideas. Here alone do the various branches of philosophy, gnosticism (ʿerfan), and the mystical schools of Sufism converge and unify. Where theology and dogma divide, the ideas of metaphysics unite, and are bound in a nexus of resounding common themes. These are by no means unique to Islamic civilization, nor to Iran alone, but in no other culture were they developed with such astonishing refinement, or borne so far from their heartland through the medium of the arts they informed.

The most consistent of these is the notion of an ordered universe of divine origin; a map of sorts, by which the human soul is able to orient its earthly sojourn. Another is the idea of an invisible but real world of angelic or archetypal forms, sometimes called the imaginal world; a treasure trove of heavenly templates striving to be expressed in the phenomenal, visible world. This too is an ancient theme; its roots can be traced to Zoroastrian cosmology, but surfaces in Islamic Persia through the visionary meta-philosophy of Sohrawardi.* We encounter too a

---

scholarship. The geometries that relate the proportions of calligraphy to architecture, or those of carpet knots, remain similarly invisible; but perhaps one day they will be well understood by a more willing generation of interpreters.

* The enormous influence of Sohrawardi (1153–1191) in the eastern Islamic world and especially Persia can be compared to that of the Andalusian gnostic Ibn al-ʿArabi in the West. Sohrawardi's visionary blending of the perennial wisdom of pre-Islamic Persia into Islamic philosophy can be likened to such powerful intellectual syntheses as al-Ghazali's in connection with Sufism or that of St Palamas with Hesychasm's integration into Orthodox Christianity. His ideas are revived and extended by such Safavid luminaries as Mir Damad and Sadr al-Din Shirazi (also known as Mulla Sadra) in the sixteenth century. Each of these intellectual and gnostic giants held in the highest esteem the ancient

repertoire or code by which this supersensory realm is represented, as well as the techniques by which its presence may be felt.

This (at last) simplifies things. Music, painting, calligraphy, and the various arts deriving from them are considered to have a single celestial origin; all of the arts, in their highest expressions, refer back to this unifying theme. Even the design of gardens draws on this otherworldly vision of the Paradisiacal realm. As mirrors of the invisible world, they conform to a rigorous order; in poetry achieved by metre, in music by mode, in calligraphy by proportion, and in architecture by geometry. All are further refined by symmetry and rhythm; all strive for clarity, luminosity, and above all, beauty. Brush, string, reed, and compass are the tools by which this theophanic vision is expressed: all echo the longing of the divine to be expressed at the level of His vicegerent, Man. *On earth*, in other words, *as it is in heaven.*

The twin configurations of the geometric and arabesque, whose designs are not limited by their borders but strive invariably to stretch behind them, allude irresistibly to infinity; the resonance between them, to unity. Calligraphies of dazzling variety serve as bridges between the worlds of form and of literal meaning, and all are combined in strategies of ingenious harmony. Their interlacement, exploited in stone and stucco and glaze and metal and fabric, mirrors the endless complexity of creation. Yet their ultimate resolution, achieved by a universal exactitude of proportion and design, always suggests the greater and unifying design of a cosmic order.

In architecture, their expression is further refined by wizardries of composition, where light itself submits to the artist's command, scattered and absorbed from interplaying textures, sucked into opacity along intersecting vaults and galleries or sent tumbling in prismatic torrents over *muqarnas*-encrusted arches. Elsewhere its substance is amplified or subdued by colour and the

---

philosophers of both Greece and pre-Islamic Persia. Their works represent an almost inexhaustible vein of knowledge waiting to be mined by anyone who is not embarrassed by the axioms of traditional cosmology.

echoes between shade and tone. Every surface is ennobled by pattern. Kaleidoscopic stars burst and cohere in countless fragments across shimmering panels, or glissade over parabolas in reciprocating geometries. Streams of turbulent calligraphy, stretched to the limit of intelligibility, cascade between dense patterns of crystalline sobriety. The static and the mobile, the permanent and the changing, the immanent and transcendent are all articulated in these lofty visual riddles. Trapezoid meets spiral and the radiations of symmetry fuse magically with the rhythm of the volute.

At times, the mind, struggling to resolve such visual paradoxes, is lured into moments of vision and freed from the confines of ordinary thought. At others it is overwhelmed by their complexity and abundance. There, on the periphery of mentation, they begin to reveal their loveliest secrets. Under the scrutiny of language these fragile intimations seem to dissolve like snowflakes on the palm of an outstretched hand. But in their simultaneous appeal to the different portions of the human being, converging in a campaign of allied meanings upon the senses, mind, and feelings, the instruments of this art can be said to exert their wholesome genius.

Seven

Persepolis
Yazd · Kerman · Natanz
Kashan · Mashhad

✫

Money Talks · Persepolis · The Shah's Last Hurrah

Operation Ajax: The Un-Democratization of Iran

A Civilized Way to Differ · Dualities · Holy Smoke · Taxis of Evil

Rendezvous in Paradise · Rosewater · The Crazed Ones · Plus ça Change

Lessons in Profanity · To the Shrine · Full Circle

بشنوی سخن اهل دل مگو که خطاست   سخن شناس نه‌ای جان من خطا اینجاست

Do not find fault with the language of the People of the Heart
You, my friend, are no linguist: and the fault lies there

IT WAS TIME to think about money. I had run out of cash again and wanted before I left Shiraz to visit the country's most famous ancient site, Persepolis, or as Persians call it, Takht-e Jamshid. I wandered to the entrance of the bazaar, where men with bundles of banknotes would ply their trade, mostly to foreigners, chanting their mantra-like '*dollar, dollar*' at likely passers-by in the surreptitious manner of drug dealers. Nobody changed money at banks; the official rate of exchange was invariably lower and the whole process – the queuing, filling out of forms, and entering every detail in endless registers – could take hours. Shopkeepers tended give the full amount, but didn't always have the cash to spare. Moneychangers on the street took a small commission – about a pound – which I was always happy to give.

A smiling two-man team on a nearby street corner let me know the going rate, and I handed over a hundred-dollar bill. The exchange was normally a straightforward process. But occasionally it would be drawn out by a wearisome and theatrical attempt to wear down the customer, slowing the count of banknotes into his hand as the agreed sum neared, and fixing him with a look of expectation between the lengthening intervals. By thus exhausting the patience of the buyer who, it was hoped, would give up in disgust and frustration, the seller increased his chances of gaining an extra banknote or two by the end of the transaction. It was the same kind of psychological wearing-down employed by taxi drivers. I knew this performance well, and disliked it.

We were ten notes away from the end when the man I had

chosen began to slow, and then, seeing that I had no intention of giving up so soon, stopped counting altogether. His hand was poised over the remaining notes and he stared at me, wondering perhaps whether I was even more stupid than other foreigners he had met. As he did so, all the frustrations I had experienced in similar encounters seemed to rise up in a single voice. I felt my patience waver, and then collapse.

'Why are you stopping?' I asked, in the quiet and purposeful manner of one who has decided on murder. 'Have you forgotten how to count?'

He grinned a little, not quite sure what to make of my tone.

'No, *agha*.'

'Then show me you know how to count. Did you not go to school? Have you already forgotten what we agreed? Have you got sunstroke?'

'No, *agha*.' With a flicker of irritation, he put another note into my hand, then stopped again. 'It is a question of the commission.'

'What commission? You didn't mention a commission. How much commission?'

He exchanged a nervous look with his partner, whose grin had turned to a look of worry.

'It is customary, *agha*. One, two, three, four thousand ... as much or as little as you wish.'

'Two thousand is good,' said the other, with a conciliatory wince.

'Good for who? Good for me? If you wanted a commission, why didn't you say so? Did you forget? Or maybe you mistook me for a bank? Tell me: do you see a sign on my forehead, saying "BANK"?'

'God *is* merciful,' said his partner, a little sheepishly. 'And two thousand is nothing.'

'Oh, is it *nothing*?' His partner did not enjoy the extra attention and took a step backwards from me. 'Are you not making a lot of fuss over nothing? When you take a taxi, does the driver say, "Please give me nothing?" When you buy a watermelon, does the shopkeeper say, "That will be *nothing?*" ' I turned back. 'Count, and leave God out of it.'

With a look of utter dejection, he handed over the final banknotes.

'Finally! That wasn't so hard, was it? Now,' with a beneficent smile, 'please take your commission.' I fanned out the notes in front of him. His look of dejection deepened. 'One, two, three thousand. As much or as little as you wish.'

He refused, of course. Now it was time for the homily.

'If you want foreigners like me to trust you, tell them about your commission. Tell them why you take a commission. Not your life story, just a little one. They will appreciate your honesty. And they will return to you every few days, because they will trust you. Just be straightforward about it.'

I counted out several bills and tucked them into his shirt pocket.

'You are right, *agha,*' the two of them chimed sorrowfully, 'you are *so* right. But times are so hard and our economy is in ruin. Our livelihood is not safe. The city is not safe! It isn't like Europe, where you come from, where there's law. You can be robbed! There are bad people everywhere. Sometimes even the police rob you and there's nothing you can do. Only the other day—'

I cut short this whining with a friendly dismissal. Smiles of relief broke out all round, and I found myself invited to tea. And from then on, whenever I passed them in the street they would bow slightly, smiling deferentially, and enquire after my well-being in the loftiest honorific style. Muttering curses, I had no doubt, as soon as I was out of earshot.

Φ

When Alexander finally broke through the Persian lines in 330 BC, the empire's most sacred site was, after two hundred years of almost continual construction, virtually complete. The Greeks called it Persepolis, the ancient Persians Parsa, and even among the marvels of the ancient world, it was a unique and awe-inspiring site. Its magnificence, its wealth, and perhaps its sanctity may have awoken a vengeful streak in the young Macedonian. Arrian records that Alexander was advised against the destruction of the palace complex, but that he wished to punish the Persians for their earlier invasion of Greece and the burning of the Acropolis in Athens. What followed seems likely to have been an act of high vandalism. The guards at Persepolis were overcome and slaughtered, the statues of their kings toppled, and thousands of tons of silver and hundreds of gold were looted from its capacious treasury. Ten thousand mules and five thousand camels, according to Plutarch, were needed to transport the spoils. Thick layers of excavated ash betray the final moments of this fateful sequence. Two and a half thousand years of sun, wind, and rain have done the rest.

But even in ruin, Persepolis is dramatic. Its halls and palaces were built on an immense stone platform occupying over a million square feet, partially hewn from the cove of a low mountain and partially constructed from vast blocks of stone. Some of these weighed up to thirty tons and, without the aid of mortar, fitted together so precisely as to render the joints between them almost invisible. The platform commands a broad view of the surrounding plain, and was once enclosed by a high wall, parts of which were faced with coloured tiles. This perimeter wall, and the walls that formed the palaces and chambers within, were made of baked mud and have long since returned to dust. But the immense doorframes, gateways, lintels, and columns survive in various degrees of preservation, as do the long stone friezes that flank the monumental stairs and passageways.

Persepolis is built on a fitting scale for kings whose rule was divinely ordained. Persia's Achaemenid rulers did not claim to be divine themselves, but to act as agents on behalf of the Divine, as vicegerents of a cosmic being. Their titles and their architecture expressed both universality and cosmic purpose, to which scale, power and wealth were bound to adhere. The idea of empire, too, is transmitted at Persepolis by the international character of its execution: Egyptian, Mesopotamian, and Greek styles and motifs are brought together in a unique and incomparably grand amalgam of artistic ideals.

The very materials from which the site was built affirmed the great sweep of imperial rule, just as they did at the earlier capital of Susa, where a well-known inscription records cedar beams from Lebanon, gold from Sardis and Bactria, lapis lazuli from Badakhshan, turquoise from Khwarazm, silver and ebony from Egypt, and ivory from Ethiopia. The long friezes of tribute-bearers, carved in gentle relief and once brightly painted, each carry a characteristic gift from their homelands – vases, bows, skins, and precious fabrics. Others lead animals: lion cubs, bison, rams, horses, and two-humped camels. Medes, Elamites, Aryans, Babylonians, Parthians, Egyptians, Bactrians, Cilicians, Scythians, Assyrians, Lydians, Cappadocians, Ionians, Thracians, Punjabis, and Abyssinians are all represented in characteristic dress; even today they seem to advance with patient ceremony towards their audience with the King of Kings.

The great hall called the Apadana was in itself a wonder: fabulously adorned with precious and sparkling ornaments and supported on thirty-six slender, fluted columns sixty feet high. Each was topped with a stone capital weighing several tons in the shape of a kneeling bull. The timbers and panels were inlaid and gilded with precious metals and the walls draped with sumptuous fabrics. In places the black marble lintels are polished to a glassy smoothness and shine like smoked mirrors; awesome and glinting statuary, incense, and music must have raised the atmosphere of these magical spaces to one of splendour scarcely equalled elsewhere in the world.

Yet there is no mention of Iran's most famous ancient site in the Bible, as there is of other Achaemenid centres of power, and contemporary documents are strangely silent on it. Nothing excavated from the site suggests a political dimension, and for this reason Persepolis has been assigned a historical role beyond that of palace complex and a royal summer capital. Its function seems more likely to have been ceremonial. The serene orderliness of the tribute-bearers depicted on the long reliefs and the Buddha-like smiles on the lips of the giant carved faces of deities and beasts alike support an invocational purpose.

The visible, ritual climax of this idea seems likely to have been the celebration of the new year at the spring equinox, when Persepolis became a place of pilgrimage and tribute from vassal kingdoms across the empire; not only to honour the imperial ideology, but in affirmation of that most ancient and persistent of ideas, that of the human role in maintaining the equilibrium of the very cosmos.

We do not know for sure. Perhaps its function, and even its exact location, were kept secret from all but the palace intimates and the trusted tribute-bearers. Perhaps, a hundred miles distant from the sacred centre, foreign deputations were intercepted by members of the royal guard, and made the final portion of their long journeys blindfolded and under escort. I pictured them emerging from their dusty carriages, blinking and staring and looking up in awe at as they pulled up beneath the glinting wings of supernatural animals flanking the outer gates. And, it seemed quite likely, having to renegotiate the agreed fare with the carriage-drivers . . .

Φ

European voices on Persepolis have often sounded an ambiguous note, and there is a piquant tone of disapproval to early accounts. Nothing in European sculpture had prepared them for such strange creations as winged bulls with human faces, and Chardin's engravings, made in the 1670s, depict the giant statues with the heads of pit-bull terriers. Lord Curzon, writing at the end of the nineteenth century, was unimpressed:

> No one can wander over the Persepolis platform, from storied stairway to stairway, from sculptured doorway to graven pier, no one can contemplate the 1,200 human figures that still move in solemn reduplication upon the stone, without being struck by a sense of monotony, and fatigue. It is all the same, and the same again, and yet again.

Byron, being Byron, was scathing. He visited Persepolis with Herzfeld, accompanied by the great professor's pet pig and terrier. The columns he likened to mules – infertile from the architectural point of view. The crenellations on the monumental stairways are described as 'jagged excrescences'. And of the ceremonial reliefs, he wrote: 'They have art, but not spontaneous art, and certainly not great art. Instead of mind or feeling, they exhale a soulless refinement . . .' And here again – I think – the descriptions tell us more about European ways of seeing than about the works they judge. But this mental restlessness, this compulsion to compare, and characteristic resistance to quieter layers of meaning, limits the outsider's interpretative reach. Pope – by way of contrast – who for many years lived in Iran, and got to know the culture better than any outsider of the era, understood the limits of this overly intellectual manner of interpretation. Writing about Persepolis in his *Persian Architecture* (1965), he calls it:

> Western thinking: factual, literal, rationalistic. It fails to comprehend the constellation of assumptions, attitudes, hopes that had descended from the ancient orient with its ingrained reliance on emotion and symbolism.

Persepolis is still criticized for departing too radically from classical canons of architecture, for being ostentatious, and even imitative of Mesopotamian, particularly Assyrian art. But nowhere is there any representation, so common in imperial Assyrian tradition, of agony or warfare. Scenes of conflict are limited to the portrayal of lions attacking bulls; these are thought to represent the seasons and to celebrate the annual rebirth of fertility, and a huge body of literature is devoted to the astronomical basis for this interpretation.

A more traditional reading, virtually unwritten about but which passed into certain schools of Sufism from Mithraic symbolism, identifies the combat between lion and bull as a spiritual engagement, a struggle between the noble and the base components of the human soul. At Persepolis, the human-looking musculature of the lion, the decorated collar of the arrested bull, even the look of acceptance in the victim's eyes, which turns to face that of its attacker, suggest a rite rather than an event. A comparable scene, depicting Mithra plunging a dagger into the neck of a supine bull, is represented in Mithreaeums all over Europe, and occasionally Mithra himself is represented with the head of a lion. It is tempting to suppose that the same elements were adopted by Christian artists in their portrayal of St George and the dragon, where even the backward-looking gaze of the speared dragon is reproduced in countless Christian icons.

More will be decoded in time. But the importance of Persepolis to the identity of the Persian Empire has never been in question. 'It was the embodiment of a national consciousness,' writes Pope, 'and, as such, Alexander understood that he must destroy it.'

The attempt never wholly succeeded. Two and a half millennia later, the theme of royal glory was still being celebrated there when the Shah chose Persepolis for his notorious festivities in 1975. To mark the anniversary of the Persian Empire, he hosted the most spectacular — and the most ill-conceived — party of modern times. Preparations took a year, during which the area was sealed off to outsiders in a seventy-five-mile radius. Several thousand people were arrested as a precautionary measure, and the parents of suspected troublemakers were taken as hostages by the government. A huge encampment of tents built on concrete foundations was constructed at the base of the ruins: this covered a hundred and fifty acres. Each tent was fireproof and air-conditioned, and extravagantly appointed to resemble a neo-classical German palace complete with trompe l'œil in fake pink marble and gilt bronze appliqués.

Invitations were sent across the world. Queen Elizabeth, Nixon, and Pompidou declined politely. Fifty-nine countries were represented on the day by an assortment of kings, queens, sheikhs, sultans, prime ministers, presidents, foreign ministers, and governors-general. Haile Selassie attended with a black chihuahua wearing a diamond collar. Two hundred Iranian soldiers had their beards specially trimmed and were dressed in the manner of the Achaemenid royal guard.

The Shah could not be faulted for his largesse. His guests ate caviar-filled quails' eggs, lobster mousse, champagne sorbet, peacocks stuffed with foie gras and flaming roast lambs. Twenty-five thousand bottles of wine were flown from Paris by Maxim's, who oversaw the catering with a staff of 165 chefs, wine stewards, and waiters. In Shiraz, meanwhile, there were food shortages and hunger, and among the nomadic Qashgai, whose traditional migratory routes had been severed by the event so as to prevent the royal guests' embarrassment, terrible losses of livestock. To criticisms of the cost of the event, which is said to have topped a hundred million dollars, the Shah replied: 'What do they think I should feed fifty heads of state? Bread and radishes?'

It was nearly the last event to be held there. In 1979, a vociferous ayatollah called for the entire site to be bulldozed and ploughed into the ground. Saner voices, we may be grateful, prevailed.

Φ

In nearby Shiraz, I had arranged to meet the parents of an Iranian friend from London. They had grown up in the most prosperous days of the Shah, when Iran had bailed out European industries and bought submarines and jet fighters by the dozen from the

Americans. Under the spell of their charm and refinement, my routine struggle with language and the unscrupulousness of taxi drivers seemed magically allayed. We met at a grand restaurant on the outskirts of town, and were joined by a dignified pair of men in their seventies – the wife's uncles, I think – who moved with the same quiet elegance between their adopted countries and their former homes in Iran.

The husband, a retired doctor, spoke fluent English peppered with delightful colloquialisms ('I'll fish it out for you', 'they did a roaring trade', and, of his diminutive cigarettes, 'medically pretty harmless'). We ate outdoors beside lighted torches and the play of a fountain and were fussed over by waistcoated staff. As a foreigner and a guest my travels in Iran and especially Afghanistan were singled out for special praise by all except the elder brother, who recounted an instance of Afghan wickedness he had encountered in India. (I have forgotten the exact story.) But I remember how he turned to me after telling it. 'All Afghans,' he uttered gravely, 'are killers and thieves.'

It was always strange to hear Iranians speak of their neighbours as if they belonged to a different and baser race (though the same was true when Afghans described Persians as 'sandwich-eaters' or 'women'). I enjoyed this frankness but it made it difficult to talk any longer about Afghanistan and the Afghans. Perhaps, I suggested, the Afghans lacked the ingenuity of the Persians; and to lighten the tone I told a story I had heard from Louise Firouz.

During the upheavals of the revolution, some unscrupulous inhabitants of Rasht – a Caspian people with a reputation for financial cunning – had managed to acquire a lion from the Tehran zoo. Sensing its potential, they planned a country-wide display of gladiatorial contests between the noble lion, one of the icons of Iranian nationality, and a variety of lesser creatures. The first of these was to be an elderly donkey. The tickets sold overnight for a fortune, and a crammed stadium clamoured to watch the spectacle. But things had not turned out quite as expected. The lion, released into the arena, padded wearily towards its would-be victim, and sniffed at its tail. At the same moment, the donkey kicked the lion in the head and killed it instantly. An outraged crowd demanded its money back, and the not-so-wily Rashtis moved on to another scheme.*

A little later somebody mentioned Mossadeq, and my ears pricked up. I had often wondered about him, and I mentioned to the others how curious I was about the former Prime Minister and the period of his rule because it seemed so vital to an understanding of the later revolution that brought Khomeini to power in 1979. There were some nods of accord. I knew the rough sequence of events; the others helped me through the patchy parts.

It is a seldom-told but crucial story. The Shah had made Mossadeq his Prime Minister in 1951, and from the moment of his investiture Iran had become the focus of international controversy. Mossadeq's first act was to defy the British by nationalizing the oil industry. This act of unprecedented defiance earned him phenomenal popularity at home and notoriety abroad. It was a unique and promising time. Nationalism was on the rise, Mossadeq had emerged as the movement's de facto leader, and the oil industry was moving into high gear with greater than ever yields. Under Mossadeq's influence, the combination became explosive.

Oil had been discovered in quantity in 1908 and the Anglo-Persian Oil Company set up in 1912. The British were major shareholders, and paid less in revenues to the Iranians than they

---

* Perhaps they should have consulted in advance a traditional astrologer, as sensible people used to do. In the section on astrology of the *Chahar Maqale*, the story is told of the court astrologer to Mahmoud of Ghazni, at the time none other than the celebrated al-Biruni. Entering a courtyard with four doors, the Sultan asked his astrologer to predict which door he would exit by. When Biruni had written down his prediction, the wily king ordered his men to break a hole in the wall, out of which he walked. This the astrologer had predicted; and the Sultan, incensed, sent him to prison. At the intervention of the Prime Minister, the Sultan repented, and rewarded his astrologer with appropriate gifts, but not without the warning: 'if thou desirest always to reap advantage from me, speak according to my desire, not according to the dictates of thy science.'

did in taxes to their own government. At the giant refinery at Abadan, Iranian workers lived like slaves under British command, and for years the company's brazenness had been a source of humiliation to Iranians.

Mossadeq's bombshell was to propose a 50/50 split of profits with the company, as was common with oil consortiums elsewhere. But London was in no mood to negotiate. 'MOSSIE TAKES OVER BRITISH PETROL BUT THE NAVY COMES TO THE RESCUE' read one headline in England. The British imposed a blockade on Iranian oil, imposed financial restrictions, held naval firing practices in the Persian Gulf, sent paratroopers to Cyprus, and withdrew its personnel from the refinery at Abadan, crippling the industry. Plans for a British invasion were circulated in Whitehall. But Mossadeq was still enormously popular, and over the course of the year — one of the stormiest in modern Iranian history — he named himself War Minister, dissolved the Senate, and broke off diplomatic relations with Britain. He also appealed to the Court of International Justice in the Hague and to the United Nations, where support was given to the Iranian claim. He was voted Man of the Year by *Time* magazine and became known for his eccentric and theatrical behaviour, delivering impassioned speeches from the balcony of his home wearing only his pyjamas, and alternately fainting and crying in parliamentary sessions.

His intransigence took Iran to the verge of bankruptcy, but he was granted ever-greater powers by Parliament. There was much unrest. Pro- and anti-Mossadeq factions battled in the streets of Tehran, while the Shah, meanwhile, was paralysed with indecision. He made a brief attempt to thwart Mossadeq, who resigned and was then reappointed after bloody demonstrations swept the country. Mossadeq then moved aggressively against the Shah, whom he believed should rule as a constitutional monarch. He purged the army of the Shah's most loyal officers, and exiled dozens of his friends, the Queen Mother, and, eventually, the Shah himself.

Perhaps inevitably, the decision had elsewhere been made to act against Mossadeq. By mid-1953, a plan for covert intervention

– the first of its kind and a model for future operations – had been drawn up. It was incubated in Whitehall, hatched in Washington, and nourished throughout by the now-discredited notion that Iran was about to fall into the hands of the Communists. An ailing Churchill approved the plan; and the recently elected Eisenhower (Truman had rejected the idea) agreed to apply personal pressure on Mossadeq by refusing Iran the financial assistance it desperately needed. The aim of Operation Ajax, according to the now-declassified summary by its author, Princeton scholar and CIA asset Donald Wilber, was 'to cause the fall of the Mossadeq government; to re-establish the prestige and power of the Shah; and to replace the Mossadeq government with one which would govern Iran according to constructive policies...'

The plan was in essence cruel and simple: to force the country to decide between the Shah and Mossadeq, and to undermine the pyjama-wearing Prime Minister in every way possible in the meantime, depriving him utterly of any hope of rescue. Newspapers and radio stations would broadcast anti-Mossadeq propaganda; CIA- and British-sponsored agents would spread dissent among his supporters; key military officers would be enlisted in support of the Shah; and the Shah himself was to be persuaded to sign a royal decree appointing a new Prime Minister, General Zahedi.* The Shah's flamboyant sister Ashraf, who had been

---

* This was the same Zahedi whose pro-German sympathies prompted the British to have him kidnapped from his home in Isfahan during the Second World War. The task was given to Captain Fitzroy Maclean, who made a plan to insinuate himself into the general's home by impersonating a brigadier making an impromptu social call. Operation PONGO was an unqualified success. 'When,' writes Maclean in *Eastern Approaches*, 'a couple of minutes later, General Zahedi, a dapper figure in a tight-fitting grey uniform and highly polished boots, entered the room, he found himself looking down the barrel of my Colt automatic...'

One thinks inevitably of the similar fate of General Kreipe, commander of German forces in Crete, kidnapped in his own car with unsurpassed daring and elegance by British officers operating with the

exiled by Mossadeq, was to be infiltrated back into Tehran from the roulette tables of Cannes especially for the purpose. A mink coat, and promises of an appropriate allowance in the event of a failed coup, are said to have secured royal cooperation. Also enlisted for his persuasive skills was General Norman Schwarzkopf, a friend of the Shah and former commander of the Iranian gendarmerie. His son and namesake was the military commander of the 1990 Persian Gulf campaign.

Amid daily turmoil in Tehran, rioting and rumours of coups and shifting allegiances, a small team of planners led by the thirty-five-year-old Kermit Roosevelt went to work. In secret meetings, the chain-smoking Shah eventually agreed to put his signature to the decree; Zahedi organized military cooperation, and the propaganda war began. But on the day on which the decree was to be delivered, the plot was undone; Mossadeq had been warned. He announced the failed coup on radio; the conspirators were rounded up; Zahedi escaped and went into hiding at a CIA safe house; and the Shah fled to Iraq and then Rome in his private plane.

Controllers in Washington agreed to cancel the operation. But Roosevelt was made of sterner stuff. His cool nerve, clandestine wartime training, and unlimited supplies of cash allowed him to come up with an improvised plan. Thousands of copies of the signed decree were distributed around Tehran, the Shah's dismissal of Mossadeq was announced on radio, and money was lavishly distributed to wavering army units and a number of key figures promising crowds of pro-Shah supporters on the streets. The leader of the Tehran *zurkhanas*, Sha'ban 'the Brainless', provided hundreds of armed gang members; a popular and anti-

---

Cretan resistance. The General's car, which was driven through sixteen enemy checkpoints by Patrick Leigh Fermor, was found abandoned with a note on the front seat alerting the Germans to the fate of their General. The postscript read: 'We are very sorry to leave behind this lovely car.' The recollection of this encounter is recounted with characteristic poignancy in Leigh Fermor's *A Time of Gifts* (John Murray, 1977).

Mossadeq member of the clergy was paid to provide a pro-Shah crowd to march from the bazaar to the centre of the city; and the members of another crowd, paid for with $50,000 changed into small Iranian bills by the American Ambassador himself, were to masquerade as Tudeh party members in order to provoke fears of a communist takeover.

Two days later the gangs rampaged through the streets, mysteriously infected by enthusiasm for the Shah, and the day was carried. Zahedi was borne aloft through the streets by a jubilant mob, and royalist troops spread virtually unopposed through the city. Mossadeq, after a shootout at his home, fled through neighbouring gardens in his overcoat and pyjamas. Within a few days the Shah returned from Rome wearing his air marshal's uniform, greeted by cheering and flag-waving supporters. Royal power had been restored, Mossadeq arrested, and a reliable American ally secured in the world's most sensitive region. Not a single bomb had been dropped.*

Kim Roosevelt, who was thanked personally for his role in the coup by Churchill, skied annually thereafter on expenses-paid holidays with the Shah in Switzerland, and Sha'ban the Brainless was rewarded with a yellow convertible Cadillac, a brand new *zurkhaneh* and the role of trainer to the Shah's shock-troops. At the end of a trial lasting six weeks, Mossadeq was sentenced to death. The Shah interceded and his sentence was commuted to three years in prison, after which he lived under guard at his home outside Tehran. He died of cancer in 1967.

All this had made the year comparable in promise to the final

---

* Although an exploding electric razor provided by the British Secret Intelligence Service is said to have been used to eliminate a key minister. The standard work on the country in coming decades, Donald Wilber's *Iran, Past and Present*, describes the events of the fateful day of Mossadeq's defeat: 'By this time it was perfectly clear that a spontaneous uprising of the masses, including thousands who were not normally involved in parties or politics, had occurred.' This is rich, coming from the CIA agent who planned it.

moments of the Constitutional Movement in 1912. A democratically elected government had been stopped in its tracks. I could not resist asking the obvious question: what might have happened had Mossadeq not been undermined from outside?

'Exactly the same thing,' said one of the brothers darkly. 'Mossadeq had already failed. He was too stubborn – he admitted it himself.'

It was not the reply I had expected; Mossadeq was nearly a myth nowadays, a hero of nationalist sentiment, a defier of autocrats.

'What I find extraordinary,' I said, 'is that a tiny number of foreign professionals were able to engineer the course of Iranian politics.' It was perhaps a blunt confession. This time the elder brother spoke.

'Would you have preferred,' he asked coolly, 'that they had been *amateurs?*'

And this too was a strange reply. I wasn't sure if the dour tone of this judgement was an indictment of Mossadeq, or just a general distaste for all the troubles of the time. It felt wrong to pursue the issue, and a thoughtful silence fell over us all.

The Shah's power grew steadily over the next few years. Mossadeq's supporters were exiled or imprisoned, and the Communist Party ruthlessly persecuted. Almost everyone in the Shah's administration was replaced. Like his father, he made the military the instrument of his power, supported by a secret service which had been trained by advisers from both the CIA and the Israeli secret service. It was soon known not only for its efficiency but also for inventiveness of its methods of torture. The Shah survived several assassination attempts, and used them to silence his opposition with ever-greater autocracy. As his power grew, his legitimacy was correspondingly undermined, and within a decade there was widespread unrest over an ever-broader spectrum of opposition groups. Khomeini was exiled in 1964, but his sermons disputing the necessity of the monarchy were increasingly heard; a few years later he began to put forward the radical notion of the *velayat-i faqih*, the basis of theocratic rule.

Phenomenal wealth allowed the Shah to remain indifferent to cries for constitutional reform. The quadrupling of oil prices in the mid-1970s brought billions into the treasury, and huge sums were spent on American military equipment. Resentment was widespread. The number of American advisers and military personnel in the country grew to over twenty-five thousand; American teenagers rode their motorcycles through the courtyards of the Royal Mosque in Isfahan; and the Status of Forces Agreement, which exempted American personnel from Iranian law, proved universally offensive. The Shah's days were numbered. American imperialism was widely felt to have replaced that of the British; all subsequent Iranian policy was anti-American.

At this point the doctor's wife spoke up in a wistful tone. 'The others were thieves with bad taste,' she said, and sighed. 'These ones are thieves with no taste at all.'

'Things *are* better now,' said the doctor. 'At least there are *some* checks and balances.' The others nodded gravely, and the conversation shifted. A little later we exchanged addresses and, as it was cool, moved inside and prepared to leave. The doctor called a taxi for me from the front desk, and surreptitiously paid my fare in advance. We all walked to the entrance together.

'I was very happy to talk with you,' said the older brother, 'even if we have different opinions. The world would be very dull if everyone thought the same way.'

It was a civilized way to differ. He waved his walking stick from the doorway and a smile flashed from his face as the taxi pulled away. The radio in the car was on, broadcasting a discussion between two professors about Beckett's *Waiting for Godot*.

It was an evening of characteristically opposing themes. I remembered the woman I had met on my first visit to Tehran – it seemed a long time ago now – who had told me that Iranians led a 'double life'. At the time I had understood her words in a social sense, but now realized the idea went deeper. Iranian culture is permeated with Janus-like traits which puzzle, bemuse, and infuriate the outsider who, at first, has no means to make sense of them. Ever since I had arrived in Iran I had been running up against different versions of these dualities; at times the very culture seemed to thrive on them. I had noticed their pervasiveness and, some time earlier, had even made a list:

Public Private
Street Home
Conservative Reformist
Modern Traditional
Masses Elite
Extremism Universalism
Ta'arof Bi-ta'arof
Mulla Sufi
Shah Ayatollah
Qur'ān Divān of Hafez
Geometric Vegetal
Iran Turan
Farmer Nomad
Ali Rostam
Wife Woman
Tourist price Iranian price
Ahura Mazda Ahriman
Modern Ancient
Visible Invisible
Darkness Light

But there are shadows here and shades of grey, which part under the cold blade of analysis and regather behind it. I had begun to notice my own willingness to collaborate with these behind-the-lines networks of meaning and fifth columns of concept; and many things that had at first appeared contradictory now seemed closer to a kind of resolution at which it was impossible to arrive intellectually. A dawning sense of the complexity of ordinary life had loosened my thinking about so many issues which had first appeared to lie in opposition. But perhaps in the end there was nothing contradictory about contradictions.

All that was needed was a reconciling element to bridge the intervening void: one had only to be Iranian.

Φ

South of the famous cities of Shiraz and Isfahan, the geography begins to change. The landscape pales, unfolding from the roadside in yellowing sheets which merge with the sky along a mirage-fringed horizon. Moving against these desiccated expanses, one feels like a survivor, adrift without bearings. Then strange mountains rise in the distance. No grassy slopes or gentle foothills introduce their ascent. They drive upwards from the flatness with the suddenness of switchblades, climbing at frenzied angles in profiles that resemble the temperature charts of the delirious. Their flanks are wreathed in a purplish haze, which lightens as it rises, bearing the evaporated traces of rose-pink and lilac-purple and merging with bands of half-formed cloud that patrol the uppermost slopes. Above these, the mountains erupt in clusters of shimmering rock like the spires and battlements of weightless metropolises. These resolve illogically as one approaches into unexpected shapes, split apart by ragged valleys or extended by new ranges like convoys of airborne sharks' fins which stretch for miles. Around them the colours regroup in bleeding spectrums of bleached celestial inks that seem borrowed from some cruelly arid planet. Then, without warning, they falter, as if responding en masse to some cosmic warning signal, and moments later sink and collapse downwards into plains barer than the sea.

The desert voice is heard in the architecture too. Palm trees, rather than cypress, plane, or pine, cluster above the houses here. There are small mosques with narrow windows circling the bases of their domes, a design I hadn't seen before. Two other new shapes appear: in place of the flat roof, the dome surmounted by a small central chimney becomes common. The ensemble gives the impression of a female breast. There are also rectangular homes with arched fronts resembling the microscopic offspring of Ctesiphon. All are unseen in the north and give a taste of how heterogeneous the architecture of the country must have been until nearly yesterday.

I had hired a car and driver for half a day to cross one such stretch of landscape. Gazing at ease from the window I felt very glad to have been spared the need to cross it on foot or horseback. You feel a kind of awe when looking across such dehydrated fastnesses for all those who endured the crossing of them in the days before the trusty Peykan.* The English explorer Frye, travelling north through Iran in 1680, captured the cruel atmosphere of his summer route

> ... up hill and down hill, through broken rocks and unsteady stones, through kindled fires from sulphurous caverns, and the more raging effects of the burning orb, enlightening and enlivening all the world beside; here it kills and consumes the unnurtured plants, leaving them dry and sapless; as if the great heaps of rocks were made for no other end but to counterpoise the more fruitful part of this terrestrial globe ...

My driver for the day was called Reza, a barrel-chested, jovial man who talked about the old days with heavy sighs and frequent moppings of his brow. I felt inexplicably sad for him. He was transparently kind and good-natured; for some reason I pictured him as a benevolent feudal khan, dispensing favours from his veranda to petitioning villagers. But squeezed into his decrepit car, ferrying strangers to and fro for a pittance, he seemed as tragic as a dancing bear.

A puncture brought us to a halt half an hour from our starting point. Reza wheezed over the jack as I loosened the wheel-nuts, and we changed the wheel in the blazing desert light. The sunshine was so strong it seemed to push through my shirt like a blunt knife.

'We'll be all right now,' muttered Reza with an unconvincing smile. He settled back into his seat with a '*Ya Ali!*' and wiped the sweat from his forehead with the back of a hand. Not long

---

* The Paykan is the national car of Iran, modelled on the Hillman Hunter.

afterwards, the engine began to stutter. We pulled over. Our clothes were wet against the seats. Reza wiped his brow again, muttering to himself in an anxious sing-song. He opened the bonnet of the car, removed the air filter, beat it several times against the engine, looked at it for a moment or two, and then flung it into the desert. I got out to see if I could be useful. Things didn't look good: coolant was pouring from the radiator at the front, and petrol from a leak at the back. But we topped up the water level and tightened up the hoses with some spare wire and moved on until, at a desolate checkpoint surrounded by pale outcrops of desert rock, a soldier waved us down.

From the nearby post a lean and deeply sunburned young man wearing a dark blue track suit and flip-flops crossed the road towards us. This was a police officer. He came to the window, demanded papers, looked them over for a moment, then ordered Reza from the car.

'*Chasm*,' he replied, placing the palm of his hand over his eye. As I watched this untranslatable gesture of obeisance I felt the hair go up on the back of my neck. It was the equivalent of the tugging of a forelock and a sudden reminder of the humiliations which people endure daily without even the possibility of protest. I asked if I could help but he begged me to stay in the car, nervously retrieved some more documents from the dashboard, and, stammering explanations, returned to the officer with the papers fanned out in front of his body like an offering.

I was impressed by such thoroughness at a checkpoint as lonely as this. Even the engine number of the car was checked: Reza held the bonnet of the car open while the officer typed it into a laptop resting on the engine. Then the two of them walked a little way away together, and I watched from the window as the officer barked questions, and as Reza, growing steadily more obsequious under salvoes of abuse, bowed slightly between apologies.

I had taken a dislike to the police officer's manner as irrationally as the protectiveness I now felt for Reza, and had a strong urge to intervene on his behalf. I got out of the car, wondering what the worst might be that could happen. I pictured a confrontation, and asked myself how far I would be prepared to take it. It would be a bad place to be imprisoned, and a thirsty one.

I walked over to them to assert some kind of presence, and stood a few feet away with my arms folded. Then I glimpsed the butt of an automatic pistol tucked into the officer's waist, and realized it was the not the moment to compliment him ironically on the cut of his uniform, or to remind him that his behaviour was un-Christian. He ignored me, fortunately, and the tirade drew to an end. But as he turned, our eyes met for an instant, and I realized I was wishing for him to challenge me. His expression was as brutal as I had ever seen, and I sensed the sudden presence of that thread-like line dividing peace from conflict, and that against all sensible judgements I had been savouring its closeness.

We drove on for a while in silence.

'I was very unhappy,' I said, 'to see you apologizing to that dog-for-a-father.'

'It's nothing,' he said like an old nurse, but he was visibly upset. 'It's a game, that's all. He plays it, I play it. That's how it works.'

Φ

I now moved through a string of towns: southwards to Yazd, Kerman, and Bam, then north again via Natanz and Kashan. These are all ancient places with rich histories, the centres of once-powerful and virtually autonomous provinces. I was drawn to them not only by curiosity but by a faint sense of duty, since they are well-known sites. I had briefly entertained a plan to buy a car and move around more independently between less obvious destinations. But the expense for this scheme was too great, and I took up the route again by bus, arriving at odd hours in deserted suburbs, or rising for an early departure in the cool grey of dawn.

I had imagined Yazd, unique among Iranian towns for its desert architecture and setting, to be a sleepy sort of place, where donkeys padded along dusty lanes. I was of course wrong again.

The donkeys, and the magnificent city walls, chevroned and crenellated, have long since disappeared, though the centre is small enough to explore on foot. On my first evening I found a noisy and unfriendly hotel, and was pursued by a persistent teenage boy on a motorcycle. Each time I managed to evade him by ducking into side streets, he would be waiting for me at the far end with a nonchalant grin. Eventually I relented and he took me as his passenger on a tour of town. We ended up at an old hammam that had been converted into a restaurant, where garish lighting and shiny white tiles gave the impression of a municipal swimming pool.

I soon found another hotel, this time in the heart of the old town. It was a sensitively restored Qajar home at the end of a long cobbled entrance tunnel. Urns big enough to hide in dotted the periphery of the spacious courtyard, where the noise of the town was unheard. Behind a balustrade on the second floor were some grand bedrooms, and some crypt-like windowless rooms below ground, one of which I chose.

In the daytime I ate outside on a platform in the courtyard, and in the evenings in a small but ornate dining room. Its walls were decorated with panels of floral plasterwork delicately inlaid with mirrors, and the windows with tessellating and multicoloured slivers of stained glass. Elsewhere the room itself would have been a museum.

There were half a dozen other guests: a Czech tennis coach and talented amateur artist; two young and clean-looking Swiss, and a middle-aged couple hunched gloomily over their menus. They had a vaguely unkempt and fugitive air about them and I wondered where they might be from. They were speaking too quietly for me to hear until a waiter came to their sides, notepad in hand, and the man looked up expectantly.

'Have you got any chips?' he asked in a thick Liverpudlian accent. The waiter looked blank.

'Chips. Potato chips! French fries!'

'*Pommes frites,*' tried the woman, to no avail.

Overhearing this exchange, I leaned back into the shadows

with the instinctive aversion that an Englishman feels on encountering his own kind when abroad. But the waiter, knowing I spoke Persian, enlisted me to translate. I sat at a neighbouring table and broke the news to them that there weren't any chips, and suggested a few alternatives from the menu. They looked very sad, and it seemed quite likely they had arrived in Iran by accident, like fish that are said to be swept up into hailstones and deposited hundreds of miles away.

'We only wanted to get some beer and chips,' said the man, in a tone of infinite reproach.

Later I joined the Swiss couple. They were backpacking across Asia on the final leg of a long journey and were planning to get married on their return home. They were healthy and earnest, radiated a mixture of naivety and self-assurance, and recounted the unusual and delightful things they had seen on their travels with a consistently cheerful and disconcerting lack of feeling.

I studied their clear and untroubled faces — her blonde hair bobbing above a smooth and tanned forehead, their uniformly strong teeth, his wide blue eyes behind delicate gold-rimmed glasses — and I was not sure whether I envied them or not. They seemed the kind of people to whom nothing bad ever happens. It seemed likely they had never known grief, debt, or uncertainty. No tragedy, cravings, or dark nights of the soul hindered their ambitions; and to their very journey was a calculatedness of which I felt incapable. They respected foreign culture, so long as not too much of it ever came to Zurich, and their lives were marvellously planned. But we didn't talk for long; it was time for bed, to which, like figures returning to the twin doors of a cuckoo clock, they punctually retired.

The manager was an affable young man called Hussein, who took me aside the following morning, wanting to talk about cures for menstrual pain and about war in Iraq. On the former he confessed he knew nothing, and wondered if I could help; on the latter he was extraordinarily pragmatic. So for a few minutes we talked about hot-water bottles, aspirin, and evening-primrose oil; and then, for a little longer, about war.

War was always a moral issue for Westerners, he said, because we had forgotten what war was really like on the receiving end, and the very way we thought about war was a kind of intellectual luxury most other cultures couldn't afford. Westerners would never admit to the practical necessity of war; in this, he said, apologizing for using the term, lay their *do-rui*, hypocrisy.

This was an intriguing premise, with which I happened to agree. Iranians, he went on, understood American pragmatism better than the American people themselves, not being fooled by the official reasoning. The war in Iraq wasn't about terrorism, he said, although it was bound to make terrorism worse: everybody knew that. It wasn't even about oil.

'You need a war to *sell* stuff,' he said cheerfully. 'Arms and computer systems, mostly. Construction. Roads, factories, and all that. That's how the Americans maintain their economy. Big economies need wars every few years, just to survive.'

It was refreshing to hear this from a citizen of the very country that America was now poised to attack. Yet it was characteristically broad-minded. In the course of all these journeys around the country I had never heard a word against Americans; only expressions of a kind of resignation, and deep sadness at the contemporary American perception of Iran.

I asked him whether he believed politicians had a responsibility to avert bloodshed; I had seen what bombs did, I said, and the results were never pleasant.

'You'd never be a politician,' he chuckled, and deftly flicked the butt of his cigarette into a nearby urn. 'Politicians can't afford to care,' he said. 'It's like this: if politicians were the humanitarians you'd like them to be, they wouldn't be politicians, because politicians have to start wars to keep their economies going. They'd have to kill themselves if they faced up to the truth.' This, he added, was the very reason that religious men didn't make good politicians, as in Iran: they had to lie for their work, and lying was bad religion. The West didn't have that problem: lying was much easier for us. He mentioned a Persian saying, 'If you work with your feet, your shoes wear out; if you work with your head, your hat wears out', which I wasn't quite sure if I understood. Then he asked if I had tried the quail on the lunch menu, and said he'd bring it up to me on the roof. So I wrote up our conversation on the terrace in the sunshine, wanting to record it before I forgot the details. A little later, Hussein appeared with a roast quail, flattened and skewered and sprinkled with rose petals. On the tray was a vase with a purple flower in it.

Φ

In Yazd, unlike almost all other Iranian towns, a large portion of the traditional architecture has been preserved, and transmits a powerful sense of antiquity. From the roof of the Friday Mosque one can see that the surrounding structures have been kept to a manageable scale; the size of the human being in the street still has meaning against the buildings around him, and vice versa. Its unique feature is the roofline, which is dotted with rectangular shapes like watchtowers; these are called *badgirs* or wind-catchers, and their ingenious design once provided cool air to the hottest of homes. Their design is functional, but like even the most utilitarian of structures they are sensitively decorated, often with arched mouldings and scalloped cornices. Air enters these structures through tall vertical grilles, and descends into narrow, finned channels, over which it cools as it is impelled downwards. Two such towers are positioned at opposite ends of an interior porch, providing a cross-current of cooling air. I would not have guessed at their efficiency had I not discovered an abandoned but still grand home in the old town, where the *badgirs* were still intact. It was late afternoon but still very hot, and I sat down absentmindedly on the porch. Suddenly I felt a cool and gentle wind across my face. It seemed impossible to believe that such coolness could be naturally produced. Until the relatively recent arrival of electricity, homes were supplied with water by underground *qanats* from mountains up to twenty miles distant and cooled in giant reservoirs by the evaporative action of the wind; the city owes its very existence to such ingenious and humane technologies.

In the winding clamour of the bazaar, I met a sugar-maker,

who showed me the vats where the quartz-like crystals are grown on lengths of string; and weavers whose fabrics, still unique to the region, dazzle and mystify by their richness and complexity. Their colours preserve an antique fascination for the spectrum; an instinctive reply, perhaps, to the harshness of the natural surroundings. I found the tomb of Ruknaddin, and the Daylamite Mosque of the Twelve Imams from the eleventh century, and climbed the dramatic facade of the Amir Chaqmaq complex. After all the exploring among the shadows and light and dust, I was aching for a glass of tea.

'Tea?' The question evoked puzzled looks from shopkeepers and passers-by. 'W'allah, not around here. You could try in the bazaar...' Old men would scratch their chins and gaze towards the horizon with troubled expressions, as if I had asked the whereabouts of some long-disappeared relative, and not for a sample of the national drink. 'Tea...' they seemed to say, 'yes, we've heard of it...'

Eventually I found a restaurant where the cook, a bear-like man with a gentle manner, at last brought me a glass of a tea. He lingered by the table, studying me with the absence of self-consciousness to which foreigners are unaccustomed.

'A foreigner,' he repeated. This got him thinking. Did I like films? he asked. 'We used to have good ones here,' he said wistfully, wiping a hand absent-mindedly on his filthy apron as he spoke. I asked him what his favourite had been. He thought for a while, then his bushy eyebrows rose at the instant of recollection.

'Samson and Delilah! Yes ... that Delilah was a wicked one.' His outraged tone suggested all the gravity of a historical event. 'She cut all his hair off.' A pair of greasy fingers snapped at the phantom locks. 'Today's movies are no good.' He heaved a sigh of resignation. 'They've got no plot.'

Or rather, they all had the same plot. I had seen a good number of films by now, most of them on buses. In all, the protagonist, having fallen foul of some villainous or powerful agency, struggles with a period of terrible injustice. In one, a man who loses custody of his only child is killed in a shootout with the police in a failed kidnapping; in another, a debt-ridden student takes on the drugs mafia; and in another a villager defies a corrupt tribal leader. One member of the enemy is secretly in sympathy with the underdog, but is powerless to help. After the hero's death, it is this character who transmits the martyr's sacrifice to the next generation, sustaining thereby the notion of a sacred cause. A sense of holy doom pervades these stories; they all end bloodily and on a note of tragic redemption.

One evening, outside a stall in the bazaar, a row of giant wooden clubs caught my eye. I chatted for a while with the carpenter who had made them, and asked if he knew the where-abouts of the town's *zurkhaneh*. It was difficult to find, he said, being used only by locals who knew the place; nine o'clock was the time to go. He drew me a rough map, and a little later I was ducking through an unmarked door in a tiny street. The men were gathering and, being the only visitor, I was ushered to a place above the central pit, where the wall was stepped like a miniature amphitheatre.

The routine was just as I had seen in Tabriz: an hour of flexing and twisting to the rousing chant of martial poetry. Then club-twirling by even the youngest members, whose matchstick-sized arms looked as if they might snap under the weight; then spinning, one by one, young and old, at an incredible speed. Finally, a youthful champion wielded an iron bow above his head with unnatural strength. Gleaming with perspiration, the men clambered out of the ring and dispersed.

I stood up to leave, feeling satisfied to have found this coven-like sanctuary of such an ancient and little-known system of training. No one had noticed I was a foreigner; it was obvious they did not see many. As I approached the door, an old man sitting nearby raised his arm and waved a small piece of paper at me. I wondered what it could be: perhaps the phone number of the place. Perhaps the chief trainer would invite me to become a member ... It was about the size of a raffle ticket and blank on one side. I turned it over and read:

ZURKHANE:
Ancient Persian Sport
Price for Forinear: 5,000 *rials*

Oh yes, I laughed as I handed over the money, partly to conceal my own disappointment; getting money out of foreigners was indeed a very ancient Persian sport! The old man looked up at me with bleary and uncomprehending eyes. I tried to make the joke again. But he was deaf, I think, and heard nothing: neither my joke, nor my indignant muttering as I crossed the threshold and ducked into the street beneath a blanket of stars.

Φ

Two conical hills, several hundred feet high and resembling extinct volcanoes, dominate the well-known Zoroastrian site on the outskirts of the town. They are called the Towers of Silence, I am not sure why, though the name is fitting enough for the place where the Zoroastrian community once exposed the bodies of their dead to the elements. The deserted circular platforms at their peaks are reached by clambering through a small rocky aperture, where I half-expected to disturb a few vultures hopping among piles of sun-bleached bones. There was no trace of either; nor of silence. The taxi driver, whom I had hoped to outwalk on the way up, followed me persistently and chattered nervously without a break.

We walked among the half-ruined structures below; a caravan-serai, said the driver, and a cluster of vaulted brick buildings built on an ancient and characteristic cruciform design. These, he said, were abandoned temples of the *atesh-parastan*, or fire-worshippers, as the Zoroastrians are sometimes – and inaccurately – called. But his constant talking had a numbing effect, and my mind was wandering off.

I was thinking of the universality of fire-rites of different kinds, and of the broad extent to which the symbolism of both fire and light had penetrated Iranian tradition, both in the era before Islam and afterwards. Even the etymology of the word minaret, derived from the Arabic *nur*, light, carried in it the echo of fire as an arbiter, purifier, and spiritual renewer. The Zoroastrian veneration of fire is well known; and perhaps it is not surprising that the concept of illumination should have become so central to the later, mystical Islamic philosophies of Persia. In Zoroastrian lore, a lantern was used specifically to ward off evil spirits, just as the Yuletide log and the lighting of candles around a bier was traditionally supposed to do, and I wondered if anyone had studied the origins of this same prophylactic impulse.

Perhaps the customs had arisen independently and were the expressions of a common human urge; but perhaps not. We are back to the problem of the inherent and the acquired; and I had run up against the same difficulty in thinking about the symbols and motifs appearing in art across similar distances. Historically, one can trace obvious similarities in a rough and ready sort of way, speculating backwards and tentatively towards origins. One can compare, say, the winged Victories in the spandrels of Marble Arch on the edge of Hyde Park with the deities that float almost identically above the arch of Khosrow at Taq-e Bostan; or the profile of Brunelleschi's famous dome with that of the Mausoleum of Uljeitu at Soltaniyeh. But one can also picture them as the expressions of a universal impulse, archetypal in essence and residing, as it were, beyond the reach of temporal cause and effect. These two approaches are poles apart in concept and as irreconcilable as Darwin and Lamarck, but between them all other methodologies lie.

Were these towers of silence, then, the surviving beacons of an ancient and conflagratory sweep of worship, transmitted steadily westward by human tapers and metamorphosing into the torchlight processions of the Eleusinian Mysteries and the Hestia Prytaneion of the ancient Greeks and the fire-festivals of the Druids? Or had the sanctity of flame erupted irresistibly into human consciousness as mysteriously as the hexagon into the intelligence of the bee?

History, on its own, makes it impossible to link the November joy-fires in Japan with the riotous bonfires that once lit the skies of the Celtic world, or the apotropaic fire-walkers of Polynesia with the barbarous Mayan rite of rekindling the annual fire on a living victim's breast. But it is easier, if not tempting, to speculate on an ancestral relationship between the Babylonian deity Bel and the Beltane fires of the Celtic world; or between Agni, the Vedic god of fire of the Indian world, and the Holy Ugnis of Slavic tradition.

There is much to connect the popular vestiges of these ante-diluvian cults. The notion of a holy fire kept by virgins has its parallels as far apart as Peru and among the Damaras in Africa; in Celtic ritual it appears almost intact in the cult of Brigindu, the female deity adopted by the Church as St Brigit of Kildare, and her fire-tending vestals as nuns. The link with fire is preserved in the blessing of lights at Candlemas at the same time as the saint's day and the veneration of a special candle, traditionally lit with flints.

I had never seen it, but an annual festival of the re-kindling of a sacred flame with flints said to have been captured at Jerusalem during the First Crusade still takes place every year at Easter in Florence at the SS Apostoli. All other candles at the ceremony are lit from the first, *de lumino benedicto*, and a cart teetering with fireworks outside the doors of the church is lit by a mechanical dove, ending in riotous celebrations. Here a much earlier Eastern origin is preserved. The Miracle of the Holy Fire, overseen by the Greek Orthodox Patriarch in Jerusalem, occurs at the same time of year at the tomb of the Holy Sepulchre. It is identical in almost every ritual detail, and is one of the oldest continually celebrated festivals in Christendom; the fire is said to arise spontaneously and not to burn the faithful. A seventeenth-century description has the ceremony culminating in a bacchanalian frenzy 'prophaning the holy places in such manner that they were not worse defiled even then when the heathens here celebrated their Aphrodisia...' and perhaps it echoes pre-Christian festivities associated with the rite.*

---

* *A Journey from Aleppo to Jerusalem at Easter*, 1697, by Henry Maundell

There must have once been many others. Christmas, with all its ritual echoes of light and flame, remains the outstanding example. Here, perhaps, the Mithraic veneration of the cypress tree can be allowed a look-in. It is all very patchy from the historical point of view, but it was fun to contemplate a bridge of tradition stretching from the Towers of Silence to the Yuletide log. Fortunately for acquisitive children, not even all the puritanical loathing of Cromwell and Knox for the pagan-inspired excesses of the Christmas festival failed to extinguish it; and, as we know, it was revived nearer to our own time by an unlikely saviour from the Saxe-Coburg-Gotha line. By the time Prince Albert had persuaded the English to adopt the fir tree as the centrepiece of the rite, most of the work had already been done ...

The driver dropped me near the hotel, where he asked for more money, saying that the fare we had originally agreed had not included waiting time. I had no wish to argue. But as I handed over the notes, I hoped I might evoke a twinge of shame.

'Iran! The country where everything comes down to money!'

'Yes,' he said, grinning malevolently, 'especially Iran. Much more than most places.'

Φ

That evening, I made another list: of all the excuses I had been given by taxi drivers for overcharging me at the end of a journey. These, at least, were the ones I had been able to understand. They were rarely used singly, but deviously combined in a sorrowful heaping-up of guilt. 'But, *agha*,' the driver would say ...

My brother is ill
My family is ill
I am ill
I am poor
I am poor, and you are:
   i) my friend
   ii) rich
   iii) a foreigner

It is very early
It is very late
It is dark now
You should have pity on me
You must have misheard the price
It is a fair price: it is the law
It is a fair price: there is no law in Iran
The price is fixed by the agency
Are you out of your mind?
Are your brains rotten?
I shall never find other passengers on the way back
I shall never find my way back at all
What is 5,000 *tomans* to you?
Times are hard
You cannot know the price of things in Iran
Petrol and oil have gone up
Everything has gone up
We have gone into my free time
It makes no difference to you
It is very little
It is nothing
I thought you wanted to go somewhere else
We came further than I expected
It took longer than I expected
I got a big fine this morning from the police
My shop was robbed
I have a family to support
I have lost everything
You have ruined my car
You have ruined my livelihood
You have ruined my whole life

But the prize for sheer deviousness went to a driver I met a few days later. I had asked a friend to call an agency for the car, and to confirm the price in advance. But as soon as we were en route I checked with the driver to be sure. We had not yet reached the outskirts of town when it had already gone up to six hundred *rials* a kilometre.

'When I telephoned your agency a few minutes ago,' I pointed out, 'they said it would cost me three hundred *rials* per kilometre.'

'They must have made a mistake,' he grumbled.

'Then perhaps you wouldn't mind turning around and taking me back there, just so that I can let them know.'

'Well, let's say five hundred, then, and be done with it.'

'I really think we should turn back.'

'All right! Four and a half.'

I opened the door as if to jump from the car.

'*All right!* Four hundred . . .'

To confirm our agreement, I shook his hand on it, and wrote down the mileage. There was no way he could get out of it. For the rest of the journey, I was able to relax, satisfied that I was at last getting the hang of how to do things.

Several hundred kilometres later, we pulled up outside our destination. I took the mileage, deducted the starting figure, and multiplied it by the rate. Tapping the figures with the point of a pen, I made sure he could see the figures.

'Here's what I owe you,' I said, holding out a bundle of notes, 'according to the price we agreed.'

But he refused to take it. I tried to press it on him physically but he stepped backwards and raised his hands as if at gunpoint.

'No, no, no,' he protested. 'That's not the price at all.'

I was dumfounded at this Houdini-like audacity.

'I tried to tell you,' he said, shaking his head with an expression of exasperation, 'but you *wouldn't* listen. My odometer is faulty! For every ten kilometres we go, it only registers eight.' He flung open the door of the car and banged his fist against the instrument panel, from which a little cloud of dust erupted. He was lying shamelessly.

'It's an old car!' he shouted. 'What do you expect? I'm *losing* money by bringing you here!'

Impressed by this ingenuity, taking sudden pity on the fact that he had but one tooth in his in his lower jaw, and to disperse the gathering crowd, I paid the amount he was asking. But not before steeling myself and letting the notes scatter to the ground by his feet.

Φ

I had come to a small village on the edge of the desert to follow an unlikely clue. Years before, I had read an enigmatic mention of a 'monastery in Persia' where visitors were said to weep spontaneously on entering a particular room. I had often wondered whether such a place might really exist, and was sceptical of the universality of the claim. There are no monasteries in Iran, but there are shrines raised to the saints of the Sufi tradition, whose followers dedicated themselves to the life of the spirit.

In one such place, a kindly dervish showed me to the shrine-room of the saint. I could not have guessed that I had found the place until, sitting there alone, I found myself sobbing uncontrollably. Not with tears of either joy or pain, but of feeling in the grip of a presence, a force of unutterable goodness. Others have described a similar experience. Religious persuasion, or the lack of it, does not seem to be relevant. All testify to an encounter with an entity of overwhelming benevolence, and a feeling of having been overcome and reduced, momentarily, as if to dust.

But the night that followed this experience, as if to balance things, was the worst I had yet spent. As evening fell a squirrel-like man with bright, inquisitive eyes and a clipped white beard attached himself to me as I was walking along the leafy lanes of the village. I was intrigued by his manner; he pestered me in English with a thousand questions, which had at first sounded like some kind of wisdom, but which I later realized were part of a strategy to wear me down.

He had a guest house, he eventually said, and begged me to stay with him. I had nowhere else to go; there were no hotels. So we drove together to his home – this was the 'guest house' – and I regretted my decision from the moment we arrived. The house was unkempt and dirty. Two unruly children were running in and out; a television was blaring, and everything seemed damaged or neglected. The wife hobbled in with a foot in plaster, leaning on a gnarled stick, looking and sounding as fearsome as a witch. Her voice was shrill, and when she shouted at the children rose to an intensity that was physically painful. It was obvious she ruled the home. She chuckled like a jailer as she caught sight of me, and ushered me mannerlessly into the main room. The television was turned up so loud it shook. A bare bulb hung from a ceiling of flaking paint, and in one corner a toothless grandfather was huddling under a mound of blankets.

The husband, so voluble at our encounter in the village, now hardly spoke, and disappeared completely when the wife returned to ask me how many nights I would be staying. It was not difficult to answer. She demanded a fortune, so I got up to leave, and we renegotiated. But it was a horrible evening, throughout which I felt a homesickness of child-like intensity.

We sat against the cold walls propped on cushions, and talked over the din of the television. I had often wondered what it might be like to shoot a television; now seemed the perfect time. A man with a huge, poodle-like head of hair was giving televised oil-painting lessons, resting a palette in the crook of his arm as he applied the final touches to a moon-tinted seascape with dolphins. Nothing could have seemed more irrelevant to the lives of ordinary people. Advertisements for stomach-trimming aids followed this, and then another episode of the series I had earlier seen, in which the beautiful female hero is a drug-enforcement agent working undercover, disabling villains with ju-jitsu armlocks and shooting others with a oversized and bucking pistol.

A couple arrived, the wife with a big pot of strange, blubbery stew which we peered at in turn, and then, as I had feared we might, began to eat. Some dirty plastic bowls were distributed for the purpose by our hostess, whose limp had grown noticeably worse after the arrival of her guests. Then another couple arrived; a sister and brother-in-law, I think, and a similarly ill-mannered kind of people, with brutal laughs and gestures. The wife carried a swaddled infant which she laid on the floor and rocked roughly and absentmindedly with a foot against its abdomen. When it began to cry, the husband took a knife from the sheath at his waist and waved it menacingly in front of the tear-filled eyes. The others laughed raucously. The old man tilted over onto one side and slept. The daughter, a highly strung and undisciplined eight-year-old, presented me at her mother's suggestion with her English homework, which amid all the noise I struggled with for half an hour.

At last, overcome by fatigue, I moved into the adjoining room and made a bed of sorts. A visit to the filthy bathroom evoked a feeling of utter dread. The mattress was little thicker than a blanket, and the blanket as thin as a sheet. A sustained coldness drilled into my body from the concrete floor. Cacophonous peals of laughter erupted every few minutes from the other room; gunfire, sirens, screams, and all the sounds of destruction filled the gaps between them. It was as squalid a place as the few moments I had earlier experienced had been sublime. Yet I felt strangely detached from all these discomforts; they had acquired the insubstantial quality of something theatrical. Stranger than this, it seemed, was the range of experience that one could encounter in a single day, and how far the receptacle of the heart is able to expand in order to contain it.

Φ

Further south, in Kerman, a weary-looking guide short of clients adopted me in the bazaar. We walked idly through the bustle of the vaulted tunnels and the dust-filled slanting beams of light, past the crammed stalls a-dangle with glinting fabrics and pots and pans or buttressed with tiers of lustrous vegetables. It had a wilder quality than the bazaars further north. There were cauldrons of beaten brass big enough to hold several missionaries, bottles of medicinal juices lined up like an alchemist's boudoir, jars of pickled walnuts resembling preserved rodents' brains, sacks brimming with spices, nuts, seeds, herbs, and petals, bright and fragrant and in colours spanning the whole spectrum, boxes of live day-old chicks dyed purple and blue and green; and all the beggars and hustlers and fortune-tellers and the sad-looking traders with the sum of their goods laid out in rows on sheets of newspaper at their knees — watches and pens and sunglasses and rosaries and rings and amulets.

We passed the entrance to a subterranean reservoir, where a steep flight of narrow stairs ran downwards from the street level. It was empty now. Above the arched portal stretched a half-dome *muqarnas* ceiling, brightly and elaborately tiled: a reminder of the dignity traditionally afforded to even the most utilitarian of structures. Nearby was an open square where a portion of the walls was being restored. A team of workmen was mixing an adobe rendering and hauling it up to the roof in buckets. At the foot of the wall, barefoot and ankle-deep in a circular mound of mud and straw, a man was shovelling furiously. This was another sight that seemed brought to life from the same miniature painting I had been reminded of by the tile-cutter in Isfahan. Above the roofline ran a series of bulbous adobe swellings pierced with small windows, like the homes of visiting extraterrestrials.

Then we wandered round the square, where my guide pointed out the dragons and suns with human faces in the tilework of the portal to the madrasseh, saying they were symbols that had been taken from Mithraic tradition. Nearby we found a passage and a tiny flight of stairs leading downwards to the vaulted chamber of an old hammam. The owner was feeding goldfish in a central octagonal pool and showed us through the various rooms. One had been completely abandoned and the floor was piled with dusty tiles stripped from the walls. I asked if the place would be rebuilt; the owner shrugged his shoulders and said he couldn't afford to restore it. The tiles were heavy and hand-painted and I longed to be able to buy and rescue them.

The main chamber was still in use, and I couldn't resist returning there the following afternoon. A rank and humid smell filled the vaulted gloom, where arched entrances to the adjoining chambers gave the impression of a steam-filled mosque. Wrapped in a towel of rough cotton I sluiced myself down with hot water and stretched out. Half a dozen bodies lay inert on the warm stone floor, like corpses abandoned in a mist. A small wiry man loomed and offered a massage, rubbed my limbs with a rag like a scouring pad until the skin came off in drifts, then twisted my arms and legs into knots, put his knee into my back, walked up and down on it, and pummelled me into a state of delicious stupefaction.

I lay half asleep on the stone, drifting in and out of consciousness, dimly aware of the ebbing daylight through the star-shaped apertures overhead. A party of several young men arrived and received the masseur's treatment in turn, then set on each other in a frenzy of lathering and drenching, yelping and frolicking like hyenas. At dusk a single electric bulb came on, its brightness refracted spectrographically through water-laden eyelids. A steady drip of water fell onto my face. I watched each drop detach itself from the ceiling, feeling the tension grow in my forehead at each looming descent before the meteor-like impact.

Later on, at the hotel, I sensed something was troubling the manager. He was slumped in a chair in the lobby in front of a television. 'They will take us over,' he murmured darkly. I asked him what he meant. 'Haven't you heard? The *Afghans*! All the money they are getting to rebuild their country! For years they have come to Iran to work for us at all the jobs we wouldn't do ourselves. Now we Iranians will have to go there to find work. From the *Afghans!* The times are ruined.' Byron records an identical conversation, seventy years earlier.

Φ

Natanz was different. It is a small town today, lies off the main roads, and had just the sleepy quality I had been hoping to find, as if the place was suspended in a permanent siesta. I walked along a rising tree-lined avenue and from between the trees flashed the turquoise glint of domes perched on nearby hilltops. In a shady square I found the Ilkhanid shrine-complex I had wanted to see; a combination of two small mosques, an octagonal sanctuary, a minaret, and a turquoise-and-terracotta facade, over-hung by an ancient plane tree. There was no one there; I wandered about the interior until the keeper appeared, saying he had looked after the place for more than twenty years, and with a rattle of keys showed me into the shrine-room that lies under the pyram-idal roof. Light enters through carved stone grilles above a Kufic frieze and is scattered upward in delicate gradations across a beautiful *muqarnas* ceiling. Near the tomb of the thirteenth-century Sufi sheikh, the outline of the mehrab was clearly visible, but the tiles had been plundered from the place, leaving a ragged outline. There was, in fact, only one left; a beautiful but lonely star-shaped tile set in a blank plaster wall. I asked what had happened to all the others.

'Some people came in and took them away,' said the keeper.

'That's a terrible thing,' I said.

'They were beautiful tiles,' he nodded, gloomily. I guessed that the plunder had taken place in the aftermath of the revolution; perhaps more recently. Everyone in Iran knew — or at least talked — about the role of the government in the illegal appropriation of cultural treasures. I asked if it were known who had stolen them.

'I think,' he said, 'it was an Englishman.' This was an unpleasant revelation. I hoped it wasn't someone I knew. But what had become of them? I asked. Was it known where they had been taken?

'Oh yes,' he said. 'Let me think...' His eyes rolled upwards for a moment. 'Yes, that's it. Somewhere called "The *Victoria and Albert Museum*."'

Φ

A distant storm brooded in the east, and the mountains were gold against the darkened sky. I walked along the little streets for a rare hour of absolute tranquillity, wishing I had discovered the place earlier, and thinking how strange it was that several hundred miles overhead, satellites were busy photographing the nuclear facility that lay beyond the town. Nothing was more remote at that moment than the clamorous world of politics. Aside a tiny stream, there was a tea-house selling ice cream. I stopped there and chatted with two forlorn-looking Afghans, who confessed how irreligious they found Iran and couldn't wait to get back home. Later, a dapper man in a pilot's jump suit came to the counter with a friend. He spoke Persian to the shopkeeper but Armenian to his friend. I guessed he was a Christian from Isfahan; he was, he said. He had come with a friend to go hunting for wild boar, and they were about to set off for a few nights' camping.

'Up in the mountains,' he said, waving vaguely in the direction of the slopes beyond the town. 'We take the tent, make a big fire at night, and sleep under the stars.' He mimed an expression of soporific bliss. 'Want to come?'

'Have you got anything to drink?' I heard myself ask.

'Plenty,' he said with a wink, nodding to his partner, who was loading crates of soft drinks into the back of their car. The Armenians made their own alcohol, and were allowed a special dispensation to do so under the law. Despite all these auspicious promptings, I hesitated. And that night, instead of counting the dissolving trails of meteors, drinking wine with new friends, and learning hunter's songs in Armenian, I spent the night alone in a dreary hotel in Kashan, regretting my timidity.

Φ

The famous walled garden of Kashan, called the Bagh-e Fin, is the best-known of the Safavid era, and lies on the outskirts of the town at the end of a wide avenue built by the Shah. Today the town's most prestigious, and the ugliest, houses are being built along it. But within the garden walls, the eye is granted an unexpected haven.

The square enclosure covers several acres, and is filled with long tiled canals and bubbling fountains. Cypresses several hundred years old shelter the watery avenues, which converge under a central square pavilion, arched and decorated with floral scenes and faded royal portraits. Some picnickers were spreading blankets, and a few couples, hands intertwined, were stealing moments on secluded benches.

In the little bookshop, a young man in charge tried diligently to sell me a video about the gardens. I bought a few postcards instead.

'Are you a Muslim?' he asked, with a look of enthusiasm that I knew well, and preferred to avoid.

'God knows best,' I said. This was the wrong answer, and enflamed his curiosity. He came out from behind the counter as if in pursuit of a shoplifter, and followed me to the door.

'Sunni or Shi'a?'

'God knows.'

'You know why we disagree with the Sunnis, don't you?'

'Yes I do.'

'You know what today is, don't you?'

'No.'

'The celebration of the martyrdom of Fatima. You know who killed her sons, the Imams Hassan and Hussein?'

'Yes. Yazid.'

'So you do know! And who was he?'

'He was Caliph.'

'A *Sunni*! That's why the Sunnis cannot be trusted!' I had managed meanwhile to get outside, but he was circling around me. 'You know the Mehdi, the Imam of the Age? He will return and wipe out injustice! Only the righteous will remain!'

'*Insh'allah.*'

'And then we will see who was right!'

'*Insh'allah.*'

He studied me for a few moments. Then, unexpectedly, his expression broke into a warm smile, and he flung his arms around me. 'I will see you in Paradise, for sure.'

'*Insh'allah.*'

Φ

One has only to walk for half an hour in the devouring heat of summer to realize the deliciousness, and the heavenly connotations, of shade and the hypnotic murmur of flowing water. In a nearby courtyard, where the water bubbled noisily into a pool and stone-lined channel, I had tea and ice cream and wrote up my diary with a water pipe at my side. A dozen other visitors were lounging, and a man was cooling his feet in the flow.

A small party of Scandinavians, laden with backpacks and cameras, came in loudly and settled on one of the platforms. A few glances, embarrassed and curious, fell on them from their neighbours, who covertly studied the strange spectacle of European women. Their sunburned faces glowed like pools of molten lava from the black folds of their chadors, and their hiking boots heightened the impression of having arrived from a different planet; in a transgression of social norms almost unthinkable for Iranian women, they smoked openly in public.

A solemn cleric, flanked by two obsequious underlings, appeared in the doorway and cast a disapproving look around the courtyard. I sensed a conscious effort to deprive him of any attention, and he disappeared in a swish of robes. A boy refreshed the charcoal in my water pipe, and peace reigned.

At dusk, in the centre of the town, a kind of electrical tension was growing in the streets. Men on motorcycles seemed to be everywhere, others strode purposefully in groups and a preponderance of black shirts was impossible to explain by coincidence. I went to get my hair cut. Wielding a pair of scissors around my head, the young barber, also wearing a crisp black shirt, explained.

'They are the *divānegān*,' he said: the crazed ones, preparing for an evening of commemoration. The martyrdom, I now remembered, of the daughter of the Prophet. I asked if this was the reason everyone was wearing black, and he nodded solemnly, motioning with a little tug to his own lapel.

'The colour of mourning.'

Behind me, reflected in the mirror, sat three young men similarly turned out, each waiting their turn under the scissors.

'If you come back later,' he suggested, 'you could come with us.'

Images of self-flagellating mobs began to surface in my mind's eye – the very scenes of religious transport that make a Westerner's blood run cold – and I declined as politely as I could. But a little later, in a shop to which I had been drawn by the scent of roses, a similar conversation led to a similar offer. For a few minutes, the elderly owner talked about the curative effects of the different types of rosewater for which the town is famous. Bottles of all sizes lined the walls of his little shop and he reached among the shelves to let me sniff at them in turn. One had depilatory qualities; another, he explained with a circular motion suggesting regularity, was useful to women after pregnancy; another helped dissolve kidney stones. I settled on two variations suitable for cooking with and he put the pair of chosen bottles aside.

When I asked about the evening's festivities, he was adamant I visit a gathering of the *divānegān* and, shouting across the street to a fellow shopkeeper, summoned one of his sons to take me. A boy of fourteen soon appeared, and we weaved through the streets on his motorcycle. We passed a troupe of about fifty men trailing behind some flags of billowing calligraphy, and a little further on, pulled up outside an entrance to the bazaar.

Nearby a huge banner had been hung from a scaffold, depicting the veiled and winged holy figure of Fatima, set against a mist-covered sea and illuminated by a supernatural shaft of light. Stars and spinning planets dotted the background, and a swelling tear hung from a ray of the largest star. We edged forward into the melee that had gathered. A turbaned man was chanting into a microphone, perched on a platform fifty yards along the tunnel of the bazaar. There were about two hundred in the audience, lining the walls nearby, sitting and standing and all swaying to the cadence of the chant. At each beat their hands rose to their chests in unison; first on one side, then the other. The amplified voice was close to tears at moments and a few old men were wiping their eyes as the emotion of the tragic narrative rose and fell. Centuries of prejudice have taught the Westerner to feel nervous at such events, but the men were very friendly, and seeing a foreigner in their midst ushered me protectively through the growing crowd to get a better view.

We watched for a while until a tap on my shoulder by the shopkeeper's son and an expression of disappointment signalled our retreat. When we got back to the shop, the owner looked downcast at our report: it had been very tame, we told him.

'They don't really get going till later,' he said. Then, a little wistfully, added: 'I suppose it's much quieter nowadays.' The real event, he confided, was later in the year, when the martyrdom of Hussein and his family by the treacherous and worldly Yazid at Kerbala were re-enacted by the city's firebrands. I had often heard about the festival of Ashura, and dimly assumed that the event was something beyond the reach of outsiders. The twin spectres of primitivism and violence almost always hung over foreign depictions of the event. But seeing the kindly expression on the faces of the others was a reminder of how skewed my ideas had been.

'You really ought to come back at Moharram,' he said, rubbing a thumb and finger over the two halves of his silvery moustache with a sigh of nostalgia, 'when they recreate the whole thing in the desert, just to get the feeling of the burning heat and how terrible the whole thing was.' His hand rose and parried a phantom sword. 'They fight it out themselves,' he said, 'with all the horses and camels and tents, just like it was on the day.' The sons nodded enthusiastically. 'We could go together,' he added cheerfully, as he wrapped the bottles, packed them carefully into a plastic bag, and handed them over to me. 'Don't forget us.'

Φ

Beyond the centre of the town, high walls conceal an ensemble of nineteenth-century houses once belonging to wealthy merchants. It is impossible to guess, from the unextraordinary exterior walls, what grandeur lies within. Nor is it quite right to call them houses; they are little palaces really, with so many interlocking spaces that one is soon lost among them. Gloomy entrance tunnels lead onto large bright courtyards with rectangular pools flanked by trees and flowerbeds, and the open spaces are linked by archways and arcades, overlooked by airy facades. The largest of these buildings, the Tabataba'i House, was being turned into a luxury hotel when I found it, and workmen were applying the final touches to the plasterwork on the columns and niches. Abundant patterns of vines, vases, and cypress trees ran over every surface in powder blue and buff like bands of oriental Wedgwood. Inside the rooms, the sun's glare was reduced to gently glowing spectrums by stained glass set in delicate wooden traceries. A tall vaulted living room with tiny mirrors for wallpaper glittered spectacularly. Here too, wind-towers propelled cooling breezes through the rooms, conspiring magically with the sound of running water from the fountains.

The Borujerdi House is less spectacular in scale, though richer in original features. The dome above the reception hall is exceptional for a private home, and the plaster lattice of diminishing triangles faintly echoes the spectacle of the Lutfullah Mosque in Isfahan. There are painted romantic vignettes of European life on the walls – the equivalent of Eastern scenes in Victorian homes – enclosed in elaborate floral stucco. I wanted to photograph the roof, a request the staff refused, saying that the structure was too fragile, and then, when I persisted, that it was un-Islamic. I argued that it was the most photographed rooftop in the whole country, but to no avail. In a defiant mood I walked to the outskirts of the town, climbed onto the eroded platform of the ancient walls, and photographed the rooftop from the opposite side, from where the view was even better.

Later, the heat drove me into a shop to buy water, where a trio of women gave vent to their curiosity. It was a familiar exchange; one of hundreds like it that I had already had, but by which I never failed to be touched.

'Are you a foreigner? We thought you might be. England? Which is better – here or there? There, of course – where everything's more free! A book? What kind? History? That's good – Iran's got plenty of that! But you don't want us asking all these questions ... Can you come to our house for lunch? *Ta'arof nakon!* Don't be polite! We're not terrorists, don't worry. Haven't you got a Persian wife yet? Lots of foreigners have! You're tired, come and eat ...'

Φ

A long bus ride took me to Tehran; I realized now I hadn't many of these journeys left. I knew the routine quite well, and what feelings to expect; though remembering that my travels were nearly at an end threw each moment into new relief. Always there is the clamour at the ticket office, and the uncertainty of which bus to run for, and a moment of submission as you watch your baggage hurled into the belly of the bus, disappearing like a cherished letter, and a shudder of doubt as to whether it will really arrive with you at the far end. There is a last-minute flurry of the dispossessed, who clamber aboard on their crutches or with their withered hands, dispensing prayers and muttered blessings; then a final scooping-up of passengers on the outskirts of town, making you wonder why you went to so much trouble to hurry to the bus station and buy your ticket in advance. There is a teenage girl two rows behind you, sobbing at her parting from loved ones, a crying baby, a crone with a piercing voice, and a young man with wild eyes who looks as though he's on the run. There is always the same glare returned from the landscape, and the same line of mountains in the distance, glimpsed in half-sleep from curtains which emit little clouds of dust like a puff-ball as you try to shake them free from the railings overhead; a ruined fort shimmering in the heat-haze which you wish you had the time and means to visit, and a bad film played on the television with the volume turned up too loud. Then long stretches, when you find yourself contemplating your motives and achievements, ambitions, and lost opportunities, resolutions, the spectre of unwritten letters, kindnesses you have forgotten to repay, scores you'd like to settle but know you never will, plots for short stories you'll never write, severed fragments of dreams and conversations ... plans ... hopes ... until your head finds the niche between the adjoining seat, and sleep closes in on you.

Φ

Sorush was still away when I telephoned from the bus station, and his housekeeper told me he would be away for a few more days. The news left me unexpectedly bereft. I returned to the same hotel where I had spend my very first night in Tehran, feeling like an habitué now. It was a national holiday, the traffic in the streets was reduced to a trickle, and in the absence of the usual clamour and pollution I felt for the first time something close to affection for the city.

I wandered about the streets for a day to no great purpose, then, feeling at a loose end, called the number I had been given by a friend back in London.

A young woman's voice with a Persian accent answered.

'British Embassy.'

I asked to be put through to the name I'd been given. There was a pause, then an Englishman's voice with a barely perceptible lisp, and I thought involuntarily of the ritual games played by Etonians. There was a friendly exchange of courtesies, and a feeling of delight at a warm invitation to dinner and accommodation at the embassy. But there was more.

'I must just ask you one important question,' said the voice.

'Please do,' I said, but my mind raced. Had I associated with terrorists on my travels? Would I submit to a cavity search? Perhaps I would have to sign the Official Secrets Act.

'Do you have a pair of swimming trunks?'

A taxi took me to the chevroned barrier of the embassy. I walked a little way along the leafy paths of the compound, where in Louise's day the hunt used to meet at the weekends, and reached the door of one of the residences. Here the man I had earlier spoken to greeted me with nothing but a towel around his waist. Times had changed. I hoped that this informal streak would survive his eventual promotion to ambassador; and pictured him greeting dignitaries on porches and verandas the world over wearing a batik wrap, a kashmiri shawl, kaftan, pattu, or perhaps a Kamchatkan bearskin around his lower half.

High ceilings, the dark gleam of oak, and a smell of furniture polish reminded me how diligently the English have always replicated their homes abroad; beside the lavatory lay a collection of malapropisms uttered by George Bush. Two Burmese cats slinked inquisitively over a sideboard as cocktails were prepared, and a few minutes later we were joined by an equally feline, and equally handsome, young Iranian woman. Her appearance added to the general feeling of the surreal, and as she crossed the compound with us to the swimming pool, my heart went out to any lurking gardeners.

We swam in the broad octagonal pool at dusk, and dressed, a little, for dinner. We were joined by another couple, and shared our impressions of Iran. These were not the kind of observations one was likely to hear at home, and turned on a refreshing axis of intelligence. My host expressed the opinion that Iran was the most stable, potentially prosperous, and democratic nation of the entire region. Every factor was in place for its evolution, which it would be a pity to usurp. Yes, someone agreed; the Iranian experience was far ahead of would-be Islamicist states; they understood the limitations of theocratic rule better than any other Islamic nation, and the ongoing debates on the nature of rulership were probably the world's most intellectually sophisticated.

I asked if it was true that an American embargo on high technologies meant that the drug smugglers bringing opium from Afghanistan were better equipped than the police and army units trying to stop them. It was; though occasionally the drug-interdiction teams fought gun battles from Vietnam-era helicopters. 'They should let it all through,' said someone. 'Then the Americans would come running to help them.'

Φ

Feeling oppressed by Tehran and with several days' wait for Sorush to return, I went exploring in the vicinity of Mount Damavand. This was Iran's highest peak, and only an hour from the city. A taxi took me to a tiny village at the base of the mountain, where I began a three-day circuit, walking for most of the day and sleeping in the open at night. Goaded by the presence above me, I made a futile attempt on the summit, and was beaten back by cold and the horrible nausea of high altitude. Someone at the embassy had mentioned it was an easy climb, and popular with old women on Friday afternoons: I cursed him all the way.

After a gruelling descent, I reached a settlement at the base of the slopes, where an elderly watchman saw me hobbling past and ushered me inside. His eyebrows flexed in waves of benevolent disbelief as he fussed over a Primus stove.

'Up there? That's no place for a man to be!'

I agreed: an unpleasant encounter with a snow-filled ravine had made my fingers feel as though they had all been slammed in a heavy door, and my nails were rimmed with blood. I emptied the gravel from my boots, which the trackless rocks had torn open at the seams, and contemplated my blistered feet.

'Where did you sleep? Weren't you afraid of wolves?'

I hadn't thought of that; though I had seen what looked like a bear, loping across the rocks about six hundred yards away. I rested for a while in the kindly company of the watchman, then, restored by ample doses of tea, struggled back into my boots.

A final few miles led me to the valley floor, where a little later I flagged down a local farmer in a battered truck. With one hand on the passenger door I asked how much he would want to take me to the main road. He dismissed this with an expression of loathing and waved me in over the rattle of the engine.

'Don't worry about the money,' he chuckled. 'I'm not one of those thieving Tehrani taxi drivers. They're not even Muslims! You to your religion and me to mine – we're both men, and that's the point. What's money? God doesn't care about that sort of thing.'

'I'll give you ten thousand,' I said.

'Why not give me fifteen,' he said, 'and I'll drop you at the bus stop.'

Φ

At last I caught up with Sorush again at his home, and shared my plans with him. Time was running out and I wouldn't be able to make the journey to Khorasan that I had hoped. I would go to Mashhad instead and then, as I'd wished to for years, cross the border into Afghanistan from Tayyebad.

He seemed disappointed I didn't have the chance to explore Khorasan; there was much to see there, he said, though being a Sunni region, like Kurdistan, the government had taken less interest in its development.

'Is lucky,' he winked, 'for survival of traditional life.'

It had also been the centre of the Assassins, the powerful and mysterious entity that had led resistance against the Seljuk Empire in the twelfth century. Claiming descent from the Nizari line of Shi'a Imams, its fearless devotees operated throughout the Middle East, and struck terror into both Sunni leaders and Crusaders alike. Their most famous headquarters, one of many near-impregnable castles, was at Alamut in the Alburz Mountains, a day's drive from Tehran.

Sorush shook his head. 'Alamut was political centre. Khorasan was for training.'

I had heard the well-known stories, popularized by Marco Polo and virtually unchanged in the intervening centuries, about the sect's fanatical adepts. Drugged by their master and trans-ported to heavenly gardens and tended by nubile maidens, they believed themselves in Paradise, and by this subterfuge their devotion was secured.

'All is romance,' he scoffed. They were *professionals!* 'In East, drug was for purpose, never pleasure. Was *science*, like music — was only part of training. First they frustrate them.'

I wasn't sure what he meant by this until he made a slashing motion with one hand, and the other cupped under it. 'Then twenty years of training. Twenty years! Then one man go — Damascus, Aleppo — with just donkey, in disguise like peasant. Not *one* fail!'

He asked if I'd like to meet some other friends who'd been forced to leave Iran twenty-five years ago but who'd recently returned. We drove across the city the following evening, and were greeted warmly by a man in his mid-forties called Mehdi, who had returned to Iran from America with his family a couple of years earlier. He was friendly and voluble and held forth over a sumptuous dinner with lots of funny stories, recounted with a theatrical air.

After the meal we settled in carved oak chairs too heavy to lift, and admired a silk carpet whose colours changed according to the angle of view. I sat near one of the other guests, a quiet man with the burned-out look of an old rock star, and asked him how life in America had been.

'Stayed too long,' he said in a low, gravelly voice. I asked him why. 'Got caught by the greed,' he chuckled, and drew deeply on his cigarette. 'Car dealerships. Easy money.'

Mehdi appeared by my side, poured me an ample whisky, and delivered several ice-cubes from an engraved glass bowl. I confessed that meeting him and his friends made me want to ask how they were adjusting to life in Iran, after having lived for so long abroad.

'Life must have changed so much for you,' I said.

He spun the ice cubes in his glass and looked thoughtfully at them. 'Life hasn't changed,' he said. 'What's changed?' He looked up. 'Nothing's changed.'

This was an understatement. It was impossible to reconcile the Iran of the present with the days when the Shah had loaned billions of dollars to European industries, endowed chairs at

American universities, threw fancy-dress balls wearing a lion-suit, and had a swimming pool built in the palace gardens for Her Majesty's pet seal.

'Your political system has changed,' I said. 'Your government has changed. Your country's orientation to the world has changed. Your whole society has changed.'

He brushed all this aside with a sweep of his arm.

'You don't get it,' he said patiently. 'In my youth, what did my parents do? Drank a little whisky, kept their beautiful things around them, and talked about life. Well? What are we doing now?'

'The same.'

'So! I do what my parents did!' He took a fortifying sip of Johnny Walker. 'What's changed? Instead of one bunch of criminals running the country, we have another. For families like mine, nothing has really changed. We lost things, of course – we had property, we had homes – but deep down we're the same people. The rich are still rich. And the poor stay poor.' He shrugged his shoulders. 'Where's the change? If the opposition had something to offer, we would listen to them, but nobody takes them seriously here. How can we, while they sit on their asses in Europe and America?' He paused, and sighed, then said quietly: 'We've been through too much and survived.'

The others were all nodding, gravely and silently. I suspected Mehdi of protesting a little too much, in order to drive home a point he felt an outsider should grasp. To those who remembered the revolution of 1979 but were strangers to its complexities, Iran's dramatic resurgence on the world's stage was bound inextricably to Islam, to the iconic scowling of Khomeini, and to a word no one had really heard before: fundamentalism. I had learned by now that this was the wrong word to describe Khomeini's political philosophy; it was anything but fundamentalist. But the association had stuck.

I said that elsewhere in the world, and particularly in America, people perceived the revolution as an act of international defiance, a political transformation inspired by religion.

'Of course they do! But that totally misses the point. The revolution was about two things which Westerners can't possibly understand because they have no idea what they are: one is tradition, and the other is hunger. They don't understand that it's *hunger* that causes revolutions.'

'But the religious aspect . . .' I began.

'There was nothing "Islamic" about the revolution, if that's what you're thinking. Look at the proof! Now that we actually have an Islamic government, nobody wants *anything* to do with religion. This government has *killed* Islam. There is no religious feeling among the young.' He paused, then added: 'This is the saddest thing of all.'

'It's true,' said one of the others. 'When kids hear the call to prayer, they say: "*Shut that guy up!*" They don't even understand what he's saying.'

I had witnessed this myself, and been shocked, too.

'Even in my family,' Mehdi went on, 'yes, we gambled, we drank whisky — but there was always a place of respect in our hearts for the Prophet and the Imams. Now the young look at this government and they see a system which can excuse anything. Seventy per cent of them are under twenty-five, and there's no jobs! So they look at us,' his arm swept across the room and returned accusingly to his own chest, 'at *me*, at the generation that supported the revolution, and you know what they say? *This is your fault.* Then they look at Khomeini's tomb and they think: maybe all the imams were the same. Maybe the other imams killed half a million people too and got away with it. They feel very let down by our generation. The revolution means nothing to them.'

In an odd reverse, I found myself defending the notion of the revolution as a reaction against interference from abroad. For years, foreign governments had interfered in Iranian affairs; recent events had brought the theme new intensity.

'Well?' he replied. 'I don't blame them. The US wants to look after its people. The British destroyed a former government in Iran for oil. Its their job to look after their people. But the

Iranian government hasn't looked after *its* own people. You know what a rich country Iran is. But do you know how many people live below the poverty line here? The *Iranian* poverty line?'

Like most revolutions, no one was thinking very much about the long term.

As we drove back home, Sorush waved a hand at the lines of streaking headlights on Vali-Asr Avenue.

'When first I came here, was not one car.'

We stayed up late. 'Now you know what you will write in your book?' he asked. I had fairly good idea, I said. There were lots of books about politics, but fewer about art. I had no background or training in the subject but I wanted to write about what I had found; I reminded him that this, after all, was what he had advised me to do a long time ago.

'Now I know,' he said, nodding with his sad look of approval. 'I was afraid you will write about politics. Art is much better – is eternal. Come back with new book.'

Φ

Tehran's main train station is in the south of the city, where the gloss on life begins to thin. I made my way there at dusk by taxi, fighting traffic for more than an hour and realizing I had hardly ventured into the less prosperous portion of the city. As we edged our way southward through the tide of cars, the surroundings grew steadily more decrepit, as if an old witch was being shed of her make-up. The smog thickened, and the buildings began to lose their verticality and sparkle. The broad and tree-lined avenues of the northern neighbourhoods gave way to derelict-looking squares, where it was impossible to tell if the structures on them were half built or half destroyed. The very faces on the streets seemed to change, robbed now of the vanity and leisure of privilege, growing more drawn and anxious as we drove deeper into the atmosphere of poverty. Stupefied clusters of drug addicts huddled in boarded-up doorways, men hauled carts like refugees fleeing a city under bombardment, and the luxuries I had experienced over the past few days – the Filipino housekeeper at

the embassy residence had even washed and ironed all my shirts
— seemed all the more incongruous.

The station was a vast and Soviet-looking building of dark
brick. Inside, its stern rectangularity was offset by a giant chan-
delier, hanging above the centre of the main hall. It was full of
people: purposeful businessmen, young soldiers, students, beggars,
and little encampments of families spread out on blankets as if
they'd been living there for several days. I bought a couchette on
the overnight train to Mashhad and found my way to the platform.

The train had the air of a dragon straining at its leash. Steam
poured from under the carriages and billowed upwards through a
yellowish light thrown by powerful sodium lamps overhead.
Figures loomed through the sulphurous wisps from the darkness
beyond, there were shouts and whistles and the clang of iron
buffers, and I half-expected to see Poirot emerge from the
shadows in a trilby, dark suit, and spats, or a gang of SS men in
leather overcoats.

There were four seats in the compartment, and the first of
three other passengers arrived just as I was making myself
comfortable. We introduced ourselves; he was a jewellery merchant, he said, going to visit relatives in Mashhad. I had learned
my lesson pretending to be from Azerbaijan, and explained that I
was English. He seemed unsurprised, tossed a worn leather bag
into the rack above our heads, and asked if I knew what time we
would arrive the next morning. A brief first impression had
persuaded me he was a travelling salesman, but as he spoke my
opinion began to change.

'Not like the TGV!' he said cheerfully. 'Paris to Avignon in
four and a half hours! It's the new high-speed line. Have you ever
done it?' I hadn't, I admitted. 'I was in Paris the other day,' he
went on, 'but I went to see friends in Marseilles. Then it was on
to Stockholm and Frankfurt — not my favourite places! Did some
good business in Hong Kong before that, though. Have you ever
been?'

'Paris and Marseilles? Yes, both.'

'No – Hong Kong.'

'Never.'

'Japan?'

'No, actually.'

'Africa's my favourite.'

'I've been to Morocco,' I pointed out, but he shook his head and tutted.

'No, I mean *real* Africa – Ivory Coast, Guinea, Mali. I was in Senegal a month ago, but Mali's the best. Beautiful women. And very friendly . . . you really ought to go.'

'Now wait a minute,' a voice seemed to say. 'You are an impoverished Muslim xenophobe from a repressive country. I'm the one who does the travelling around here . . .' This disturbing train of thought was interrupted by the next of my fellow passengers. The door slid open, and a big man, turning sideways as he entered, greeted us with a kind of grunt and settled into the seat opposite. His skin was almost black and his cheeks bulged like a hamster's. He had curly hair and small watchful eyes which darted between us as we made small talk, and a few minutes later, after a rueful glance at the no-smoking sign, lit his first cigarette. The door slid open again and the final passenger, a smartly dressed young man with glasses and an attaché case, settled into the seat opposite me. He had a quiet and studious air and a gentle smile. In a convention very different from home, professions and incomes became the immediate subjects of mutual enquiry. Clockwise, we were: banana merchant (good money), jewellery trader (up and down), writer (none), and – I couldn't understand the last. The young man across from me took off his glasses and wiped them on a corner of his shirt.

'I design image-processing software,' he said in English, 'for warships.' His name was Iman, and we were to become friends of a sort. The train jolted forward and gathered speed. Soon a trolley arrived outside the door and delivered neat airline-style trays with portions of tasty chicken kebab, rice, and salad. As we ate, two small television screens on either side of the compartment flickered to life with a badly dubbed American drama about mutant rats which dragged their decapitated victims through the sewer system of Los Angeles. The banana merchant ate without taking his eyes off the screen, and threw the discarded bones from his meal under the seat.

After we had eaten, Iman nodded towards the door, and we walked together to the dining car. It was the survivor of a different era: lace curtains hung across the windows, the doors were padded with green leather and studs, and there was a bar in the corner serving soft drinks and coffee, and a dozen little tables with trembling lamps of frosted glass. Behind the far door there was even a small adjoining library of about a hundred books.

I chatted with Iman over a hot chocolate, wishing it were a brandy. We were joined by two young men desperate to travel to Europe, who launched into a long interrogation about the border controls in Belgium, visa requirements in Scandinavia, and marriage laws in England. I couldn't offer much advice or help, and felt deeply for them. Iman fielded me protectively back to our compartment, where we unfolded our beds in the darkness. The others were already snoring.

Φ

I woke at dawn, and glimpsed a different world beyond the window. The land was streaked by the golden light of the morning and long shadows thrown by low and barren hills. The air was cold. There was frost on the ground, and the architecture had changed again. Clusters of tiny houses made from timber and mud-brick resembled Afghanistan. I felt a tug of recognition, and a flurry of memories like a party of unexpected visitors.

Then came the first water towers; then the apartment blocks of the outskirts of Mashhad; then the first rubble-strewn allotments. We pulled in an hour after dawn, and I walked with Iman from the train in the cool air. A hundred yards from the station, we heard a cry; it was the banana merchant, wheezing and puffing, and holding out in his hand a pair of glasses that Iman had left in the compartment.

'He didn't believe you were English,' he grinned.

I asked where he'd thought I was from.

'Azerbaijan...'

Φ

He helped me find an inexpensive hotel, and promised to return in the evening. I spent the day re-reading Byron's account of his visit to the shrine around which the city had grown. It was not only the holiest sanctuary of the nation, being the resting place of the eighth Imam, but, architecturally a marvel on a par with the Naqsh-e Jahan in Isfahan. Its buildings spanned several centuries, the most famous of them — apart from the shrine itself — the mosque commissioned at the turn of the fifteenth century by one of the most remarkable women in history.

Gohar Shad was the daughter-in-law of Tamerlane and wife of Shah Rukh, King of Herat at the zenith of the Timurid renaissance. Many stories are told of her humanitarian vision. At Mashhad she is said to made provision for the animals carrying the building materials to the site, providing water and fodder at regular intervals and denying their owner the right to beat them. A humble workman is recorded as having glimpsed her royal face, falling into a mortal swoon of longing. Rumour of the poor man's fate reached the queen, who visited him at his bedside, and offered herself to him in marriage if he would only recover and spend a period in prayer. The man recovered, realized his folly, and released the queen from her pledge. The more one reads of this kind of story, the less one is inclined to dismiss them as fiction; and it is irresistible to picture the queen of the most powerful Islamic empire of the day, kneeling to hear the dreams of a love-stricken bricklayer.

The character of this scarcely known but extraordinary woman would be virtually unmentioned were it not for the glorious quality of the buildings she had built across Khorasan during her husband's reign. I had seen her mausoleum and the sole surviving minaret of her college at Herat, and been deeply moved by their beauty. But the main structure of the college was demolished by the British in the nineteenth century; only the minarets

397

remained, felled one by one by earthquakes, war, and neglect. The comparable fifteenth-century mosque in Tabriz that I had earlier seen is resurrected from fragments, and only hints at the marvel of the original building. From this unique era, only the mosque at the heart of the shrine complex in Mashhad has survived intact.

Byron, accompanied by Sykes, visited the complex on his journey in 1934, having daubed his face with burnt cork for a brief night-time visit to lessen the chances of recognition. Wanting to see the mosque in daylight, he had stubbornly returned alone for a glimpse of the place the next morning, disguised for the purpose in 'brown shoes with tight black trousers four inches too short; grey coat; gold stud instead of a tie; our servant's mackintosh; and a black Pahlevi hat which I aged by kicking it...'

In Byron's day the entire complex was forbidden to non-Muslims; the rules have softened since then, though the shrine itself remains strictly off-limits. But his brief vision of the courtyard of the mosque confirmed his belief that 'the mosque of Gohar Shad must be the greatest surviving monument of the period, while the ruins of Herat show that there was once a greater.'

Φ

At dusk there was a knock at the door: Iman had returned. We ate together at a charmless local restaurant and then returned to the hotel and talked until it was late. Iman was from an old family near the Afghan border, he said. I longed to visit this part of Iran. It was still called Khorasan, the surviving portion of a vaster area which once embraced much of Turkmenistan, Uzbekistan, and western Afghanistan. Centuries earlier its cities had been the glittering showpieces of Persian culture. He told enticing stories about castles and treasure and ancient sites unknown outside the region: one was a giant pipeline which had provided water to the region until it was destroyed by the Mongols. It was a predominantly Sunni region and neglected for this reason by the government. Life was still hard there; his ancestors, he said, had been 'as tough as Afghans', and told the story of a villager who, after a recent foray across the border, had returned with twelve Russian watches on his wrists, each taken from the corpse of an enemy soldier.

I wished we had met earlier; we might have travelled there together. My Persian, at least, would have improved under his influence. He didn't shy from correcting me, and our evening led to the kind of session one cannot get from books and which acquaintances are too polite to engage in. He pointed out that the expression 'to get used to something', which I had evidently been misusing, had several closely allied forms. The use of a different auxiliary verb could change the meaning significantly, and this is what I had been doing.

Iman explained. Whenever I had been cheerfully saying, 'I'm getting used to it!' in response to some question about adapting to life in Iran, I had in fact been saying, 'I have become a drug addict,' and 'My period has become regular.' I had also been confusing the Persian words for married, *isdavaj*, and mistake, *ishteba*, though in my own case this had not impinged on the truth.

I admitted to my ongoing frustration with taxi drivers, and to my feelings of helplessness whenever I suspected I had been overcharged. I didn't mind so much about the money, I said; it was the assumption that all foreigners were millionaires and fools that grated.

Quite right, he agreed, and went on to explain the solution. It was all very easy: the thing to do, he said, was to lose one's temper. Leaning back onto the bed, he held up one hand and counted the methods on his outstretched fingers.

The best way was to throw the money onto the passenger seat and walk away without looking back; this would often prompt the driver to return some of the money out of shame. But the chances of this, he admitted, were slim. Better still was to throw the money on the ground so that the driver would have to get out and pick it up, giving one more time to escape. If that didn't work, one should demand without hesitation to go to the police. Almost all drivers would concede at this point.

It seemed like a lot of effort just to pay for a taxi fare. Couldn't one simply reason with an unscrupulous driver? This democratic approach evoked a look of scepticism. If I was determined to get into a discussion, which he advised strongly against, I could look aghast at the mention of the fare, and say, 'What are you talking about?' or 'Don't talk rubbish,' and if these didn't work, 'Shut up, stupid!' He wrote down these handy phrases in my notebook. But there was more. 'Dog-father' and 'burnt-father' came next in this ascending scale of insult. These I already knew; they had their close equivalents in English — son-of-a-bitch and bastard. I then learned that all the worst words in Persian began with the letter K.* Finally, I was instructed in the use of a series of expressions linked to the rudest term possible. These could be used to indicate in turn one's feelings towards a victim's speech, face, and brain. The last of these seemed a bit too strong for everyday purposes. Who, I asked, would I ever call by such a name?

He thought for a moment, then said: 'George Bush!'

He rolled back on the bed in fits of laughter, and I remember thinking how strange it was to hear such irreverence from a face as serious and studious-looking as his. It had been an instructive evening. Then, at eleven, just as it seemed time to turn in, he asked if I knew how much Persians loved gardens. I did, I said; and he suggested we go to one.

We took a taxi through the deserted streets and ended up at a public park somewhere across the city. The long pools and

---

* A story is told of the presentation of the Greek Ambassador Kyriakos to the court of Reza Khan. 'Kir' in Persian denotes the male organ, 'kos' the female. 'Ya' means 'or'. 'Well?' demanded the outraged Shah from a stammering chamberlain. 'Which is he — *kir* or *kos*? If he hasn't made up his mind, throw him out!' Diplomatic relations between Iran and Greece were severed the same day.

intersecting pathways were, unsurprisingly, deserted, and for a moment I wondered whether he had brought me there for some darker purpose, and that perhaps a gang of his friends were preparing in the shadows to rob me. But it was quickly obvious that we had come for no reason other than to stroll through a freezing park at midnight. Walking along the edge of one of the pools, Iman slipped into the cold water up to his knees, and we laughed out loud at his silliness. He took off his shoes and poured the water from them with a comic expression of regret. Then, looking up, he saw me chuckling to myself and asked me what I was thinking.

'I was thinking,' I said, 'that this, too, is life.'

For some days now the prospect of leaving the country had been at work in my feelings, and seemed to press more insistently from beneath the surface of events. Our midnight walk was not the ending for my journey that I had pictured, any more than its beginning had conformed to my early predictions. Yet this moment, along with so many others like it that I had at first unconsciously assigned to a kind of wilderness of lost experience, now felt pregnant with significance.

It struck me that the whole of life lay behind it, akin to the winding film that people claim to glimpse on the point of death; and I had a sudden feeling that, were it not for the habitual shortfall in one's awareness, every moment might achieve such quantum-like connectedness to all of life, and one's participation in it. The displacement, uncertainty, and trials of travel bring to the fore a sensitivity to this, rewarding one with a quality of freedom that makes itself felt at just such moments and, over time, makes it possible to tread more lightly across life.

Φ

We had planned to meet again the following morning, and to visit the shrine complex together. Two hours after the agreed time, I gave up and waiting and decided to go alone. Iman appeared as I getting ready to leave, mumbling apologies. I was glad he did.

We walked together to the gates of the complex at the very centre of the city, an ensemble of buildings and courtyards mercifully free of motorized traffic. The periphery of the site bristled with cranes and scaffolding where an entirely new courtyard was under construction. Concrete minarets, planned to be several hundred feet high and the highest in the country, were rearing into the sky. Beneath our feet a parking lot was being constructed for several thousand cars.

Yet nothing of the scale of these modern additions can compete with the quality of the interior buildings, against which the latest efforts are made grotesque. As we wound towards the centre, moving between shadow and light, the shabbiness of the city fell away, yielding to courtyards each grander and more beautiful than the last. Golden minarets and domes hovered beyond the rooflines, realigning themselves at each transition. We stopped at a bookshop, and looked into an unexpectedly modern library housing thousands of rare volumes. I had been quite unaware of the scale of the site; there are several mosques and famous shrines, including that of Sheikh Baha'i, whose statue I had admired in Isfahan; seven different courtyards, and four traditional areas of *bast* or sanctuary.

Iman walked quietly by my side, guiding my attention with gentle gestures of his hand or head. I had soon lost all sense of bearing, but knew at once when we passed under another long archway and entered the courtyard of Gohar Shad. The force and luminosity of the tilework was unmistakable. It seemed to fly outwards from a double gallery of arches saturated with coloured patterns and calligraphy of an intensity matched only by its precision. At the southern end rose the vast turquoise dome of the mosque, looking as fragile as a heavenly pigeon's egg. And at the north end, two hundred yards away, was the smaller dome of the shrine itself, wrapped in a gleaming coat of solid gold.

A strange feeling of recognition informed this sudden vision. The spirit of the patterns was familiar to me from the Timurid monuments I had seen seven years earlier in Herat, as if a language I had long ago studied and largely forgotten was being spoken again. We walked towards the entrance. The dome subsided like the sun of a different planet, and the portal was soon towering over us. Its marble revetments give way to giant Kufic calligraphies and, further up, enclosed in a web of unglazed brick turquoise-rimmed lozenges framing even tinier mosaics, each describing one of the ninety-nine names of God.

There is no entrance door; the huge portal is open to the courtyard, where a thousand pilgrims were flowing across the space like iron filings across invisible lines of force. The interior dome is hemispherical and shallower than the greater shell above, and balances exquisitely on the uppermost portions of the interior *ivāns*, as if supported by an act of grace.

Then we came out again, and walked under the arcades, marvelling at the intricacy of the designs, the fluid bands of calligraphy, and the restless ingenuity of designs as bright as the day they were constructed six hundred years earlier. The effect was overwhelming, as it is intended to be; and the eye must rest at intervals before discovering new harmonies and correspondences like the interweaving themes of a symphony.

At the far end, set in the arched wall of the portal above the door of the sanctuary itself, a mosaic panel caught my attention. It was made from hexagons and diamond shapes in blue and yellow, held in a matrix of white borders. It transformed itself as I looked at it, calling out to be reconfigured in three dimensions, then retreating again into new and unexpected layers of pattern. I had not seen this pattern since I had glimpsed it in Herat, seven years earlier. It was the very same design which had danced before my eyes one evening at dusk, whispering questions which had first set me thinking about art. The intervening years seemed suddenly compressed to a moment; I felt I had come full circle.

We walked to the portal, and lingered among the seated lines of pilgrims lining the walls at its base. The heavy doors were open, their frames smoothed by the caresses of numberless hands, lips, and foreheads. From the entrance stretched carved blocks of jade, bordered with inscribed panels of solid gold and silver, glittering half in the sunlight and half from the light of the

chandeliers within. Then the echoes of the courtyard began to
fall silent, supplanted now by the deeper chant of prayer, over
which sobs of ecstasy rose and fell like waves breaking above a
sea of souls.

Without knowing it, I had crossed the threshold. Inside, the
decoration was even more intricate, gleaming in every colour. The
shrine was nearby, a golden cage against which a hundred hands
stretched from the encompassing throng of bodies. Soon we
reached a space where the walls and ceilings were made entirely
of tiny mirrors, glittering kaleidoscopically; and by now the
ordinary world seemed to have faded completely away, as if we
had stepped into the interior of a jewel.

A sudden feeling that I had strayed too far made me turn my
head in search of Iman, whose presence I had forgotten. But I
needn't have worried. He was walking calmly beside me, and
there was no sense in retreating now; I had come too far. He
smiled warmly, and with a wink and gentle movement of his
head, nodded me forward.

'TAMAM SHUD'

Appendage

PERSIAN PICNIC

'Mamluk! Get the Baghdad! There's a Parthia.'

(Assassin terrain)   'All right, sunni. We'll stop Behzad this hejira,
Khodabend in the river.'

'Fine Ali!'

'Did you put the Saladin? It wazir earlier.'

'I put Alid on it, to keep Tabriz off. Here,
un-Tigris.'

(pirs)   'Mmm ... khamsa and egg tempera, Mashhad
potatoes, Ja'far cakes, Mithradates and
Twelver Namaz bars. Anything Tughril?'

(Ismaels)   'Qiblas, but ... Damavand! They've Gombad.
Who turned off the Phrygia?'

'Danishmendid. But we're up Darius in
Salamis!'

'*Chaldiran!* Khomeyni-Shah feud! Merv over,
Amina, that's Moghul.'

Children: '*There's no Rūm! Hezbollah's bigger than mine! We want
Kurds! There's Bactria on my plate!*'

(Roman Aria)   'Right, I'll make a fire ... Abu Bakr in a
minute. Bazaar ... gnostics!'

'Salman *farsi?*'

'Nawa'i not?'

'Pass your Platea. You'll get as Fath as Omar.'

'– Khayyām, Ardeshir greed! But don't Babylon
about it!'

(A sayeed)	'I'm Hafez size, and Erzerum for more . . .'
	'Mede? Russian campaign? Shapour?'
	'Rhyton time!'
	'*Shiraz!*'
	'*Shiraz!*'
	'. . . Junaid another? There's a Ferdowsi here.'
(ribbing)	'Dome mind if I do . . .'
(shifting Kushans)	'. . . Nicea . . . I'm a Lutfullah now. What's the matter, sunni? Lost your Apadana? A minaret hers — maidan effort.'
(Timurid)	'Dad . . . Ahmad up my mind! Iwan to Seleucid Paykans! Kashan hand.'
(Balkhs, taken Abbas)	'You're as madrasseh hatter!'
	'*Come Bakhtiar senses! It's completely Sassanian!*'
	'But *Isfahan!*'
	'Ayatollah before, Anatolia again: you need to carve a Nishapur yourself. Besides, it's Veramin to your parents. Think of Imam.'
	'I khan take it any more! Ottoman way!' *(jumps into cataphract)*
	'*Shi'ite!* Sunni, Toqtamesh!'
	'It's Nowruz! Grab his Zand!'
	'Uljeitu, if I can.'
	'*Well chai-khana!*'
(leaps Zagros)	'Kerman . . . Atabeg. Put this Thermopylae on, and take a Valerian. You'll sufi better.'
(uncontrollable sheikhs)	'You Magus be right. Afghan too far — I Firuzabad, dad.'
(weak frontiers)	'Your father's *bagh* is worse than his *bayt*.'
	'That's all in the Pars. Let's have a ziggurat, and Turcoman toman . . .'
	'I'll never Ulugh-Beg.'

PRIVATE VIEW

An artistic reunion in Isfahan, c. 900

'Tyler! You were just an idol painter when we met. Still devoted to
mural?'

'As you are to Art. But I've experimented a bit since then: strapwork,
Zaidism, Manicheism, golden ratios...'

'You've expanded. I remember your friends – always getting stoned!'

'Well ... It was illegal to have hookahs in our studios.'

'I see you were fond of foreign models – especially Arabesque and
Hellenic.'

'I explored a good variety: sometimes several at the same time. The
curvilinear Greek used to be my favourite.'

'But this one's Chinese: a fine white body, delicate lines, and no
underglaze.'

'Occasionally I had to borrow norms.'

'What's this? Tulips enclosing a raised niche?'

'That's my favourite, polychrome.'

'Ceramic's brilliant progeny?'

'Yes: intense, immensely flexible, and perfect for naturalism.'

'I thought your principles were Platonic.'

'They were, at first ... but after I fired all the others, I fell in love
with polychrome. My first glimpse was in the mosque ... such
finely mitigated curves and swellings! The sheen of those stalactites
and lacy tendrils...'

'Polychrome's rich and successful. Was it a great relief?'

'Turned out to be a facade.'

'Did heretics cause problems? Or were the Copts involved?'

'My approach was too Byzantine. I tried to be realistic, but was
driven to abstraction.'

'Isn't it all a matter of perspective?'

'I found Christians used too much gilt.'

'That's why you began to work just for the mullah?'

'Yes ... one day I woke up with an advanced symbolism.'

'Bet you needed a doctrine for that.'

'And an aesthetic.'

'Avicenna again?'

'Just metaphor fun.'

'Oh, Tyler ... for years I've wanted to put you behind me.'

'And you're still divinely proportioned.'

'Care to exhibit me? Without my cloisonné?'

'Buff, or transparent white slip? I'll use bold vertical strokes in an unhurried tempo, free but rhythmic, with developing inventiveness over a long period.'

(The shapes are carefully outlined by hand, then after a few minutes' rasping, squeezed inseparably into a soft bed.)

'A perfect balance between stress and resolution, subordination and dominance, surprise and fulfilment.'

(glazed) 'It's a *synthesis*.'

Index

Abaqa, Sultan 206
Abbas I, Shah 56–8, 59, 85, 87, 292
    and the arts 79
    final years of 79–80
    and the Sheikh Lutfullah Mosque 70
    threats to the reign of 57–8
Abbas II, Shah 80
Abbasids 159, 262
al-Abedin, Zein, Fourth Imam 171
abjad numerological system 298
Abu Bakr 171, 173
Abu Nasr Parsa mosque, Balkh 167
Achaemenids 7, 23, 25–6, 79, 97,
    130–1
    gardens 48, 53–4
    Greek descriptions of 211
    and Hamadan 225
    and Pasargadae 287
    and Persepolis 342
    and the Sasanians 247
    and Takht-e Soleyman 204
    see also Cyrus the Great
Afghanistan 5, 11, 64, 81, 230, 233,
    389
    and the Soviet Union 189–90, 313
    Timurid monuments of 73–4, 167
Afshar, Nader Quli 81
Agha Mohammad Khan 82
Ahl-e Haqq 196, 197, 223
Ahmad, Jalal al-e 213
Ahmad, Sultan 85

Ahmadiyya 170
Alamut 389
Alborz Mountains 13, 47, 106, 389
Alexander the Great 12, 25, 114, 131,
    132, 212, 244, 341–2, 346
Alfarabius see al-Farabi
Alhambra 322, 328
Alhazen see ibn al-Haytham
Ali, the First Imam 88, 170–1, 173,
    174, 175–7, 179, 180, 268
Ali Qapu Palace, Isfahan 59, 279, 281,
    294, 298–9, 303, 304–6
Allahverdi Khan Bridge (also the Si o
    Se Bridge), Isfahan 284
Anahita 137, 218
Ansari-i Hezbollah 170
Apadana, Persepolis 343
    Apadana reliefs 113
Arabs 204
    and Poitiers 129
    and Tabriz 165
Arāmgāh, Shiraz 249–50, 255
architecture 167–8, 218–20, 279–88,
    293–5, 334
    caves and 314
    and the Golden Mean 279–81,
    288, 294
    Mongol 160, 163–6
    Parthian 136
    Sasanian 136, 218–19, 237,
    244–7, 262–3, 309

architecture (*cont.*)
  of the Sheikh Lutfullah Mosque
    59–60, 70–4, 265, 277–84,
    288–90, 293–4, 296–301, 303
  see also specific buildings
Ardashir I 26, 135, 237, 244
arg (citadel), Tabriz 165–6
art 73–5, 79, 318–35
  floral 68, 74–5
  geometric 286–7
  Mongol 160–1
  mosaics 227
  nature and 68, 74–5, 262–3, 267
  see also Islamic art
Ashraf, Princess 351–2
Ashura, Festival of 383
al-Askari, Hasan, Eleventh Imam 171
Assassins 97, 158, 389–90
'Attar 8, 16
Averroës *see* Ibn Rushd
Avicenna *see* Ibn Sina
'Ayn Jalut (Goliath's Spring) 133, 159
Azerbaijan 57, 81, 167, 234–5
  East 165
  Iranian 47, 165

Baba Taher 227
Babakin, Ardashir 15
Babylon 24, 25, 117, 134, 213, 218,
    326, 369
Bactria 117, 129, 343
Badakhshan 343
badgirs (wind-catchers) 364
Bagh-e Fin garden, Kashan 380
Baghdad 12–13, 158
Baha'i, Sheikh 292–3, 402
Bahram Gur 8, 26
Bakhtiari Mountains 23
Balkh 74
Bam 360
Baqir, Muhammad, Fifth Imam 171
Bayazit, Sultan 133

Benyamin, Pir 223
al-Biruni 288
Bokhara 82, 158
Borujerdi House, Kashan 384
Bridge of Thirty-Three Arches, Isfahan
    291–2
British Embassy, Tehran 12, 15, 110,
    386–8, 394
Brunelleschi, Filippo 163, 164, 368
Byron, Robert (author of *Road to
    Oxiana*) 36, 66, 72, 111, 163,
    165, 236–41, 247, 249, 264,
    277, 304, 315, 345, 378, 397,
    398
Byzantium 204, 205, 214–15, 323–4,
    332

Caliphs of Baghdad 115, 129, 170–1
calligraphy 263–5, 287, 322, 324,
    334–5
Cambyses 24
Carrhae 133
Caspian horses 97, 98, 100, 112–14,
    115–17
Caspian Sea 47, 57, 107
Chahar Bagh Avenue, Isfahan 53–4,
    58, 78, 90, 281–2, 289–92, 301
Chaldaea 326
Chardin, Jean (author of *Travels in
    Persia*, 1673–77) 54, 56, 165,
    344
Chehel Sutun Pavilion, Isfahan 284,
    304
China 132, 158, 160, 244, 261
  cultural influence of 160–1
Chingiz Khan 158, 250
Crassus 114, 132–3
Crusades 115, 159, 369, 389
Ctesiphon 12, 26, 131, 134, 160, 204,
    244, 245, 357
Cyrus the Great 15–16, 23–4, 88,
    211

establishes Pasargadae 287
gardens of 53–4
tomb of 287

Damavand, Mount 388–9
Darius I 24, 27, 211
  seal of 113
Darius III Codommanus 25
Dasht-e Kavir 47
Democritus 213
al-Dinawari 7

Ecbatana (now Hamadan) 218
  see also Hamadan
Egypt 24–5, 134, 159, 279, 326,
  342–3
Ethiopia 26, 343
Euphrates 132, 134

al-Farabi 7
Farahani, Qa'em Maquan 15
Fardid, Ahmad 213
Fars province 5–9, 24, 97, 237, 244
Fatima 268, 380, 382–3
Fatimid caliphate 171
Ferdowsi (poet) 8, 16, 22, 88, 130,
  222, 231, 303
Firouz, Louise 97–102, 106–18, 123,
  182, 196, 387
  horse work 112–17, 144–5
  horseback trip with author 128,
    130, 139–41, 143–6, 147, 149,
    150
Firouz, Narcy 98–9, 100
Firuzabad 238, 239–49, 267, 309–18
Friday Mosque, Hamadan 225–6
Friday Mosque, Isfahan 261–3, 284,
  322
Friday Mosque, Yazd 364

gardens 328–9, 334, 380
  Achaemenid 48, 53–4

domestic 77
of Tabriz 177–8
theme of in art 68, 74–5
Gaugamela 25
Gayomart 22
al-Ghazali (Algazel) 6
Ghazan Kahn 161, 163
Ghaznavids 28
Gibran, Khalil 182
Gohar Shad 397–8, 402
Golden Mean (Divine Proportion)
  279–81, 288, 294
Golestan National Park 149–51
Gombad-e Khirqa (Taj al-Molk) 264
Gombad-e Qabus 107, 123–4, 322
Gombad-i Alaviyan 226

Hafez (poet) 8, 16, 33, 138, 190, 232,
  250–5
  shrine of (Arāmgāh) 249–50, 255
Hakim Mosque, Isfahan 284
Halabja 198
Hamadan 218, 225–8
Hamadani, 'ayn al-Qudat 7
Hasht Behest (Eight Paradises)
  Pavilion, Isfahan 290, 292
Hassan, Second Imam (son of Ali)
  170, 268, 380
ibn al-Haytham 327
Hazrat-e Massumeh shrine 267
Hedayat, Sadeq 191–2
Herat 57, 74, 80, 158, 397–8, 402–3
Herodotus 114, 211, 212, 225
Hidden Imam *see* Muhammad, Twelfth
  Imam (the Mahdi)
horses 144–5
  Arab 113, 114, 115
  Caspian 97, 98, 100, 112–14,
    115–17
  Turkoman 114–15, 116, 128, 145
Hulegu Kahn 158–9
Husayn 80

Husayn (*cont.*)
Hussein, Third Imam (Prophet's grandson) 88, 171, 173–4, 176, 268, 362–4, 380, 383
Hyrcanian steppe 129

Ibn al-Haytham (Alhazen) 7, 327
Ibn al-Hayyam, Jabir 7
Ibn Battuta 160
Ibn Rushd (Averroës) 327
Ibn Sina (Avicenna) 6, 227, 327
Ikhwān al-Safā' (Brethren of Purity) 175
Ilkhanids 13, 28, 97, 160–3, 165, 206, 226, 262, 378
Imam Mosque, Isfahan *see* Royal Mosque
Iman 395–6, 398–404
India 24, 28, 58, 83, 87, 233, 244, 326, 332
Isfahan 13, 37, 51–81, 89–90, 96, 97, 138, 188, 189, 247, 259–63, 264–7, 277, 289–308, 357
    Ali Qapu Palace 59, 279, 281, 294, 298–9, 303, 304–6
    Chahar Bagh 53–4, 58, 78, 90, 281–2, 289–92, 301
    Friday Mosque 261–3, 284, 322
    great maidan (Naqsh-e Jahan Square) 58–9, 65–6, 70, 72–3, 277–85, 287, 288, 293–5, 300–1, 303
    Hasht Behest pavilion 290, 292
    imperial complex of 53–6
    Royal Mosque *see* Royal Mosque
    Sheikh Lutfullah Mosque *see* Sheikh Lutfullah Mosque
Islamic art 27–9, 262–5, 318–35
    features of 321–7
    geometric 286–7
    nature in 262
    symbolism 28–9, 333

Ismael I 57, 171
Ismaelis (Seveners) 170, 171
Istanbul 138
ivān (monumental archways) 136, 218, 237, 262, 266–7, 403
Iznik ceramics 320

Jahan Shah 167
Jahan-Nama (World-Viewing Pavilion), Isfahan 55, 284
al-Jahiz 7
Jamalzade 191–2
Jami (poet) 7, 16
Jerusalem 26, 138, 204, 369
Jundishapur 213

Karaj 97–102, 105–6
Karim Khan 82
Kashan 360, 379–85
kashgul (begging bowl) 296, 322
al-Kazim, Musa, Seventh Imam 171
Kerbala, Iraq 171, 174, 383
Kerind 223
Kerman 82, 247, 360, 376–8
Kermanshah 202, 211, 216–19, 221–5
khatam (inlay) 60–2
Khayyām, Omar 6, 8, 16, 303
Khidr 108, 117–18, 122–7, 139–40, 143, 147, 149–50
Khomeini, Ayatollah Ruhollah 6, 88, 109, 155, 347, 391–22
    conspiracy therapies regarding 104
    exiled 88, 354
    gains power 349
    popular disregard for 59, 78–9, 203
    returns from exile 89
    on war 190
Khorasan 57, 96, 158, 174, 389, 397–8
Khosrow, arch of, Taq-e Bostan 368

Khosrow II 204, 218
Khwarazm 158, 343
al-Kindi 7
Kopet Dagh 107, 129
Kurdistan 49, 96, 182, 183, 183–208,
    389
Kushans 26, 132, 247

Lebanon 170, 343
Lutfullah Mosque, Isfahan *see* Sheikh
    Lutfullah Mosque, Isfahan
Lydians 23

Madinat al-Zahra, Cordoba 74
Mahmud, Shah 80, 81
Majid 184–7, 191, 192–204, 205–6
Majlesi, Mohammed Baqir 80
Mamluks 133, 159, 319
Maragheh 167
Mashad 57, 80, 82, 171, 389, 394,
    396–404
Masjed-e Kabud (Blue Mosque), Tabriz
    167
Massagetai 24
Mazanderan 106
Mecca 67, 72, 174, 277
Mehdi 390–2
Merv 133, 158, 160
Mesopotamia 28, 132, 134
Mir Damad 15, 175
Mirza Razi 54–5
Mithra 137–8, 346
Mithradates 25, 131, 132
Mithraism 136–8, 345–6, 370, 376
Mo'aven al-Mulk 222
Moghul Empire 5, 58, 79, 233, 322
Moghul India 58, 233
Mongols 8, 47, 79, 133, 158–63,
    167, 204, 250, 321, 398
    Ilkhanids 13, 28, 97, 160–3, 165,
        206, 226, 262, 378
    Persianization 161–2

and Shiraz 233
and Tabriz 165
mosaics (polychrome, faience) 227,
    296, 301–2, 378–9, 402
Moshiri, Fereydun (poet) 303
Mosque of Ali, Isfahan 284
Mosque of the Shaking Minarets 77
Mosque of the Twelve Imams, Yazd
    365
Mossadeq, Mohammed 104, 111,
    349–54
Mowlavi *see* Rumi
Mu'awiya 173
Muhammad (the Prophet) 268, 313,
    330
    succession 170, 171, 173, 174, 176
Muhammad, Twelfth Imam (the
    Mahdi) 14, 105, 171–2, 175,
    380
Muhammad Ali, Shah 85
Muhammad Reza, Shah 5, 87, 88–9,
    97, 104, 109, 190–1, 230, 380,
    390–1
    calendar of 16
    exiled 350, 352, 353
    growing power of 354–5
    and horses 115, 123
    land reforms 186
    and Mossadeq 349, 350, 351–2,
        353
    nostalgia regarding 4, 13, 45, 98,
        235
    and Persepolis 346–7
al-Mulk, Nizam 264
Mulla Sadra 175
mullas 13, 16, 37, 191
muqarnas (form of vault) 188–9, 206
Muzafferuddin Shah 85

Nachivan 234
Nader Shah (Nader Quli Afshar) 15,
    81–2

al-Naqi, Ali (Tenth Imam) 171
Naqsh-e Jahan Square (great maidan),
    Isfahan 58–9, 65–6, 70, 72–3,
    277–85, 287, 288, 293–5,
    300–1, 303
Nasir-i Khusraw 16
Nasruddin Tusi 6
Natanz 360, 378–9
National Museum, Tehran 18, 22, 27,
    50, 135
New Mosque, Isfahan 284
Nezami (poet) 48
Nishapur 158
Nizami 7, 251
Nizaris 170, 389
Nurshirvan 26

Office for Cultural Heritage, Isfahan
    296, 299
oil 85, 86, 87, 349–50, 355
Omar 173
opium 46, 119–20, 122, 124, 200–1,
    387–8
Orumiyeh 182
Orumiyeh, Lake 183
Ottoman empire 5, 13, 57, 79, 82,
    320, 322

Parthians 12, 23, 25–6, 27, 79, 108,
    130–7, 204
    culture 135–6
    religion 136–7
    and the Romans 132–4, 135
Pasargadae 53–4, 117, 287
Persepolis 24, 25, 27, 88, 97, 113,
    160, 212, 225, 244, 304, 339,
    341–7
    statues of 344–6
Persian Empire
    anniversary of the 346–7
    capital cities of the 12–13
    fall 26–7

rise of the 23–5, 79
Plato 213, 215
poetry 8, 232–3, 250–4, 302–3
    garden theme 329
    ghazal verse 252–3, 254, 255
    rhetorical devices 252
    see also specific poets
Poitiers 129
Polo, Marco 160, 389
Pope, Arthur Upham 98, 111, 164,
    264, 345, 346
Prezewalski's horse 116
Publius 133
Pythagoras 286

Qabus 128
Qajar dynasty 13, 82–5, 103, 165,
    187, 218, 233, 299, 361
Qala-e Dokhtar 240–4, 309, 310
qanats (underground water channels)
    47–8
Qandahar 82
Qay Khosrou 22
Qay Qubad 22
Qazvin 13, 97
Qom 267, 268
Qur'ān 173, 250
    art and the 327–8, 329–30
    miniature versions 322
    Mongol 160

Rafsanjani, Akbar Hashemi 52
Ramadan 183, 184–5
Rashid ud-Dun 160
Razi, Fakhruddin 6
Reza, Eighth Imam 171, 267, 397
Reza Khan 104
Reza Shah 86–7
Roman Empire 7–8, 25, 26, 204, 213,
    247
    and the Parthians 132–4, 135
    religion 137

and the Sasanians 133–4
and the Seleucids 132
Royal Mosque, Isfahan 59, 66–7, 72,
74, 278, 293, 294, 299–302,
303, 307, 355
Rudaqi (poet) 16, 231–2
Rukh, Shah 82, 397
Ruknaddin, tomb of 365
Rumi (Mowlavi/Jelalludin Balkhi)
(poet) 7, 9–10, 16, 249, 303

Sa'di (poet) 8, 16, 217–18, 232, 249,
302–3
Sadiq, Ja'far, Sixth Imam 171
Safavids 15, 54, 79–81, 97, 288, 299
Ali Qapu Palace 304
capital 13, 56, 72
gardens of 380
monuments 66, 167, 291
scholars 175
and Tabriz 165
and the Turks 133
see also Abbas I, Shah
Safi, Shah 80
Samarqand 158
Sana'i 8, 16
Sanandaj, Kurdistan 183–93, 218
Sanjar, Sultan 160
Sardis 53, 117, 343
Sari 106
Sasanian dynasty 97, 130, 159, 222,
226
architecture 22, 53, 79, 136,
218–19, 237, 244–7, 262–3,
309
art 79, 218–19, 323–4, 332
and Ctesiphon 12
and the Roman Empire 134
and Takht-e Soleyman 204
Scythians 24, 129, 247
burial sites 140–1, 145–6
Seleucids 25, 131, 132

Seljuks 13, 28, 79, 97, 160, 226, 262,
264, 266, 388
Sha'ban 'the Brainless' 352–3
Shabestar 182
Shah Mosque, Isfahan 72
Shams of Tabriz 255
Shari'ati, Ali 14
Sheikh Lutfullah Mosque, Isfahan
59–60, 70–3, 74, 265, 277–84,
288, 289–90, 293, 294, 296–9,
300–1, 303
Shi'ism 58, 70, 87–8, 103, 105, 138,
170–7, 268, 380–1
Shiraz 81, 82, 88, 97, 99, 110, 230,
232–8, 255–9, 308–9, 339–41,
347–9, 355–7
Sohrawardi 7, 137, 175, 333
Soltaniyeh 13, 97, 160, 163–5,
164–5, 167
Sufism 9, 16, 137, 161, 176, 226,
250, 253–5, 293, 294, 297,
333, 345, 373
Suleiman 115
Suleyman 80
Sunnis 170–1, 172–3, 174–6, 268,
380, 389, 399
Susa 27, 343
Syr Darya 158
Syria 159, 199, 321
Syrian Antioch 132

Tabataba'i House, Kashan 384
Tabriz 13, 57, 85, 97, 165–71,
177–82, 398
gardens of 177–8
under the Mongols 160, 161
zurkhaneh 179–81
Tahmasp 81
Taj Mahal 233, 288, 322
Takht-e Jamshid 15
Takht-e Soleyman (Solomon's throne)
202–8

Taleghani 15
Tamerlane (Timur) 13, 133, 167, 233, 250, 325, 397
Taq-e Bostan 218–19, 222, 368
al-Taqi, Muhammad, Ninth Imam 171
Tarpan (horse) 116
Tayyebad 389
Tehran 3–5, 9–12, 13–22, 27–34, 39–45, 49–51, 95–6, 169, 183, 228–30, 259, 260, 267–74, 289, 355, 385, 386–94
  Ministry of Islamic Guidance 49–51
  Museum of Islamic Arts 27–9
  National Museum 18, 22, 27, 135
  parks 32
  Parliament building 85
Timur see Tamerlane
Timurids 28, 79, 397
  monuments 73–4, 167, 402–3
Towers of Silence 367, 368, 370
Turkmen 57, 82, 100, 107–9, 112, 117–20, 122–7, 139–44, 147–51
Turkmenistan 113, 122
Turkoman horses 114–15, 116, 128, 145
Turks 133, 165, 169

Ugnis 369
Uljeitu 163, 262, 322
Uljeitu mausoleum, Sultaniyya 163–4, 368
Umayyads 88, 129, 171, 173, 174
United States 390, 392
  contemporary Iranian intervention 229–30
  and the last Shah 87, 104, 348
  technological embargo against Iran 387–8
  and war 363
  see also Americans
Urartuans 23
Uthman 173
Uzbeks 57, 59, 82

Vakil Mosque, Shiraz 233–4
Vali-ye Asr, Tehran (formerly Pahlavi Avenue) 14
Vatican 138, 163
velayat-i faqih 354

wind-catchers see badgirs

Xenophon 212
Xerxes 24, 27, 227

Yazd 220, 360–7, 370
Yazid 88, 171, 174, 380, 383

Zagros mountains 47
Zaidis (Five-Imam Shi'a) 170, 171
Zand dynasty 82, 233
Zanjan 163
Zayandeh River 51–2, 56
Zoroaster 8, 218
Zoroastrians 26, 137, 268, 303, 333
  fire-rites 367–8
  persecution of 80
  temples 76–7
  Towers of Silence 367, 368, 370
  traditions 288
zurkhaneh (house of strength/force)
  Tabriz 179–81, 186
  Yazd 366–7